新形态教材

21世纪高等院校国际经济与贸易专业规划教材

国家级一流本科专业建设点教材

广西壮族自治区社会科学优秀成果奖

国际商务合同双语教程 第三版

INTERNATIONAL BUSINESS CONTRACTS
BILINGUAL COURSEBOOK　3rd Edition

杨　静　杨鑫坡　主　编

刘艳萍　杨　洁　副主编

东北财经大学出版社
Dongbei University of Finance & Economics Press　大连

图书在版编目（CIP）数据

国际商务合同双语教程 / 杨静，杨鑫坡主编．—3版．—大连：东北财经大学出版社，2024.1（2024.12重印）

（21世纪高等院校国际经济与贸易专业规划教材）

ISBN 978-7-5654-5110-2

Ⅰ．国…　Ⅱ．①杨…②杨…　Ⅲ．国际贸易-贸易合同-双语教学-高等学校-教材　Ⅳ．F740.4

中国国家版本馆CIP数据核字（2024）第015401号

东北财经大学出版社出版

（大连市黑石礁尖山街217号　邮政编码　116025）

网　　址：http://www.dufep.cn

读者信箱：dufep@dufe.edu.cn

大连图腾彩色印刷有限公司印刷　东北财经大学出版社发行

幅面尺寸：185mm×260mm　　字数：433千字　　印张：16.75

2024年1月第3版　　　　　　　2024年12月第2次印刷

责任编辑：蔡　丽　张晓鹏　　　　　责任校对：一　心

　　　　　吉　扬　刘慧美

封面设计：原　皓　　　　　　　　　版式设计：原　皓

定价：52.00元

教学支持　售后服务　联系电话：（0411）84710309

版权所有　侵权必究　举报电话：（0411）84710523

如有印装质量问题，请联系营销部：（0411）84710711

第三版前言

当今中国进一步放开国内市场，以更稳健、自信的姿态走向国际市场，国际经济合作日趋紧密，经济交往更加频繁。国际上的一切经济活动，如贸易、金融、投资等都离不开相互制约的合同。因此，懂得国际商务合同的基础知识、语言特征、结构、词汇，会翻译、起草合同成为商务人士或相关从业人员必须具备的技能，只有这样才能在业务实操中游刃有余，收获颇丰。

为减少经济活动中的合同纠纷、普及国际商务合同的基本知识，帮助合同当事人在经济活动中切实有效地保护自己的合法权益，本教材编者在阅读大量原版教材的基础上，参考了国内外商务英语、商务基础理论和知识等多种教材，编写了这本双语教程。在编写过程中，本教材编者努力解决相关专业知识的理论性、实用性和语言上的可读性之间的矛盾，使其适合中国国情，达到专业知识传授和语言技能培养的统一，突出前沿性、新颖性、实用性，紧跟社会需求和时代发展，符合国际商务、国际经济与贸易、商务英语等专业的人才培养目标。

本教材内容充实、完整，其中包括对国际商务合同结构的较为精细的剖析和归纳，导入的案例贴近实际；附录中吸纳了编者从事国际商务合同谈判和制作合同的宝贵经验，提供了多份操作性强、实效性高的国际商务合同样本，其中包括采购合同、销售确认书、销售合同、加工合同、代理合同、经销协议。此外，本教材还在东北财经大学出版社官网上为授课教师提供了免费的教学资源，其中包括电子课件、章后习题参考答案，以及寄售协议、补充贸易合同、来料加工装配合同、独家代理协议、销售代理协议、独家经销协议、易货合同、合资经营企业合同、股权转让协议、技术转让合同和雇佣合同等国际商务合同样本。

本教材第三版的主要特色是注重思政引领，融入党的二十大精神。党的二十大报告指出："用社会主义核心价值观铸魂育人，完善思想政治工作体系，推进大中小学思想政治教育一体化建设。坚持依法治国和以德治国相结合，把社会主义核心价值观融入法治建设、融入社会发展、融入日常生活。"本教材第三版更新了部分资料，增设了二维码形式的"即测即评"习题。尤为重要的是，本教材第三版融入课程思政元素，思政栏目名称是"Ideological & Political Gardens"（思政园地），结合党的二十大报告内容，引导学生深入社会实践，关注现实问题，使他们加强对专业知识的内化吸收与灵活应用，坚定中国特色社会主义道路自信、理论自信、制度自信、文化自信，努力践行习近平新时代中国特色社会主义思想进教材、进课堂、进头脑，达到价值塑造、知识传授、能力培养三位一体的育德树人之效。

本教材由广西财经学院的杨静和杨鑫坡担任主编，刘艳萍和杨洁担任副主编，段艳平、刘松竹、魏格坤、戴君益、凌华参与了编写工作。编者在编写过程中得到了广西财经学院多位老师和学生的帮助。美国外教 Shawn Frazier 教授为本教材英文校对做了大量工作。

在本教材的编写和修订过程中，编者参考和引用了大量文献，但由于不具备广泛且深入地查询馆藏资料的条件，以及电子数据资源的覆盖范围有限，在脚注和"主要参考文献"中没有列全资料来源，或者所列的可能不是最早来源的作者的作品，请相关作者谅解；若相关作者与编者联系，编者愿意根据引用作品的篇幅而提供相应的字数报酬。在此，编者向所有的相关作者表示衷心的感谢。

由于编者水平和学识有限，书中难免出现差错、疏漏的地方，敬请读者不吝指正。

编　者

2023年10月

目　录

Chapter 1

Basic Knowledge of International Business Contracts
国际商务合同的基础知识

Learning Objectives

◆ 重点掌握英语合同的用语、用词特点；掌握英语合同的句式特点；了解英语合同的基本概念、构成内容、分类。

Guide Case

Selling Water for China

1.Case Story

Overview: Acqua International (AQ) is a Europe-based multinational company that has interests in water and other environment-related businesses. In China, the company has joint ventures with medium-size and large municipalities to produce potable water. To increase its investments in China, the AQ Group arranged through its local subsidiary Pacific Acqua International (PAQ), to enter into a strategic alliance with Tak Foy Co., a Chinese conglomerate with strong roots in China in the service industry (mainly leisure-related). The ventures is called Haoyu China Limited (HCL).

2.The Scene

These negotiations concerned an urban water supply system providing potable water to around one million people. Through an agent in the province, the China subsidiary PAQ had secured a contract to construct a water treatment plant for the system.

Some time after the completion and commissioning of the plant, PAQ learned from the same agent that the municipality was short of funds for some urgent development projects. One of its options was to privatize the municipality's water supply facilities.

The sale value of the facilities was set by the municipality and bidders were sought from within its jurisdiction, there would be no recourse to the central government for approval. HCL, located in the municipality, submitted a purchasing proposal to buy the facilities, to set up a joint ventures with the municipality's water company on a 3 : 1 ratio and to operate the facilities on a twenty five-year contract.

The unresolved issues when bids were called for were:

Initial water charges. The only thing that had been agreed on up to this date was how much would be invested in the facilities and spent on improvements.

The demand for water. To make the business financially viable, a take-or-pay mechanism would have to be introduced and local wells would have to be closed.

The formula to calculate annual water tariff revisions. Devaluation of the Yuan would affect foreign exchange-based investment.

The new company's structure. Who would be the shareholders, board members, and those responsible for its day-to-day management?

3.Selling Negotiations Begin

At the request of the Chinese, a memorandum was signed by HCL and the municipality to record the issues still outstanding.

It was only then that PAQ-and through it HCL-was informed by the local PAQ agent (who was supposedly very close to high levels in the municipality) that other international competitors had also visited the municipality in connection with the same project.

After meeting high-ranking officials in the city, the PAQ team was advised to lower its starting price for water supply if it wished to remain the preferred partner.

In a bid not to lose the municipality's interest, PAQ organized visits to PAQ operations in other provinces for a group of municipal officials whose reaction was positive. Then believing it a good time to start negotiations, PAQ submitted a revised proposal, which it followed up by visits requesting discussion.

The mayor's office arranged a negotiating session to be attended by representatives of all the municipal departments concerned, at which PAQ and HCL were represented by four people: John King, Hans Christian, Cheng Peng Li, and Xu Jing.

For several weeks the unresolved issues and other matters were discussed, and every evening the municipality hosted a formal banquet, which lent ambiance to the talks. Cheng and Xu were the representatives on these social occasions, while King and Christian remained in the background.

4.Strategy Applied

PAQ did not begin negotiating using the water rates as the deciding factor in the belief that, were its ideas not well accepted, the entire project might be placed on hold. Instead, it picked secondary issues with no critical impact to give both parties some wins to balance the losses.

Discussions started with water demand... Next to be negotiated was the tariff adjustment formula... Due to PAQ's favorable reputation, agreements on the shareholding structure and management were reached without too much difficulty. Last came the water rate negotiations.

PAQ impressed on the municipality that, as an old friend, it was right for the project, being technically and financially sounds with a good track record in China. PAQ's sincerity was demonstrated by the number of Chinese staffs on its team.

Agreement was reached in two weeks, with the mayor himself voicing his support. Wishing to give face to their lead negotiator and aware of Chinese sensitivity to pricing, PAQ then offered to reduce the starting water rate. In return, to give face to PAQ, the municipality offered preferential tax treatment over a five-year period.

资料来源　MARCH. Chinese water selling negotiation[EB/OL]. [2023-12-02]. http://www. negotiations. com/case/selling-water-china.

思考题：

（1）描述案例中提到的公司的基本情况，如公司间的业务关系。

（2）合同当事方是谁？合同的关键条款是什么？当进行上面所提到的合同谈判时，难题是什么？什么策略适用于处理这些难题？

（3）对于本案例中的合同谈判，欧洲方面通常会面临什么样的问题？这些问题最终是如何解决的？

（4）假设你代表中方与外商谈判，哪些文化问题可能会影响你的谈判？请给出一些合同谈判的技巧。

1.1　Basic Concept of Contracts
　　合同的基本概念

Contracts are so much a part of living in a society that nobody can calculate how many contracts are made every day. In the broadest sense, a contract is simply an agreement that defines a relationship between two or more parties. However, this notion is simply too broad to cover commercial matters which are different from everyday's life. So, to come down a little, a commercial contract, in simplest terms, is merely an agreement made by two or more parties for the purpose of transacting business.

Any contract may be oral or written. Written terms may be recorded in a simple memorandum, certificate, or receipt. Because a contractual relationship is made between two or more parties who have potentially adverse interests, the contract terms are usually supplemented and restricted by laws that serve to protect the parties and to define specific relationships between them in the event that provisions are indefinite, ambiguous, or even missing.

合同是社会生活的一部分，没有人可以计算出每天有多少合同产生。广义上讲，合同是一项定义了两个或两个以上当事人之间关系的协议。然而，这个概念太宽泛，不能覆盖所有有别于日常生活的商务事项。因此，简单地说，商务合同仅仅是一项由两个或两个以上当事人为了交易目的而缮制的协议。

商务合同可以是口头合同，也可以是书面合同。书面条款可以用简单的备忘录、证书或收据来记载。由于合同关系是因两方或多方潜在的相对利益而建立的，因此为了保护当事人和定义特定关系，合同条款如果是不确定的、模糊的甚至缺失的话，它们通常通过法律来补充和限制。

1.2　Main Features of International Business Contracts
　　国际商务合同的主要特征

Contracts are agreements between equal natural persons, legal persons and other organizations for the purpose of establishing, altering and terminating mutual civil rights and obligations. According to this definition, we can understand the general legal characteristics of the contract.

合同是平等主体的自然人、法人、其他组织之间设立、变更、终止民事权利和义务关系的协议。根据这个定义，我们可以了解一般合同的法律特征。

1.2.1　Contract Is a Legal Act
　　　合同是一种法律行为

This refers to certain rights and obligations relations between the parties for a certain purpose, which are protected by the state coercive power. Any party, who fails to perform the contract or incompletely perform the contract, should bear legal responsibility.

这是指当事人之间为特定的目的而产生的一定的权利和义务关系，而且这种权利和义务关系受国家强制力的保护，任何一方不履行或不完全履行合同，都要承担法律责任。

1.2.2　Contract Is a Legal Law Behavior
　　　合同是合法的法律行为

It is an agreement reached by both sides in accordance with the requirements of the legal norms, which result in legal consequence expected by the parties, and it is a legal behavior which can be recognized and protected by the country.

合同是双方当事人按照法律规范的要求达成的协议，产生双方所预期的法律后果。它是一种合法行为，因而为国家所承认和保护。

1.2.3　Contract Is an Agreement Between the Parties
　　　合同是双方或多方当事人之间的协议

It is not said that any agreement is a contract between the parties; it is only an agreement between the parties about the establishment, change or termination of civil rights and obligations relations.

这并不是说当事人之间的任何协议都是合同，它只是当事人之间关于设立、变更、终止民事权利、义务关系的协议。

1.2.4   Contract Is Civil Juristic Act of the Parties on the Basis of Equality, Voluntariness
合同是当事人在平等、自愿的基础上所作出的民事法律行为

International business contract is of duality of law and English. The first attribute is a contract. As standard legal documents, international business contracts should meet the general requirements of form and content legality, which have the normative in structure, words, and elements etc. The second attribute of international business contracts is English, which belongs to a kind of practical English writing. Investigated its characteristics, as a highly professional practical writing, international business contracts need to meet firstly is requirements of formatting and specifications, fixed expressions, whose format should be fixed, sentence patterns and structure should be exquisite, wording should be accurate, and professional and has long, conservative, accurate and other characteristics.

国际商务合同具有法律和英语双重性。其第一属性是合同，作为制式法律文件，国际商务合同应满足形式和内容合法性的一般要求，具备结构、文字表达、要素等方面的规范性。国际商务合同的第二属性是英语，它属于英语应用文的一种。究其特点，作为专业性极强的应用文，国际商务合同首先要满足的是格式化要求和规范、固定的用语表达。其格式固定，句式与结构考究，用词准确专业，具有冗长、保守、精确等特征。

1.3   Categories of International Business Contracts
国际商务合同的种类

At the very moment when an offer is accepted, the transaction is completed and a contractual relationship between the seller and buyer is concluded. However, according to international trade practice, the seller and buyer still have to sign a written contract or a confirmation, binding on both parties, to further define their rights and obligations respectively. In international trade, contracts vary in both names and forms. The names that often appear are contract, confirmation, agreement and memorandum. According to the different trade forms, the contract can be classified into different types as follows:

① Contract of International Goods Sales, Sales Confirmation/Sales Contract, Purchase Confirmation/Contract for Purchase;

② Agency Contract, Sole Agency Agreement, Sole Distributorship Agreement, Exclusive Sales Agreement;

③ Contract for Assembling, Agreement on Compensation Trade;

④ Finance Lease Agreement, Contract of Operating Lease, Contract for International Leasing Affairs;

⑤ Joint Venture Contract, Contractual Joint Venture Contract;

⑥ Labor Service Contract;

⑦ International Technical Consultancy Service Contract, Contract for Technology Transfer and Importation of Equipment and Materials, Technology Transfer and Technical Assistance

Agreement;

⑧ International Loan Agreement;

⑨ Contract for Works of Civil Engineering Construction;

⑩ Outsourcing Agreement;

⑪ Service Agreement;

⑫ Venture Capital Management Agreement;

⑬ Share Transfer Agreement;

⑭ Tripartite Cooperation Agreement;

⑮ Escrow Agreement;

⑯ Nondisclosure Agreement.

当要约被接受，交易就达成了，卖方和买方之间的契约关系就建立了。然而，根据国际贸易惯例，买卖双方还必须签订对双方都有约束力的书面合同或确认书，进一步定义各自的权利和义务。在国际贸易中，合同的名称和形式各式各样。经常出现的名称是合同、确认书、协议和备忘录。根据不同的贸易形式，合同可以被分为如下不同的类型：

① 国际货物买卖合同，即售货确认书/售货合同和购货确认书/购货合同；

② 代理合同，主要有独家代理协议、独家经销协议和包销协议；

③ 来件装配合同和补偿贸易协议；

④ 融资租赁合同、经营租赁合同和国际租赁合同；

⑤ 合资经营企业合同和合作经营企业合同；

⑥ 劳务合同；

⑦ 国际技术咨询服务合同，技术转让和设备、材料进口合同，以及技术转让和技术援助协议；

⑧ 国际贷款协议；

⑨ 土木建筑工程承包合同；

⑩ 外包合同；

⑪ 服务合同；

⑫ 风险投资管理协议；

⑬ 股权转让协议；

⑭ 三方合作协议；

⑮ 第三方支付协议/第三方账户监管协议；

⑯ 保密协议。

1.4　Role of International Business Contracts
　　国际商务合同的作用

The creation of an international business transaction and an international contract are a more complex process than the formation of a contract between parties from the same country and culture. In a cross-border transaction, the parties usually do not meet face-to-face, they have different societal values and practices and their own national laws. These factors can easily lead to misunderstandings, and therefore the contracting parties should define their mutual understanding in contractual and preferably written terms. Thus, the role of a contract in an international commercial transaction is of a special value and importance for the parties involved.

When one party enters into a commercial contract with an unfamiliar and distant party across a country border, a contract takes on added significance. The role of a contract in an international commercial transaction is of particular importance with respect to the following aspects:

国际贸易和国际合同的产生比来自相同国家和相同文化的各方间形成的合同要复杂。在跨境交易中，当事人通常不进行面对面的会谈，他们有不同的社会价值观和惯例以及自己国家的法律。这些因素容易导致误解，缔约双方在合同中最好用书面条款来定义彼此的理解。因此，国际商务合同的作用是合同当事方的一种特殊价值和重要性。

当一方当事人与跨境的另一方陌生的当事人签订商务合同时，合同就具有了特定的意义。国际商务合同的作用在以下方面尤为重要：

1.4.1 Balance of Power
势力均衡

The essence of a contract is the mutual understanding reached by two parties who hold adverse positions against each other. In most contractual situations, one party will have a stronger position than the other. For example, a large corporation that offers goods for sale may be able to insist on contract terms that are highly favorable to the corporation while restricting the rights of individual buyers. The corporation may offer a standard form sales contract with non-negotiable terms–take it or leave it–to the buyer.

合同的本质是拥有不同利益的当事人达成的相互理解。在大多数合同中，一方比另一方更强势。例如，一家出售商品的大公司会坚持对本公司十分有利的合同条款，而这些条款却限制买家的权利。大公司可能会提供带有不可转让条款的标准销售合同——对买方来说，可接受也可放弃。

1.4.2 The Party Who Drafts the Contract
起草合同方

The balance of power between contracting parties usually tips in favor of the party who drafts the written contract. Even if the essential contract terms have already been negotiated and agreed by both parties, the drafting party will typically include provisions that are more skewed to his or her favor. To illustrate, a seller who drafts a sales contract may provide trade terms by which the risk of loss passes to the buyer at the first possible moment of the transfer.

缔约方之间的势力均衡通常倾向于起草书面合同方。即使基本的合同条款已经由双方协商并同意，起草方通常也会把更偏向于他（或她）的条款写进合同。为了说明这一点，起草销售合同的卖方会使用把风险损失第一时间转移给买方的贸易术语。

1.4.3   The Party Familiar with Written Contracts
熟悉书面合同方

In cross-border transactions, the balance of power may tip toward the party who is most familiar with written contracts and whose country has a more highly developed system of contract enforcement. This party may insist on terms that are common in his or her domestic contracts, and the other party, with less or no understanding of those terms, may simply acquiesce. As an example, clause that is commonly inserted into contracts in the United States is, "Time is of the essence". If such a clause is included, failure to perform the contract within the time allowed is considered a material breach of the contract, entitling the other party to claim damages or other remedies. In cultures that place more emphasis on continuing business relationships, this clause has little meaning because contract terms are commonly renegotiated to allow for a party's difficulties in performing the contract. The ongoing relationship is more important than the one-time deal.

在跨境交易中，势力均衡倾向于最熟悉书面合同方，并且被倾向方所在国有高度发达的合同执行系统，他（或她）可能会坚持（订立）在其所在国国内常见的合同条款；另一方对这些条款了解得很少或根本不理解，可能只能默许。例如，美国合同通常会插入"时间就是生命"的条款。如果合同中有这样的条款，一方没有在约定的时间内履行合同，会被认为是重大违约，另一方有权要求损害赔偿或采取其他补救措施。在更强调持续发展贸易关系的文化中，这一条款没有意义，因为在一方履行合同困难时，通常允许重新协商订立合同条款。持续发展的贸易关系比一次性的交易更重要。

1.4.4   Enforcement of One-Sided Contracts
片面合同的执行

In the context of enforcement, the balance of power can work against the stronger party in a contract negotiation. Courts and arbitrators often refuse to enforce terms that unreasonably burden one party or that are otherwise unconscionable. Furthermore, contract provisions are typically given a strict interpretation against the party who drafted the terms, since that party had the opportunity to draft a dear and definite contract.

Tip: Because of the problem with enforcement, parties to cross-border transactions should avoid taking unfair advantage. A contract that is in accord with fair business practices will encourage both parties to perform their obligations, and therefore the need for enforcement and the need to outlay the costs to attendant to enforcement may be avoided.

在实施的情景下，在进行合同谈判时，势力均衡对强势的一方不利。法院和仲裁员通常会拒绝对一方存在不合理负担的条款或者在其他方面不合理的条款的执行。此外，合同条款通常给起草条款方以严格规定，因为这一方有机会起草明确的合同。

提示：由于执行的问题，跨境交易各方应避免利用不公平的优势。符合公平贸易惯例的合同将鼓励贸易双方履行各自的义务，所以执行的需要和随之而产生的成本应该被避免。

1.4.5   Cross-Border Rights and Obligations
跨境权利和义务

In any contractual arrangement, it is important to establish clearly the rights and obligations of each party. If these terms are absent or ambiguous, the parties will probably not be able to perform the contract without first modifying the terms. Moreover, enforcement will be unpredictable, because a court will have to imply terms based on what the court believes would have been the intent of the parties.

在任何合同安排中，明确双方的权利和义务都很重要。如果这些条款缺失或模棱两可，不先修改条款，各方可能就无法执行合同。此外，执行将是不可预测的，因为法院必须执行其认为有当事人意图的那些条款。

1.4.6   Differences in Business Practices
贸易惯例的差异

For contracts made between parties within the same country, missing or indefinite terms may be filled in by local regulations or practices. The rationale is that the parties likely intended to follow the local regulations and practices with which they were familiar.

If the parties are from different countries, their intentions cannot be so easily implied because they herald from different legal systems and no doubt utilize dissimilar business practices. For this reason, it is essential for your international contract to spell out in definite terms the rights and obligations of each party.

对于同一国家各方间订立的合同，缺失或不明确的条款会通过当地法规或惯例被写进合同中。其基本原理是，当事人可能旨在遵循他们所熟悉的当地法规和惯例。

如果当事人来自不同的国家，毫无疑问，他们的意图不能轻易隐含，因为他们代表着不同的法律体系，采用不同的商业惯例。出于这个原因，对国际合同来说，在明确的条款中指出双方的权利和义务是很重要的。

1.4.7   International Laws
国际法

In recognition of the difficulties that parties face in contracting across country boundaries, the international community has begun to adopt systems of laws and rules to be applied instead of local laws in transactions between parties located in different countries. The intent behind adopting uniform, international laws is to ensure that all parties to a cross-border transaction are subject to the same set of rules, regardless of whether the laws of their home countries are dissimilar. If parties to an international sales contract are nationals of countries that have acceded to an international treaty or pact, such as the United Nations Convention on Contracts for the International Sale of Goods (CISG), they may rely on international laws to determine at least some of their rights and obligations.

In general, it is unwise to rely on the law, even international laws, for implied contractual terms. The application of international laws to the interpretation of a contract can lead to unexpected and even unfavorable results. Thus, if an international contract of sale fails to provide a delivery time and the buyer sues for breach when the seller fails to deliver within one month, the contract may be deemed invalid under the local laws of the buyer's country because of the absence of an essential term. But if a court applies international laws, it may imply a reasonable delivery time of two months in accordance with the practice of the industry and therefore may enforce the contract.

在认定跨境合同中各方面临的困难时，国际社会已经开始采用可适用的法律系统和规则，而不是不同国家间交易各方当地的法律。采用统一的国际法的意图是确保各方跨境交易采用相同的一套规则，而不论他们本国的法律是否不同。如果一份国际销售合同的当事人是加入国际条约或协定的国家公民，如《联合国国际货物销售合同公约》（CISG），他们可以依靠国际法来确定他们最基本的权利和义务。

一般来说，对于含蓄的合同条款，靠法律即使是国际法也是不明智的。用于合同解释的国际法的应用，会导致意想不到的甚至是不利的结果。因此，如果国际销售合同未能提供交货时间，买方可起诉卖方违约；如卖方未能在一个月内发货，那么在买方国家的本土法律看来，因为这个重要条款的缺失，该合同可能会被视为无效合同。但如果法院采用国际法，这可能意味着两个月的合理交货期，按照行业惯例，可以执行该合同。

1.4.8 *Preciseness and Predictability*
严谨性和可预测性

To avoid an unfavorable and uncertain result, it is best to define your rights and obligations in a written contract when you are dealing across country borders. Hopefully your contract terms will be sufficiently explicit that both parties will understand what they are supposed to do and what they are entitled to receive. In the event of a breach, there is a greater chance that a court will enforce explicit terms (unless the provisions are unconscionable), and thus the parties can more closely predict the outcome.

为了避免不利和不确定的结果，当开展跨境贸易时，最好在书面合同中确定你的权利和义务。希望合同条款足够明确，使得双方了解他们应该做什么，他们可以得到什么。当发生违约时，法院将会强制执行明确的条款（除非规定是不合理的），从而使双方可以更精准地预测结果。

1.4.9 *Cross-Cultural Expectations*
跨文化的期望

Well-drafted contracts can help to ensure that parties who have diverse cultural backgrounds reach a mutual understanding with regard to their rights and obligations. All contracting parties come to the table with individual expectations, which in turn tint their understanding of the terms. What is reasonable to one may not be to the other, in which case mutual understanding an essential element in the creation of an enforceable contract is lacking.

The key is in the drafting of the agreement. You should write the provisions to reflect the culture of the foreign party, while at the same time keeping in mind your own requirements. Such drafting requires that you have an understanding of the other party's culture and the extent to which it differs from your own. Your contract provisions may need to be simplified so that they can be clearly understood, particularly if the contract will have to be translated into the other party's own language. You should review the provisions for shorthand phrases, legalese, and slang familiar to you but not to the other party-these provisions should be written in plain terms to ensure mutual understanding.

Further, you will need to determine the extent to which the other party is familiar with international business. If the other party has been trading internationally for some time, he or she is more likely to have gained an understanding of cross - cultural transactions. During your negotiations, you should explore the business history of the other party so that you can draft your contract to the appropriate level of sophistication.

A contract that reflects the cultural expectations of each party is more likely to be performed to the satisfaction of both. Mutual understanding means not only that each party knows its rights and obligations before signing the contract, but that the parties are in complete agreement as to each other's rights and obligations. Disputes typically arise when one party interprets a right or obligation differently than the other party. A contract drafted to ensure mutual understanding of culturally diverse parties will help to avoid, or at least to settle, subsequent disagreements over performance.

起草得好的合同有助于确保有不同文化背景的各方在权利和义务方面相互了解。所有的缔约方都是带着各自的预期和他们对条款的理解来谈合同的。对一方是合理的，可能对另一方就是不合理的，在这样的情况下，会缺乏对可执行合同成立必不可少的因素的相互理解。

关键是协议的起草。你应该写反映外方文化的条款，同时别忘了自己的需求。这样的起草要求你了解不同于你方的对方的文化，特别是当合同必须翻译成对方国家的语言时，合同条款必须简化，以便被清楚地理解。你应该审核简写的短语、法律术语和你熟悉但对方不熟悉的俚语——这些条款应该被写为普通条款，以确保彼此相互了解。

此外，你需要确定对方熟悉国际贸易的程度。如果对方从事国际贸易已经有一段时间，他或她对跨文化交易可能能有更多的理解。谈判期间，你应该了解另一方做贸易的经历，以便你能根据合同的复杂性起草适当的合同。

反映交易各方文化期望的合同更有可能使双方都满意。相互理解不仅意味着在签订合同前各方了解其权利和义务，而且当事方完全认同彼此的权利和义务。当一方对权利或义务的解读与另一方不同时，争端通常会出现。起草的合同要确保有文化差异的各方相互理解，避免或至少能解决后续的分歧。

1.4.10　*Personal Commitment*
个人承诺

When dealing with a distant party in another country, you may be uncertain of the extent to which that party is making a commitment to perform the contract. While you are no doubt serious about the bargain, you have no evidence as to whether the other party has equal resolve. Does timely delivery of your order have the same importance to the other party as it does to you? Is the other party committed to producing quality products that meet or even exceed your expectations? Trust is built on the personal commitment that each party demonstrates to the transaction, and therefore this aspect of any transaction whether domestic or international is especially significant.

Gaining evidence of commitment in cross-border transactions, in which parties usually operate by different business practices, can be more difficult than in domestic transactions in which parties typically share the same business practices. A party who orally agrees to become obligated has made a commitment to the other party, but the terms of that commitment depend exclusively the word of one party against the other. In many cultures, bargains are struck only when the parties meet personally; a handshake seals the promise. Other cultures insist on the signing of written informal or formal contracts before a final commitment is made.

In transacting business with a person of another culture, you should keep in mind the way in which they are likely to show their commitment. You will need to decide in advance of negotiating the bargain whether to accept the other party's evidence of commitment, insist on your own, or reach a compromise. If you meet the other party personally, shake hands, and gain that parties' respect and trust, you may decide that an oral agreement is sufficient to express commitment to the transaction.

If you do not feel comfortable with an oral arrangement, consider the other party's culture before you act. The other party may be from a culture where contracts are usually in writing, and thus without much fuss, you may simply mention that you will put the contract in writing and send it for signing. On the other hand, the other party's common practice may be to operate on a handshake, and that party may be insulted if you insist on a written contract. In that event, you may have to find an indirect approach. Then, if your host seems open to the idea, you might suggest an informal letter or memorandum as a compromise. If not, you may take or leave the handshake bargain, depending on whether you want the business and whether you can afford the risk.

If you have previously done business with the other party, you might well be willing to accept a handshake to seal the bargain, but such practice should be the exception not the rule. When dealing internationally, it is always best to insist on written evidence of personal commitment, even if you simply exchange a memorandum. In relative terms, there is more cost—in time and money—involved in cross border transactions than in domestic ones. When you agree to sell or buy goods internationally, you are also responsible for complying with import, export, customs, consumer product, marking, transport, and other trade-regulating laws of two or more countries. It is wise to ensure that the other party shares the same commitment.

当与另一个国家遥远的一方做交易时，你可能不确定另一方作出履行合同承诺的程度如何。当你认真做交易时，你没有另一方同等认真做交易的证据。及时交付你的订单对你来说与对另一方来说都一样重要吗？另一方会致力于生产出优质产品来达到甚至超过你的期望吗？信任是建立在交易各方都能证明的个人承诺基础之上的，因此无论是国内还是国际交易，这方面都尤其重要。

获得跨境交易承诺的证据可能比获得国内交易承诺的证据更难，因为跨境交易方通常依不同的贸易惯例进行交易，而国内交易方通常依相同的贸易惯例进行交易。口头同意的一方对另一方作出了承诺，但承诺的条款完全取决于一方针对另一方的执行。在许多文化中，只有当双方见面时讨价还价才发生，以握手印证承诺。而在其他文化中，在作出最后的承诺之前，则坚持要求书面的非正式或正式合同的签名。

当与另一种文化的一方做交易时，你应该记住他们表达承诺的方式。你需要提前决定交易谈判是否接受另一方承诺的证据，是坚持你自己的，还是妥协。如果你亲自与对方见面、与对方握手，并获得对方的尊重和信任，你可能认为口头协议足以表达对交易的承诺。

如果你对口头协议不满意，在行动前要先考虑对方的文化。对方的文化可能要求合同以书面形式出现，对此无须大惊小怪，你只要注意需签名的书面合同并将其寄送就可以了。另一方面，另一方的通常惯例可能是握手就表示达成交易，如果你坚持以书面合同达成交易的话，那么另一方可能觉得受侮辱了。在那种情况下，你可能需要找到一种间接的（处理）方法。如果你的客人看上去想法比较开明，你可以建议采取非正式的信件或备忘录作为和解（的方法）。如果不是（他看上去想法不是很开明），你可以采取或不采取握手交易，这取决于你是否想要达成那笔交易和你是否能承受风险。

如果你以前与另一方做过交易，你可能愿意以握手来表示达成交易，但是这样的做法应该是例外而不是规则。在开展国际交易时，最好坚持书面证据的个人承诺，即使你只是交换备忘录。相对而言，跨境交易比国内交易涉及更多的成本——时间和金钱。当你同意在国际上出售或购买商品时，你还要遵守相关进口、出口、海关、消费产品、标记、运输和两个或两个以上国家间其他贸易调整的法律。确保对方采用同样的承诺是明智的。

1.4.11   *Governing Law*
适用的法律

When trading internationally, parties frequently assume that they can operate in accordance with their own domestic laws and practices. This assumption is erroneous and can lead to grave misunderstanding. When you trade across country borders, you are subject to not only the law of your own country but to the law of other countries where you do business. You need not physically enter another country to become subject to its laws-merely selling goods by mail or electronic means may establish a sufficient connection to bring you within the jurisdiction of another country's courts.

To a certain extent, you may control the application of a country's law to your particular transaction by expressly setting forth the law that will govern the contract. However, parties do not have complete freedom of contract in choosing the governing law. Most countries have laws that mandate domestic over particular types of contractual arrangements, such as those involving land transactions.

Even in the absence of a statute, the determination as to which laws will be applied is nearly always left to the discretion of the court, which may or may not respect the choice you have made. In practice, courts tend to uphold the expressed intent of the parties provided it is not contrary to statute. An express provision on governing law therefore has a significant effect on which laws will be employed to interpret contractual rights and obligations in international transactions.

当进行国际交易时，当事方经常认为他们可以按照自己国内的法律和惯例来行事。这种假设是错误的，会导致严重的误解。当进行国际交易时，你不仅要遵守你自己国家的法律，也要遵守与你做生意的一方所在国家的法律。你不需要进入另一个国家去遵守该国的法律——仅仅通过邮寄或以电子手段销售商品就足以让你建立起与国外商家的联系，从而把你带入另一个国家法院的管辖权内。

在某种程度上，通过明确设定合同适用的法律，你可以控制针对于你特定交易的某国法律的应用。然而，在选择合同适用的法律时，当事方没有绝对的自由。大多数国家的法律在国内授权于特定类型的合约安排，如涉及土地交易。

即使没有法律条例，适用何种法律的决定也总是留给法院裁决，这可能会或可能不会尊重你的选择。在实践中，如果不违背条例，法院倾向维护当事人的表达意图。适用法律的明示条款因此将被用来解释国际交易中合同双方的权利和义务。

1.4.12 *Enforcement*
执行

As you move from a domestic to an international setting, enforcement issues increase in complexity. Local laws and practices will usually determine the evidence required to prove contract terms. An oral contract may be sufficient in one country, while another may require a written and even notarized agreement.

TIP: You should always try to secure the best possible proof of your agreement—which is a precisely drafted, written contract—in the event that enforcement becomes necessary. Remember, even if you avoid a court action, you will have more power in negotiating amended terms if you have clear and definite proof of your agreement.

Most jurisdictions require certain contracts to be written to be enforceable. Typically, contracts for the sale of goods with a total value exceeding the amount specified by the law must be in writing to be enforceable. Contracts for the sale or lease of real property may have to be written to be enforced. Although parties may make such contracts orally and may voluntarily agree to perform the terms to completion, their contractual rights will not be involuntarily enforced if a dispute should arise.

当你从国内环境转向国际环境时，执行问题就变得复杂了。当地的法律和惯例通常会决定证明合同条款所需的证据。在某一国家口头合同可能就足够了，但在另一个国家可能需要书面甚至是公证的协议。

提示：你应该总是试图保护协议中的有利证据——这是一份严谨的书面合同——如果执行是必要的话。记住，即使你避免法院执行，如果你的协议中有清晰而明确的证据，你也将更有权去协商修改相关条款。

大部分司法都要求某些书面合同是可执行的。通常情况下，总价值超过法律规定金额的货物销售合同必须以书面形式订立才是可执行的。销售或租赁不动产合同也必须以书面形式订立才是可执行的。尽管当事方可能订立口头合同并且可能自愿同意履行相关条款，但如果引起争议，他们的合同权利不会被非自愿地执行。

1.4.13　*Choice of Remedies*
补救的选择

Most contracting parties expect that all will go smoothly and that both parties will mutually benefit from the transaction. These positive expectations are most likely to be realized if you have provided for contingencies. Even in the simplest transactions, you must think about the possible problems that may develop latest.

TIP: The first rule of a successful international business transaction is also the last decide how to resolve disputes before they happen.

The best time to decide how to handle a conflict is at the time the contract is made when both parties are feeling positive toward the bargain. The contract should include provisions as to which remedies a party may seek in the unlikely event that the other party fails to perform the requisite obligations. If you are unable to reach an agreement on the choice of remedies when drafting the contract, you are even less likely to do so after a problem arises. By selecting a mutually acceptable remedy in the beginning, both parties will know what to expect should performance fail.

多数合同当事方都希望一切顺利进行，双方都从交易中获益。如果你遇上突发事件，这些积极的期望是最有可能被意识到的。即使最简单的交易，你也必须考虑可能出现的问题及问题的最新进展。

提示：成功的国际交易的第一条准则也是最后决定是在争端发生之前解决它。

决定如何处理冲突的最好时间是合同双方对交易都有积极期望的时候。合同应包括当不太可能发生事故的另一方不履行必要义务时，合同一方可能会寻求的补救条款。当起草合同时，如果不能在补救措施的选择上达成协议，问题出现后，你更不可能这样做。一开始，通过选择一种双方都能接受的补救措施，双方就会知道预计的事情不会发生。

1.4.14　*Necessary Terms*
必要条款

In most countries, parties to commercial transactions may make their own bargains free of legal restraints. However, in most jurisdictions, the courts will enforce a contract only if the parties have agreed to the following four basic terms: ①The description of the goods in terms of type, quantity, and quality; ②The time of delivery; ③The price; ④The time and means of payment.

These terms are considered essential because they cannot be easily implied by the law-they are the necessary parameters to the contractual relationship. Every international contract should provide for these terms.

多数国家的交易当事方可能会使他们自己的交易不受法律限制。然而，在大多数管辖范围内，法院只有在合同当事人同意以下四个基本条款时才执行合同：①货物的种类、数量和质量条款；②交货时间条款；③价格条款；④支付时间和支付方式条款。

由于法律不轻易隐含这些条款，因此它们被认为是至关重要的，是合同关系成立的决定性因素。每个国际合同都应该包含这些条款。

1.4.15 *International Trends*
国际趋势

As a brief aside, a current trend in the law of several nations—and eventually, no doubt, in international laws among nations—is to recognize contracts that are the basis of commercial transactions even if they fail to provide the essential terms. If a dispute arises and any of the essential terms are missing or ambiguous, the intent of the parties may be implied from customary trade or financial practices. The bottom line is that judges, arbitrators, rule makers, and law makers prefer to uphold a bargain made by business folks—who are presumed to know what they are doing. In comparison, private individuals and consumers are given more protection against bad bargains that do not cover all of the essential agreement terms because there is a presumption that they are at the mercy of the business folks. In any event, it is best not to rely on trends or implied contract terms. You should always state your intent in clear and definite written terms.

简而言之，目前有几个国家的法律的趋势——最终，毫无疑问，在涉及以上几个国家间的国际法中——是即使不能提供必要的条款，也会承认基于商业交易的合同。如果发生争议以及任何必要条款缺失或含糊不清的话，在传统的贸易或金融实务中，当事人可能会隐含他们的意图。底线是法官、仲裁员、规则制定者和法律制定者倾向于维护由业务人员达成的交易——他们被推测知道他们自己在做什么。相比之下，个人和消费者被给予更多的保护，使他们免做不包括所有基本协议条款的坏交易，因为有一种推定认为他们会受业务人员的摆布。在任何情况下，最好都不要依赖趋势或默示合同条款。你应该在书面条款中清晰和明确地说明你的意图。

1.4.16 *Payment and Delivery Terms*
付款条款和交货条款

Two of the essential terms take on further significance in international business contracts: the payment terms and the delivery terms. In international transactions, it is essential to establish the payment terms. It may be assumed in a domestic transaction that the traders intend to exchange goods for domestic currency. When dealing cross - border, there will probably be a choice of currencies. You may also be subject to foreign exchange restrictions on the currency. Payment terms should be clearly defined to ensure that the contract will be enforceable.

In an international business contract, a clear definition of the transport and delivery term is also essential. This term can have different meanings in domestic as opposed to international contracts. If each party interprets this provision differently, a breach of the contract is quite likely, and there is a greater risk of incurring a loss on the sale. Mutual agreement on the meaning of the transport and delivery term is extremely important.

在国际商务合同中有两个具有更深层意义的重要条款：付款条款和交货条款。在国际交易中，订立付款条款至关重要。在国内交易中，交易者往往用本国货币交换商品。进行跨境交易时，可能要选择货币。你可能要接受外汇货币的限制。为了确保合同的执行，应该明确定义付款条款。

在国际商务合同中，对运输和交货条款的清晰定义也是必不可少的。该条款在国内与国际合同中的含义是不同的。如果双方对这一条款的解释不同，很有可能导致违约，从而导致较大的销售损失风险的发生。关于运输和交货条款的共同协议是极其重要的。

1.5　Issues Affecting International Business Contracts
　　 影响国际商务合同的问题

1.5.1　*Cultural Issues*
　　　 文化问题

Your success in foreign trade will depend on how flexible you are in recognizing and respecting the culture of other people. Cultural differences will affect not only your negotiations with foreign traders, but also the acceptance of your goods or service in foreign markets. In a business context, culture is a set of rules that govern the way in which commercial transactions are conducted between nationals of particular nations. These rules dictate the etiquette, traditions, values, communication, and negotiating styles of a group of people. You must be aware and sensitive to other cultures, and you must adapt your products and services to the preferences of the foreign market.

Culture should be considered as applying to people, not to nations. Although it may be possible to identify an overall culture for a particular country, many subcultures are likely to exist. Even if you have identified a foreign trader's country and have learned the rules that you think will apply, you should avoid clinging to preconceived notions. In today's world, people are on the move, and even more importantly, cultures are crossing country borders and cultural rules are constantly evolving.

Cultural awareness will be most important in the initial contact and negotiation, since in subsequent contacts you will have figured out many of the rules. In making initial contact, you should first establish whether the general protocol in the country tends to be rigidly applied. The next step is to determine what that protocol is, especially for the issues that will arise at the first stage of contract negotiations. These issues include greetings, courtesies, business ethics, decision making, gender, meeting formalities, and business attire. The final step should be to ensure that you are approaching cultural issues with the proper attitude. Once you have researched the rules, learned what you believe is the proper protocol, and made an attempt to practice it, be willing to laugh at yourself. Cultural missteps are inevitable and will be made on both sides. Humor will usually ease even the tensest situation. Pull out your cultural pocket guide, show the rules and illustrations to your host, and have a good laugh together.

Cultural notes of negotiating contracts:

你在外贸上的成功将取决于你认识和尊重他人的文化有多灵活。文化差异不仅会影响到你与外国商人的谈判，而且会影响到你的产品或服务在国外市场的接受度。在商业背景下，文化是一套规则，这些规则管理着某些国家间的交易方式。这些规则规定/支配着一群人的礼仪、传统、价值观、沟通和谈判风格。你必须对其他文化有所了解和敏感，你必须使你的产品和服务适应国外市场的偏好。

文化应适应人类，而不是国家。尽管认定某个国家的整体文化是可能的，但许多次文化可能存在。即使你已经确认了交易国并了解了你认为将要适应的规则，你也应该避免抱着先入为主的观念。在当今世界，人们不断迁移，更重要的是，文化正在跨越国界且文化规则正在不断发展。

由于在随后的联系中你会想到许多规则，所以在最初的沟通和谈判中，文化意识是最重要的。当初次沟通时，你应该首先确定在该国通用协议书是否严格适用。下一步是确定协议书是什么，特别是合同谈判的第一个阶段出现的问题。这些问题包括问候、礼节、商业伦理、决策、性别、会议手续和职业装束。最后一步应该是确保你用正确的态度接触文化问题。一旦你研究了这些规则，了解了你所相信的是正确的协议，你就试图去实践它，并愿意自嘲。文化误解对双方来说将是不可避免的。幽默通常会缓解紧张的形势。你可以拿出你的袖珍文化指南，给你的客户看并解释这些规则，而后一笑了之。

就合同谈判时应注意的文化事项：

1.5.1.1 When You Meet a Foreign Trader
当你接待外商时

Do use a title to show respect and wait for the other party to initiate informality. Reply to inquiries immediately, preferably by telephone. Be enthusiastic but not overbearing. Allow the other trader equal speaking time.

Don't be in a hurry. Determine in advance whether it is common business practice in the other party's country to "grow" deals over time. If not, make your deal. If so, plan to establish a professional relationship before you sign a contract. If you are seeking more than a one-time sale, you may need months or even a year to reach a long-term arrangement.

请用头衔表示尊重并等待对方开始非正式会谈。最好通过电话立即回复询盘。热情但不傲慢。允许对方说话的时间与你一样长。

不要急，要提前确定在对方国家超时谈生意是否是常见的。如果不是，就要尽快达成交易。如果是这样，签合同前先建立贸易关系。如果你寻求的不是一次性销售，你可能需要几个月甚至一年才能达成长期协议。

1.5.1.2   When You Confront Gender or Race Bias
当你面对性别或种族偏见时

Do keep your appearance subdued, your demeanor professional, and your approach formal. Present a business card, speak quietly with knowledge and authority, and take a firm attitude. If possible, bring a business partner or coworker who is of the same race or gender as the foreign trader and who is prompted in advance to acknowledge your authority and aptitude. Find out whether you can deal with a different representative of the company: Don't try to make a statement about rights. If the deal is important, try not to take personal offense and refrain from lecturing the other party. Do not assume that others from the same company or even the same country share the same bias.

保持你的外表温和、你的举止专业和你的方法有条理。呈上名片，用知识和权威轻声地说话，并采取坚定的态度。如果可能的话，带一个业务合作伙伴或同一种族或同一性别的业务同事，他一早就了解你的权力和能力，并清楚你是否能与不同的公司代表做交易：不要试图声明你的权力。如果交易很重要的话，尽量不要责怪某人和避免训斥对方。不要假设他人与你一样来自同一家公司甚至是同一个国家而有相同的偏见。

1.5.1.3   When You are at the Negotiating Table
当你谈判时

Do show firm authority. Be aware of your host's level of eye and physical contact and remain within the bounds established. Do research common cultural traits and business practices of the foreign trader. Determine in advance the points on which you can be flexible so that you start the negotiations above your bottom line. Insert humor when appropriate, balanced with reserve when the discussion is serious.

Don't appear inflexible on all points. Avoid overt conflict or belaboring a point. Don't jump to fill every conversation gap; silence can yield golden results. Refrain from sudden shifts in your tone of voice or changes in your demeanor.

你要显示公司的权威。注意客户的眼睛水平线并且注意身体接触保持在一定范围内。研究常见的文化特质和外商的贸易惯例。事先确定可以灵活谈判的点，这样你可以在你的底线上开始谈判。在适当的时候幽默一下，当讨论严肃时，有保留地平衡气氛。

不要出现不可转变点。要避免公开的冲突或过度说明一个点。不要跳出来填补每一次谈话的空缺，有时候沉默是金。要避免突然地转变你的语调或改变你的举止。

1.5.1.4   When You are Faced with Legal Issues
当你面对法律问题时

Do find out whether negotiations will be merely preliminary or whether the other party intends to make a deal. Ask your host for a list of who will be present at the meeting, and if legal counsel for your host plans to attend, consider bringing your own attorney. Consult an attorney if negotiations are serious and you are uncertain of the risks.

Don't agree to any deal or sign any contract unless you are absolutely certain that you fully understand and agree to all rights and obligations of both parties to the agreement.

要清楚谈判是否只是开始还是另一方打算达成交易了。询问你的客户出席会议的人员名单，如果你的客户的法律顾问参加会议，你可以考虑带上你自己的律师。如果谈判比较庄重而你不确定风险的话，可以咨询律师。

除非你绝对肯定你完全理解并同意协议双方的所有权利和义务，否则不要同意任何协议或签署任何合同。

1.5.1.5　When You Socialize
　　　　 当你交往时

Do accept an invitation if your host graciously extends it. Go prepared with several conversational topics that might be of interest to your hosts other than the business at hand. Research the cultural norms of gift exchanging, and consider a gift that is representative of your country.

Don't offer to socialize if your host sticks to business and places time constraints on the meetings. Avoid criticizing your host's country, and do not raise sensitive topics such as politics, personal privacy, or religion. Be careful not to consume too much alcohol.

如果你的客户亲切邀请的话，要接受邀请。要准备几个手头业务外的你的客户可能感兴趣的话题。研究礼物交换的文化规范，考虑选择一份在你的国家有代表性的礼物。

如果你的客户坚持召开业务会议，且对会议有时间限制的话，不要提供社交项目。要避免批评客户的所在国，不要提及敏感话题，如政治、个人隐私或宗教。小心不要喝太多酒。

1.5.2　*Trends toward Globalization and Uniformity*
　　　　全球化趋势和统一性

When you begin to research the global marketplace, you will find an expanding horizon. Although some countries continue a self-imposed isolation most have come to recognize that development and refinement of a global economic strategy is important to the growth and maintenance of a strong economy. Trade barriers among countries are being reduced and infrastructures for foreign transportation and communication are improving. Trade and business journals are devoting more and more space to international news, governments are revising laws to provide more uniformity for cross-border transactions, and dispute and enforcement systems are being improved.

Much of the pressure toward globalization is bubbling up from the private business sector. Underlying the trends in government policies are the needed demands of the populace, and in particular of businesses, which have the means to be influential. Large companies and individual traders alike are seeking cross-border opportunities, and they are finding ways to make deals within the evolving international marketplace. In turn, their activities are encouraging the trend toward a uniform international law of commerce in recognition of the difficulties of applying national laws across country borders.

当你开始研究全球市场时，你会发现市场是不断扩展的。尽管一些国家继续自我孤立，但大部分国家都已认识到，全球经济战略的发展和改进对一个强大的经济体的增长和维护是很重要的。国与国之间的贸易壁垒正在减少，对外运输和沟通的基础（设施）在不断改善。贸易和商业期刊正投放越来越多的国际新闻，政府为跨境交易的统一性不断修改法律，并且异议与执行系统在不断地改善。

太多针对全球化的压力正从私营企业中显现出来。分析政府的政策趋势是民众的需求，特别是交易需求，这样的需求具有影响力。大公司和个体交易者都在寻求跨境机会，他们正在寻找方式使交易在国际市场得到发展；反过来，在适用跨境国家法律的难点问题上的认可方面，他们所做的是鼓励国际商法的统一（趋势）。

1.5.3 Role of Politics
政治的作用

Political events have a major impact on the economy of a country. Instability can be devastating to a country's markets, while a stable government can be a great asset. A strong and growing economy will in turn have a calming effect on political turmoil. Although some would argue that politicians should take less of a role in regulating the commercial affairs of private traders, the influence of politics will no doubt always be a major factor because these two forces are so entwined.

International trade plays such a significant role in a country's economy that governments throughout history have used direct and indirect trade barriers to force changes in the governments and policies of other countries. Trade barriers include boycotts, quotas, tariffs, import and export prohibitions, licenses, consumer and labeling requirements, and environmental regulations. Trade sanctions are often used to influence another country's domestic policies or practices and to protest a country's aggressive actions toward its neighbors. Favorable trade preferences are granted to countries that implement the changes thought to be desirable.

As an international trader, you must stay in touch with political trends. The stability or instability of a region will indicate whether you will succeed in establishing long-term arrangements there.

TIP: As regulations and trade barriers are relaxed in a particular country, look for new opportunities. Take advantage of your own government's incentives for trading with other countries. Before making a commitment to do business in a particular market, you should consider whether the country's political past and current political climate are conducive to your trade.

政治事件对一个国家的经济会产生重大影响。政治不稳定可能会毁灭一个国家的市场，而一个稳定的政府本身就是一笔巨大的资产。一个强大的和日益增长的经济愿景将反过来平静地舒缓政治动乱。虽然有些人主张，在调节个体交易商的商务事件时，政客们应该少起作用，但由于这两股力量总是交织在一起，政治影响无疑会永远是一个重要因素。

　　国际贸易在一国的经济中扮演着重要角色，政府在其历史/发展史上一直使用直接和间接贸易壁垒迫使其他国家的政府和政策发生变化。贸易壁垒包括抵制、配额、关税、进出口禁令、许可证、消费者和标签要求以及环保法规。贸易制裁经常被用来影响另一个国家的国内政策或实践、抗议一国对其邻国的侵略行为；而贸易优惠则被给予想要改变且实施改变的国家。

　　作为一名国际贸易商，你必须了解政治趋势。地区的稳定与否对你是否能成功地建立起长期的贸易安排起着预示作用。

　　提示：当某个特定国家的法规和贸易壁垒放松的时候，就会寻找到新的（贸易）机会。（你可以）利用你所在国政府的激励机制与其他国家开展贸易。决定在某个特定市场做交易之前，你应该考虑这个国家过去的政治情况和当前的政治气候是否有利于你的交易。

1.5.4 *Regulatory Laws*
监管法律

　　It is your responsibility to know the law. Lack of knowledge is not a defense to a criminal charge, penalty proceeding, or civil lawsuit. It is essential that you know and understand the legal implications and boundaries of trading in your own country and abroad. An attorney with international legal experience can advise you on the issues that you should know.

　　Countries are exploding with laws regulating the import, export, and sale of goods. Developing countries are taking their cues from the laws of developed countries. New and revised laws are being introduced throughout the world countries come under pressure to join the globalization trend. In the world economy, most countries are recognizing that they have to offer domestic and foreign traders a business-oriented environment. At the same time, they are striving to protect the rights of their own nationals, wherever you transact or plan to transact business, you should be aware of existing regulations governing import, export, antitrust, anti-bribery, consumer protection, intellectual and industrial property rights, and environmental issues. You must also keep watch for changes in those laws and regulations.

　　了解法律是你的责任。缺乏（法律）知识不是刑事指控、罚款或民事诉讼的防御措施。至关重要的是，你要知道和理解国内外贸易的法律含义和界限。有国际法律经验的律师会建议你应该知道这些问题。

　　当前，各国正在不断调整进出口和商品销售的有关法规。发展中国家正在从发达国家的法律中提取（制定本国相关法规）线索。新制定的和新修订的法律被引入迫于压力加入全球化趋势的世界各国。在世界经济中，大多数国家都认识到它们必须向国内外商人提供以商业为导向的交易环境。同时，它们正努力保护本国公民的权利，无论你在哪里交易或计划在哪里交易，你都应该知道涉及进口、出口、反垄断、反贿赂、消费者保护、知识和工业产权、环境问题的相关法规。此外，你还必须继续留意这些法律、法规的变化。

1.5.5   *Internet Issues*
互联网问题

The potential of the Internet, a new electronic marketplace, is an exciting concept for traders today. In just a few minutes, you can find a particular populace by search criteria and send off your advertisement. You can develop your own web site to improve customer access to your company. Sales can be made at electronic speed, suppliers can be sought worldwide, and classified advertising has taken on a global meaning.

Traders on the Internet must be aware of the pitfalls. Security of the information that passes through electronic channels remains a problem. Before using the Internet for confidential information, you should be certain to encode that information. The Internet is a public domain. If you place your intellectual property-trademarks, copyrighted or patented materials, designs, etc.- on the Internet, you should first ensure its protection from infringement.

Use of the Internet to advertise and transact business in countries home might be a sufficient minimum contact to subject you to the jurisdiction of the courts in those other places. You could also become subject to business income, and sales taxation in those countries, and your activities may be regulated by local country laws such as those governing antitrust, consumer fraud and unfair trading practices. Similarly, you may be required to comply with business and profession licensing requirements in jurisdictions where you do business. Be certain that you understand the legal implications of using the Internet before you take the plunge.

互联网的潜力，一个新的电子市场，今天对交易者来说是一个令人激动的概念。通过搜索条件并发出你的广告，在几分钟内，你就可以找到一个特定的人。你可以开发自己的网站来改善链接，使客户访问你的公司。（通过互联网）以电子化的速度营销，可以在全球寻找供应商，并且可以做全球分类广告。

互联网上的交易者必须谨防陷阱。通过电子渠道传输的信息的安全仍然是一个问题。在使用互联网传递私密信息之前，你应该对信息进行编码。互联网是一个公共领域。如果你把你的知识产权——商标、版权或专利材料、设计等——放在互联网上，你应该首先确保其免受侵犯。

使用互联网做广告和在国内进行交易可能与地方法院接触最少。你的交易收入和这些国家收取的销售税以及你的活动可能由当地的（国家）法律进行调整，如反垄断、消费者欺诈和不公平贸易行为等方面的法律。同样，在你做生意的地方，在司法管辖区内，你可能被要求遵守商业和职业许可方面的规定/要求。在你全身心投入你的交易之前，你要确保你理解了使用互联网的法律含义。

Ideological & Political Gardens

取消普惠制待遇，我国外贸依然保持稳健增长

2021年12月，一则海关总署公告在业界引起较大关注。公告说："自12月1日起，对输往欧盟成员国、英国、加拿大、土耳其、乌克兰和列支敦士登等已不再给予中国普惠制关税优惠待遇国家的货物，海关不再签发普惠制原产地证书。"

有观点认为，欧盟成员国等国家正取消对中国的最惠国待遇，也有人认为这将冲击我国的出口。更有甚者，"脑补"出新的经贸摩擦。事实如何？

先说最惠国待遇。单从字面上看，"最惠国"似乎意味着得到的优惠很大，其实不然。最惠国待遇是现代国际贸易关系中的正常贸易关系待遇。目前，中国的主要贸易伙伴，包括世界贸易组织的所有成员，都与中国有最惠国待遇关系。即便是在某些时候某些国家违反WTO规则对华加征关税，也都没有到全面取消最惠国待遇的地步。

再说"普惠制"。相比最惠国待遇，普惠制中"惠"的意味更浓、更实。通常，发达经济体可以给予发展中经济体普惠制等关税待遇，发展中经济体也可相互给予优惠待遇。在这个待遇中，给惠国可以根据受惠国的发展情况等，适时取消，也就是业界通常所说的"毕业"。

欧盟（包括当时仍属于欧盟的英国）和土耳其在2015年1月1日就取消了对中国的普惠制待遇。加拿大、瑞士和列支敦士登取消的时间是2014年7月1日。乌克兰则在更早的2012年就取消了对中国的普惠制待遇。

换言之，这份公告所提到的国家在几年前就已取消对中国的普惠制待遇。要说冲击出口，按道理也应该是几年前的事了。然而，事实是，即便取消了普惠制待遇，我国外贸近年来依然保持稳健增长。2021年前10个月，我国外贸进出口总值达到31.67万亿元，同比增长22.2%，比2019年全年还高出1 300亿元。此次海关不再签发普惠制原产地证书，只不过是海关的一个"技术性处理"。

其实，这也不是海关总署第一次发布类似公告。在2021年10月的一则公告中，海关总署决定从2021年10月12日起，不再对输往俄罗斯、白俄罗斯、哈萨克斯坦3个欧亚经济联盟成员国的货物签发普惠制原产地证书。输往上述相关国家货物的发货人需要原产地证明文件的，可以申请领取非优惠原产地证书。在中国，原产地证书已实现自助打印，足不出户即可完成全套申领流程。

截至2021年12月，给予我国普惠制待遇的国家还剩3个：澳大利亚、新西兰、挪威。业内人士认为，普惠制原产地证书在未来可能会彻底退出历史舞台。

实际上，得益于我国与越来越多的经济体签署自贸协定，企业完全可以根据自身情况选择最有利的关税安排。比如，我国与日本通过《区域全面经济伙伴关系协定》（RCEP）建立了自由贸易伙伴关系，协定于2022年1月1日生效后，企业可以申领RCEP项下原产地证书，享受相应的协定税率。

业内人士建议，企业要充分利用自贸区建设等合作成果，提高自贸协定利用率，不断优化出口市场结构，打造竞争新优势。

党的二十大报告指出："我们实行更加积极主动的开放战略，构建面向全球的高标准自由贸易区网络，加快推进自由贸易试验区、海南自由贸易港建设，共建'一带一路'成为深受欢迎的国际公共产品和国际合作平台。我国成为一百四十多个国家和地区的主要贸易伙伴，货物贸易总额居世界第一，吸引外资和对外投资居世界前列，形成更大范围、更宽领域、更深层次对外开放格局。"

资料来源 刘红霞. 新闻分析：没了普惠制原产地证书，出口会遭殃吗？[EB/OL].（2021-12-01）[2023-12-22]. https://baijiahao.baidu.com/s?id=1717945015023101575&wfr=spider&for=pc.

Exercises

Chapter 1 即测即评

Ⅰ.Single-choice.

1.A contract is simply a(n)_____ that defines a relationship between two or more parties.

A.letter　　　　　B.record　　　　　C.agreement　　　　　D.confirmation

2.A contract refers to an agreement enforceable at law. An agreement consists of _____.

A.inquiry and reply　　　　　　　　B.negotiation and bargaining

C.offer and counter-offer　　　　　　D.offer and acceptance

3.A commercial contract, in simplest terms, is merely an agreement made by parties _____ for the purpose of transacting business.

A.one or more　　　B.more than two　　　C.two or more　　　D.three or more

4.The contract terms are usually supplemented and restricted by laws that serve to protect the parties and to define specific relationships between them in the event that provisions are as follows except _____.

A.ambiguous　　　　B.complete　　　　C.indefinite　　　　D.missing

5.In an international sales contract, the balance of power between contracting parties _____.

A.is equal in most contractual situations because of mutual understanding

B.usually tips in favor of the party who does not draft the contract

C.usually tips to the party who is not familiar with written contracts

D.can work against the stronger party in a contract negotiation

6.When making a commitment to perform an international commercial contract, _____.

A.parties usually operate by same business practices

B.consider the other party's culture before you act

C.accept a handshake to seal the bargain

D.insist on written evidence of personal commitment

7.When trading internationally, you are subject to _____.

A.the laws of your own country　　　　B.the laws of other countries

C.the laws of international community　　D.any of the above is possible

8.Most jurisdictions require that certain contracts should be _____ to be enforceable.

A.oral　　　　B.parol　　　　C.written　　　　D.witnessed

9.By selecting a mutually acceptable _____in the beginning, both parties will know what to expect in case a performance fails.

A.formation　　　B.execution　　　C.subsidy　　　D.remedy

10.The four basic terms of a contract include _____.

A.description of goods, delivery, price, and payment

B.description of goods, inspection, price, and payment

C.inspection, price, payment, and warranty

D.insurance, delivery, price, and payment

Ⅱ.Gap-filling.

Contracts are so much a part of living in a society that you are probably unaware of how many contracts you make every day. In the broadest sense, a contract is simply an (1)_____(协议) that defines a relationship between two or more parties. Any contract may be oral or written. Written terms may be recorded in a simple (2)_____(备忘), certificate, or receipt. Because a contractual relationship is made between two or more parties who have potentially (3)_____(双方利益), the contract terms are usually supplemented and restricted by laws that serve to protect the parties and to define specific relationships between them in the event that (4)_____(条款) are indefinite, ambiguous, or even missing.

When one party enters into a commercial contract with an unfamiliar and distant party across a country border, a contract takes on added significance. The creation of an international contract is a more complex process than the (5)_____(订立) of a contract between parties from the same country and culture. In a cross-border transaction, the parties usually do not meet face-to-face, they have different societal (6)_____(价值) and_____(习惯), and the laws to which they are subject are imposed by different governments with distinct (7)_____(法律体系). These factors can easily lead to misunderstandings, and therefore the contracting parties should define their (8)_____(共识) in contractual, and preferably written terms. The role of a contract in an international commercial transaction is of particular importance with respect to the following aspects, such as balance of power, cross-border (9)_____(权利和义务), governing law, (10)_____(救济选择), and the like.

Ⅲ.Discussion.

1.What is a contract? What is the role of contracts in international commerce?

2.What is the typical situation concerning balance of power between the parties to a contract? If you are a weak party, what are the countermeasures to protect your rights?

3.Why should you make your rights and obligations definite in a transaction? How to do it?

4.What is the importance of culture in an international contract? How to deal with it?

5.What are different ways to make a commitment in an international transaction? How do you get to know the extent to which a party is making a commitment?

6.What laws may govern an international contract? How to choose the governing law for an international commercial contract?

7. What are the requirements for a contract to be enforceable? Must a contract for international sales be made to be enforceable?

8.What is the importance of remedies for a transaction? What are the basic types of contract remedies and how to apply them in practice?

9.What terms or clauses are essential for a contract to be valid? How does China's Civil Code govern the terms of a contract?

10.Philosopher Confucius said,"Human life can not avoid the cycle of birth, aging, sickness, and death."Neither can an international contract. What are the birth, the aging, the sickness, and the death of a contract? Describe the life of a contract.

Ⅳ.Case study.

Enterprise P. Boucher Ltee. v. Henan Yuanfeng Leather Manufacturing Co., Ltd.

13 August, 2007, Xinxiang Intermediate People's Court District Court, China

Case Story

...

Position of the Parties

A.Seller's Claims

Seller alleges that:

Based upon the introduction of the intermediary and the trust between the parties, Seller and Buyer orally made a goods import agreement in May, 2005. They agreed that Seller would provide to Buyer ten containers of wet-blue cattle hides from abroad. Later, from July to the end of November, 2005, Seller delivered the goods aforementioned to China. Buyer received them successively from August to December, 2005 and issued a Confirmation Note on 3 March, 2006. The total amount owed for the goods was USD437,800. However, although Seller reminded Buyer several times to pay for the goods, Buyer always delayed the payment. Until now, Buyer has not paid anything, which breached the contract and lost Buyer's faith seriously. Thus, Seller has the following requests:

1.Buyer should pay Seller USD437,800 for the goods plus USD36,000 for demurrage fees, which is USD473,800 (equal to CNY3,790,000) in total;

2.Buyer should undertake the lawsuit fee and preservation fee of this case.

B.Buyer's Rebuttal

Buyer alleges that:

1.There was no sale of goods contractual relationship between Seller and Buyer, since the parties did not sign any written sales contract. Both Seller's home country, Canada, and Buyer's home country, China are, Parties to the United Nations Convention on Contracts for the International Sale of Goods. Because China has declared a reservation to Article 11 of this Convention, the People's Court should find that the contractual relationship between Seller and Buyer was not established. Therefore, Buyer has no obligation to pay for the goods, let alone the demurrage fees.

2.The parties actually established a processing contractual relationship. Since Seller has not yet provided Buyer the processing remuneration (加工费), Buyer has the right to detain the products that have been processed. As Seller did not pay the processing remuneration, it has no right to pick up the goods.

Buyer Counterclaims that:

Due to the introduction of the intermediary and the trust between the parties, Buyer and

Seller made an oral agreement on the processing of cattle hides. They agreed that the Buyer would process cattle hides for Seller and Seller would buy them back after Buyer processed the cattle hides into leather. Then Seller delivered ten containers of wet-blue cattle hides to Xingang, Tianjin, China, asking Buyer to transport these goods to Qinyang, Henan Province to process them. Because of this, Buyer paid a large amount for port fees, loading and discharge fees for transportation, and warehousing fees. Besides, Buyer actively imported quantities of high-qualified chemical raw materials according to Seller's request, and organized its staff to process these goods. Most of the wet-blue cattle hides have now been processed into finished goods or semi-finished goods, and are waiting for Seller to take them back to Canada for sale. Nevertheless, while Buyer was working positively to perform the processing contract, it received the judicial process of payment for the goods requested by Seller, which brought Buyer a great shock.

Buyer believes that the parties have established a processing contractual relationship, and Buyer has performed the main obligation of the contract. If Seller disobeys the principle of good faith and does not perform the obligation of buying back the goods, it will undoubtedly bring a big loss to Buyer, which not only includes various fees that have paid by Buyer, but may also involve loss of customs payment, available profits, etc. To avoid these unnecessary losses, Buyer files a counterclaim with this Court, requesting that:

1. Seller should compensate Buyer for the following losses: entry-exit inspection and quarantine fee, CNY10,264;

2. The lawsuit fee of this case should be undertaken by Seller.

Facts Identified by the Court

Based upon the parties' statements, evidence adduced and opinions, the Court identifies the facts of the present case as follows:

In May, 2005, Seller and Buyer made an oral import goods agreement, providing that from July to November, 2005, Seller would send ten containers of cattle hides to Buyer. In that period, Buyer drafted a sales contract by itself and made a record to Zhengzhou Customs. In that contract, the Seller was Enterprise P. Boucher Ltee., while the Buyer was Yuanfeng Co., Ltd. After Buyer received the goods, it issued a Confirmation Note to Seller on 3 March 2006, confirming that it had received Seller's ten containers and noted the quantities and price for the goods, as well as stating that "these products will be used to produce the export orders of Seller, the order contract will be discussed separately". On 13 March 2006, 24 March 2006, and 5 April 2006, Seller faxed Buyer to remind it to pay for the goods, but Buyer has not paid for the goods as of now.

资料来源　佚名. CISG case presentation [EB/OL]. [2023-11-22]. http://cisgw3.law.pace.edu/cases/ 070813cl.html.

Case Discussion:

(1) What is the governing law of contract in the case? Why?

(2) Brief the facts and the key issues of the case.

(3) What judgment will the court make? Why?

(4) What do you learn from this case? Discuss the form and governing law of the contract.

Case Summary:

This case is the Chinese and foreign goods' business cases. The case is about the dispute over oral goods' agreement reached between Yuanfeng company in China and P. Boucher company in Canada. Based on the introduction of the middleman and trust to Canada party, Chinese party reached an oral export agreement of wet-blue cattle hides with the Canadian side. According to the agreement, China party delivered USD437,800 of goods to Canada, the Canadian side accepted the goods and issued a confirmation, but did not make payment. Therefore China filed a lawsuit. The Canadian side counterclaimed that there was no contract relationship between both parties because both parties are members of the CISG, and Article 11 of CISG are reserved in China. That is, for Chinese party, the international sales of goods contract should be made in writing.

This case involved the issues of the form of contract, enforcement and applicable law. It reflects the importance of a written contract in international business, namely it will be better that the international sales of goods contract between Chinese and foreign should be concluded in written form to facilitate the contract performed smoothly, avoid and solve contract disputes, also it can prevent the other legal loophole.

Chapter 2
Language Features in International Business Contracts
国际商务合同的语言特征

Learning Objectives

◆　重点掌握国际商务合同中常用的词语与句式；掌握国际商务合同中同义词连用的语言特点；了解国际商务合同中一词多义和易混淆词的语言特点。

Guide Case

A Case of Contract Termination and Default

The sellers agreed to sell to the buyers 12,000 tons of citrus pulp pellets CIF Rotterdam for use as animal feed. Clause 7 of the contract provided for "shipment to be made in good condition". One shipment arrived in the "Hansa Nord" with 1,260 tons of pellets in No.1 hold and 2,053 tons in No.2 hold. Much of the cargo in No.1 hold was found to be damaged while that in No.2 hold was in substantially good condition. The buyers rejected the whole cargo. Mocatta J., on a case stated from arbitration, upheld the board's award in favour of the buyers and held that the term "shipment in good condition" was a condition of the contract, breach of which justified rejection of the goods. The sellers appealed to the Court of Appeal.

The judge held that, in contracts for the sale of goods, a stipulation must either be a "condition" or a "warranty" and that there could be no tertium quid. Accepting that distinction, he held that this stipulation "shipped in good condition" was a "condition" and not a "warranty". So that, for any breach of it by the seller, the buyer was entitled to treat the contract as repudiated...

The general law apart from the sale of goods. For the last 300 or 400 years the courts have had to grapple with this problem: in what circumstances can a party, who is in breach himself of a stipulation of the contract, call upon the other side to perform his part or sue him for non-performance? At one time the solution was thought to depend on the nature of the stipulation itself, and not on the extent of the breach of its consequences. A plaintiff had to aver and prove that he had performed all conditions precedent or that he was ready and willing to perform them. The question, therefore, was whether the stipulation (which he had broken) was a condition precedent or not or whether it was an independent covenant (the breach of which did debar the plaintiff because the performance by the other was dependent on the plaintiff performing his).

Although that division was treated as exhaustive, nevertheless, when the courts came to apply it, they had regard to the extent of the breach. This was done by Lord Mansfield in 1777 in the great case of Boone v. Eyre (Note) (1779) 1 H. Bl 273；126 E. R. 160. In the language of those times, if the breach went to the whole consideration, the covenant was considered to be a condition precedent and the defendant could plead the breach in bar of the action: but if the breach went "only to a part, where a breach may be paid for in damages, there the defendant has a remedy on his covenant, and shall not plead it as a condition precedent".

In short, if the breach went to the root of the matter, the stipulation was to be considered a condition precedent, but if the breach did not go to the root, the stipulation was considered to be an independent covenant which could be compensated for in damages.

Apart from those cases of "breach going to the root", the courts at the same time were developing the doctrine of "anticipatory breach". When one party, before the day when he is obliged to perform his part, declares in advance that he will not perform it when the day comes, or by his conduct evinces an intention not to perform it, the other may elect to treat his declaration or conduct as a breach going to the root of the matter and to treat himself as discharged from further performance: see Hochster v. De la Tour I (1853) 2 E. & B. 678；118 E. R. 922. By his prior declaration or conduct the guilty party is said to repudiat the contract. The word "repudiation" should be confined to those cases of an anticipatory breach, but it is also used in connection with cases of an actual breach going to the root of the contract (see Heyman v. Dar-wins Ltd. (1942) A. C. 356, 378-379, per Lord Wright). All of them were gathered together by Lord Blackburn in his famous speech in Mersey Steel and Iron Co., Ltd. v. Naylor, Benzon & Co. (1884) 9 App. Cas. 434, 443-444:

"The rule of law, as I always understood it, is that where there is a contract in which there are two parties, each side having to do something (it is so laid down in the notes to Pordage v. Cole (1669) 1 Wms. Saund. 319,320；85 E. R. 449,450), if you see that the failure to perform one part of it goes to the root of the contract, goes to the foundation of the whole, it is a good defense to say...I am not going on to perform my part of it when that which is the root of the whole and the substantial consideration for my performance is defeated by your misconduct. I repeatedly asked Mr. Cohen whether or not he could find any authority which justified him in saying that every breach of a contract...must be considered to go to the root of the contract, and he produced no such authority. There are many cases in which the breach may do so；it depends upon the construction of the contract."

Those last words are clearly a reference to a "condition" strictly so called, in which any breach entitled the other to be discharged from further performance, but the earlier words are quite general. They refer to all terms other than conditions strictly so called.

THE SALE OF GOODS ACT

Such was the state of the law when the Sale of Goods Act 1893 was passed on 20 February 1894. I have studied the current edition of Benjamin, Sale of Personal Property (4th ed., 1888), and the little books which Judge Chalmers wrote before 1890 and after the Act (Chalmers' Sale of Goods Act, 1893 (1st ed., 1894)), and the proceedings in Parliament. These show that until, the year 1893 there was much confusion in the use of the words "condition" and "warranty". But that confusion was removed by the Act itself and by the judgment of Bowen L. J. in Bentsen v. Taylor, Sons & Co. (1893) 2 Q. B. 274,280. Thenceforward those words were used by lawyers as terms of art. The difference between them was that if the promisor broke a condition in any respect, however slight, it gave the other party a right to be quit of his obligations and to sue for damages: Unless he by his conduct waived the condition, in which case he was bound to perform his future obligations but could sue for the damage he had suffered. If the promisor broke a warranty in any respect, however serious, the other party was not quit of his future obligations. He had to perform them. His only remedy was to sue for damages...Now that division was not exhaustive—it left out of account the vast majority of stipulations which were neither "conditions" nor "warranties" strictly so called, but were intermediate stipulations, the effect of which depended on the breach. The cases about these stipulations were legion. They stretched continuously from Boone v. Eyre to Mersey Steel and Iron Co., Ltd v. Naylor, Benzon & Co.

I can not believe that Parliament in 1893 intended to give the go-by to all these cases; or to say that they did not apply to the sale of goods. Those cases expressed the rules of the common law. They were preserved by s. 61(2) of the Act of 1893, which said: "The rules of the common law, including the law merchant, save in so far as they are inconsistent with the express provisions of this Act...shall continue to apply to contracts for the sale of goods."

There was nothing in the Act inconsistent with those cases. So they continued to apply.

In 1962 in the Hongkong Fir Shipping Co. Ltd v. Kawasaki Kisen Kaisha Ltd. (1962) 2 Q. B. 26, the Court of Appeal drew attention to this vast body of case law. They showed that, besides conditions and warranties, strictly so called, there are many stipulations of which the effect depends on this: if the breach goes to the root of the contract, the other party is entitled to treat himself as discharged; but if it does not go to the root, he is not. In my opinion, the principle embodied in these cases applies to contracts for the sale of goods just as to all other contracts.

The task of the court can be stated simply in the way in which Upon L. J. stated it at (1962) 2 Q. B. 64. First, see whether the stipulation, on its true construction, is a condition strictly so called, that is, a stipulation such that, for any breach of it, the other party is entitled to treat himself as discharged. Second, if it is not such a condition, then look to the extent of the actual breach which has taken place. If it is such as to go to the root of the contract, the other party is entitled to treat himself as discharged; but, otherwise, not. To this may be added an anticipatory breach. If the one party, before the day on which he is due to perform his part, shows by his words or conduct that he will not perform it in a vital respect when the day comes, the other party is entitled to treat himself as discharged.

SHIPPED IN GOOD CONDITION

This brings me back to the particular stipulation in this case: "Shipped in good condition". Was this a condition strictly so called, so that any breach of it entitled the buyer to reject the goods? Or was it an intermediate stipulation, so that the buyer cannot reject unless the breach is so serious as to go to the root of the contract?

If there was any previous authority holding it to be a condition strictly so called, we should abide by it just as we did with the clause "expected ready to load" (see...The Mihalis Angelos (1971) 1 Q. B. 164). But, there is no such authority with the clause "shipped in good condition". I regard this clause as comparable to a clause as to quality, such as "fair average quality". If a small portion of the goods sold was a little below that standard, it would be met by commercial men by an allowance off the price. The buyer would have no right to reject the whole lot unless the divergence was serious and substantial...Likewise with the clause "shipped in good condition". If a small portion of the whole cargo was not in good condition and arrived a little unsound, it should be met by a price allowance. The buyers should not have a right to reject the whole cargo unless it was serious and substantial. This is borne out by the difficulty which often arises (as in this case) on a CIF contract as to whether the damage was done before shipment or took place after shipment: for in the latter case the buyer would have no claim against the seller but would be left to his claim against the insurers. So, as a matter of good sense, the buyer should be bound to accept the goods and not reject them unless there is a serious and substantial breach, fairly attributable to the seller.

In my opinion, therefore, the term "shipped in good condition" was not a condition strictly so called, nor was it a warranty strictly-so called. It was one of those intermediate stipulations which gives no right to reject unless the breach goes to the root of the contract.

On the facts stated by the board of appeal, I do not think the buyer was entitled to reject these installments of the contract. The board only said that "not all the goods in hold No.1 were shipped in good condition". That does not say how many were bad. In any case, their condition cannot have been very bad, seeing that all of them were in fact used for the intended purpose. The breach did not go to the root of the contract. The buyer is entitled to damages, but not to rejection...

思考题：
（1）根据本案判决解释"条件""担保""中间条款"的含义。
（2）在本案中，法院是如何确定卖方违约的性质的？其理由是什么？

Besides the differences between English contract and Chinese contract in structure, its content and language expression way are very different from common English: long sentences, special word order, special sentence patterns and expressions, all the sentences are relatively independent. Language in English contract is long, conservative and accuracy.

英语合同除了篇章结构与中文合同有所差异外，其内容和语言表达方式与普通英语也大为不同：句子偏长，语序特别，句式和用语特别，各句子相对独立。英语合同的语言具有冗长性、保守性和精确性的特点。

2.1 Characteristics of Words in International Business Contracts 国际商务合同的词语特点①

International business contracts have definite characteristics (such as a nominalization structure instead of a verb structure, noun phrases, prepositional phrases and adjectives phrases instead of verb phrases, less adjective usage, nor enforcing adverbs such as very and rather, the pronouns and nouns "such, same, hereof" etc. refers to repetition.)

国际商务合同具有明确的用语特点（诸如名词化结构替代动词化结构，名词短语、介词短语和形容词短语替代动词短语，形容词用量少，very 和 rather 等加强性副词不用，用 such、same、hereof 等代词和名词表示重复等）。

2.1.1 *Formal Legal Term—Big Words Used*②
使用正式的法律用词——大眼词

Because an important international business contract is a legally binding document, the architect should be used to take the form of a written contract, use the legal words to show the formality, solemnity of the contract and the accuracy, specifications and majesty of language features.

E.g.1: In convening a general meeting of shareholders, notice shall be dispatched to shareholders. ("Convene" is more formal than "hold" and "assemble", "dispatch" is formal than "spread out" and "hand out".)

E.g.2: The accounting principles employed shall be the same as those applied in preceding years. ("Employ" is more formal than "use".)

E. g. 3: It hereby covenants that the Consignee guarantees the payment of all bills and accounts for goods. ("Covenant" is a legal term, said formally signed a legally binding contract.)

E.g.4: Except AAA's prior written consent, no party shall enter in or assume any mortgage. ("Consent" is a noun, which means "yes" in the contract and is in the alternative use of "agreement".)

E.g.5: This Agreement shall supersede all previous commitments. ("Supersede" are more

---

① 傅伟良. 英文合同写作指要 [M]. 北京：商务印书馆国际有限公司，2002.

② 兰天. 国际商务合同翻译教程 [M]. 大连：东北财经大学出版社，2007.

formal than "take the place of". "Commitments" said "promise", which is more formal than "promise".)

E. g. 6: The licensee shall not dispute or object to the validity of said Letters Patent. ("Object" in the contract should be translated as "against" or "dissent". "Against" can be said as "disagree" in general desk.)

E.g.7: The Principal shall be obliged to pay the commissions to the Sales Agent. ("Oblige" is a typical legal term, instead of "have the responsibility to do sth.", or "compelled to do sth.".)

E.g.8: If any of the terms or conditions of this Agreement is substantially breached by either Party, the other Party shall have the right to terminate this Agreement. ("Terminate" can replace "stop" in the legal documents.)

E.g.9: Party A shall repatriate the patient to China and bear the cost of his passage to Beijing. (Compared with "send back", "repatriate" is a formal written language.)

In contracts, some words and phrases are used in a high frequency and repeatedly. To sum up them as two categories: substantive words and empty words.

重要的国际商务合同，由于是依法成立的具有法律约束力的文件，所以合同的草拟者要习惯采用书面的形式，使用法律词汇，以显示合同正规、庄严、准确、规范以及威严的语言特色。

例1：要召开一次股东大会，需将通知发给各股东（convene 比 hold 和 assemble 要正式，dispatch 比 spread out 和 hand out 要正式）。

例2：所使用的会计原则要与以往各年的会计原则相一致（employ 比 use 要正式得多）。

例3：兹订立契约，承销人保证付清一切票据款及账款（covenant 是法律用词，表示签订有法律约束力的正式合约）。

例4：除非经甲方事先书面同意，任何一方不得参与或承担任何抵押（consent 作名词，在合同中表示"同意"，替代常用词 agreement）。

例5：本协议将取代以前的一切承诺（supersede 比 take the place of 要正式。commitments 表示"承诺"，比 promise 要正式）。

例6：许可证受证人不应对所述专利证书的有效性提出争议或异议（object 在合同中应被翻译成"反对"或"异议"。在普通文书中，"反对"可以用 disagree 表示）。

例7：委托人对经销代理商负有支付佣金的义务（oblige 是个典型的法律用词，替代 have the responsibility to do sth. 或者 compelled to do sth.）。

例8：如果当事人任何一方实质上破坏了本协议中所签订的条款或条件，那么另一方有权终止该协议（terminate 在法律文书中可以替代 stop）。

例9：甲方应将病人遣返回中国，负担他返回北京的费用（与 send back 相比，repatriate 是正式的书面用语）。

在合同中，有一些单词和短语会被反复使用。其总体分为两类：实词和虚词。

2.1.1.1 Empty Words
虚词

The most common empty words are: notwithstanding, above-mentioned, according to, subject to, in accordance with, as per, as provided in, pursuant to, under or in accordance with, prior to, include but not limited to, from...(time) to...(time), no later than, on or before, without prejudice to, whereas, hereto, herein, hereby, hereinafter, hereunder, thereof, the following, as follows, as of the date.

(1)Notwithstanding

It's a prep, similar to "in spite of" or "despite" in meaning. It'll be put at the beginning of one sentence.

E.g.1: Notwithstanding any other provisions to the contract herein, insurance coverage and limits shall be subject to approval of all the parties.

E.g.2: Notwithstanding Article 2.2, the parties may agree to extend the expiration date to such date as is reasonable in the circumstances if any of the conditions precedent referred to in Article 2.1 is not satisfied, or waived on or before the expiration date, any such agreement or waiver to be in writing.

(2)As

It may serve as prep, conjunction, pronoun and may use in several ways. To some extent, the flexible usage of "as" in contract clauses plays an important role.

E.g.1: For purpose of this, capital accounts shall be adjusted as provided for in Sections 4.6 herein.

E.g.2: Based on their respective venture interests as set forth in section 5.2 hereof.

E.g.3: The parties may agree to extend the expiration date to such date as is reasonable in the circumstances.

E.g.4: The venture may relocate its office from time to time or have additional offices as the ventures may determine. (Attention: "as sth. may determine" refers to "so it is with".)

E.g.5: The term of the venture shall commence as of the date hereof.

E.g.6: Except as otherwise provided in section 6.0 and 9.0 hereof.

E.g.7: Sales Representative shall be free to utilize his time, energy and skill in such manner as he deems advisable to the extent that he is not otherwise obligated under this agreement.

(3)Foregoing, Aforesaid, the Said, Aforementioned, Above-Mentioned

E.g.: During the arbitration, the parties hereto shall continue to perform the undisputed part of the contract mentioned above.

(4)According to, under, Subject to, in Accordance with, as per, as Provided in, Pursuant to, under or in Accordance with, as Provided Herein

E.g.: Subject to the supervision and pursuant to the orders, advices and direction of employer, employee shall perform such duties as are customarily performed by one holding such position in other business or enterprises of the same or similar nature.

(5)Including but not Limited to, Including without Limitation, Including by Way of Illustration but not Limitation

E.g.: Party B shall pay sums equal to taxes (including without limitation of sales, value added and similar taxes) and customs duties paid or payable, however designed, levied, or based on amounts payable to party A hereunder.

(6)Prior to, no Later than, on or Before

E.g.1: The buyer shall advise the seller the date of the unpacking inspection as early as possible no later than 15 days in advance.

E.g.2: Shipment shall be made on or before August 15, 202×.

E.g.3: Notification shall be made by the employee to the employer by whom he is employed one month prior to the actual date of termination of labor relation.

(7)With Prejudice to, without Prejudice To

E.g.: This court adjudged with prejudice to that.

(8)Hereof, Hereto, Herein, Hereby, Hereinafter, Hereinbefore, Hereunder, Thereof, Therefrom, Whereby, Hereunto Etc.

E.g.1: Section 10 hereof=section 10 of this contract/agreement.

E.g.2: Article 6 thereof=article 6 of that contract/agreement.

E.g.3: Parties hereto=parties to this contract.

E.g.4: Set my hand and official seal hereunto=set my hand and official seal unto the document.

E.g.5: Terms and conditions provided herein=terms and conditions provided in the contract.

E.g.6: Hereunder=under the contract.

E.g.7: The failure of either party to enforce, at any time, any of the provisions of this agreement, or to require at any time the performance by the other party of any of the provisions hereof, shall in no way be construed to be a waiver of such provisions. Nor in any way affect the validity of this agreement or any part thereof, or the right of the said party thereafter to enforce each and every such provisions.

E.g.8: Now, therefore, in consideration of the mutual promises and covenants herein contained, the parties hereto agree as follow. (Herein contained=contained in this contract)

E.g.9: All amounts due hereunder are payable in full to party B without deduction and are net of taxes (including any withholding tax and custom duties). (All amount hereunder=all amount under this contract)

(9)Attributable to, by Virtue of, on Account of, due to (These Phrases Equal to "Because of", but They are More Formal in Contracts)

E.g.1: Party B hereby undertakes as from the effective date to perform and discharge all obligations and liabilities whatsoever from time to time to be performed or discharged by party A under or by virtue of the amended management agreement as from the effective date in all respects as if party B were the original party to the amended management agreement as a party in place of party A.

E.g.2: The seller shall be liable for any damage of the commodity and expenses incurred due to improper packing and for any rust attribute to inadequate or improper protective measures taken by the seller with regard to the packing.

最常见的虚词有：尽管、上面提到、根据、以……为条件、依照、按照、规定、依据、根据或按照、在……之前、包括但不限于、从……到……、不晚于、在……时或在……之前、毫无偏见、然而、到此为止、于此、以此方式、以下、依此、下面、如下、截至……日。

（1）尽管

它是介词，和"不管"的意思相似。它通常被放在一个句子的开头。

例1：尽管有与本合同相悖的规定，保险范围和责任限制也应以合同各方同意为准。

例2：尽管本合同第2条第2款规定，如上述第2条第1款规定的先决条件在合同到期日之前既未实现又未放弃，合同各方应该根据具体情况，约定合理延长合同的到期日。

（2）作为

它既可以作为介词、连词、代词，也可以多种方式使用。在某种程度上，as的灵活使用在合同条款中起着重要作用。

例1：为此目的，应依照本合同第4条第6款调整资金账户。

例2：基于本合同第5条第2款规定的各方在合资公司中的权益。

例3：合同各方亦可同意根据具体情况合理延长合同到期日。

例4：合资公司有时可迁址或增添营业场所，视投资者的决策而定。

例5：该合资公司的有效期限自本合同签订之日开始。

例6：除本合同第6条和第9条规定外。

例7：销售代表应以他在本协议下无其他义务但他认为适当的程度，自主利用其时间、精力和技能。

（3）前面所述的、前述的、上述的、上述提到的、上述

例：仲裁过程中，本合同各方仍将继续执行上述合同未产生争议的部分。

（4）关于、依照

例：员工应依照用人单位的监督命令、建议和指示，履行在相同或类似企业同一位置的员工通常所履行的职责。

（5）包括但不限于

例：乙方向甲方支付的总额应等于已交或应交的各种税费（包括但不限于消费税、增值税和其他类似的税种）和关税，无论是指定的、征收的还是基于应付给甲方的款项。

（6）在某日之前、提前多少日

例1：买方应尽早通知卖方开箱日期，最早应提前15日发出通知。

例2：装船应在202×年8月15日前（包括15日当天）。

例3：在实际中止劳动关系1个月前，雇主应通知雇员解除劳动关系的事宜。

（7）有损于……、有偏见、在不损失……情况下、无偏见

例：法庭作出了有偏袒的裁决。

（8）于此、到此为止、此中、据此、在此之后、在此之前、在此之下、关于、自此、凭借等

例1：此条款10=本合同/协议条款10。

例2：关于条款6=合同/协议条款6。

例3：关于当事方=本合同当事方。

例4：在此盖我的手印和公章=在文档上盖我的手印和公章。

例5：此处的条款和条件=合同中的条款和条件。

例6：在此之下=合同下。

例7：任何一方当事人未能执行本协议的任何规定，或未要求另一方履行合同的任何规定，都不得解释为放弃上述规定，也不得影响本协议或其任何部分的效力，以及上述一方以后执行任何和全部此种规定的权利。

例8：因此，双方本着相互承诺和契约特约定如下。

例9：本协议规定的所有到期款额应向乙方足额交付，不得抵扣，所交税款为完税后净款额（包括任何待扣款项和关税）。

（9）归因于，凭借……，因为，由于（这些短语等同于"因为"，但用在合同中它们更正式）

例1：乙方在此保证，自本契约生效之日起替代甲方作为上述经变更的《管理协议》的一方，履行自本契约生效之日起，经变更的《管理协议》规定应由甲方履行的责任和义务。

例2：卖方应对因包装不当而发生的货物损坏和费用以及因此采取不充分或不恰当的保护措施而发生的货物生锈承担责任。

2.1.1.2 Substantive Words
实词

(1)Provide, Stipulate, Prescribe, Describe, Set Forth

E.g.1: As provided for in Section 4.6 herein.

E.g.2: The goods should conform to the relevant clauses stipulated in the contract.

(2)Represent, Warrant, Undertake, Guarantee

E.g.1: Party A hereby represents and warrants to party B that.

E.g.2: The seller guarantees that the quality and performance of the contracted equipment furnished by him will be in accordance with the specification requirements as in the contract.

(3)Principal Place of Business, Domicile, Business Premise (Attention: Domicile Is a Legal Term Meaning "Address")

E.g.1: The partnership's principal place of business shall be_____.

E.g.2: The employer is a engaged in_____and maintains business premises at_____.

(4)Chapter, Article, Clause, Section, Paragraph, Sub-Paragraph

E.g.: Party A agrees to hire, train and support sufficient sales and technical staff to meet its obligations under this Agreement and to provide Party B with reasonable proof thereof under section 4.

(5)Has/Reserve Right to, Be Entitled to Have Authority to Do Sth., at One's Option

E.g.1: No party shall have the right to withdraw his capital contributions or demand or receive the return of his capital contributions or any part thereof, except as otherwise provided in this agreement.

E.g.2: The seller shall, at his option, choose the best method, offering either complete or partial replacement or shall depreciate the equipment according to the state of the defects. The buyer shall be at liberty to eliminate the defects himself at the seller's expenses after getting the written approval from the seller.

(6)Have the Legal Obligation to Do, Be Obliged to, Be under the Obligation to Do, Shall Be Liable to, Shall Hold Responsible for, Shall Take the Responsibility For

E.g.1: Under such circumstances, the seller, however, is still under the obligation to take all necessary measures to hasten the delivery of goods.

E.g.2: The seller is obliged to provide the shipping documents with a certificate issued by the relevant authorities of the country or the region attesting that the wooden packing materials have been treated with anti - parasite and anti - mold agent so as to enable the buyer to apply for quarantine inspection at the entry port of animal and plant quarantine.

(7)Incur=Cause but More Formal=Accrue

E.g.1: All banking charges shall be borne by the incurred party.

E.g.2: The losses incurred within the responsibility of the insurance company should be lodged as a claim against the insurance company.

（1）提供、规定、指定、描述、提出

例1：依照（本合同）第4条第6款的规定。

例2：货物应符合本合同有关条款的规定。

（2）代表、担保、承担、保证

例1：甲方向乙方声明并保证。

例2：卖方保证其提供的设备的质量与性能符合合同要求。

（3）主营业地址（注意：domicile是法律用语，意思是"地址"）

例1：本合伙企业的主营业地位于_____。

例2：雇主从事_____业务，营业地位于_____。

（4）章、条款、章节、段落、分段

例：甲方同意雇用、培训、维持足够的销售和技术人员，履行本协议规定的义务，且向乙方提交与本协议第4条相关的合理证明。

（5）保留权利、有权做某事、由……选择

例1：除非本协议另有规定，任何一方都无权撤回其全部或部分出资，也不得要求或接受全部或部分出资的返还。

例2：卖方应自己决定采取最佳方案，或更换全部或部分零件，或根据设备瑕疵的具体情况折价处理。买方有权在得到卖方的书面同意后自行销毁瑕疵零件，费用由卖方负担。

（6）有义务做……，被迫做……，有义务，应当承担责任，要负责，承担……责任

例1：在此情况下，卖方仍有责任采取必要措施加紧交付货物。

例2：卖方有义务提供由相关国家或地区官方签发的装船单据，证明木质包装材料已经过防虫蛀、防霉变的处理，以便买方在入境口岸申请动植物检疫。

（7）发生

例1：所有银行费用都由发生方负担。

例2：如发生保险公司责任范围内的损失，应当向其提起索赔。

2.1.2 Series Synonyms Used[①]

同义词连用

Because of polysemy of many English words, unclear meaning may occur in the sentence and both parties in the contract may understand according to his intent. In order to ensure that the words aren't misinterpreted, using synonyms such as doublets, couplets and triplets etc. in order to guarantee the accuracy of the content, make the contract with careful and rigorous characteristics; in order to reduce vulnerability and controversy and maintain the independence of legal documents.

E.g.1: This agreement is made and entered into by and between party A and party B. （"Made and entered into" is a set of synonyms, said "sign agreements". "By and between" is another pair of synonyms, said signature by party A and party B.)

E.g.2: Nothing contained in this Agreement shall be deemed to obligate Seller to permit Buyer to examine any patent application of Seller otherwise than upon a secret and confidential basis and upon the written request of Buyer.

E.g.3: Change in the Work shall mean any modification of, amendment of/to, or alteration in the Work. （"Modification of" "amendment of/to" and "alteration" in the sentence are three synonymous phrases.)

E.g.4: The Contractor shall always have the sole responsibility for the due and proper execution and performance of all of its rights and obligations under the Contract. （"Execution" and "performance" in the sentence are synonyms.)

E.g.5: Any such consent shall not relieve the Contractor from any liability and obligation under this Contract. （"Liability" and "obligation" in the sentence are synonyms.)

E.g.6: This Agreement, and all rights vested in the Second Party, shall forthwith become null and void, if the Second Party shall violate, or omit to perform, any of the following terms and conditions. (In the sentence, "null" and "void" is a pair of synonyms, "terms" and "conditions" is another group of synonyms.)

Common law matching words or triple in contracts, that are the synonyms and phrases which we understand are as follows:

（1）Acknowledge and Agree

The Parties acknowledge and agree that Joint Venture Company shall be formed forthwith upon satisfaction of the following condition.

（2）Authorize and Grant

You are authorized and granted exclusive authority to conduct an absolute auction sale.

---

① 兰天. 国际商务合同翻译教程 ［M］. 大连：东北财经大学出版社，2007.

(3)Cease and Terminate

Any and all obligations of the Company to the Operator under this Agreement shall immediately cease and terminate upon payment of the Company's dues.

(4)Each or Any

The Guarantor hereby covenants that the Creditors, and each or any of them, may extend the time of payment.

(5)Each and Every

The Borrower agrees to repay the loan to the Lender paying (amount) on the first day of each and every following month, after the date hereof.

(6)Fair and Equitable

Fair and equitable treatment has become one of the most controversial clauses in international investment agreements.

(7)Final and Conclusive

Acceptance of the Work by the Owner shall be final and conclusive except as regards latent defects etc.

(8)Force and Effect

This Agreement shall commence on_____ (date) and shall continue in full force and effect until_____(date).

(9)Fraud and Deception

If a sale has been made through fraud or deception, the Sales Company shall retain an amount equal to the commission paid out to the salesman.

(10)Free and Clear

The Consignee shall keep the consigned goods free and clear of all taxes.

(11)Keep, Observe and Perform

The Second Party shall keep, observe and perform all of the terms, provisions, covenants and conditions of this Agreement.

(12)Remise, Release and Quitclaim

The First Party remised, released, and forever quitclaimed to the Second Party all the right, claim and demand of the First party in and to the following described property.

(13)Right, Interest and Title

AAA represents that it is the owner of the entire right, title and interest in and to_____ (country) Letters Patent No. _____.

(14)Save and Except

No share in the capital stock of the Joint Venture Company can in any way be assigned save and except for directors' qualifying shares.

(15)Sole and Exclusive

The Author hereby grants and assigns to the Publisher the sole and exclusive right to publish in book from a work now entitled_____.

There are a lot of synonyms in English, which often appear in English contracts, and of which we must make the right choice when translating. Otherwise, if a synonym for improper selection, the light one can affect the rights and obligations of both sides, the heavy one can cause the performance dispute. In addition to the above list of words, there are the following common combinations: ①acknowledgment and acceptance; ②affect or prejudice; ③agree and covenant; ④agree and undertake; ⑤aid and abet; ⑥annul and act aside; ⑦any and all; ⑧assign and transfer; ⑨authorize and empower; ⑩bind and obligate; ⑪cease and desist; ⑫duties, obligations or liabilities; ⑬entered into and concluded; ⑭construe and interpret; ⑮entirely and completely; ⑯examine and certify; ⑰fair and equitable; ⑱fit and proper; ⑲for and in consideration of; ⑳force and effect; ㉑full faith and credit; ㉒give, devise and bequeath; ㉓give and grant; ㉔in lieu of and in place of; ㉕in relation to and in connection with; ㉖in truth and fact; ㉗knowledge and belief; ㉘legal and valid; ㉙ownership and title; ㉚part and parcel; ㉛pay, meet and discharge; ㉜represent and warrant; ㉝set forth and prescribe; ㉞successors and assigns; ㉟supersede and replace; ㊱release and discharge; ㊲have and hold; ㊳rest, residue and remainder; ㊴vague, nonspecific and indefinite; ㊵withdraw and rescind.

由于许多英语单词都具有一词多义的特点，在句子中会出现意思不明的情况，合同双方可能会按各自的意图来理解。为了确保所用词不被曲解，可采用同义词连用，如双词式、对句和三词并列等形式，以保证内容准确，使合同具有周密、严谨的特点，减少漏洞和争议，维护法律文件的独立性。

例1：本协议由甲方和乙方（共同）签署（在本句中，made 和 entered into 是一对同义词，表示"签订协议"。by 和 between 是另一对同义词，表示由甲方和乙方签署）。

例2：除了在保守机密的情况下和买方书面要求以外，本协议并未谈到责成卖方允许买方对卖方的专利申请书加以检查。

例3：工程的改变应指工程项目的任何变更、修订或更换（modification of、amendment of/to、alteration 在句中是三个同义短语）。

例4：根据合同的规定，承包商的唯一职责就是如期严格地执行和履行其全部的权利和义务（在句中，execution 和 performance 是同义词）。

例5：任何此类同意均不应解除合同规定的承包商的责任与义务（liability 和 obligation 在句中是同义词）。

例6：如乙方违反或忘记执行以下条款及条件，则本协议及赋予乙方之所有权利，将立即失效（在句中，null 和 void 是一对同义词，terms 和 conditions 是另一组同义词）。

合同中常见的法律配对词或三联词即我们所理解的同义词和短语有：

（1）确认与同意

各方确认并同意在下列条件得到满足时立即创办合资公司。

（2）授权与授予

兹授权并授予你完全的独家拍卖经营权。

（3）取消与终止

公司对经营者的一切合同义务在公司付款后，应立即予以取消与终止。

（4）每一个或任何一个

保证人特此约定，债权人中的每个人或任何人都可以延期支付。

（5）每一个

借款人同意在本文规定的日期以后的每月第一日付款（总额），以偿还贷款人的贷款。

（6）公平和公正

国际投资协定中的公平和公正待遇目前已成为最具争议性的条款之一。

（7）决定性的和结论性的

除了关于潜在的缺陷以外，业主验收的工程应是决定性的与结论性的。

（8）生效

本协议从_____日开始，而且直到_____日为止，都应完全生效。

（9）欺骗

假如交易是由于欺骗达成的，则销售公司应保留一笔款项，这笔款项相当于支付给推销员的佣金。

（10）免除

承销人应使所承销的货物免除一切税金。

（11）坚持、遵守并执行

乙方应该忠实地坚持、遵守并执行本协议的各项规定。

（12）出让、让与并放弃

对于下述财产，甲方愿立契出让、让与并永远放弃对乙方的一切权利和要求。

（13）权利、利益和权益

甲方表示，它是_____（某国）_____号专利证书的全部权利、利益与权益的所有者。

（14）除……之外

除董事的资格股外，合资公司的资本股一概不能转让。

（15）独家的

为此，作者指定并授予该出版商以独家权利，出版现名为_____的这本书。

同义词在英语中为数不少，在英语合同中也时常出现，但翻译时必须作出正确选择；否则，如果同义词选用不当，轻者会影响双方的权利、义务，重者可能造成履约争议。除了上述列举的词语外，还有以下常见的组合：①承认；②影响；③同意、约定；④同意、承担；⑤同谋，教唆；⑥取消和清除行动；⑦任何，所有；⑧转让；⑨授权；⑩约束；⑪制止；⑫义务和责任；⑬订立、缔结；⑭解释；⑮完全地；⑯检验；⑰公允；⑱适当的；⑲作为……的对价，考虑到……；⑳效力；㉑完全诚信；㉒遗赠；㉓授予；㉔替代；㉕与……有关；㉖真相、事实；㉗获悉、了解；㉘合法有效；㉙所有权；㉚部分；㉛付款，偿付；㉜声明并保证；㉝规定；㉞继承人；㉟替代；㊱解除；㊲享有；㊳剩余；㊴模糊的、不确定的；㊵取消。

2.1.3 *Words with Mule-Interpretations*
一词多义

In English contracts, polysemy or more than one righteous word phenomenon is relatively common. To thoroughly understand the meaning of the words, it must be combined with the context, close scrutiny. Contract style has a strong logicality. There always are interdependence, mutual restriction between words, between two paragraphs, between the terms and conditions. Avoid understanding the meaning of the clause isolated, unilaterally and motionlessly. Should understand and choose the meaning comprehensively and objectively.

(1)Considering the Part of Speech

There are a lot of English words in the same written form, which are in different parts of speech. And if parts of speech are different, meaning is also different. Therefore, we must firstly determine the word part of speech in the original, and then determine its meaning further according to the part of speech.

E.g.1: Unless the claims are fully paid, ZZZ shall not be discharged from the liabilities.

E.g.2: Subject as hereinafter provided, the lay time allowed to Buyer for discharging a Cargo shall be seventy - two (72) running hours after the arrival of the vessel at the discharge port including Sundays and holidays.

E.g.3: The invalidation, cancellation or discharge of a contract does not impair the validity of the contract provision concerning the method of dispute resolution, which exists independently in the contract.

E.g.4: Routine duties of the Joint Venture Company are to be discharged the general manager appointed by the Board of Directors.

(2)Considering the Profession

English contract can be involved in all kinds of different business. In different business, the meaning of some words also needs to be adjusted accordingly.

E.g.1: All the rights and interests of the Salesman shall cease and/or terminate upon his breach of any of the preceding Articles. ("Interest" in the contract has the meaning of "benefit" .)

E. g. 2: Should either Joint Venture fails to pay the contribution on schedule according to Clause 5, the default party should pay the other 10% interest one month after the deadline. ("Interest" in the sentence has the meaning of "interest" in the contract.)

E.g.3: Loss or damage to any fixed or movable object or property or other thing or interest whichever, other than the Vessel, arising from any cause whichever in so as such loss or damage is not covered by Clause 17. ("Interest" in the sentence refers to "the subject matter insured" in the insurance business.)

(3)Considering the Collocation

Collocation refers to the connection, resulting in when one word is used with another. There is a meaning when a word is alone, but it may have different meaning when they are used with other word collocation.

E.g.1: In case of late delivery or non-delivery due to Force Majeure, the time of shipment might be duly extended, or alternatively a part or whole of this contract might be canceled, but the Seller shall advise the Buyer of the occurrence mentioned above and send to the Buyer for its acceptance a certificate issued by the surveying institute where the accident occurs as evidence thereof within 14 days.

E.g.2: This Clause 9 shall in no case extend or be deemed to extend to any sum which the Assured may become liable to pay or shall pay for or in respect of.

E.g.3: No claim under this Clause 11 shall in any case be allowed where the loss was not incurred to avoid or in connection with the avoidance of a peril insured against.

E.g.4: In the case of dangerous and/or poisonous cargo(es), the Seller shall be obliged to take care to ensure that the nature and the generally adopted symbol shall be marked conspicuously on each package.

E.g.5: The method of payment shall in all cases be determined by the sales company.

在英语合同中，一词多义或一义多词的现象较为普遍。要透彻地理解这些词义，必须结合上下文，仔细推敲。合同文体具有很强的逻辑性，词与词之间、段与段之间、条款与条款之间总是相互依存、相互制约的。要避免孤立、片面和静止地去理解条款中的词义，应全面、客观地去理解和选择词义。

（1）根据词性确定词义

英语中有许多书写形式相同的词，却有着不同的词性，而词性不同，意义也有差异。因此，首先要判定这个词在原文中的词性，根据词性再进一步确定其词义。

例1：除非这笔债款全部清偿，否则，乙方不能免除承担该债务的责任。

例2：在下列所列条件下，每艘船的卸货时间为船舶抵港后72小时，含星期日和节假日。

例3：合同无效、被撤销或解除，不影响合同中独立存在的有关解决争议方法的条款的效力。

例4：董事会任命的总经理负责履行合资公司的日常职责。

（以上四个句子中都含有discharge，在不同的合同条款中，其词义也有很大的不同。第一个句子中的discharge是动词，词义为"免除"；第二个句子中的discharge也是动词，表示"卸货"；第三个句子中的discharge是名词，意思为"合约的解除"；第四个句子中的discharge是动词，意思为"履行"。）

（2）根据行业来确定词义

英语合同会涉及各类不同的行业，行业不同，某些词语的词义也就需要进行相应的调整。

例1：在违反上述任何条款时，应停止和/或终止推销员的所有权利与利益（句中的interest在合同中有"利益"的含义）。

例2：如果合资一方未能按本合同第5条之规定按期付款，违约方应在逾期后1个月内付给另一方10%的利息（句中的interest在合同中表示"利息"）。

例3：除了船舶以外的任何固定或可移动物体或财产或其他物品或无论何种保险标的物的灭失或损害，由除第17条承保责任之外的任何其他原因所致（句中的interest在保险业务中指"保险标的物")。

（3）根据词的搭配关系确定词义

搭配关系，是指一个词与另一个词连用而产生的意义上的联系。一个词单独存在时是一个意思，但与其他词搭配使用就可能产生不同的词义。

例1：一旦发生不可抗力造成迟延交货或不能交货，卖方可延长交货时间或者解除合同的部分或全部，但卖方必须在14天内通知买方并提交买方可接受的公证机构出具的不可抗力事件的证明（句中的介词短语 in case of，其含义为"假使""如果"，引出状语）。

例2：在任何情况下，第9条皆不扩展或视为对被保险人可能有责任支付或应支付的任何金额的扩展（句中 case 的介词短语 in no case，意思是"决不"，具有副词性质，用作状语）。

例3：如果损失不是为避免承保风险而发生或与之有关，根据第11条提出的索赔在任何情况下均不予认可（句中 case 的介词短语 in any case，意思是"无论如何"，具有副词性质，在句中作状语）。

例4：如果是危险及/或有毒货物，卖方负责保证在每件货物包装上明显地标明货物的性质说明及习惯上被接受的标记（句中 case 的介词短语 in the case of 表示"假使""如果"）。

例5：在所有情况下，付款方式都应由销售公司决定（句中 case 的介词短语 in all cases，意思是"在所有情况下……"）。

2.1.4　*Easily-Confused Words*
易混淆的词

There are some confusing words in the international business contract. Though some handwriting of these words is basically the same, the content is a big difference: Some can express the same concept, but they are used on different occasions; Some words produced the change of rights, obligations and so on due to the distortion.

(1)Attention to Meaning

In the English contract, there are many words on basic same handwriting, but there is a big difference in content. In particular, when some phrases are replaced with a preposition or added with a word, the content will be greatly different.

E.g.1: The buyers are requested always to quote the number of this sales confirmation in the Letter of Credit to be opened in favor of the Sellers. (The phrase "in favor of sth." in the sentence, means "...for the beneficiary" or "help to..." .)

E.g.2: The quality of the goods in the previous contract was much in favor on the European Continent. (The phrase "in favor" in this sentence means "welcome" and "popular" .)

E.g.3: In the event we are not favored with the award of the Contract, this proposal shall be returned to us forthwith. (The phrase "be favored with" in the sentence means "support" or "yes" .)

(2)Attention to the Relation

In English contracts, some words' concept alone is consistent, but in the specific application of terms, the performance of the rights and obligations relations is different from the wording specification or not.

国际商务合同中还有一些易混淆的词，这些词有的书写虽基本相同，内容却有很大差别：有的可以表达同一概念，但使用场合有别；还有一些词语由于发生变形，产生了权利、义务的改变等。

（1）注意书写基本近似但意义不同的词

在英语合同中，有许多词书写上基本相同，但在内容上却存在较大差异，特别是一些短语，更换一个介词或添加一个冠词，其内容就会有很大的不同。

例1：买方要在开立的以卖方为受益人的信用证上填注本销售确认书号码（句中的短语 in favor of sth. 意思是"以……为受益人"或"有利于……"）。

例2：之前的合同中的货物质量在欧洲大陆颇受好评（短语 in favor 在这个句子中表示"受欢迎""受好评"）。

例3：如果我们不接受合同的仲裁裁决，要立即将申请书归还给我们（句中的短语 be favored with 表示"支持"或"赞同"）。

（2）注意同一概念但表达不同权利、义务关系的词

英语合同中的某些单词，单独看，其概念是一致的，但在条款的具体应用中，其表现出的权利、义务关系与用词的规范与否是不同的。

2.1.5 *Choice of Synonyms*
同义词的选用

(1)Words Choice Considering the Connotation

E.g.1: The ownership of any improved and developed technology shall belong to the party who has improved and developed the technology. （"Belong to" is the keyword in the sentence. The optional synonyms are own, possess and belong.)

E.g. 2: Within the validity of the Contract, both parties shall provide each other with the improvement and development of the technology related to the Contract Products free of charge. （"Provide" is the keyword in the sentence, the optional synonyms are "supply" and "offer". "Supply" and "offer" are very casual, which are not suitable for the serious expression of the legal document; but "provide" says "to give sb. sth. free of charge", which is very close to the sample's meaning.)

E.g.3: A deduction of...per day will be made for every calendar day after the above completion date if the Contract is not completed in every detail. (In the sentence, "finished" is the keyword, the synonyms associated with "completion" is "finish", but "completion" is the contract term.)

(2)Words Choice Considering the Grammar

In the international business contract, the choice of some English synonyms is required according to sentence structure and collocation, which should avoid to appear the syntactic collocation errors.

E.g.1: The Contractor shall observe and abide by all applicable laws, rules and regulations in connection with the Work. (The synonyms of "obey" in this sentence are "observe", "abide by" and "comply with" etc. As the subject in the sentence is parties of the contract, "observe" and "abide by" should be chosen according to the matching relationship of this sentence.)

E.g.2: All the activities of a joint venture shall comply with the provision of laws, decree and pertinent regulations of the People's Republic of China. (As the subject in the sentence is "activities", "comply with" should be chosen according to the matching relationship of this sentence, which means "to act in accordance with a provision, rule or demand".)

E.g.3: "Reasons" in international business contracts are often appeared by means of a set phrase "due to, owing to, in the view of, because of, considering and in consideration". Please compare the following sentences:

(a)The Landlord shall not be liable for any failure to supply such heat, water, or electricity, not due to gross negligence on its part.

(b)His failure is due to causes beyond the control of Area Franchisee such as strike, weather, etc.

(In sentence a and sentence b, phrases arisen out of the phrase "due to" belongs to nature of adjectives, respectively as attributive and predicative in the sentence, which generally does not elicit adverbial. The phrases which lead adverbial, said "because of" and "owing to" are often chosen.)

E.g.4: A tender price offered by a tender shall remain unchanged during the performance of the Contract, and shall not be modified because of any reasons. According to Clause 24 of the Notice, tender documents containing any adjustable prices will be rejected as non‐responsive tenders.

E.g.5: Neither the Seller nor the Buyer shall be held responsible for late delivery or non‐delivery owing to generally recognized "Force Majeure" causes.

(3)Words Choice Considering the Writing Style

Basic requirements of International business contracts are standard formal words in accordance with conventional meaning. When choosing a synonym, the characteristic of contract text should be fully considered, standard formal words should be chosen, which conform to the style of formal and standard contract, to avoid arbitrariness in word choice.

E.g.1: We reserve the right to revise any part of this proposal, if we deem it necessary to do so. (Ownership clauses in international business contracts mostly choose "to have the right to" or "keep the right". But this sentence chose "reserve the right to do sth." which is more formal than the other two sentences, because "reserve" itself belongs to the special words in legal English, said "to have a specified power of right in law".)

E.g.2: The Sales Agent shall, under no circumstances, be required/requested to maintain a showroom. (In this sentence, though "ask", "require" and "request" means "demand", "require" and "request" are more formal than "ask".)

E. g. 3: Seller shall immediately make full payment of the balance. (In this sentence, "immediately" should choose "forthwith" because "forthwith" is more formal and rigorous than "immediately" or "at once".)

E.g.4: This Agreement shall not be assigned by the Sales Agent without the Principal's prior written consent. (Generally, "transfer" will be chosen in the sentence, but "assign/assignment" is a formal legal writing word, said "to transfer property, rights to sb. in accordance with the laws". "Transfer/transference" only said "to hand over the possession of the property, etc.")

（1）根据合同的内涵进行选词

例1：对于改进和开发的技术，其所有权属于改进和开发技术的一方（belong to是该句的关键，可选择的同义词有own、possess和belong）。

例2：在合同有效期内，双方对合同产品涉及的技术如有改进和发展，应相互免费将改进和发展的技术提供给对方使用（provide是该句的关键词，可选择的同义词有supply、offer。supply和offer较为随意，不太适合法律文书的严肃表达；provide表示to give sb. sth. free of charge，非常贴近例句的用意）。

例3：如果不能在每个细节上完成合同，那么，就应按上述完工日期期满后的每一日历日计算，每天扣除……（在句中，"完成"是关键词，与completion相关的同义词是finish，但completion是合同用词）。

（2）根据语法要求进行选词

在国际商务合同中，有些英语同义词是按句子结构和搭配（要求）选择的，此时应避免出现句法搭配上的错误。

例1：承包商必须遵守和服从与该工程有关的一切适当的法律、规章和条例（上述句子中obey一词的同义词有observe、abide by、comply with等。由于句子中的主语是合同的当事方，应根据句子的搭配关系选择表示"遵守"的词汇，因此选择observe和abide by）。

例2：合资经营企业的一切活动都应遵守中华人民共和国的法律（由于句子的主语是activities，所以按照句子的匹配关系就要选择comply with，表示to act in accordance with a provision，rule or demand）。

例3：国际商务合同中经常出现的"由于"，常用due to，owing to，in the view of，because of，considering，in consideration等短语来表达。请比较下列句子：

（a）如果不是因为房主方面的重大疏忽，房主对不能供应暖气、水或电不负责任。

（b）他的失误是由于地区特权持有人所无法控制的原因，如罢工、天气骤变等造成的。

（在句子a和b中，由due to引出的短语均为形容词性质，分别在句中作为定语和表语，一般不引出状语。引出状语、表示"由于"的短语往往选用because of和owing to。）

例4：投标人所报的投标价在合同执行过程中是固定不变的，不得以任何理由予以变更。根据本须知第24条的规定，以可调整的价格提交的投标文件将作为非响应性投标文件而予以拒绝。

例5：由于一般公认的不可抗力原因而延迟交货或不能交货，卖方或买方都不负责任。

（3）根据合同的文体进行选词

国际商务合同的基本要求是用词规范、正式，符合约定俗成的含义。在选择同义词时，应充分考虑合同文本的特点，选择符合合同文体的正式和规范的词汇，避免在用词选择上的随意性。

例1：如果我们认为有此必要，那么我们对建议的任何部分都保留修改的权利（对于条款中的"所有权"，国际商务合同中大多选择 to have the right to 或 keep the right。但该句选用了 reserve the right to do sth.，比前两种表达更正式，因为 reserve 本身就属法条英语中的专用词汇，表示 to have a specified power of right in law）。

例2：不管什么情况都不能要求销售代理商维修陈列室（在这个句子中，尽管 ask、require、request 都有"要求"的意思，但 require 和 request 更正式）。

例3：卖方应立刻支付全部余额（在句中，"立刻"应该选择 forthwith，因为 forthwith 是公文体，比 immediately 或 at once 要正规、严谨）。

例4：未经委托人事先书面同意，本协议不允许经销代理人转让（句中的"转让"一词，一般情况下多数译者会选用 transfer，但 assign/assignment 是正式的法律文体词，表示 to transfer property, rights to sb. in accordance with laws，而 transfer/transference 仅表示 to hand over the possession of property, etc.）。

2.2　Characteristics of Patterns Used in International Business Contracts[①] 国际商务合同中的句式特点

International business contracts have the following characteristics: long sentences, diversification of pattern expressions, simplicity, hierarchy and equivalence of sentences, the habitual structure of passive voice, position flexibility of attributive, adverbial, special word order, negation in advance and phrases instead of clauses etc. There are many common patterns and idioms, and the specialization is strong. International business contracts use generic post positions and do not adopt semantic principles of everyday English such as judgment by common sense.

国际商务合同有句子长、句式表达多样化、表达简化性、句子的层次性和对等性、被动语态的惯用结构、定语和状语的位置灵活性、特殊语序、否定提前和短语代替从句等特点。常用句型和惯用语有很多，专业性强。国际商务合同使用类属后置，在常识判断等日常英语中不采用语义原则。

2.2.1　*Long Sentences*
句子长

International business contracts always have long sentences. It is not difficult to find that hundreds of words and complex structure of a single sentence constitute a certain clause in an international business contract. It constitutes a unique style different from others, whose style and length are a bit similar to the following: The rights and liabilities of the parties hereto will bind and inure to the benefit of their successors, executors or administrators, provided however that Party B may not assign or delegate this agreement of any of its license, rights or duties under this agreement, whether by operation of the law or otherwise, without the prior written consent of Party A except to a person or entity into which it has merged or which has otherwise succeeded to all or

---

①　刘川，王菲. 英文合同阅读与翻译［M］. 北京：国防工业出版社，2010.

substantially all of its business and assets to which this Agreement pertains, by merger, reorganization or otherwise, and which has assumed in writing or by operation of the law its obligation under this Agreement.

This is an article about the terms of the transfer. The whole sentence consists of 111 words, both synonyms, coordination of related words, and four attributive clauses which are led by prepositions adding which or which. The trunk of the whole sentence is: The rights and liabilities of the Parties hereto will bind and inure to the benefit of...provided however that Party B may not... except to a person or entity into which...or which...to which...and which...The sentence means to the effect that: The rights and responsibilities of the agreement on both sides come into effect and bind on heirs, executors or administrators of the agreement. But without the prior written consent of Party A, Party B shall not use legal or other means, without authorization, to transfer, by other ways, to designate any licence, other rights or obligations specified in this agreement, which belongs to oneself. Party B will be transferred or assigned to the creditor's rights and debts of the combined party personal or of the business, or will be transferred or assigned to the creditor's rights and debts inherited from the relevant part of this agreement or virtually all properties of the individuals or the enterprises, and the individuals or the enterprises in written form or to perform the contract obligations according to the law the rights and responsibilities, it is not subject to this restriction.

The content information held, of each sentence in contracts, is big, complete and strict. In order not to be distorted, misread, choose to use long sentences is necessary. But the successful use of long sentences in international business contracts, in addition to benefit from the rigorous logical thinking and the legal language, there must be a guarantee for the basis of English syntactic and lexical.

For example, a certain project contract wrote when appointting the obligations of the customer at the site: Where servants, agents or subcontractors of the Company carry out work under the direction of the Client, the Client shall be fully responsible for, and must indemnify and hold harmless the Company against any claim, loss or damage of any kind, whether arising in the contract, in negligence, in equity or by statue or under any Law connected in any way with the services, the project or the relationship established by this Agreement.

The sentence is a complex sentence led by "where" adverbial clause, with total 70 words. The clause part is not confusing, but the part of the main clause is not easy to be understood. This is not because of many new words. Even if checking out the new words, the complex structure may be still found in the main clause. After analyzing, we found that there were two predicates in the sentence, to declare that the client had two obligations under the contract: one was "shall be fully responsible for" the said part of the object; second, "must indemnify and hold harmless", said that the compensation must be paid for the object in the sentence and guarantee that the company must be protected from damages compensation. A lot of the rest left is afraid to be, in one breath, "compensate for whom" (main body compensated) and "what compensate specifically" including compensation basis (in contract, in negligence, in equity or by statute or under any Law), the scope of compensation (connected in any way with the services, the project or the relationship established by this Agreement), the compensation object (any claim, loss or damage of any kind in respect of the acts or omissions of the company, its servants, agents or subcontractors). In this way, the obligations of the client object are very clear. The sentence's object only took two past participle phrases "connected in any way with" and "established by" to simplify expression, instead of attributive clause modifying antecedent respectively, otherwise, the sentence would be more complex. This sentence means to the effect that the company employees, agents or subcontractors by the client to perform the work, the customer for the company employees, agents or subcontractors act or omission of any claim, loss or damage caused by both should bear all responsibilities. Whether the compensation happens based on the contract, negligence, equity law, and enacted law which are based on the relationship with the services, the project or the agreement to establish the relevant laws and regulations, also regardless of the size, they must carry on the compensation to the company, and ensure the company pay damages.

Long sentences in international business contracts are numerous to enumerate, such as:

"The Company in general meeting may, upon the recommendation of the Directors, resolve that it is desirable to capitalize any part of the amount for the time being standing to the credit of any of the Company's reserve accounts or to the credit of the profit and loss account or otherwise available for distribution and not required for the payment or provisions of the fixed dividend on any share entitled to fixed preferential dividends and accordingly that such sums be set free for distribution among the members of the Company who would have been entitled thereto if distributed by way of dividend and in the same proportions on the condition that the same be not paid in cash but be applied either in or towards paying up any amount for the time being unpaid on any share held by such members respectively or paying up in full unissued shares or debentures of the Company to be allotted and distributed credited as fully paid-up to and amongst such members in the proportion aforesaid, or partly in the one way and partly in the other, and the Directors shall give effect to such resolution provided that a share premium account and a capital redemption reserve fund may, for the purpose of this Article, only be applied in the paying-up of unissued shares to be issued to members of the Company as fully paid bonus shares."

There are 232 words in this sentence. The backbone is "The Company may resolve that...and accordingly that... and the Directors shall give effect to such resolution", which is A and B compound sentence. Among them, "upon the recommendation of the Directors" is the condition of "may resolve". Phrase "standing to the credit of" is the attributive of the antecedent "amount", in parallel of "credit". Phrase "entitled to" is "shares" antecedent's post positive attributive; "to be allotted" and "to be issued" are post positive attributive of the preceding antecedents respectively, which says behavior result to happen. "On the condition that" clause limits the realization condition of the former sentence "such sums be set free for distribution" to realize the distribution. "Provided that" limits the realization condition of "the Directors shall give effect to such resolution".

Another example: Every Director, Managing Director, President, Vice-President, Manager, Secretary, Assistant Secretary, Treasurer or other officer of the Company and their heirs and personal representatives shall be entitled to be indemnified and held harmless out of the assets of the Company against all actions, proceedings, costs, damages, expenses (including reasonable legal and/or other professional fees), claims, losses or liabilities which he may sustain or incur in or about the execution of the duties of his office or otherwise in relation thereto, including any liability incurred by him in defending any proceeding, whether civil or criminal, in which judgment is given in his favor or in which he is acquitted, and no Director or person as aforementioned shall be liable for any loss, damage or misfortune which may happen to or be incurred by the Company in the execution of the duties of his office or in relation thereto provided that he acted in good faith and in a manner reasonably believed by his to be in the best interests of the Company and provided further that his actions did not involve negligence, willful default, fraud or dishonesty.

The structure of the sentence is A and B, in all 185 words. The backbone is "A, B, C...shall be entitled to be indemnified and held harmless...against A, B, C...which he may sustain or incur... proceedings, in which judgment is given..., and no Director or person...shall be liable for something which may happen or be incurred... provided that... and provided further that..." Among them, "provided that...and provided further that" is the restrictive provision of the A and B in the front.

Another example: In the event of Client's breach of any of the foregoing representations and/ or warranties, the Factor shall have, in addition to all other rights under this Agreement, the right to charge back to the Client immediately the full amount of the Receivables affected thereby together with interest, but such charge back shall not be deemed a reassignment thereof, and the Factor shall retain a security interest in such Receivables and in the merchandise represented thereby until such Receivables is fully paid, settled or discharged and all Client's Obligations (as hereinafter defined) to the Factor are fully satisfied.

The structure of the long sentence is A but B until C, the adverbial clause illustrates to cancel B condition. A consists of "Factor shall have the right to charge back", B consists of two sentences: "such charge back shall not" and "the Factor shall retain", C consists of a compound sentence connected with "and". The whole sentence consists of 93 words.

Thus it can be seen that the sentences in international business contracts overall are long and are piled up into by subordinate clauses, phrases or vocabularies.

国际商务合同总是有长句。在国际商务合同中不难发现字数上百、结构复杂的单一句子构成某条款的现象。它构成了有别于其他文体的、国际商务合同独有的一大特征，其风格和长度与下句有点类似：The rights and liabilities of the parties hereto will bind and inure to the benefit of their successors, executors or administrators, provided however that Party B may not assign or delegate this agreement of any of its license, rights or duties under this agreement, whether by operation of the law or otherwise, without the prior written consent of Party A except to a person or entity into which it has merged or which has otherwise succeeded to all or substantially all of its business and assets to which this Agreement pertains, by merger, reorganization or otherwise, and which has assumed in writing or by operation of the law its obligation under this Agreement.

这是一条关于转让的条款。全句由 111 个单词组成，句中既有同义词、关联词搭配，又有介词加 which 或 which 引导的 4 个定语从句。整个句子的主干是：The rights and liabilities of the Parties hereto will bind and inure to the benefit of...provided however that Party B may not...except to a person or entity into which...or which...to which...and which.... 该句大意是：协议双方的权利、责任对协议的继承人、执行人或管理人生效，对其有约束力。但未经甲方事先书面同意，乙方不得运用法律或其他手段，擅自转让或指定或采取其他方式转让、指定本协议规定的属于自己的任何许可权、其他权利或义务。乙方将债权、债务转让或指定被合并后的个人或企业，或将债权、债务转让或指定给继承了与本协议的相关部分或实际上全部财产的个人或企业。这些个人或企业以书面形式或依法履行合同义务的方式享有权利、履行责任时，则不受此限。

合同中的每个句子包含的信息量很大、完整和严密。为了不被曲解、误读，选择使用长句乃不得已而为之。但国际商务合同中成功使用长句的，除得益于严谨的逻辑思维和法律用语外，一定会有英语句法和词汇的基础作为保障。

例如，某工程合同在约定客户在工地的义务时写道：Where servants, agents or subcontractors of the Company carry out work under the direction of the Client, the Client shall be fully responsible for, and must indemnify and hold harmless the Company against any claim, loss or damage of any kind, whether arising in the contract, in negligence, in equity or by statue or under any Law connected in any way with the services, the project or the relationship established by this Agreement.

该句是由 where 引导的状语从句复合句，共 70 个单词。从句部分并不费解，而主句部分就不易理解了。这不是生词多的缘故。即使查完生词，可能还是觉得主句结构复杂。经过分析，我们发现该句有两个谓语，是为了说明客户在该合同项下有两项义务：一是 shall be fully responsible for，表示对句子的宾语部分应当承担责任；二是 must indemnify and hold harmless，表示对句子的宾语部分必须赔偿并保证公司免于赔偿。剩下来的一大堆恐怕是在一口气说完"赔谁的"（获赔主体）和"具体赔什么"，包括赔偿依据（in contract，in negligence，in equity or by statute or under any Law）、赔偿范围（connected in any way with the services, the project or the relationship established by this Agreement）、赔偿对象（any claim，loss or damage of any kind in respect of the acts or omissions of the company，its servants，agents or subcontractors）。这样，客户对象的义务就非常明确了。该句具体表述宾语时只用了两个过去分词短语 connected in any way with 和 established by 来简化表达，分别替代定语从句修饰先行词；否则，该句会更复杂。该句大意是：公司员工、代理人或分包商经客户委托履行工作的，顾客对因公司员工、代理人或分包商的作为或不作为而造成的任何索赔、灭失或损毁均应承担全部责任。无论基于合同、过失、衡平法、制定法而发生还是基于与服务、项目或本协议确立的关系相关的法律规定而发生，也无论程度大小，都必须就此向公司进行赔偿，并保证公司免于赔偿。

国际商务合同中的长句不胜枚举，比如：

The Company in general meeting may, upon the recommendation of the Directors, resolve that it is desirable to capitalize any part of the amount for the time being standing to the credit of any of the Company's reserve accounts or to the credit of the profit and loss account or otherwise available for distribution and not required for the payment or provisions of the fixed dividend on any share entitled to fixed preferential dividends and accordingly that such sums be set free for distribution among the members of the Company who would have been entitled thereto if distributed by way of dividend and in the same proportions on the condition that the same be not paid in cash but be applied either in or towards paying up any amount for the time being unpaid on any share held by such members respectively or paying up in full unissued shares or debentures of the Company to be allotted and distributed credited as fully paid-up to and amongst such members in the proportion aforesaid, or partly in the one way and partly in the other, and the Directors shall give effect to such resolution provided that a share premium account and a capital redemption reserve fund may, for the purpose of this Article, only be applied in the paying-up of unissued shares to be issued to members of the Company as fully paid bonus shares.

该句有 232 个单词。主干是 "The Company may resolve that...and accordingly that...and the Directors shall give effect to such resolution"，是个 "A and B" 的并列句。其中，upon the recommendation of the Directors 是 may resolve 的发生条件；standing to the credit of 短语是先行词 amount 的定语，与 credit 在文中并列；entitled to 短语是 shares 先行词的后置定语；to be allotted 和 to be issued 分别为前面先行词的后置定语，表示将要发生的行为结果；on the condition that 从句限定了前句 such sums be set free for distribution 的实现条件；provided that 限定了 the Directors shall give effect to such resolution 的实现条件。

又如：

Every Director, Managing Director, President, Vice-President, Manager, Secretary, Assistant Secretary, Treasurer or other officer of the Company and their heirs and personal representatives shall be entitled to be indemnified and held harmless out of the assets of the Company against all actions, proceedings, costs, damages, expenses (including reasonable legal and/or other professional fees), claims, losses or liabilities which he may sustain or incur in or about the execution of the duties of his office or otherwise in relation thereto, including any liability incurred by him in defending any proceeding, whether civil or criminal, in which judgment is given in his favor or in which he is acquitted, and no Director or person as aforementioned shall be liable for any loss, damage or misfortune which may happen to or be incurred by the Company in the execution of the duties of his office or in relation thereto provided that he acted in good faith and in a manner reasonably believed by his to be in the best interests of the Company and provided further that his actions did not involve negligence, willful default, fraud or dishonesty.

该句又是个 "A and B" 结构的并列句，全句有 185 个单词。主干是 "A, B, C...shall be entitled to be indemnified and held harmless...against A, B, C...which he may sustain or incur... proceedings, in which judgment is given..., and no Director or person... shall be liable for something which may happen or be incurred...provided that...and provided further that..." 其中，provided that...and provided further that 是前面 A 和 B 的限定性规定。

再如：

In the event of Client's breach of any of the foregoing representations and/or warranties, the Factor shall have, in addition to all other rights under this Agreement, the right to charge back to the Client immediately the full amount of the Receivables affected thereby together with interest, but such charge back shall not be deemed a reassignment thereof, and the Factor shall retain a security interest in such Receivable and in the merchandise represented thereby until such Receivable is fully paid, settled or discharged and all Client's Obligations (as hereinafter defined) to the Factor are fully satisfied.

该长句的结构是"A but B until C",其中状语从句说明取消B条件。A由Factor shall have the right to charge back 构成,B由 such ctwo predicates in the senteharge back shall not 和Factor shall retain两个句子并列构成,构成C的是由and连接的并列句。全句由93个单词构成。

由上可以看出,国际商务合同的句子总体上比较长,长句多由从属的从句、短语或词汇构成。

2.2.2   *Diversification of Pattern Expressions*
句式表达多样化

2.2.2.1   Big Change of Word Orders, and Inserts and Adjustable Sequence Techniques to Phrases and Clauses
语序变化大,对短语、从句采用插入、调序手法多

This is another big characteristic of contract English sentences, i. e. adverbial phrases or clauses insert or switch in main clauses by original positions, use commas to separate. Contract English does not like ordinary English, it always puts time adverbials at the first of sentences to separate by commas from main clauses, or in the end of sentences, but uses an idiomatic insertion method to put adverbials, appositives or attributives between subjects and predicates, or between predicates and objects, or other parts of sentences.

In general English, it will affect fluency of contracts and readers' mind if there are too many commas in sentences. But in contract English, the reason why it is so idiomatic to use processing technique of insert and sequence with commas, still probably is in order to cause parties to attention of parts in special positions of expressions in addition to pursue expressing effect of diversification.

For example: "The applicant shall, within 30 days after receiving the approval notice by the competent authority of the industrial and commercial registration formalities." The average person is likely to choose the expression as: The applicant should go through formalities for industrial and commercial registration within 30 days upon receipt of the notice of approval from the competent authority. The general expression for contract English like: The applicant, within 30 (thirty) days upon receipt of the notice of approval from the competent authority, shall go through formalities for industrial and commercial registration.

Another example: "Upon termination or dissolution of the Partnership, the Partnership will be promptly liquidated, with all debts being paid first, prior to any distribution of the remaining funds." In the sentence, the partnership liquidation condition "with" the guide of prepositional phrase, "with" is between the time adverbial phrase "prior to" and the predicate, which is afraid to intend for the partners to notice that to meet the premise condition, may be assigned to the remaining property. The sentence means to the extent that when termination or dissolution, partnership ventures should be immediately liquidated and paid off all the debts before being allocated to the remaining property.

Another word order characteristic of contract English is that adverbial clauses are often put between connection words and a subject, using commas to separate. Such as: "If, after 60 (sixty) days from the date of commencement of friendly negotiations, the parties hereto fail to reach any agreement, either party hereto may submit the dispute to arbitration for settlement." In this sentence, phrase "after 60 (sixty) days from the date of commencement of friendly negotiations" is the adverbial of the clause "If the parties hereto fail to reach any agreement", put in the position, using commas to separate. The sentence means to the extent that if the parties of this contract do not reach an agreement within 60 days of the beginning of friendly consultations, any party can submit the dispute to arbitration for resolution.

The adverbial insertion also includes the phenomenon that an entire clause is put between a subject and a predicate in a main clause, using commas to separate. Such as: "Party B shall, if required by Party A, provide to Party A financial statements in such form and at such intervals as Party A may require." In this sentence, "if required by Party A" is the short form of the subordinate clause "if Party B is required by Party A". When the subject in the main clause and the subject in the subordinate clause are consistent, the subject in the subordinate and the linking verb can be achieved to omit, to change the form of clauses' predicate verbs to participle word phrases, which avoids the use of if clause and put the clause in the front of the sentence or at the end of the sentence and loss characteristics of contract English. The sentence means to the extent that Party B shall submit financial statements with the requirements of Party A in accordance with the required format and the time interval.

这是合同英语句子的另一大特点，即将状语短语或从句插入或由原位置调换进主句中，用逗号隔开。合同英语并不像普通英语那样，将时间状语要么放到句首，用逗号和主句隔开，要么放在句末，而是惯用插入法，将状语、同位语或定语插到主语、谓语之间，或谓语、宾语之间，或句子的其他位置。

普通英语中，如果句子中的逗号太多，会影响合同的流畅性和读者的思维。而合同英语之所以如此惯用插入和调序并用逗号隔开的处理手法，除了追求多样化的表达效果外，大概还为了引起当事人对处于特殊位置的表达部分的重视。

例如"申请人应自接到主管机关的批准通知后30日内办理工商登记手续"一句，一般人很可能选择的表达为：

The applicant should go through formalities for industrial and commercial registration within 30 days upon receipt of the notice of approval from the competent authority.

而合同英语一般表达为：

The applicant, within 30 (thirty) days upon receipt of the notice of approval from the competent authority, shall go through formalities for industrial and commercial registration.

又如：

Upon termination or dissolution of the Partnership, the Partnership will be promptly liquidated, with all debts being paid first, prior to any distribution of the remaining funds.

该句将规定合伙清算条件的由 with 引导的介词短语放在了时间状语短语 prior to 和谓语之间，恐怕是有意让合伙人注意，在满足什么前提条件下方可分配到剩余财产。该句大意是：合伙企业终止或解散时，应在分配到剩余财产之前对合伙企业立即清算，清偿所有债务。

合同英语的另一语序特点是常将状语从句放在从句的连接词和主语之间，用逗号隔开。例如：

If, after 60 (sixty) days from the date of commencement of friendly negotiations, the parties hereto fail to reach any agreement, either party hereto may submit the dispute to arbitration for settlement.

本句中，短语 after 60 (sixty) days from the date of commencement of friendly negotiations 是从句 If the parties hereto fail to reach any agreement 的状语，放在该位置，用逗号隔开。该句大意是：本合同当事人未在开始友好协商之日起 60 日内达成一致的，任何一方可将争议提交仲裁解决。

这种状语插入还包括将整个从句放在主句的主、谓语之间，用逗号隔开的现象。例如：

Party B shall, if required by Party A, provide to Party A financial statements in such form and at such intervals as Party A may require.

本句中，if required by Party A 是从句 if Party B is required by Party A 的简略形式。在主句主语和从句主语一致时，就可将从句主语和系动词省略掉，将从句谓语动词变成分词短语形式，从而避免因使用 if 从句和将该从句放在句首或句末而丧失合同英语的特点。该句大意是：经甲方要求，乙方应按照甲方要求的格式和时间间隔提交财务报表。

2.2.2.2　One Meaning, More than One Sentence Pattern
一个含义，多个句式表达

English is widespread in contracts as a phenomenon of one meaning, multiple sentence expressions. This is another big performance of English sentences to express contract variety. The following is the most representative, the most frequently used pattern-assume pattern.

In general English, the most commonly used English patterns to express "if" and "in case" are subordinate clauses or phrases led by if or as long as. So the people who look to start a career in contracts think that the patterns to express assumption generally fall into two categories and mistake assumption patterns in English contracts are these a few kinds. In fact, "if" and "in case" patterns in English contracts are extremely rich.

Besides "if" adverbial clauses, there are at least the following words led adverbial clauses, which associate with "if" and "in case": if and whenever, in the event that (phrase as in the event of), where, should, in case (phrase in case of), on the condition that (plural form as on the conditions that), in so far as, when, and in the form of noun phrases appeared in subject position of assumptions. As long as clause is generally not used in English contracts.

(1)If and Whenever

From the sense, "whenever" after "if", means "whenever", expressing more closely, which covers more widely. When express "if" and "doing sth." in international business contracts, consider using "if and whenever" instead of "if".

E.g.: If and whenever the attorney at law designated by Party B comes to work with Party A, Party A shall offer all sufficient and necessary facilities, arrange the said legal adviser with an office, appoint a company officer to assist legal adviser with his functions, provide relevant information and write and print legal draft for such legal adviser.

(2)In the Event That and in Case

The two clauses of "in the event that" and "in case" are said the meaning of "if in any case", generally in the beginning of sentences, and the predicate in clauses generally uses present tense. "In the event that", "in case", "in the event of", and "in case of" are followed by a noun phrase, of course.

英语合同中广泛存在一个含义、多个句式表达的现象，这是英语合同句式表达多样化的另一大表现。本书仅列举最有代表性的、使用最频繁的句式——假定句式。

普通英语中，表达"如果""假如"的英语句型最常用的是if或as long as引导的从句或短语。因此，初涉合同的人对假定句型表达一般也无外乎这两种，也误以为英语合同的假定句子也就这几种。实际上，英语合同中"如果""假如"的句型表达极其丰富。

除了if状语从句外，至少还有下列词引导状语从句与"如果""假如"相关：if and whenever，in the event that（短语为in the event of），where，should，in case（短语为in case of），on the condition that（复数形式为on the conditions that），in so far as，when，以及以名词短语形式出现在主语位置的假定。as long as从句一般不被用于英语合同之中。

（1）无论何时

从意义上讲，if之后加上whenever后又多了一层"无论何时"的含义，表达更严密，涵盖面更广。国际商务合同中想要表达"如果""在做什么事"时，不妨考虑用if and whenever替代if。

例：If and whenever the attorney at law designated by Party B comes to work with Party A, Party A shall offer all sufficient and necessary facilities, arrange the said legal adviser with an office, appoint a company officer to assist legal adviser with his functions, provide relevant information and write and print legal draft for such legal adviser.（该句大意是：乙方律师到甲方工作时，甲方应充分给予方便，安排法律顾问住所，选派公司领导协助法律顾问工作，为其提供有关信息、缮写和打印法律稿件等。）

（2）如果在什么情形下

in the event that和in case两个从句都表示"如果在什么情形下"的意思，一般放于句首，且从句中的谓语一般用一般现在时。in the event that、in case、in the event of和in case of后接名词短语，当然亦可。

2.2.3　Patterns Commonly Used in International Business Contracts
国际商务合同中的常用句型

(1)If/in Case/Provided That/in the Event That/in so Far as+Clauses

E.g.1: In the event that Party B becomes delinquent in the payment of any sum due hereunder,

Party A will have the right to suspend performance until such delinquency is corrected, and initiate termination for causes in accordance with Section 10.2.

E.g.2: In case the accident lasts for more than eight weeks, both sides of the contract should make joint measures to carry out the obligations of the contract.

E.g.3: Notwithstanding the completion of the sale and the purchase of ordinary shares in the company, the terms and conditions of this agreement shall remain in full force and effect as between the parties hereto in so far as the same are not fulfilled.

E.g.4: Should the Seller fail to make delivery on time as stipulated in the contract, with the exception of Force Majeure causes specified in Clause 14 of this contract, or causes by the Buyer in written form prior to such delay, the Buyer shall agree to postpone the delivery on the conditions that the Seller shall be obliged to pay liquidated damages which shall be deducted by the paying bank from the payment under negotiation for such delay in delivery at the following rates.

(2)Unless Otherwise Stipulated/Except as Otherwise Provided

E.g.1: Unless the context of these Articles otherwise stipulated...

E.g.2: Except as otherwise provided by the law or this Agreement, the Venturers shall not be required to make any further capital contributions to the Venture.

E.g.3: Unless otherwise stipulated, to refer to some terms refers to the present contract.

(3)So Agreed

At the end of a lot of English contract text, sometimes occurs such a sentence "So agreed, this＿＿＿＿day of＿＿＿＿(month), 202×", which is another express form of the sentence "IN WITNESS WHEREOF, the parties set their hands and seals hereunto as of the date hereinabove mentioned."

(4)Save That/Save As

E.g.: Save as supplemented and varied by clause 2, the management agreement shall continue in force and effect in all other respects. The management agreement and clause 2 shall be read and constructed as one document and clause 2 shall be considered to be a part of the management agreement. Without prejudice to the generality of the foregoing, where the context allows references in the management agreement to "this agreement", however, expression shall be read and constructed as references to the management agreement as supplemented and varied by clause 2.

（1）if/in case/provided that/in the event that/in so far as+从句

例1：乙方未按期支付本协议项下任何到期款项，甲方有权暂停协议履行，直至该违约行为得以纠正；同时，甲方有权于协议第10条第2款规定的事由出现时终止本协议的履行。

例2：如果事故持续8周以上，则合同双方应共同采取措施来履行合同义务。

例3：尽管公司普通股的销售和购买已结束，但是只要该行为尚未履行完毕，本协议条款对双方仍然完全有效。

例4：卖方未依照合同约定按时交付的，本合同第14款规定的不可抗力事件或延迟交付前买方书面通知的原因除外，如卖方采取由其付款行在货款议付时直接扣除的形式，按照下列比率支付由于延迟交付而应付的违约金，买方应同意延迟交付日期。

（2）除非另有规定

例1：除非条款另有规定……

例2：除非法律或本协议另有约定，不得要求投资方向企业另行出资。

例3：除非另有规定，参照某条款指参照本合同的条款。

（3）因此同意了

在不少英语合同正文末尾，有时出现"So agreed, this＿＿＿＿ day of＿＿＿＿（month），202×"这样的句子，这是句子"IN WITNESS WHEREOF, the parties set their hands and seals hereunto as of the date hereinabove mentioned."的另一种表达形式。

（4）……者例外

例：除第2条补充和变更的地方外，《管理协议》的其他部分继续有效。《管理协议》和第2条应一并阅读，作为一个完整的文件来理解，应将第2条理解为《管理协议》的一部分。在不影响上述整体性的情况下，在本协议允许之处，《管理协议》中明示的参见"本协议"应理解为参见本协议第2条补充、变更后的《管理协议》。

2.3　Characteristics of Tenses Used in International Business Contracts[①] 国际商务合同中的时态特点

2.3.1　*Future and Present Tenses Are Frequently Applied Because Contracts Are to Be Performed but Still Have Not*
因为合同将要执行，但仍没有执行，所以经常应用将来时态和现在时态

"Shall or should or to do" is used to express the future tense. The present tense is used in subordinate clauses.

E. g.: Should any dispute arise between the contracting parties, it shall be settled through friendly negotiation, but if there is no agreement to be reached, the disputes arising out of the execution or performance of this contract shall be submitted by the parties for negotiation.

shall、should或to do被用来表达将来时态，从句使用现在时态。

例：如果合同双方产生争议，那么应友好协商解决；若未能达成一致，双方将执行或履行合同过程中产生的争议提交仲裁解决。

2.3.2　*More Present Tense, Less Future Tense*
多用现在时态，少用将来时态

Although clauses are stipulated in contracts after signing, but still often use the present tense for the principle.

E.g.1: Before the completion of the project, Party A may at any time increase or decrease the quantity of the project.

---

① 王相国. 鏖战英文合同：英文合同的翻译与起草［M］. 最新增订版. 北京：中国法制出版社，2014.

E.g.2: The Licensee may terminate this Contract 90 days after a written notice thereof is sent to Licensor upon the happening of one of the following events:

① The Licensor becomes insolvent or a liquidator of the Licensor is appointed.

② The patent described in Article 2 is not issued within 30 days from signing.

③ The Licensor in this Contract falls to perform its obligations under this Contract.

尽管合同的条款是规定签约以后的事项，但是仍通常以使用现在时态为原则。

例1：在工程竣工之前，甲方可以随时增加或减少工程数量。

例2：当有下列事件之一发生时，被许可人在提前90天向许可人发送书面通知后，可以终止本合同：

①许可人无力偿付债务或许可人的破产清算人已被指定。

②第二条规定的专利在签约后30天内尚未发布。

③许可人未能履行其合同义务。

2.4　More Active Voice, Less Passive Voice①
多用主动语态，少用被动语态

The active voice is more natural, clearer, more direct, and more powerful than the passive voice. Try to compare:

①A.The rules and regulations of the worksite shall be observed by workers.

B.Workers shall observe the rules and regulations of the worksite.

The meaning of these two sentences is same, but because the ways of expression are different, sentence B is more natural and more powerful than sentence A.

②A.Party B is hereby appointed by Party A as its exclusive sales agent in Singapore.

B.Party A hereby appoints Party B as its exclusive sales agent in Singapore.

Sentence B is clearer and more appropriate than sentence A.

主动语态比被动语态更自然、明确、直接和有力。试比较：

①A.工地的规章制度应被工人遵守。

B.工人应遵守工地的规章制度。

这两句的意思虽然相同，但表达方式不同，B句比A句更自然、更有力。

②A.乙方被甲方委托为新加坡独家销售代理。

B.甲方委托乙方为新加坡独家销售代理。

二者相比，B句比A句更明确、更妥当。

2.5　More Direct Expressions, Less Indirect Expressions
多用直接表达方式，少用间接表达方式

For example:

---

①　吴敏，吴明忠. 国际经贸英语合同写作［M］. 广州：暨南大学出版社，2002.

①A.This Article does not apply to bond holders who have not been paid in full.

B.This Article applies only to bond holders who have been paid in full.

② A. All persons, except those who are 60 years old or older may be employed by this enterprise.

B.All persons who are less than 60 years old may be employed by this enterprise.

The above two sentence A are the negative indirect expression. Actually they are not so directly understanding, so straightforward like two sentence B.

例如：

①A.本条款不适用于尚未全部偿付的债券持有者。

B.本条款只适用于已经全部偿付了的债券持有者。

②A.所有的人，年满60岁或60岁以上者除外，都可被本企业雇用。

B.所有不满60岁的人均可被本企业雇用。

上述两个A句都是采用否定的间接表达方式，其实都没有两个B句的直接表达方式那么明白、直截了当。

2.6　Patterns Commonly Used[①]
常用句式

2.6.1　*Patterns Led by "If"*
if 引导的句式

E.g.1: If the shareholders of the New Company do not reach an agreement about any matter in relation with the Project, the opinion and the decision of the major shareholders shall be final and binding upon the other shareholders of the New Company.

E.g. 2: If the Force Majeure applies prior to the completion date, the parties will meet to discuss a revised timetable for the completion of the Project.

E.g. 3: During the enforcement of this agreement, if it is found necessary that, in addition to the machinery and equipment listed herein, some new accessories or measuring and testing instruments are needed for the completion of the project, additional orders may be made through negotiation by the parties. The new items thus added shall be incorporated in the agreement.

例1：如果新公司各股东对本工程的有关事宜不能达成协议，那么主要股东的意见和决定应是最终的，对新公司的其他股东具有约束力。

例2：如果在竣工期之前遇到不可抗力，那么双方应开会讨论修改工程竣工的时间表。

例3：在执行本协议过程中，如果发现本合同项下的机械设备在配套生产时需要继续增添新的机械设备或测试仪器，可由双方另行协商，予以增订；增订的项目仍应列入本合

---

① 乔焕然. 英文合同阅读指南：英文合同的结构、条款、句型与词汇分析［M］. 最新增订版. 北京：中国法制出版社，2015.

同范围之内。

2.6.2   Patterns Led by "Should"
should 引导的句式

E.g.1: Should any loss or damage occur, Party A shall lodge the claim against the insurer and pay a part of the indemnification received from the insurer to Party B, which shall be in proportion to the payment Party A has not made for the part of machinery involved in the loss or damage.

E.g.2: Should no settlement be reached through negotiation, the case shall then be submitted for arbitration to China International Economic and Trade Arbitration Commission (Beijing) and the rules of this Commission shall be applied.

E.g.3: Should all or part of the contract be unable to be fulfilled owing to the fault of one party, the breaching party shall bear the responsibilities thus caused. Should it be the fault of both parties, they shall bear their respective responsibilities according to actual situations.

例 1：如果发生损失或损坏，由甲方向保险人提出索赔，并将从保险人处获得的赔偿的一部分付给乙方，这部分应与受损机械设备中甲方未支付的部分成比例。

例 2：如果协商不能解决争议，则应将争议提交中国国际经济贸易仲裁委员会（北京），依据其仲裁规则进行仲裁。

例 3：由于一方的过失，本合同不能履行或不能完全履行时，由过失一方承担违约责任。如果属双方过失，则根据实际情况，由双方分别承担各自应负的违约责任。

2.6.3   Patterns Led by "Unless"
unless 引导的句式

E.g.1: On the transfer date the New Company shall transfer to B, free from any lien or encumbrance created by the New Company and without the payment of any compensation, all its right, title and interest in the infrastructure project, unless otherwise specified in the agreement or any supplementary agreement.

E.g.2: It should be returned to the buyer within the guarantee period, unless with the written agreement of the buyer.

E.g.3: Neither party shall have the right to represent the other party unless otherwise arranged.

E.g.4: Notwithstanding any reference to arbitration, both parties shall continue to perform their respective obligations under the Contract unless otherwise agreed.

E.g.5: The terms CFR and CIF shall be subject to the International Rules for the Interpretation of Trade Terms 2020 (INCOTERMS 2020) provided by the International Chamber of Commerce (ICC) unless otherwise stipulated herein.

(Pay special attention that "unless" are linked with "otherwise" and followed by the past participle.)

例 1：在转让期，新公司应将对基础设施的全部权益转让给 B，新公司不应滞留，也不能要求补偿，除非协议或补充协议中另有规定。

例 2：除经买方书面同意外，卖方应在保证期内把它归还给买方。

例3：除另有安排者外，任何一方无权代表另一方。

例4：除非另有规定，仲裁不得影响合同双方继续履行合同所规定的义务。

例5：除非另有规定，CFR和CIF均应依照国际商会（ICC）制定的《2020年国际贸易术语解释通则》（INCOTERMS 2020）办理。

（特别注意，unless常和otherwise连用，且后面接过去分词。）

2.6.4　*Patterns Led by "Provided That"*
provided that 引导的句式

E.g.1: C shall be responsible for the following provided that and after the New Company is established, responsibilities shall be transferred to the New Company and be shared by the shareholders of the New Company.

E.g.2: This Agreement shall become in full force and effect as of the date of signing this Agreement provided that C has the right of reserving the fulfillment of its obligations until the fulfillment of the following conditions.

E.g.3: Either party may at any time replace the chairman, deputy chairman or directors it has appointed, provided that it gives the written notice to the Joint Venture Company and the other party.

(Pay special attention that it cannot be invariable when being translated. In the above example, if "provided that" is translated into "if", it can not reach good results.)

例1：C应负责下述工作，但在新公司成立后，责任转给新公司，由新公司股东分担。

例2：本协议自签署之日起生效，但C有权保留履行其义务直至下述条件满足为止。

例3：任何一方可随时更换自己委派的董事长、副董事长或董事，但必须书面通知合资公司和合资的另一方。

（特别注意，在进行翻译的时候，不能一成不变。以上例子中的 provided that 如果被译成"如果"，就达不到好的效果了。）

2.6.5　*Patterns Led by "in Case of/That"*
in case of/that 引导的句式

E.g.1: The Project Cost shall be based on the feasibility study report and in case of a substantial variation in investment arising from geologic reasons, the additional part (the Project Cost) shall be approved by B.

E.g.2: In case the issue remains to be settled, it shall be finally settled by arbitration pursuant to the Rules of Conciliation and Arbitration of the International Chamber of Commerce, by three arbitrators designated in accordance with the said Rules. Arbitration shall be held in_____and shall use the_____language.

E.g.3: In case the total proceeds received by Party A from selling Color TV Sets to Party B is not enough to cover the total value of the assembly lines, the balance shall be made up by Party B with a down payment before the usance L/C opened by Party A expires, thus enabling Party A to effect payment due under the usance L/C.

例1：工程造价以可行性研究报告为基础。如果因工程地质等问题引起大的投资变化，则资金的追加部分应经B批准。

例2：如果问题仍未解决，则应根据国际商会调解与仲裁规则，由该法则指定3个仲裁员最终仲裁解决。仲裁应在_____进行，并应使用_____语言。

例3：如果甲方得自向乙方出售彩电的全部收入不足以支付甲方装配线的全部价款，则余额由乙方在甲方开出的远期信用证到期前用预付款补足，以使甲方能够履行远期信用证项下的付款。

2.6.6 *Patterns Led by "in the Event of/That"*
in the event of/that 引导的句式

E.g.: In the event that the party who holds the preemptive right fails to make a response to the assignor within thirty days of the assignor's request for assignment, the assignor shall have the right to effect assignment to a third party.

例：有优先购买权的一方须在转让方提出转让要求后30天内作出答复，否则转让方有权向第三方转让。

2.7 Other Expressions
其他表达方式

Except for the above characteristics of words, phrases and patterns, international business contracts also use the following expressions to make contracts more complete, more concise, more striking, and to make the structure tight and distinct.

①Use titles, chapters, articles, paragraphs and itemized writing. For example:

Chapter 5 Transfer of Technology

Article 12 Technical Information

12.1 Party B shall provide Party A with the following technical information within 30 days after signing the Contract:

(a)Technical know-how for processing the Products;

(b)Manuals for repair and maintenance of the equipment.

② Use appendixs (annexs), detailed lists (schedules) and other forms of certain necessary details as a part of a contract, which can make contract provisions concise, and achieve detailed and comprehensive requirements. For example:

Article 1 The Lessee hereby leases from the Lessor the Equipment as specified in the Annex, which shall constitute an integral part of this Agreement. ANNEX TO LEASE AGREEMENT NO.123.

Party B agrees to lease to Party A the following Equipment:

Specification:

Quantity:

Unit Price:

Price Terms: FOB Singapore.

Shipment:

Total FOB Value of the Equipment:

Total Rent for the Lease:

③Use definition terms in a contract, namely define recurring expressions in a contract and give shortened forms, which can not only avoid explaining differences, but also can make the contract concise. For example:

Article 1 Definitions

1.1　The terms as used herein shall have the following meanings.

1.1.1　The term "Products" means the products specified in Annex 2.

1.1.2　The term "Components" means any assembled or unassembled parts of the Products.

④Some parts to be highlighted in a contract are written in capital letters to be marked. For example:

This AGREEMENT...WITNESSES that WHEREAS and WHEREAS...NOW THEREFORE in consideration of...It is hereby agreed as follows.

⑤Using the method of "bracket + short form" to simplify some important words which recur in a contract to achieve the purpose of accuracy and conciseness. For example:

Foreign Advance Broadcasting Ltd. of Amsterdam Holland (hereinafter called "Licensor"), and China Broadcasting Products Factory (hereinafter called "Licensee") agree to sign this Contract with the terms and conditions as follows.

⑥By the way of "number+word" to emphasize and to be marked some important items, such as the amount, quantity and deadline in a contract. For example:

(a)USD4,500 (Say U.S. Dollar Four Thousand Five Hundred only).

(b)INVESTOR will assist CHINESE PARTY to construct a paper mill in Guangdong Province, China with a planned capacity of One Million (1,000,000) metric tons per year.

除了上述词汇、短语、句式的特点以外，国际商务合同还采用下列表达方式，使合同更加完整、简洁、醒目、结构严谨、主次分明。

①采用多种标题，分章、分条、分款、分项书写。例如：

Chapter 5 Transfer of Technology

Article 12 Technical Information

12.1　Party B shall provide Party A with the following technical information within 30 days after signing the Contract：

(a)Technical know-how for processing the Products;

(b)Manuals for repair and maintenance of the equipment.

②使用附件（附录）、清单（一览表）等形式详列某些必要的细节作为合同的组成部分，既可使合同规定简洁，又能达到详尽、全面的要求。例如：

Article 1 The Lessee hereby leases from the Lessor the Equipment as specified in the Annex, which shall constitute an integral part of this Agreement. ANNEX TO LEASE AGREEMENT NO.123.

Party B agrees to lease to Party A the following Equipment:

Specification:

Quantity:

Unit Price:

Price Terms: FOB Singapore.

Shipment:

Total FOB Value of the Equipment:

Total Rent for the Lease:

③在合同中使用定义条款，即把在合同中反复出现的用语加以界定意义并赋予简称，既可避免解释上的分歧，又能使合同简洁。例如：

Article 1 Definitions

1.1　The terms as used herein shall have the following meanings.

1.1.1　The term "Products" means the products specified in Annex 2.

1.1.2　The term "Components" means any assembled or unassembled parts of the Products.

④合同中某些需要强调的部分用大写字母书写，以资醒目。例如：

This AGREEMENT... WITNESSES that WHEREAS and WHEREAS... NOW THEREFORE in consideration of...It is hereby agreed as follows.

⑤用"括号+简称"的方式把合同中反复出现的某些重要词语简化，以达到准确、简洁的目的。例如：

Foreign Advance Broadcasting Ltd. of Amsterdam Holland (hereinafter called "Licensor"), and China Broadcasting Products Factory (hereinafter called "Licensee") agree to sign this Contract with the terms and conditions as follows.

⑥用"数字+文字"的方式把合同中某些重要的项目，如金额、数量、期限等加以强调，以资醒目。例如：

(a)USD4,500 (Say U.S. Dollar Four Thousand Five Hundred only).

(b)INVESTOR will assist CHINESE PARTY to construct a paper mill in Guangdong Province, China with a planned capacity of One Million (1,000,000) metric tons per year.

Ideological & Political Gardens

为稳外贸跑出"海关速度"

为打造便捷高效的通关环境，天津市推出进口货物"船边直提"，大力推广出口货物"抵港直装"，实现船舶抵港"零等待"装车、企业"不到场"查验、离港"一站式"验放，减轻外贸企业负担，为稳外贸跑出"海关速度"。

一、"船边直提"创新举　"海关速度"外贸忙

以前进口货物需在港口码头卸箱落场后向码头预约时间、办理提箱，现在对于无须海关查验的进口集装箱，抵港后即可放行，并实现企业车辆从船边直接接卸提货，提箱用时由原先的一两天，最短压缩至1.5小时。这样的口岸通关方式是天津海关与天津港口部门推广实施的"船边直提"天津模式。

在货船抵港前，贸易公司就已通过"单一窗口"向海关提前办理报关申报、单证审核、税款缴纳等通关手续，并在线办理了预约提箱手续。在"天津港电子商务网服务号"微信公众服务平台上，贸易公司能随时了解货轮的卸船进度、集装箱等待排位、预计提箱时间等一系列物流节点信息。

二、疏通堵点破难点　提升企业"获得感"

货物的快放快提，减少了码头堆存及向港外堆场转运货物的数量，也压缩了企业港口物流成本。

以前集装箱在港口堆存短则一天，长则两天，如果内装水果，就需要插电打冷才能保证集装箱内低温。现在每个冷藏集装箱每天能省出300多元的堆存和打冷费用。

提升企业"获得感"的背后是天津海关积极破解改革推行中的各类难点、堵点，小到岸桥如何准确吊卸集装箱到车辆上，大到海关方与港口方、船方和企业方之间的无缝衔接和协调配合。

在"船边直提"政策推行初期，传统的港口作业系统不具备船舶卸箱时间与提箱车辆进入码头时间精准匹配的功能，偶会出现车等卸箱时间长、已卸箱车未到等情况。

天津海关会同港口部门探索开发了"船边直提"货物卸箱时间预测功能，主动推送及重点提示待提货物卸船进度、预计等待时间等信息，便利企业合理调度进场提箱时间。

三、通关便利稳外贸　"晴雨表"里展活力

天津港集装箱吞吐量不断创历史同期新高。数据的背后与天津海关的各项通关便利化改革密不可分，在服务功能和通关效率上"做加法"，在服务费用和环节上"做减法"，减轻企业负担，稳定外贸基本盘。

"船边直提"作业模式实现物资"即到即提"零等待，有关货物可从港口码头直通企业生产车间。

天津海关通过实施海铁联运过境货物"港场直通"作业改革，将有关货物纳入"船边直提"范围，货物运抵天津港到铁路堆场等待装车发运的时间从原来的2至3天最短压缩至3小时，有效提升跨境班列发运效率，进一步畅通了物流运输通道。都说港口是经济的"晴雨表"，从天津港能够看到外贸增长的活力与潜力。

党的二十大报告指出："依托我国超大规模市场优势，以国内大循环吸引全球资源要素，增强国内国际两个市场两种资源联动效应，提升贸易投资合作质量和水平。稳步扩大规则、规制、管理、标准等制度型开放。"天津海关正是践行了此文件精神。

资料来源　张宇琪.为稳外贸跑出"海关速度"[EB/OL].[2023-12-22].https://baijiahao.baidu.com/s?id=1674725414951685821&wfr=spider&for=pc.

Exercises

Chapter 2 即测即评

Translate the following contract clauses into Chinese. Pay attention to the usage of the words underlined.

1. If, <u>as a result of withdrawal</u> or other reasons, an arbitrator fails to perform his duties as an arbitrator, another arbitrator shall, in accordance with the provisions <u>hereof</u>, be selected or appointed.

2. All disputes arising from the performance of this contract shall, through amicable negotiations, be settled by the parties <u>hereto</u>. Should, through negotiations, no <u>settlement</u> can be reached, <u>the case in question</u> shall then be submitted for arbitration to China International Economic and Trade Arbitration Commission, Beijing. The <u>award</u> of the arbitration shall be final and binding upon the parties <u>hereto</u>. The arbitration fee shall be borne by the losing party.

3. "Patented Technology" means such letters patents, and applications <u>therefore</u> as are presently owned or acquired in the future by Party B and/or as Party B has or may have the right to control or grant license <u>thereof</u> during the <u>effective period</u> of this contract in any country or all countries of the world, and as are applicable to or may be used in the manufacture of contract products.

4. <u>Whereas</u> Party B <u>has the right, and agrees to</u> grant Party A the right to use, manufacture and sell the contract products of patented technology, Party A derives to use the patented technology of Party B to manufacture and sell the contract products.

5. The representatives authorized by the parties to this contract have, <u>through friendly negotiations</u> agreed to enter into this contract under the terms, conditions and provisions specified as follows.

6. A sales contract refers to a contract <u>whereby</u> the seller transfers the ownership of an object to the buyer and the buyer pays the price for the object.

7. <u>If, notwithstanding sub-clause 5.1</u>, any damage occurs to any bridge or road communicating with or on the routes to the site due to the transport of materials or plant, the contractor shall notify the engineer of the matter in question, with a copy to the employer, as soon as he becomes aware of such damages or as soon as he receives any claim from the authority entitled to make such a claim.

8. <u>Notwithstanding</u> any other provision of the contract, if the contract intends to claim any additional payment <u>pursuant to</u> any clause of these conditions or other provisions, the contractor in question shall, within 28 days after the event giving rise to the claim, has first arisen, notify the Engineer of his intention, with a copy to the Employer.

9. These articles shall apply to all <u>documentary credits</u> including standby L/C, to the extent to

which the credits in question shall be applicable, and shall be <u>binding upon</u> the parties to the contract, <u>unless otherwise</u> expressly agreed by the parties <u>thereto</u>.

10. <u>Unless otherwise</u> specified in the credit, banks will accept a document <u>bearing</u> a date of issuance prior to that of the credit, subject to such document being <u>presented within the time limit</u> specified in the credit and in these articles.

11. The staff and workers of a company may, <u>in accordance with</u> the law, organize a trade union to carry out union activities and protect the lawful <u>rights and interests</u> of <u>the staff and workers</u>. The company shall provide the necessary conditions for the activities of the trade union of the company.

12. The notice in question shall state the discrepancies <u>in respect of</u> which the <u>issuing bank</u> refuses to the documents and also state whether the bank will hold the documents waiting for the disposal of, or it will return them to, the holder of <u>bill of exchange</u> (remitting bank or the beneficiary, as the case may be).

13. <u>In the event that</u>, either party hereto fails to comply with the terms or conditions of this agreement, and, within 90 days after the written notice is issued by the other party <u>hereto</u>, fails to remedy such failure, the party giving notice, may forthwith notify the other party of the matter in question and <u>terminate</u> this agreement.

14. An <u>irrevocable</u> credit shall be deemed to constitute a definite undertaking of the issuing bank. <u>Provided that</u>, the stipulated documents are presented and are complied with the terms and conditions of the credit, and if the credit provides for <u>sight payment</u>, the payment shall be made or shall be guaranteed to be made.

15. <u>For the purpose of these articles</u>, the date of issuance of a transport document shall <u>be deemed to</u> be the later between such date of the issuance and such date of the <u>receipt stamp</u> as is indicated on the transport document.

16. <u>In case</u> the quality, quantity or weight of the goods are not <u>in conformity with</u> the provisions of the contract after <u>arrival of the goods</u> at the port of destination, the buyer may, <u>under survey report</u> issued by an inspection organization <u>agreed</u> by the parties thereto, <u>lodge claim</u> with the seller, <u>with the exception</u>, however, of those claims for which the insurance company or the shipping company shall be responsible.

17. <u>Should</u> the carrying vessel has arrived at the port of shipment as advised and the seller fails to have the quantity of the goods ready for loading in time specified, the seller shall be liable for any dead <u>freight</u> or <u>demurrage</u>.

18. <u>In testimony whereof</u>, this contract shall <u>come into effect</u> after the contract in question is made and signed by the parties hereto in duplicate, and either party will hold one copy.

19. The securities purchased and sold by the parties to a securities transition may be in the form of scrips or <u>such other forms</u> as are specified by the securities regulatory authorities under the state council.

Chapter 3

Structures of International Business Contracts

国际商务合同的结构

Learning Objectives

◆ 重点掌握英语国际商务合同篇章结构的特点；掌握国际商务合同目录的特点；了解国际商务合同的封面。

Guide Case

Hadley v. Baxendale

9 Ex. 341, 156 Eng. Rep. 145

The plaintiffs, who operated a mill at Gloucester, sued the defendants, who were common carriers, for the damages for the breach of a contract of carriage. The declaration contained two counts but prior to the trial plaintiffs entered a nolle prosequi as to the first. In the second count the plaintiffs alleged that they were forced to shut their mill down because the crank shaft of the steam engine, by which their mill was operated, became broken; that they arranged with W. Joyce & Co., of Greenwich, the manufacturers of the engine, to make a new shaft from the pattern of the old one; that they delivered the broken shaft to the defendants who, in consideration of the payment of their charges, promised to use due care to deliver it to W. Joyce & Co. within a reasonable time but that the defendants failed to do so; that by the reason of the defendants' negligence the completion of the new shaft and the reopening of the plaintiffs' mill were delayed five days longer than would otherwise have been the case; and that during that period the plaintiffs were compelled to pay wages and lost profits aggregating £300 for which amount the plaintiffs sought judgment. The defendants pleaded that they had paid £25 into the Court in satisfaction of the plaintiffs' claim; the plaintiffs replied that this sum was insufficient for that purpose; and the issue was joined upon this replication.

At the trial before Crompton, J., at the last Gloucester Assizes, it appeared that the plaintiffs carried on an extensive business as the millers at Gloucester; and that, on the 11th of May, their mill was stopped by a breakage of the crank shaft by which the mill was worked. The steam-engine was manufactured by Messrs. Joyce & Co., the engineers at Greenwich, and it became necessary to send the shaft as a pattern for a new one to Greenwich. The fracture was discovered on the 12th, and on the 13th the plaintiffs sent one of their servants to the office of the defendants, who were the well known carriers trading under the name of Pickford & Co., for the purpose of having the shaft carried to Greenwich. The plaintiffs' servant told the clerk that the mill was stopped and that the shaft must be sent immediately; and in answer to the inquiry when the shaft would be taken, the answer was that if it was sent up by twelve o'clock any day, it would be delivered at Greenwich on the following day. On the following day the shaft was taken by the defendants, before noon, for the purpose of being conveyed to Greenwich, and the sum of £ 24 was paid for its carriage for the whole distance; at the same time the defendants' clerk was told that a special entry, if required, should be made to hasten its delivery. The delivery of the shaft at Greenwich was delayed by some neglect; and the consequence was, that the plaintiffs did not receive the new shaft for several days after they would otherwise have done, and the working of their mill was thereby delayed, and they thereby lost the profits they would otherwise have received.

On the part of the defendants, it was objected that these damages were too remote, and that the defendants were not liable with respect to them. The learned Judge left the case generally to the jury, who found a verdict with £ 25 damages beyond the amount paid into the Court.

Whateley, (for the defendants) in last Michaelmas Term, obtained a rule Nisi for a new trial, on the ground of misdirection.

(The arguments of counsels were omitted. After they were completed the court took the case under consideration until the next term.)

The judgment of the Court was now delivered by Alderson, B. We think that there ought to be a new trial in this case; but, in so doing, we deem it to be expedient and necessary to state explicitly the rule which the Judge, at the next trial, ought, in our opinion, to direct the jury to be governed by when they estimate the damages.

It is, indeed, of the last importance that we should do this; for, if the jury were left without any definite rule to guide them, it would, in such cases as these, manifestly lead to the greatest injustice. The Courts had done this on several occasions; and, in Blake v. Midland Railway Company, 21 L. J., Q. B. 237, the Court granted a new trial on this very ground, that the rule had not been definitely laid down to the jury by the learned Judge at Nisi Prius.

"There are certain established rules," this Court said, in Alder v. Keighley, 15 M. & W. 117, "according to which the jury ought to find." And the Court, in that case, added: "And here there is a clear rule, that the amount which would have been received if the contract had been kept is the measure of damages if the contract is broken."

Now we think the proper rule in such a case as the present is this: Where two parties have made a contract which one of them has broken, the damages which the other party ought to receive in respect of such a breach of contract should be such as may fairly and reasonably be considered either arising naturally i. e., according to the usual course of things, from such a breach of contract itself, or such as may reasonably be supposed to have been in the contemplation of both parties, at the time they made the contract, as the probable result of the breach of it. Now, if the special circumstances under which the contract was actually made were communicated by the plaintiffs to the defendants, and thus known to both parties, the damages resulting from the breach of such a contract, which they would reasonably contemplate, would be the amount of injury which would ordinarily follow from a breach of contract under these special circumstances so known and communicated. But, on the other hand, if these special circumstances were wholly unknown to the party breaking the contract, he, at the most, could only be supposed to have had in his contemplation the amount of injury which would arise generally, and in the great multitude of cases not affected by any special circumstances, from such a breach of contract. For, had the special circumstances been known, the parties might have specially provided for the breach of contract by special terms as to the damages in that case; and of this advantage it would be very unjust to deprive them. Now the above principles are those by which we think the jury ought to be guided in estimating the damages arising out of any breach of contract. It is said, that other cases, such as breaches of contract in the nonpayment of money, or in not making a good title to land, are to be treated as exceptions from this, and as governed by a conventional rule. But as, in such cases, both parties must be supposed to be cognizant of that well - known rule, these cases may, we think, be more properly classed under the rule above enunciated as to cases under known special circumstances, because both parties may reasonably be presumed to contemplate the estimation of the amount of damages according to the conventional rule. Now, in the present case if we are to apply the principles above laid down, we find that the only circumstances here communicated by the plaintiffs to the defendants at the time the contract was made, were, that the article to be carried was the broken shaft of a mill, and that the plaintiffs were the millers of that mill. But how do these circumstances show reasonably that the profits of the mill must be stopped by an unreasonable delay in the delivery of the broken shaft by the carrier to the third person? Suppose the plaintiffs had another shaft in their possession put up or putting up at the time, and that they only wished to send back the broken shaft to the engineer who made it; it is clear that this would be quite consistent with the above circumstances, and yet the unreasonable delay in the delivery would have no effect upon the intermediate profits of the mill. Or, again, suppose that, at the time of the delivery to the carrier, the machinery of the mill had been in other respects defective, then, also, the same results would follow. Here it is true that the shaft was actually sent back to serve as a model for a new one, and that the want of a new one was the only cause of the stoppage of the mill, and that the loss of profits really arose from not sending down the new shaft in proper time, and that this arose from the delay in delivering the broken one to serve as a model. But it is obvious that, in the great multitude of cases of the millers sending off broken shafts to the third persons by a carrier under ordinary circumstances, such consequences would not, in all probability, have occurred; and these special circumstances were here never communicated by the plaintiffs to the defendants. It follows, therefore, that the loss of profits here cannot reasonably be considered such a consequence of the breach of contract as could have been fairly and reasonably contemplated by both parties when they made this contract. For such losses would neither have flowed naturally from the breach of contract in the great multitude of such cases occurring under ordinary circumstances, nor were the special circumstances, which, perhaps, would have made it a reasonable and natural consequence of such a breach of contract, communicated to or known by the defendants. The Judge ought, therefore, to have told the jury that, upon the facts then before him, they ought not to take the loss of profits into consideration at all in estimating the damages. There must therefore be a new trial in this case.

思考题：

（1）涉及对损害赔偿金的限制，法官阐明了哪些规则？这些规则之间的关系是什么？

（2）导致本案判决结果的关键事实是什么？

No matter what name and what type the contract is, a formal business contract usually consists of three parts: preamble, main body, and ending.

不管什么名称和什么类型的合同，一份正式的商务合同通常由三部分组成：前言、正文和结尾。

3.1　Preamble of a Contract[①]
合同的前言

A preamble is a preliminary statement to introduce the general reasoning of an agreement, the principle of reaching an agreement, or the scope of authority. It usually includes the title and number of the contract, the date and place of signing the contract, the names and addresses of both parties and the preface or recitals, etc.

The control number, as an identification code, is useful for filling and the reference for the implementation of a contract, which is usually written at the beginning of a contract.

The date of signing a contract is the time that a contract comes into force, which can be written at the beginning of a contract or at the end of it.

The place of signing a contract will be related to the governing laws. However, it can be ignored if the parties concerned sign a contract at the different place.

---

① 乔焕然. 英文合同阅读指南：英文合同的结构、条款、句型与词汇分析［M］. 最新增订版. 北京：中国法制出版社，2015.

The parties concerned in a contract must have capacity and cannot be minors or persons not mentally competent. The parties concerned must not be the same party but two or more parties with the qualification of the legal representative. The name of the parties concerned must be written in full to indicate its legal identity, however, the abbreviation of the partys' name can be used in the body of a contract.

The address of the parties concerned must be specific and in detail. This address must be permanent but not temporary and should not be the address of its branch or subordinate. The address of the parties concerned will be used for communication by letters, identifying the parties and when the litigation comes, choosing relative litigation authority.

The preface is the paragraphs at the beginning of a contract that usually summarizes the agreement or provides background information related to the deal. The preface is not a mandatory part of any contract and some contracts skip it entirely. But it can assist outsiders who are trying to understand the contract with description of what the parties intend to do in the contract. The preface is often in the form of a "Whereas Clause" and just for this reason we have called this section the "WHEREAS". The function of a preface is filled in the background, the hope, and the general reasoning of the parties, it is not the part of a contract. In fact, it is written in front of the words "it is hereby agreed…". Everything after those words is the part of a contract. So don't put any important term in the preface unless you clearly repeat them in the body of a contract. The value of a whereas-clause is that it may be helpful for interpreting a contract if any trouble arises later.

Model 3–1

Contract No.:

Date of execution of contract:

Place of execution of contract:

Buyer:

Register No.:

Legal person:

Legal address:

Contract address:

P. O. Code:

Bank:

A/C No.:

Taxpayer identification No.:

Contact person:

Tel:

Fax:

E-mail:

```
Seller:
Legal person:
Legal address:
Contact address:
P. O. Code:
Bank:
A/C No.:
Taxpayer identification No.:
Contract person:
Tel:
Fax:
E-mail:
```

Model 3-2

This contract is made on 14th of April, 202× by and between Romantz Ltd. (hereinafter referred to as the Buyer) with its registered office at No.703 London Street, ××, USA and Arthur Industrial Corporation (hereinafter referred to as the Seller) with its registered office at No.43 Silver Road, Wuhan, China, through friendly negotiations. Both parties have hereby agreed on the terms and conditions stipulated hereunder...

前言是介绍协议的一般理由、达成协议的原则或权限范围的初步声明。它通常包括合同的标题和编号、签订合同的日期和地点、当事人的姓名和地址、前言或说明条款等。

作为识别代码的管理号码，有助于撰写合同，并且可作为履行合同的参考，其通常被写在合同的开始部分。

签订合同的日期是合同生效日，可以写在合同的开始或结束部分。

签订合同的地点与法律的管辖有关。然而，如果当事人在不同的地点签合同，它可以被忽略。

合同的相关当事方必须有行为能力，且不能是未成年人或者智力不健全的人。相关当事方必须不是同一方，但可以是具有法定代表人资格的双方或多方。当事方的名称必须是书面全称，用以表明其合法身份，不过当事方的名称的缩写可用于合同的主体。

当事方的地址必须详细具体。这个地址必须是永久性的，不是暂时的，不应该是其分支机构或下属单位的地址。当事方的地址将用于通信联系、确定当事方和诉讼时选择相关的诉讼权。

前言通常是合同开头的段落，总结协议或提供交易相关的背景信息。前言并不是任何合同的必需部分，一些合同完全跳过前言，但它有助于局外人通过描述合同中当事方打算做什么来理解合同。前言的形式往往是一个"鉴于条款"，只是因为这个原因，我们将这部分称为"鉴于"。前言的作用是介绍背景、期望和当事方的一般理由，它不是合同的一部分。事实上，它写在"特此同意……"的前面。那些单词后面的每句话都是合同的一部分。除非你在合同的正文中清楚地重复了它们，否则不要把任何重要措辞放在前言中。鉴于条款的价值在于，如果以后出现任何麻烦，它可能有助于解释合同。

模板 3-1

合同号：

合同的执行日期：

合同的执行地点：

买方：

登记号：

法人：

法定地址：

合同地址：

邮编：

银行：

账号：

纳税人识别号：

联系人：

电话号码：

传真号码：

电子邮箱：

卖方：

法人：

法定地址：

联系地址：

邮编：

银行：

账号：

纳税人识别号：

联系人：

电话号码：

传真号码：

电子邮箱：

模板 3-2

这份合同是Romantz有限公司（以下简称买方，注册办公地址是美国××市伦敦街703号）与亚瑟工业公司（以下简称卖方，注册办公地址是中国武汉市银路43号）通过友好协商在202×年4月14日签订的。双方特此同意本合同规定的如下条款……

3.2　Main Body of a Contract[①]
合同的正文

A body usually includes general clauses, commonly used clauses and operational clauses.

General clauses include the following: ① definition clause; ② representation and warranty clause; ③indemnification/hold harmless clause; ④confidentiality clause; ⑤terms and terminations clause; ⑥assignment and modification clause; ⑦entire agreement clause; ⑧severance/severability clause; ⑨non‑waiver clause; ⑩force majeure clause; ⑪non‑competition clause; ⑫intellectual property rights clause; ⑬default clause; ⑭dispute resolution clause; ⑮other clauses.

Commonly used clauses include the following: ①conditions precedent clause; ②insurance clause; ③independent contractor relationship clause; ④taxation clause.

Operational clauses actually are a specific contract specifically agreed by the parties, which marks this contract is not that contract.

Model 3-3

　　1.Name, Specifications and Quality of Goods

_____ .

　　2.Quantity

_____ .

　　3.Price

At _____ per ton of 1,000 kilograms, cost, insurance and freight to _____ .

　　4.Total Amount

_____ .

　　5.Period of Shipment

As per bill(s) of lading dated or to be dated _____ .

　　6.Shipment and Classification

Shipment from _____ . Shipment to be made in good condition, direct or indirect, with or without transshipment by first class mechanically selfpropelled vessel(s) suitable for the carriage of the contract goods, classed Lloyds 100A1, or equivalent class, or in accordance with the Institute Classification Clause of the Institute of London Underwriters.

　　7.Extension of Shipment

The contract period for shipment, if such be 31 days or less, shall, if desired by the Shipper, be extended by an additional period of not more than 8 days, provided that the Shipper serves notice claiming extension by telegram or telex sent not later than the next business day following the last day of the originally stipulated period. The notice need not state the number of additional days claimed, and such a notice shall be passed on by the Seller to his Buyer in due course after

---

① 吕昊，刘显正，罗萍.商务合同写作及翻译［M］.武汉：武汉大学出版社，2005.

receipt. The Seller shall make an allowance to the Buyer, to be deducted in the invoice from the contract price, based on the number of days by which the originally stipulated period is exceeded as follows: for 1 to 4 additional days, 0.5% of the gross CIF price; for 5 to 6 additional days, 1% of the gross CIF price; for 7 to 8 additional days, 1.5% of the gross CIF price. However, after having given a notice to the Buyer as above, the Seller fails to make shipment within such 8 days, then the contract shall be deemed to have called for shipment during the originally stipulated period plus 8 days, at the contract price less 1.5%, and any settlement for default shall be calculated on that basis. If any allowance becomes due under this clause, the contract price shall be deemed to be the original contract price less the allowance and any other contractual difference shall be settled on the basis of such reduced price.

8.Appropriation

A notice of appropriation stating the vessel's name, the port of shipment, the date of the bill of lading and the approximate weight shipped, shall within 10 consecutive days (unless otherwise agreed), from the date of the bill of lading be dispatched by or on behalf of the Shipper direct to his Buyer or to the Selling Agent or the Broker named in the contract. In case of resale, the notice of appropriation shall be passed on without delay. The Non-business Days Clause shall not be applied.

9.Payment

Final invoices may be prepared by either party and shall be settled without delay. If not settled, either party may declare that a dispute has arisen which may be referred to arbitration as herein provided.

10.Interest

If there has been unreasonable delay in any payment, the interest appropriate to the currency involved shall be charged. If such charge is not mutually agreed, a dispute shall be deemed to exist which shall be settled by arbitration. The interest shall be payable only where specifically provided in the terms of the contract, or by an award of arbitration. This clause does not override the parties' contractual obligations under the Payment Clause.

11.Shipping Documents

Shipping documents shall consist of:

(1)Invoices.

(2)Full set of on board Bills of Lading and/or Ship's Delivery Orders and/or other Delivery Orders in negotiable and transferable form.

(3)Insurance Policy(ies) and/or Insurance Certificate(s) and/or Letter(s) of Insurance in the currency of the contract. The Letter(s) of Insurance should be certified by a recognized bank if required by the Buyer.

(4)Other documents as called for under the contract. Should shipping documents be presented with an incomplete set of bill(s) of lading or should other shipping documents be missing, the payment shall be made, provided that delivery of such missing documents be guaranteed, such a guarantee to be signed, if required by the Buyer, by a recognized bank. The acceptance of this guarantee shall not prejudice the Buyer's rights under this contract. No clerical error in the documents shall entitle the Buyer to reject or to delay the payment provided that the Seller furnish at the request of the Buyer a guarantee, to be countersigned by a recognized bank, if required by the Buyer. The Seller shall be responsible for any loss or expense incurred by the Buyer on account of such an error. The Buyer agrees to accept the documents containing the Chamber of Shipping War Deviation Clause and/or other recognized official War Risk Clause.

12.Duties, Taxes, Etc.

All export duties, taxes, etc., present or future, in the country of origin, shall be for the Seller's account. All import duties, taxes, levies, etc., present or future, in the country of destination, shall be for the Buyer's account.

13.Discharge

(Omitted)

14.Weighing

(Omitted)

15.Sampling and Analysis

Samples required for the purpose of the contract shall be taken and analytical instructions shall be given in accordance with the GAFTA Sampling Rules Form No. 124. When superintendents are required for the purpose of the supervision and sampling of the goods in accordance with these Rules, superintendents shall be appointed from the GAFTA Approved Register of Superintendents.

16.Insurance

The Seller shall provide insurance on terms not less favorable than those set out hereunder, and as set out in detail in the GAFTA Form 72 viz risks covered:

(1)Cargo Clauses (W.A.), with average payable, with 3% franchise or better terms−Section 2 of Form 72.

(2)War Clauses (Cargo)−Section 4 of Form 72.

(3)Strikes, Riots and Civil Commotions Clauses (Cargo)−Section 5 of Form 72.

17.Prohibition

In case of prohibition of export, blockade or hostilities or in case of any executive or legislative act done by or on behalf of the government of the country of origin or of the territory where the port or ports of shipment named herein is/are situated, restricting export, whether partially or otherwise, any such restriction shall be deemed by both parties to apply to this contract and to the extent of such total or partial restriction to prevent fulfillment whether by shipment or by other means whatsoever and to that extent this contract or any unfulfilled portion thereof shall be cancelled. The Seller shall advise the Buyer without delay with the reasons therefore and, if required, the Seller must produce proof to justify the cancellation.

18.Force Majeure

The Seller shall not be responsible for the delay in shipment of the goods or any part thereof occasioned by any Act of God, strike, lockout, riot or civil commotion, combination of workmen, breakdown of machinery, fire or any cause comprehended in the term "Force Majeure". If the delay in shipment is likely to occur for any of the above reasons, the Shipper shall give notice to his Buyer by telegram telex or by similar advice within 7 consecutive days of the occurrence, or not less than 21 consecutive days before the commencement of the contract period, whichever is the later. The notice shall state the reason(s) for the anticipated delay. If after giving such notice an extension to the shipping period is required, then the Shipper shall give either notice not later than 2 business days after the last day of the contract period shipment stating the port or ports of loading from which the goods were intended to be shipped, and shipments effected after the contract period shall be limited to the port or ports so nominated. If shipment be delayed for more than 30 consecutive days, the Buyer shall have the option of canceling the delayed portion of the contract, such option to be exercised by the Buyer giving notice to be received by the Seller not later than the first business day after the additional 30 consecutive days. If the Buyer do not exercise this option, such delayed portion shall be automatically extended for a further period of 30 consecutive days. If the shipment under this clause be prevented during the further 30 consecutive days extension, the contract shall be considered void. The Buyer shall have no claim against the Seller for delay or non-shipment under this clause, provided that the Seller shall have supplied to the Buyer if required, satisfactory evidence justifying the delay or non-fulfillment.

19.Notices

All notices served on the parties pursuant to this contract shall be served by letter, delivered by hands on the day of writing, or by telegram or by telex or by other method of rapid written communication. A notice to the broker or the agent shall be deemed a notice under this contract. For the purpose of a time limit, the date and the time of the dispatch shall unless otherwise stated, be deemed to be the date and the time of the service. In case of resales, all notices shall be passed on without delay by the Buyer to his Seller or vice versa.

20.Non-Business Days

Saturdays, Sundays and the officially recognized and/or legal holidays of the respective countries and any day which the GAFTA may declaim as non-business days for specific purposes shall be non-business days. Should the time limit for doing any act or giving any notice expire on a non-business day, the time so limited shall be extended until the first business day hereafter. The period of shipment shall not be affected by this clause.

21.Default

In default of the fulfillment of the contract by either party, the following provisions shall apply:

(1)The party other than the defaulter shall, at their discretion have the right after giving notice by letter, telegram or telex to the defaulter to sell or purchase. As the case may be, against the defaulter and such sale or purchase shall establish the default price.

(2)If either party be dissatisfied with such default price or if the right at (1) above is not exercised and the damages cannot be mutually agreed, then the assessment of the damages shall be settled by arbitration.

(3)The damages payable shall based on the difference between the contract price and either the default price established under (1) above or upon the actual or estimated value of the goods, on the date of the default, established under (2) above.

(4)In all cases the damages shall, in addition, include any proven additional expenses which would directly and naturally result in the ordinary course of events from the defaulter's breach of contract but shall in no case include the losses of profit on any sub-contracts made by the party defaulted against or others unless the arbitrator(s) or board of appeal, having regard to special circumstances, shall in his/their sole and absolute discretion think fit.

(5)The damages, if any, shall be computed on the quantity appropriated, but if no such quantity has been appropriated then on the mean contract quantity, and any option available to either party shall be deemed to have been exercised accordingly in favor of the mean contract quantity.

(6)The default may be declared by the Seller at any time after the expiry of the contract period, and the default date shall then be the first business day after the date of the Seller's advice to his Buyer. If the default has not already been declared, then (notwithstanding the provisions stated in the appropriation clause) if the notice of appropriation is not passed by the 10th consecutive day after the last day for appropriation laid down in the contract, where the appropriation clause provides for 7 or more days for the dispatch of the notice of appropriation, or if the notice of appropriation is not passed by the 4th business day after the last day for appropriation laid down in the contract where the appropriation clause provides for less than 7 days for the dispatch of the notice of appropriation, the Seller shall be deemed to be in default, and the default date shall then be the first business day thereafter.

22.Insolvency

If before the fulfillment of this contract, either party shall suspend payments, notify any of the creditors that he is unable to meet debts or that he has suspended or that he is about to suspend payments his debts, convene, call or hold a meeting of the creditors, propose a voluntary arrangement, have an administration order made, have a winding-up order made, have a receiver or manager appointed, convene, call or hold a meeting to go into liquidation (other than for reconstruction or amalgamation), become subject to the Interim Order under Section 252 of The Insolvency Act 1986, or have a Bankruptcy Petition presented against him (any of which acts being hereinafter called an "Act of Insolvency"), then the party committing such Act of Insolvency shall forthwith transmit by telex or telegram or by other method of rapid written communication, a notice of the occurrence of such Act of Insolvency to the other party to the contract and upon proof (by either the other party to the contract, receiver, administrator, liquidator or other person representing the party committing the Act of Insolvency) that such notice was thus given within 2 business days of the occurrence of the Act of Insolvency. The contract shall be closed out at the market price on the business day following the giving of the notice. If such a notice be not given as aforesaid, then the other party, on learning of the occurrence of the Act of Insolvency, shall have the option of declaring the contract closed out at either the market price on the first business day after the date when such party first learnt of the occurrence of the Act of Insolvency or at the market price on the first business day after the date when the Act of Insolvency occurred.

In all cases the other party to the contract shall have the option of ascertaining the settlement price on the closing out of the contract by repurchase or resale, and the difference between the contract price and the repurchase or resale price shall be the amount payable or receivable under this contract.

23.Domicile

The Buyer and the Seller agree that, for the purpose of legal or arbitrational proceedings, this contract shall be deemed to have been made in ×××, and to be performed there, my correspondence in reference to the offer, the acceptance, the place of payment, or otherwise, notwithstanding, and the Courts of ××× or arbitrators appointed in ×××, as the case may be, shall, except for the purpose of enforcing any award made in pursuance of the Arbitration Clause hereof, have exclusive jurisdiction over all disputes which may arise under this contract. Such disputes shall be settled according to the law of ×××, whatever the domicile, the residence or the place of business of the parties to this contract may be or become.

24.Arbitration

Any dispute arising out of or under this contract shall be settled by arbitration in accordance with the Arbitration Rules, such rules forming part of this contract and of which both parties hereto shall be deemed to be cognizant.

25.International Conventions

(Omitted)

正文通常包括通用条款、常用条款和操作性条款。

通用条款包括：①定义条款；②陈述与保证条款；③赔偿与免责条款；④保密条款；⑤期限与终止条款；⑥转让与变更条款；⑦完整协议条款；⑧可分性条款；⑨不弃权条款；⑩不可抗力条款；⑪竞业禁止条款；⑫知识产权条款；⑬违约条款；⑭争议解决条款；⑮其他条款。

常用条款包括：①先决条件条款；②保险条款；③独立合同关系条款；④税收条款。

操作性条款实际上是当事人针对特定合同所作的特别约定，它们标志着此合同非彼合同。

模板 3-3

1.货物名称、规格和质量

_____。

2.数　量

_____。

3.价　格

以每吨成本、保险和运费价格_____运至 _____。

4.总　值

_____。

5.装运期

根据提单日期或日期为_____。

6.运输和分类

从_____装运。货物状态良好，由适航的头等机械自航船以直接或间接、转运或不转运的方式运输，Lloyds 100A1类或同等类，或者根据伦敦保险人协会的协会船级条款分类的合同货物。

7.装运期展期

如果承运人要求合同的装运期是31天或少于31天，同时如果承运人要求展期的电报或电传通知在不晚于原来规定装运期的下一个工作日的最后一天发送，那么装运期可延长不超过8天。通知不需要说明展期的天数，并且卖方在收到这个通知后，在适当的时候应通知买方。卖方应当考虑在发票中从合同价格金额中扣除超过原定的天数，比如，超出1到4天，就扣除CIF价格总值的0.5%；超出5到6天，就扣除CIF价格总值的1%；超出7到8天，就扣除CIF价格总值的1.5%。不过，如果已经像上面那样通知了买方，而卖方不能在8天内装运，那么合同装运期将被视为要求在原定装运期加上8天，合同价格减少1.5%，结算违约将在此基础上计算。如果在此条款下任何差额到期，合同价格应少于原合同价格，并且应在此降价的基础上解决合同其他的差异。

8.拨款

拨款通知说明船名、起运港、提单日期，并且托运人或托运代理人应从提单日期起连续10个工作日内（除非另有约定）把约计装运重量货物装运出去，直接发货给他的买方或销售代理或合同指定的经纪人；如果转售，应当及时传递拨款通知。非业务日条款不适用。

9.付款

任何一方都可以备妥最终的发票，并应毫不延迟进行结算。如果不结算，任何一方可以提出有可能被提交仲裁的争议。

10.利息

如果有不合理的延迟付款，应付适当的利息。如果这些费用没有达成一致意见，存在的争端应通过仲裁解决。应付的利息，只有合同条款或仲裁裁决书上特别提出才会付。这一条款的内容不会取代支付条款下当事方的合同义务。

11.装运单据

装运单据包括：

（1）发票。

（2）议付和可转让的全套已装船提单和/或船的交货单和/或其他交货单。

（3）合同货币的保险单和/或保险凭证和/或保险函。如果买方要求，保险函由经认可的银行证明。

（4）合同要求的其他单据。如果是一套不完整的提单或者其他装运单据丢失了，只要提交这些缺失装运单据的由认可银行签署的保证函（如果买方要求），就可以付款。这个保证的接受不影响买方在本合同项下的权利。单证如无笔误，如果卖方根据买方的要求提供由公认的银行加签的担保，买方有权拒绝或延迟付款。卖方应负责由买方的这种错误产生的任何损失或费用。买方同意接受包含航运协会战争绕航条款和/或其他被公认的官方战争险条款的单据。

12.关税和税款等

原产国现在或将来的所有出口关税和税款等应当由卖方来付。所有目的地国现在或将来的进口关税和税款等应由买方负担。

13.免责

（略）

14.称重

（略）

15.取样和分析

为了合同的目的，应采样品。分析说明应按照谷物与饲料贸易协会第124号抽样规则。为了监管的目的，应当需要监管人。货物的采样应根据谷物与饲料贸易协会第124号抽样规则，指定谷物与饲料贸易协会认可的监管人。

16.保险

卖方提供的保险条款应不低于如下规定，如同谷物与饲料贸易协会表格72所详细列出的，即承保风险包括：

（1）货物条款（水渍险），平均支付，3% 免赔额或更好的条款——表格72第2节。

（2）战争条款（货物）——表格72第4节。

（3）罢工、暴动和民变险条款（货物）——表格72第5节。

17.禁止

如果禁止出口、封锁或敌对行动，或如果由原产国政府或位于装运港口所在国政府或代表作出任何政府部门或立法的行为，限制出口，不管是限制部分出口还是限制全部出口，合同双方都视任何这样的限制适用于本合同，并且在一定程度上，防止履行不管是装运或任何其他方式的限制的全部或部分出口，并且在一定程度上应当取消本合同或任何未完成部分。卖方应当及时通知买方延迟的原因，因此，如果需要，卖方必须出示证据来证明取消的原因。

18.不可抗力

卖方对任何天灾、罢工、停工、暴动或民变、游行示威、机械故障、火灾或其他构成不可抗力条款的原因导致的货物延迟装运不负责。如果延迟装运可能由于任何上述原因而发生，托运人应当在连续发生故障7天或不晚于合同期限开始前21天内以电报、电传或类似的通知形式通知买方，两者以较迟者为准。通知应当说明延迟的原因。如果通知后，还要求延迟装运期，那么托运人应当不迟于合同装运期最后一天的2个工作日内通知，说明港口或货物装运的起运港口，合同期间后的装运应当限于某个港口或指定港。如果货物被推迟装运连续超过30天，买方有权选择取消合同的延迟部分，这样的选择可由买方通知卖方，卖方收到通知不迟于额外连续30天后的第1个工作日。如果买方不如此选择，推迟部分有效期将自动延长连续30天。在进一步展期连续30天内，如果该条款下的装运被禁止，则合同应当被认为是无效的。在该条款下，买方不能因为卖方迟运或不装运货物向卖方提出索赔；如果需要，卖方应提供令买方满意的证明延迟或不装运的证据。

19.通知

依照本合同，送达当事人的所有通知应当通过信函送达，或在写信当天亲自送达，或通过电报、电传或其他快速书面交流的方式送达。通知经纪人或代理人应被视为在本合同项下的通知。为了限制时间，除非另有说明，发货日期和时间应被视为服务的日期和时间。如果转售，所有通知应毫不延迟地由买方向卖方发出；反之，亦然。

20.非工作日

各国的星期六、星期日和正式承认和/或法定假日，以及谷物与饲料贸易协会规定为非工作日的任何特定日子，应被视为非工作日。如果进行任何行为或给予任何通知在非工作日到期，到期日应延长至第1个工作日以后。装运期不受到这一条款的影响。

21.违约

任何一方在履行合同时违约，都适用以下规定：

（1）除了违约方的当事方，在通过信函、电报或电传通知违约方后，其应当有权自由选择销售或采购。由于此情形是针对违约方的，所以这些销售或采购应当设违约价。

（2）如果任何一方对此违约价不满意或者上面（1）条款没被执行，并且损害赔偿不能达成一致意见，那么损失的评估应通过仲裁解决。

（3）应付赔偿应当基于（2）条款订立的违约日期的合同价格和（1）条款订立的违约价或货物实际或估计价值之间的差额。

（4）此外，在所有情况下，损失包括任何额外费用，这将直接和自然导致违约方一般情况下的违约，但在任何情况下应包括由于一方或其他方违约引起的分包合同利润损失，除非仲裁员或申诉委员会考虑到特殊情况，否则其将认为他/他们唯一和绝对的裁决是合适的。

（5）如果产生损失，应按恰当数量计算；但是如果没有恰当的数量，那么按平均合同数量，并且任何一方的选择都应被视为按平均合同数量在执行。

（6）在合同期满后的任何时间里，卖方可能提出违约，违约日期应是卖方通知买方日期后的第1个工作日。如果违约尚未提出，那么（尽管拨款条款说明有7天或者更多时间用于发送拨款通知）在合同规定的拨款最后1天后的连续10天里，若拨款通知没有被发送，或若拨款通知没有在合同规定的拨款最后1天后的第4个工作日内被发送（合同拨款条款规定在7天以内发送拨款通知），那么卖方可能会被视为违约，并且违约日期将是此后第1个工作日。

22.破产

如果在履行本合同前，一方暂停支付，通知任何一位债权人，他无法偿还债务或他已经或者将要暂停支付其债务，召集、要求或举行债权人会议，提出自愿偿债安排，得到行政命令，启动清盘令，指定接管人或管理者，召集、要求或举行会议进行清算（除了重建或合并），受辖于1986年《破产法》第252条下的"暂行法令"，或向他提出破产申请（以下简称"破产行为"），然后提出破产一方应当立即以电传或电报或以其他快速书面沟通的方式，通知合同另一方破产的发生和（由合同的另一方、接管人、管理者、清算者或其他代表破产执行方的人）作出的证明通知应在破产发生的两个工作日内发出。合同应在裁决后的第1个工作日以市场价格结束，之后发出通知。如果上述通知没有发出，那么另一方在了解破产发生后，有权声明合同或者以另一方首次获悉破产发生后的第1个工作日的市场价格结束，或者以破产发生日后第1个工作日的市场价格结束。

在所有情况下，合同另一方有权在合同结束时通过回购或转售选择确定结算价格，并且合同价与回购或转售间的差额应是本合同项下的应付金额或应收金额。

23.注册地

买方和卖方同意，为了诉诸法律或仲裁，本合同应视为在×××国制作和执行，要约、承诺、付款地要对应；否则，×××国法庭或案件在×××国被指派的仲裁员，除了执行根据仲裁条款规定的任何裁决目的外，将对合同下的所有争议有专属管辖权。无论本合同当事人的注册地、居所或营业场所在哪里，此类争议应依×××国法律解决。

24.仲裁

凡由本合同引起的或本合同项下的任何争议，应按照仲裁规则提交仲裁委员会来解决。这些规则构成本合同的一部分，应当视为双方已认知的。

25.国际公约

（略）

3.3 Ending
结尾

The ending includes three parts: the attestation, the signatures and the appendixes. The appendixes are the unnecessary parts of a contract. The attestation part includes the languages to be used in the contract and their effectiveness.

Model 3-4

The contract shall be written in Chinese and English. Both versions are equally authentic. In the event of any discrepancy between the two versions, the Chinese version shall prevail.

Model 3-5

The contract shall come into effect as soon as it is duly signed by both parties and shall remain effective for two years.

Model 3-6

1. The appendixes drawn up in accordance with the principles of this contract are the integral parts of this contract, including: the project agreement, the technology transfer agreement, the sales agreement, etc.

2. The contract and its appendixes shall come into force commencing from the date of approval of the Ministry of Commerce of the People's Republic of China (or its entrusted examination and approval authority).

3. Should the notices in connection with any party's rights and obligations be sent by either Party A or Party B by telegram or telex, etc. The written notices shall be also required afterwards. The legal addresses of Party A and Party B listed in this contract shall be the postal addresses.

4. The contract is signed in _____ , China by the authorized representatives of both parties on _____.

Sometimes the parties to an international business contract may consult to set out the appendixes in the contract. In this case, it must be declared that the appendixes are the inseparable parts of the contract.

结尾由证明、签名和附件三部分组成。附件为合同的非必要部分。证明部分包括合同中使用的语言及其有效性。

模板 3-4

合同应当用中文和英文撰写。两个版本都有法律效力。在两个版本之间存在任何歧义，以中文版本为准。

模板 3-5

双方一旦正式签约，合同即生效，有效期为两年。

模板 3-6

1. 依本合同原则制定的附件是本合同不可分割的一部分，包括项目协议、技术转让协议、销售协议等。

2. 本合同及其附件应自中华人民共和国商务部（或其委托的审批机关）批准之日起开始生效。

> 3. 甲方或乙方应该通过电报或电传等方式发出与任何一方的权利和义务有关的通知，之后还要求发书面通知。列在本合同里的甲方和乙方的合法地址应当是邮政地址。
>
> 4. 本合同于_____年__月__日由双方的授权代表在中国_____签署。

有时，国际商务合同双方当事人可以协商撰写合同附件。在这种情况下，必须宣称附件是合同不可分割的一部分。

Ideological & Political Gardens

中国贸易金融跨行交易区块链平台

2020年8月28日，中国银行业协会（以下简称中银协）组织召开"中国贸易金融跨行交易区块链平台"（以下简称CTFU平台）建设座谈会。会上，中银协与中国工商银行、中国农业银行、中国银行、中国建设银行、交通银行共同签署《CTFU平台服务协议》，正式拉开CTFU平台应用投产的序幕。

CTFU平台将主要发挥以下方面的作用：

一是实现跨行贸易金融产品交易信息的标准化、电子化和智能化，促进供应链金融发展；

二是提高贸易融资效率，降低融资成本，增强金融服务实体经济质效；

三是利用区块链技术"分布式存储、交易可溯、不可篡改"等特点，有效防控贸易金融业务风险；

四是有利于资源共享和利用，提升协会服务会员的水平。

未来，要扎实做好信息安全保障和市场推广工作，加速推进新业务功能落地应用，积极探索与第三方机构开展合作，以科技赋能金融，以合作促进发展，携手各会员单位打造全新的贸易金融生态圈。

为推动银行业数字化转型发展，增强服务实体经济和中小微企业的能力，并有效防范愈加复杂的国际形势所引发的不确定性风险，中银协牵头组织筹建CTFU平台。

2019年12月，中国银保监会、商务部和外汇局联合印发了《关于完善外贸金融服务的指导意见》，其中明确要求："银行业和保险业自律组织应加强调研，深入了解银行保险机构外贸金融业务诉求，在推动完善法律法规、规范展业标准、运用金融科技建设贸易金融信息平台等方面发挥积极作用。"随后，中银协联合五大行全力推进平台有关建设工作。

CTFU平台建设响应国家区块链战略号召，采用分布式账本底层技术，利用其公开透明、不可篡改、集体维护和隐私保护等特点，满足银行贸易金融业务数字化转型的发展需求。平台整体设计采用弱中心、多节点的联盟链组织形式。中银协负责平台运营与管理，保障平台的中立性与公信力；中国工商银行、中国农业银行、中国银行、中国建设银行、交通银行五大行加盟平台，共同议定平台发展方向，共同担负平台发展重任；中银协会员单位均可依据自身需求自愿申请加入平台，共享平台资源。

中银协SaaS共享节点的建立使平台具备了为中小行、外资行提供零成本、快速接入平台业务系统的服务能力，可有效避免机构层面的重复投资，有机整合行业优势资源，实现行业乃至社会层面的资源共享和有效利用。CTFU平台采用自主研发、安全可控的分层多链式总体结构，具有基础平台一次建设重复使用、业务场景灵活适配、应用服务快速上线等特点。

CTFU平台一期上线福费廷二级市场业务功能，立足于解决福费廷业务发展中长期存在的信息不对称、交易流程脱节、缺乏统一规范、交易主体受限、"半手工操作"效率低等痛点，便利银行间福费廷资产买卖信息交互，提高福费廷领域的贸易融资效率，降低企业融资成本，从而有效提高银行业服务中小微企业、服务实体经济质效。二期拟上线保理、再保理等贸易融资产品，中长期将探索追加供应链金融应用场景及其他贸易金融业务相关信息查询功能等。

CTFU平台在建设期间得到中国建设银行、中国银行、中国工商银行、中国农业银行、交通银行、中信银行、招商银行、中国民生银行、上海浦东发展银行、中国光大银行、国家开发银行、汇丰银行（中国）等中银协贸易金融专业委员会常委单位的积极参与和大力支持，在制定平台系统开发需求方案、业务标准及主协议，编写功能测试案例集，以及开展业务联调测试、业务上线验证等多项工作中均发挥了重要作用。2018年12月，CTFU平台完成首笔跨行国内信用证线上验证；2019年11月，完成首笔福费廷二级市场跨行交易线上验证。

党的二十大报告指出："推动货物贸易优化升级，创新服务贸易发展机制，发展数字贸易，加快建设贸易强国。"CTFU平台为进一步发展贸易创造了条件。

资料来源　吴丛司．中银协联合五大行共建"中国贸易金融跨行交易区块链平台"应用投产［EB/OL］.［2022-02-22］. http://news.xinhua08.com/a/20200828/1953318.shtml.

Exercises

Chapter 3 即测即评

Ⅰ.Please read the following English contents, and point out respectively which part they belong to: A.title; B.introduction; C.body; D.ending.

1. After the friendly consultations conducted in accordance with the principles of equality and mutual benefit, the parties have agreed to (describe the subject matter of the Contract) in accordance with the Applicable Laws and the provisions of this Contract.

2. No lawsuit, arbitration or other legal or governmental proceeding is pending or, to its knowledge, threatened against it that would affect its ability to perform its obligations under this Contract.

3. Joint Venture Contract.

4. IN WITNESS WHEREOF, each of the parties hereto has caused this Contract to be executed by its duly authorized representative on the date first set forth above.

Ⅱ.Please classify the structure of the following English contract.

Stock Purchase Agreement

THIS AGREEMENT is made on the _____ th/rd/nd day of _____(month), ____(year), by and between ×××, a corporation authorized to do business in YYY (the Corporation) and the individual listed in exhibit A attached hereto (each individually, a Shareholder and collectively, the Shareholders).

RECITALS

A. The issued and outstanding capital stock of the Corporation currently consists of one thousand two hundred and thirty - one (1, 231) shares of common stock (the Shares). The Shareholders currently own all the issued and outstanding Shares.

B. The Shareholders and the Corporation desire to make provisions for future disposition of the Shares in order to prevent interference with the orderly conduct of the business of the Corporation.

C. The Shareholders and the Corporation desire that each Shareholder shall be prohibited from engaging in any business or activity that competes with the business of the Corporation, as long as he owns the Shares of the Corporation.

Now, therefore, in consideration of the mutual premises and covenants made herein, and for other good and valuable consideration, the receipt and sufficiency of which are hereby acknowledged of the parties do hereby agree as follows:

1.Restrictions on Transfer

No Shareholder will sell, transfer, donate, exchange, pledge, assign or in any way alienate, encumber or dispose of its ownership of any of its Shares of capital stock of the Corporation, whether now owned or hereafter acquired, whether voluntarily or by operation of law, without the prior written consent of the Corporation and all the Shareholders, unless such transfer is in accordance with the provisions of this Agreement.

1.1   Void Transfers. The Corporation shall not transfer on its books any Shares sold or transferred other than pursuant to the provisions of this Agreement. No transferee of the Shares in violation of the provisions of this Agreement shall be a record owner of such Shares nor will such a transferee have the right to receive dividends or other distributions payable to the record owner of such Shares. Any transfer of the Shares in violation of the terms and conditions of this Agreement shall be void and without effect in transferring any interest in such Shares to the transferee.

1.2   Lifetime Transfers. Any Shareholder desiring to transfer the Shares of the Corporation during his lifetime (the Transferring Shareholder) must give notice (the Notice) of intent to transfer in writing to the Corporation and to the remaining Shareholders at least ninety days before the date of the proposed transfer. The Notice shall specifically name the proposed transferee, the number of the Shares to be transferred and the proposed price and terms of the transfer. The following procedures shall be followed:

(A)Purchase by the Corporation. Within thirty days after receipt of the Notice, the Corporation may elect to purchase the Shares of the Transferring Shareholder at the price and terms indicated in the Notice, or, at the option of the Corporation, the price and terms indicated in paragraph 1.4 herein. The Transferring Shareholder shall abstain from participating in any decision of the Corporation to exercise or refrain from exercising the purchase options provided herein, except that at the direction of the holders of the majority in interest of the outstanding Shares not held by the Transferring Shareholder, the Transferring Shareholder will vote its Shares and take such other action as may be required by such majority.

(B)Purchase by the Shareholders. In the event that the Corporation either affirmatively elects not to exercise the above-described option or allows the period for exercise of the option to lapse, the remaining Shareholders shall have an additional sixty-day period beginning with the end of the thirty-day period specified in subsection (A) above in which to elect to purchase all the Shares of the Transferring Shareholder at the price and terms indicated in the Notice, or at their option, the price and terms indicated in paragraph 1.4 herein. Any Shareholders so electing shall deliver to the president of the Corporation a written notice indicating the Shareholders' intent to purchase such Shares and the number of the Shares which such Purchasing Shareholders exceed the number of the Shares to be transferred by the Transferring Shareholder, the Shares of the Transferring Shareholder shall be allotted among the Purchasing shareholders in any manner on which the Purchasing Shareholders may agree; however, if they are unable to agree the shares shall be allotted among them so that each Purchasing Shareholder shall purchase the fractional portion of the Shares to be transferred which is equal to the fractional portion of the total number of outstanding Shares held by the respective Purchasing Shareholder (the Pro Rata Amount). Should the Pro Rata Amount of a respective Shareholder exceed the Purchase Commitment of the respective Shareholder, the excess of each Pro Rata Amount exceeding the Purchase Commitment shall be allocated among the remaining Purchasing Shareholders in any manner on which the remaining Purchasing Shareholders may agree; however, if they are unable to agree, the Shares shall be allotted among them as equally as possible per capital, without creating fractional Shares, the preference shall be given to the Purchasing Shareholders in order of their respective holdings of the Shares of the Corporation, with the holder of the greatest number of the Shares receiving the first preference.

(C)Interim Death of Transferring Shareholder. In the event a Shareholder dies or dissolves alter having sent the Notice but prior to the transfer of the ownership of the Shares pursuant to the terms of this Agreement, this paragraph 1.2 shall Lapse or Refusal. If the options to purchase all the Shares of the Transferring Shareholder are not exercised by either the Corporation or the remaining Shareholders, the Transferring Shareholder may then transfer its shares pursuant to the provisions described in the Notice, but such transfer must be the original transfer at the purchasing price and under the provisions specified in the Notice within one hundred days following the original date of receipt of the Notice by the Corporation. Additionally, such transfer will not be effective unless the transferee executes and becomes bound by this Agreement prior to the transfer of the Shares to such transferee.

1.3　Death or Dissolution of a Shareholder. In the event of the death or dissolution of a

Shareholder, the executor or personal representative or corporate representative of the deceased or dissolved Shareholder shall sell and the Corporation shall purchase all of the Shares then owned by the deceased or dissolved Shareholder at the price and terms provided in paragraph 1.4 of this Agreement. The Corporation may, however, at its option, assign the right to purchase such Shares to the surviving Shareholders on a basis proportional to their respective ownership of the Shares in the Corporation.

1.4　Purchasing Price and Closing. In the event of the purchase of the Shares under paragraph 1.3, or at the option of the Corporation or the Purchasing Shareholders under paragraph 1.2, the purchasing price to be paid for each of the Shares shall be the net book value as of the end of the month preceding the month Shareholder notifies the Corporation of its desire to sell or lies or begins the process of dissolution. The net book value shall be determined from the Corporation's regular financial statements as prepared in accordance with Section 1.5 by subtracting the total amounts of its liabilities from the total net book value of its assets and dividing the difference thereby obtained by the number of the Shares of the capital stock of the Corporation issued and outstanding as of the date of the valuation. The appropriate adjustments shall be made, however, for the dividends and the other distributions to the Shareholders which occur after the valuation date.

The closing of the transfer of the Shares pursuant to this Agreement (the Closing) shall take place within ten days following the date on which the determination of the purchasing price for the Shares to be transferred has been completed. The Closing shall take place at the principal office of the Corporation at 12: 00 noon or at such time and place as may mutually agreed upon by the parties. The selling Shareholder or its personal or corporate representative shall deliver to Party A at closing the certificates representing the Shares being purchased along with such additional documentation and endorsements as Party A may reasonably request.

The purchasing price for any share purchased pursuant to this Agreement shall be paid in cash or by check payable to the selling Shareholder.

1.5　Financial Statements. The Corporation shall cause its financial condition and the results of its operations to be compiled at the end of each fiscal year by its accountant. The Corporation shall prepare or cause to be prepared financial statements as of the end of each month including the month that corresponds to the end of its fiscal year. These statements need not be audited and shall consist of a balance sheet and a profit and loss statement which shall contain all appropriate adjustments necessary to present fairly the financial condition and the results of the operation of the Corporation as of the end of each month and for the interim period then ended. Such year-end and monthly financial statements shall be prepared in accordance with generally accepted accounting principles consistently applied.

1.6　The Corporation shall provide the Shareholder with the Shares of the Corporation's outstanding stock for the payment of USD, the Shareholder shall relinquish his/her voting right and elect to represent the Shareholder's voting rights (excluding the rights to dividends and other rights of the holders of the Shares). If leave the employment of the Corporation (for any reason) before one year from _____ nd/rd/th of _____ (month), _____ (year), the payment of USD could be returned to the Shareholder by the Corporation with 12% interest in 30 days after the employee's departure. Should a forfeiture result in the creation of fractional share(s), the number of share(s) to be forfeited shall be rounded out to prevent the creation of fractional share(s). All stock distributed under this Agreement shall be adjusted to preserve the value of the bonus in the event of a stock dividend, stock split or reverse stock split, recapitalization, merger, consolidation, reorganization, cash or properly dividends, exchange of shares, repurchase of shares or any other change in corporate structure of or by the Corporation that in any such event materially effects the outstanding shares of stock.

(Omitted)

Name of Corporation:

By:

Name, Title:

Name of Party A

Attest:

Name, Title:

Ⅲ.Translation.

1.Translate the title of the following contract into English cover.

中国浙江宁波化工厂与韩国汇维士（Huvis）化学公司关于建设浙江天堂聚酯项目的合同，签名时间为202×年6月。

2.Translate the following English technical contract directory into Chinese.

Table of Contents

Preamble

Article 1   Definition and Interpretation

Article 2   Country of Origin and Manufacturer

Article 3   Time of Delivery

Article 4   Port of Shipment

Article 5   Port of Destination

Article 6   Terms of Payment

Article 7   Insurance

Article 8   Packing

Article 9   Terms of Shipment

Article 10   Guarantee of Quality Claims

Article 11   Claim

Article 12   Force Majeure

Article 13   Arbitration

Article 14   Checking

Article 15   Operation

Article 16   Maintenance

...

Article 20   Technical Personnel

Article 21   Languages

Appendix 1   Work Schedule

Appendix 2   Specifications

Appendix 3   Drawings

Appendix 4   Schedule of Personnel Training

3.Translate the following English parties clause into Chinese.

This Contract is made and entered into at Ningbo on the fifth day of May, 202× by and between Company A (hereinafter referred to as "Party A") and Company B (hereinafter referred to as "Party B").

4.Translate the following English certificate and signature clauses into Chinese.

IN WITNESS WHEREOF, the Principal and the Consultant hereto have caused this Consultation Agreement to be executed in accordance with their respective laws the day and year first above written.

Qi Jianchuan	Habibi
(Signature)	(Signature)
Managing Director	General Manager
Orient Lion Trading Company	Dal Handelsa Consultants Partnership

Chapter 4

Words & Expressions Following Contractual Norms
符合合同文体的规范用词及用语

Learning Objectives

◆　重点掌握法律词汇；掌握特殊副词和系指定义词；了解专用词汇。

Guide Case

Frigaliment Importing Co. v. B.N.S. International Sales Corp.

Case A

Facts:

Plaintiff, Frigaliment Importing Co., sued defendant, B.N.S. International Sales Corp., over two contracts. The first involved that defendant agreed to sell to plaintiff 75,000 lbs. of two and a half to three pound chickens, and 25,000 lbs. of one and a half to 2 pound chickens. This contract was signed on May 2, 1957. The second contract, also dated May 2, was identical to the first excepting only that it was for 50,000 lbs. of the heavier chicken, was for a slightly higher price for the smaller chickens, and was to ship on a later date, May 30. The initial shipment under the first contract was short but the balance was shipped on May 17. When the initial shipment arrived in Switzerland, the plaintiff found, on May 28, that the two and a half to three pound birds were not young chickens suitable for broiling and frying but were stewing chickens or "fowl". The plaintiff immediately protested, however shipment under the second contract was made on May 29, the two and a half to three pound birds again being stewing chicken. The defendant stopped the transportation of these birds at Rotterdam. The plaintiff claimed that, per the contract, all of the chickens were to be young. The defendant claimed that the definition of "chicken" included all types, not just young birds.

Issue:

Does the plaintiff have the burden to show that ambiguous contractual terms are used in a narrower rather than a broader sense?

Holding: Yes.

Decision/Rationale:

The court held that the word "chicken" standing alone was ambiguous. First, the contract itself must be examined to determine if it offers any aid to its interpretation. The plaintiff claimed that the size of the birds alone should indicate that they were to be young. The court found this argument to be unpersuasive. The defendant noted that the contract called not just for chicken but for "US Fresh Frozen Chicken, Grade A, Government Inspected". Therefore, the Department of Agriculture's regulations would be incorporated by reference (which favors the defendant's interpretation). The court carefully examined the negations between the two parties, and although the negations were primarily conducted in German, they used the English word chicken. During the course of negations, the defendant specifically asked the plaintiff if the term chicken was to include the German word "Huhn", which encompassed both broilers and stewing hens, and was answered in the affirmative. Next, the plaintiff contended that there was a definite trade usage of the word "chicken" which meant "young chicken". In order to establish trade usage, the law of New York required a showing that "the usage is of so long continuance, so well established, so notorious, so universal and reasonable in itself, as that the presumption is violent that the parties contracted with reference to it, and made it part of their agreement". The plaintiff provided several expert witnesses in order to establish the trade usage of the word "chicken". However, the defendant countered with industry experts as well that countered the plaintiffs' views of the usage. The defendant further showed regulations that supported his definition of the word "chicken". Also, the defendant was able to show that if the birds shipped were in fact young, due to prevailing market prices at the time, he would have been unable to deliver them properly. In effect, this would show that the plaintiff should have realized that he was paying too low a price to receive the birds he claimed he anticipated. Lastly, the defendant points to the plaintiff authorizing the final shipment of birds as proof that the plaintiff knew what they were receiving. The plaintiff countered that they had insisted on young birds in the second delivery. When all the evidence was reviewed, it was clear that the defendant believed that it could comply by delivering some stewing chickens instead of only young birds. The defendant's definition of "chicken" fit the evidence more closely than did the plaintiffs. When attempting to establish a narrower definition of "chicken" rather than the broader usage, the burden was on the plaintiff. The plaintiff did not meet that burden in this case. Judgment was entered dismissing the complaint with costs.

资料来源　佚名. Free case briefs[EB/OL].[2023-12-22]. http://www.freecasebriefs.com/frigaliment-importing-co-v-bns-international-sales-corp-1960.

Case B

Enders Colsman AG v. Guangzhou Qingchu Group Ltd.

1.Findings of the Court

On 1 October, 2006, Buyer and Seller signed Sales Contract No.6008DE in Guangzhou. The original version of the contract is in English. Buyer submitted the Chinese version translated by Guangzhou Municipal Notary Office while Seller submitted another Chinese version translated by Guangdong Provincial Notary Office. The main dispute is the Chinese translation of the English word "deposit" in the payment clause and default clause. Other agreed parts of Chinese translation of the contract are: (1)Price clause:... (2)Payment clause:... (3)Quality clause:... (4)Default clause:... In regard to the controversial Chinese translation of the word "deposit", Buyer interpreted it as "money paid" while Seller understood it as "down payment".

2.Ruling of the Court on the Merits of the Dispute

In regard to the price in dispute USD96,497.60, designated in the contract as deposit, it means "down payment", without reference to "money paid". Buyer has paid the total price of the goods during the performance of the contracts, the down payment USD96,497.60 was not used to offset the price of the goods, and Buyer did not breach any of its obligations. According to Art. 115 P.R.C. Contract Law that "The parties to a contract may, according to the Guaranty Law of the People's Republic of China, agree that one party pays a deposit to the other party as the guaranty for the creditor's rights. After the debt obligations are performed by the obligor, the deposit shall be returned or offset against the price." Buyer's request to return the deposit is supported by the Court.

资料来源　佚名. CISG case presentation[EB/OL].[2023-11-22]. http://cisgw3.law.pace.edu/cases/080000c1.html.

思考题：

（1）案例A和案例B有什么共同点？

（2）从以上两个案例中你得到什么教训？

4.1 Special Adverbs[①]
特殊副词

So far some archaic words in the contract are still used, such as hereto, thereafter, whereby. The archaic words mostly are adverbs, which are formed by "here, there, where" plus prepositions, as words in formal legal documents, as attributive or adverbial in the sentences. Its role is mainly to avoid repetition, make the style appear formal, accurate and concise, but also undertake the role of the terms of the contract. "Here" says "this", "there" says "that", "where" represents "which" which will lead to clauses.

在合同中迄今为止仍然使用一些古体词语，如hereto、thereafter、whereby。这些古体词语多为副词，由here、there、where加上介词，作为正式法律文书中的词汇，在句中做定语或状语。其作用主要是避免重复，使行文显得正式、准确、简洁，同时也起着承接合同条款的作用。here表示this，there表示that，where代表which并引出从句。

---

①　吕昊，刘显正，罗萍. 商务合同写作及翻译［M］. 武汉：武汉大学出版社，2005.

4.1.1   *The First Category:"Here"+Prepositions=Prepositions+"This"*
第一类："这里"＋介词＝介词＋"这"

(1)Hereby=by This=by Reason of This

E.g.1: The Seller hereby warrants that the goods meet the quality standard and are free from all defects.

E.g.2: The parties mutually agree that the said Agreement shall be and is hereby cancelled.

E.g.3: We hereby employ you as our Broker to bring about the sale of our Company.

(2)Herein=in This

E.g.1: The license herein granted is conditioned on B selling Licensed Devices at prices no more favorable than those followed by A.

E.g.2: The minimum royalty herein specified shall be paid by B to A.

(3)Hereinafter=Later in This Contract

E.g.1: Any complaint which either party does not wish to refer to a Conciliation Committee may then be submitted by the First Party to arbitration as hereinafter provided.

E.g.2: This Contract is made this 20th day of May, 202× by ABC Corporation (hereinafter referred to as "Seller") and XYZ Corporation (hereinafter referred to as "Buyer").

E.g.3: Party A agrees to pay to Party B an amount hereinafter called royalty equal to 5% of the gross sales.

(4)Hereinbefore= in a Preceding Part of This Contract

E.g.1: The Debtor may deem compromise with any other Creditor, in such manner as the Debtor may consider advisable, anything hereinbefore to the contrary notwithstanding.

E.g.2: If the Offeree does not advise the Offeror by notice in writing within the said period of ×× days as hereinbefore provided, then the Offeree shall be deemed to have accepted the offer of the Offeror.

(5)Hereto=to This

E.g.1: The parties hereto are fully aware that the best interests of their own and Joint Venture will be served by taking all reasonable measures to ensure increase in production and in order to achieve this goal. The Parties agree to retain sufficient earnings in Joint Venture for the expansion of production and other requirements, such as bonus and welfare funds. The annual proportion of the earnings to be retained shall be decided by the Board of Directors.

E.g.2: Joint Venture shall employ competent treasurers and auditors to keep all books of accounts, which are accessible at any time to each party hereto.

E.g.3: All disputes, controversies or differences which may arise between the parties hereto, out of or in relation to this Agreement and which the Board of Directors fails to settle through consultation, shall finally be submitted for arbitration which shall be conducted by the Foreign Trade Arbitration Commission of the China Council for the Promotion of International Trade in accordance with the Provisional Rules of Arbitration Procedure of the said commission, the decision of which shall be final and binding upon both parties.

(6)Hereof=of This Contract

E.g.1: Any failure or delay in the performance by either party hereto of its obligations under this Agreement shall not constitute a breach hereof or give rise to any claims for damages if it is caused by the following occurrences beyond the control of the party: earthquake, fire, floods, explosions, storms, accidents, war.

E.g.2: Whether the custom of the Port is contrary to this Clause or not, the owner of the goods shall, without interruption, by day and night, including Sundays and holidays (if required by the carrier) supply and take delivery of the goods. Provided that the owner of the goods shall be liable for all losses or damages including demurrage incurred in default on the provisions hereof.

E.g. 3: This Agreement shall begin on the date hereof, and shall continue for ×× years thereafter.

(7)Hereunder=under This

E.g. 1: The Principal shall not assign or transfer any of its rights, obligations or liabilities hereunder without the express prior written consent of the General Agent.

E.g.2: The obligations of the Joint Venture hereunder shall be as follows.

（1）特此，在此

例1：卖方在此保证：货物符合质量标准，无瑕疵。

例2：缔约双方彼此同意，特此取消该协议。

例3：我们特此雇用你为我们的经纪人，以促进公司的销售业务。

（2）此中，于此

例1：在这里授予的许可证是以乙方出售特许装置的价格不得优于甲方所遵循的价格为条件的。

例2：于此规定的最低使用费（租费）应由乙方付给甲方。

（3）以下，在下文

例1：如果任何一方不愿意把申诉提交给调解委员会，就可由甲方将其提交给下文所提出的机构以便仲裁。

例2：本合同由ABC公司（以下简称"卖方"）与XYZ公司（以下简称"买方"）于202×年5月20日订立。

例3：甲方同意向乙方支付以下称为特许权使用费的费用，该费用等于总销售额的5%。

（4）在上文中

例1：尽管有上述相反的情况，只要债务人认为是适宜的，他可以与任何其他债权人达成妥协。

例2：如果受要约人在上文所规定的××天内没有书面通知要约人，则受要约人被认为已经接受了要约人的要约。

（5）本协议的

例1：协议双方充分认识到，为了他们自己和合营企业的最大利益，必须尽一切可能增加生产。因此，双方同意合营企业应保留足够的收益，用于扩大生产及其他需要，如奖金和福利基金。合营企业的年留用奖金比率由董事会决定。

例2：合营企业雇用合格的财务人员和审计员，设立会计账目，合营各方可随时查看有关账目。

例3：本协议双方有关本协议的一切分歧或差异，若董事会不能通过协商解决，则提交中国国际贸易促进委员会对外贸易仲裁委员会，根据该会仲裁程序暂行规则进行仲裁。该委员会的裁决是终局性的，对双方均具有约束力。

（6）在本合同中的

例1：本协议任何一方因地震、火灾、洪水、爆炸、风暴、事故和战争等不可抗力事件，未能履行协议，不构成违约或索赔之缘由。

例2：不论港口习惯是否与本款规定相反，货主都应无间断地昼夜（如承运人需要，包括星期日和假日）供货和提货。货主对违反本款规定所引起的所有损失或损坏，包括滞期应负担赔偿责任。

例3：本协议由本日开始，此后继续××年有效。

（7）在此中

例1：非经总代理人预先书面同意，委托人不得将本协议规定的任何权利、义务或责任予以转让或转移给他人。

例2：下述合资企业各种义务如下。

4.1.2 *The Second Category:"There"+Prepositions=Prepositions+"That"*
第二类："那里"+介词=介词+"那"

(1)Thereafter=Afterwards, after That

E.g.1: This Agreement shall thereafter be automatically extended for further periods of ×× years.

E.g.2: The parties shall organize and appoint the management committee, and thereafter, such management committee shall control the operation of the Joint Venture.

(2)Thereby=by That Means, in That Connection

E.g.1: Notice of termination shall be served by post or in person and the Agreement is thereby terminated.

E.g.2: In the event of the death of any partner, this partnership shall not be thereby dissolved.

(3)Therefore=for That

E. g.: Before commencing the construction, the Contractor shall submit the plans and specifications therefore to the Owner for approval.

(4)Therefore

E.g.: It is, therefore, to the mutual benefit of Party A and Party B to establish high standard of quality in the merchandise.

(5)Therefrom=from That

E.g.: "Products" mean any and all agricultural products or any products derived therefrom.

(6)Thereof=of That, from That Source=of the Said Agreement

E. g. 1: Party A is the owner of the right to the Letter Patent together with any extensions thereof.

E.g.2: The titles to the Articles in this Agreement and in the said Exhibits are for convenience of reference only, not part of this Agreement, and shall not in any way affect the interpretation thereof.

(7)Therein=in That

E.g.1: The said Letter of Credit has just been received, but we find that some of the Clauses therein are not in agreement with the terms and conditions of the Contract.

E.g.2: Royalty shall be paid if any patented invention of A is embodied therein.

(8)Thereon=on That

E.g.: When the Licensed Products are sold, the royalty thereon shall be paid within a calendar month from the date of delivery.

(9)Thereto=to That

E.g.1: The written notice shall be sent to all directors, including copies of reports relating thereto.

E.g.2: The structure as well as equipment pertaining thereto shall be erected by the Contractor, on the Site set forth hereunder.

（1）此后，今后

例1：本协议此后应自动延长××年。

例2：当事人双方应组织并委任管理委员会，而且今后该管理委员会应负责管理合资公司的经营。

（2）因此，从而

例1：停止协议的通知应通过邮寄或派人送去，从而该协议终止。

例2：如果任何合伙人死亡，本合伙公司不因此而解散。

（3）为此，因此，由于这样

例：在开工之前，承包商应为此将各种计划、技术说明书一并提请业主批准。

（4）因此，为此

例：因此，为了甲方和乙方的共同利益，应该为商品确立高的质量标准。

（5）由此

例："产品"一词，系指一切农产品或由此衍生的任何产品。

（6）由此

例1：甲方是专利证书所有权及其任何引申权利的所有者。

例2：本协议的各条款和上述展示牌中使用的标题，仅为了查阅方便，并非本协议的构成部分，绝不影响对本协议内容的解释。

（7）其中……在那里

例1：我们刚收到该信用证，发现其中有些条款与合同条款不符合。

例2：一旦A方的任何专利发明在那里得以实现，那就应付给特许权使用费。

（8）在其上

例：特许产品售出后，该产品的专利权使用费从交货日算起，一个日历月度内付讫。

（9）向那里，另外

例1：应将书面通知送达所有的董事，其中包括有关各种报告副本。

例2：关于那里的建筑结构和设备应由承包商在下面所述场地建立起来。

4.1.3　The Third Class:"where"+Prepositions=Prepositions+"Which"
"哪里"＋介词＝介词＋"哪个"

(1)Whereby=by Which

E.g.1: In the event of accident whereby loss or damage may result in a claim under this Policy, immediate notice applying for survey must be given to our Agent.

E.g.2: This Agreement is made and concluded by and between A Corporation (hereinafter called Party A) and B Company (hereinafter called Party B) whereby the parties hereto agree to enter into the compensation trade under the terms and conditions set forth below.

(2)Whereof=of Which

E.g.1: In witness whereof, the Parties hereto have caused this Contract to be executed as of the date first written above by their duly authorized representatives.

E.g.2: In witness whereof, the parties hereto have caused their respective duly authorized representative to execute the Agreement on the ＿＿＿＿＿＿ day of ＿＿＿＿＿＿ in the year of ＿＿＿＿＿＿ .

(3)Wherein=in Which

E.g.1: A general suretyship refers to a suretyship contract wherein the parties agree that the surety shall undertake suretyship liability in case the debtor defaults.

E.g.2: A suretyship of joint and several liability refers to a suretyship contract wherein the parties agree that the surety and the debtor shall be jointly and severally liable.

（1）凭此协议，凭此条款

例1：所保货物，如发生在保险单项下负责赔偿的事故，应立即通知公司代理人查验。

例2：本协议由A公司（以下简称甲方）与B公司（以下简称乙方）签订，双方同意按下列条款进行补偿贸易。

（2）关于那事

例1：本合同由双方授权的代表于首开日期签立，特此为证。

例2：双方授权各自代表于＿＿＿＿年＿＿＿月＿＿＿日签署本协议，兹以为证。

（3）在其中

例1：当事人在保证合同中约定，在债务人不能履行债务时，由保证人承担保证责任的，为一般保证。

例2：当事人在保证合同中约定保证人与债务人对债务承担连带责任的，为连带责任保证。

4.1.4　Other
其他

E.g.: This circular decree is hereby issued in order to check resolutely the aforesaid illegal acts, and strengthen the protection of and the administration concerning the precious and rare wild animals.

例：为了坚决制止上述违法行为，加强珍稀野生动物保护管理工作，特通令如下。

4.2 "Shall" Legal Term[①]
法律词汇 Shall

"Shall" is one of the most frequently words used in international business contracts, which is one of the most main words in a unique style of the English contract. "Shall" is mainly used to indicate the specific provision in the contract, the obligation, liability and legal responsibility which shall be performed in law. Under this kind of circumstance, "should, must or have to" should not be used. "Shall" is not affected by subject of person, which can be translated flexibly, according to the specific content of the contract, can be translated into "must", "should" and can also be translated as "will" and "can" or no word.

E.g.1: The employer shall make a prepayment of 20% of the Contract value to the Contractor within 10 days after signing the Contract.

E.g.2: The board meeting shall be called and presided over by the Chairman. Should the Chairman be absent, the vice-Chairman shall, in principle, call and preside over the board meeting.

E.g.3: The Term of the Company shall be 5 years commencing from the date of issuance of the Company's business license.

E.g.4: Any amendment to this Contract or to its appendices shall come into force after the written agreement is concluded and signed by the parties hereto and approved by the original examination and approval authorities.

E.g.5: If the Buyer fails to notify and/or forward full details within the period specified above, the Buyer shall be deemed to have waived his right to assert any claim.

E.g.6: All residents shall be equal before the law.

E.g.7: Tenant shall pay for all utilities and/or services supplied to the premises.

E.g.8: Tenant shall not change or install locks, paint, or wallpaper the said premises without Landlord's prior written consent. Tenant shall not place placards, signs, or other exhibits in a window or any other place where they can be viewed by other residents or by the general public.

shall是国际商务合同中使用频率最高的词汇之一，它是构成独特英语合同文体的一个最主要的词汇。shall主要用来表示合同中各项具体的规定和表示法律上应当履行的义务、债务和应承担的法律责任，这种情况下不使用should、must或have to。shall一词不受主语的人称影响，可根据合同的具体内容灵活翻译，可译成"必须""应该"，也可以翻译为"将""可以"或不译出来。

例1：雇主应于签约后10天内向承包商支付相当于承包合同20%的预付款。

例2：董事会会议应由董事长召集并主持。如董事长缺席时，原则上应由副董事长召集主持。

---

① 胡庚申，王春晖，申云桢. 国际商务合同起草与翻译 [M]. 北京：外文出版社，2001.

例3：公司条款于颁发营业执照之日起5年有效。

例4：本合同及其附件的任何修改，必须经双方签署书面合同文件，并报原审批机构批准后才能生效。

例5：如果买方未能在上述规定的期间内通知和（或）寄出完整的详细资料，那么买方将被认为放弃提出任何索赔的权利。

例6：法律面前人人平等。

例7：租客须支付所有公用事业和/或服务设施的收费。

例8：如未事先获得业主书面同意，租客不得更换或安装住所的门锁、油漆住所或贴换墙纸，也不得将招牌、告示牌或其他展示牌置放在窗户上或其他住客或公众看得见的任何地方。

4.3　Defining Words
系指定义词

We define the word as defining words which indicate definition. Important contracts often limit the meaning of the key noun in the contract at the very start and give a unified explanation in order to avoid a disagreement in the future.

The definitions of the term "mean, shall be, is, are, shall mean etc." are often used in the contract, which say "refers", "refers to" and "means" and so on, between which there is a difference. If "definition terms" are specially appointed by both parties according to this contract, then "mean, is, are" will be used. If it is the usual definition, that is, all the definition words are used in the contract, "shall" plus "mean, be" is the correct expression.

E.g.1: "Licensed Products" are any and all the products as listed in Schedule A attached hereto and all improvements in such products which may be developed by the Licensor during the Effective Period.

E.g.2: In this Contract, Force Majeure shall mean any concurrence beyond the reasonable control of the parties preventing or delaying the performance of this Contract.

我们把表示定义的词称为系指定义词。重要的合同往往一开始就用系指定义词把合同中的关键名词的含义加以限定，给出一个统一的解释，以避免日后发生分歧。

在合同中经常使用的定义词有mean、shall be、is、are、shall mean等，表示"指""系指""含义为"等，但这些词使用起来是有区别的。如"定义词"是合同双方特别根据本合同约定的，那么就要用mean、is、are；如果是"通常的定义"，即所有合同都用该定义词，shall加上mean和be就是正确的表达。

例1："特许产品"的含义是指合同附件A中所列的所有产品和许可方在合同有效期内可能对这些产品作的全部改进。

例2：本合同规定的不可抗力指任何超出双方合理的控制力所发生的阻碍或延误本合同履行的事件。

4.4 Terminologies
专用词汇

In international business contracts, we find some words which are not commonly used frequently appear in the contract. Though the quantity of these words is small, but they are formal vocabulary in legal contract and special file and the special need of legal writing too.

在国际商务合同中，我们发现一些我们平时不常用的却频频出现在合同中的词汇。这些词汇虽然数量不多，但却是法律合同和文件中专用的正式词汇，也是法律文体的特殊需要。

4.4.1 *Whereas*
鉴于，就……而论

E.g.1: Whereas the first Party is willing to employ the second Party and the second Party agrees to act as the first Party's Engineer in_____, it is hereby mutually agreed as follows.

E.g.2: Whereas the Bank has agreed to extend a short-term credit loan for the purpose of providing general working capital to the Company, the parties thereto do hereby agree as follows.

E.g.3: Whereas Party A represents and warrants that he is the owner of the sole and exclusive rights to use the secret process of Party B in_____(country).

例1：鉴于甲方愿意聘请乙方，乙方同意应聘为甲方在_____（工程）的工程师。合同双方特此达成协议如下。

例2：鉴于该银行同意向该公司提供短期信贷作为其周转资金之用，双方同意以下各点。

例3：有鉴于甲方表示并保证他有独家的权利，可以采用乙方在_____（某国家）的秘密生产方法。

4.4.2 *In Witness Whereof*
特此立（证）据，以此立（证）据

E.g.1: In witness whereof, the parties hereto have caused this Agreement to be executed on the day and year first before written in accordance with their respective laws.

E.g.2: In witness whereof, stockholders of the Company have hereunto set their hands of the day and year first above written.

E.g.3: In witness whereof, we have hereto signed these Documents on_____(date) and accepted on_____(date).

例1：本协议由双方根据各自的法律签订，于上面所签订的日期开始执行，特立此据。

例2：特此证明，公司股东已于如上所述时间在此文本上签名。

例3：我方于_____年___月___日签署本文件，并于_____年___月___日已接受此文件，特此为证。

4.4.3 *Know All Men by These Presents*
根据本文件，特此宣布

E.g.: Know all men by these presents that we_____(bank's name) (hereinafter, called "the Bank") having our registered office at_____will be bound unto_____(the Owner's name) (hereinafter called the "Owner") in the sum of payment well and truly to be made to the said Owner, the Bank will bind itself, its successors and better assignee by these presents.

例：根据本文件，兹宣布，我行_____（银行名称）（以下简称银行）的注册地点在_____（注册地名），向_____（业主名称）（以下简称业主）立约担保支付金额的保证金。本文件对银行及其继承人和受益人均具有约束力。

4.4.4 *Now Therefore*
特此，因此

E.g.: Now therefore, the Conditions of this obligation are such that, if the Contractor will promptly and faithfully perform the said Contract (including any amendments thereto) then this obligation shall be null and void, otherwise it shall remain in full force and effect.

例：为此，本担保的条件是，如果承包商迅速地、忠实地履行上述合同（包括任何修改书），本担保规定的义务将无效，否则将生效实施。

4.5 Other Specific Phrases
其他特定词语

4.5.1 *Prior To*
在……之前

E.g.1: The Contractor shall bear all costs and damages which may result from the ordering of any materials prior to the approval of the shop drawings.

E.g.2: Not to make any structural alterations or additions to the said premises without first having obtained the written consent of the Landlord. In the event of any permitted alterations being made by the Tenant to the said premises during the said term, the Tenant shall reinstate the said premises at his own costs and expenses prior to delivering up possession thereof to the Landlord at the expiration of the said term.

例1：承包商应承担未经加工图认可的物资订货所带来的一切花费与损失。

例2：未获得业主的书面同意，不得对该楼宇作任何结构上的改变或附加建筑。万一租户在所述期间对该楼宇进行任何获准的改变，租户须在所述期届满而把楼宇所有权移交业主前，自费将楼宇复原。

4.5.2　*In Lieu Of*
　　作为……代替

E.g.: A foreign merchant who is accustomed to sign his name may notify the company of his signature in lieu of the seal impression referred to in the preceding paragraph.

例：凡习惯于亲手签名的外商，可通知他签名的公司，以代替前段所述的印章。

4.5.3　*In Accordance with/According To...*
　　根据

E.g.1: The work shall be performed in accordance with the provisions of the Contract.

E.g.2: The commission shall vary in percentage according to the kind of sale made by the salesman.

例1：此工程应按合同条款完成。

例2：根据推销员所从事的销售种类的不同，其佣金的比例也有所不同。

4.5.4　*Due To*
　　由于，因为

E.g.: The Landlord shall not be liable for any failure to supply such heat, water, or electricity, not due to gross negligence on its part.

例：如果不是因为业主方面的重大疏忽，业主对于不能供应暖气、水、电不负责任。

4.5.5　*In Favor Of*
　　以……为受益人，赞同

E.g.: This instrument shall inure to the benefit and run in favor of such Transferee, with the same force and effect as though such Transferee had originally been the Optionee herein.

例：本票据可供该受让人有效利用，其有效性一如该受让人原来就是取得优先选择权者。

4.5.6　*At the Request Of*
　　按照……的要求

E.g.: The question of law shall be submitted to arbitration by the parties, or either of them, at the request of the expert.

例：按照专家的要求，有关法律问题应由各方或其中一方提交仲裁。

4.5.7　*Pertaining To*
　　有关

E.g.: Buyer shall be fully acquainted with all other matters and things pertaining to the operation of the business of Seller.

例：买方对卖方经营的有关情况应了如指掌。

4.5.8   *In Compliance With*
依从，按照

E.g.: In compliance with your invitation for bids of the above date, the undersigned hereby proposes to furnish all labor and materials.

例：遵照你方的上述日期投标，签名人特此建议提供全部劳动力和材料。

4.5.9   *Provided That*
但是，但规定

E.g.1: Instructions given by the Engineer shall be in writing, provided that: if for any reason the Engineer considers it necessary to give any such instructions orally, the Contractor shall comply with such instructions.

E.g.2: The owner may, at its discretion, approve or reject any change proposed by the Contractor, provided that the Owner shall approve any change proposed by the Contractor to ensure the safety of the Works.

例1：由工程师发出的指令应为书面形式，但规定：如果出于任何原因，工程师认为有必要以口头形式发出指令，承包商应遵照执行。

例2：业主可赞成或拒绝由承包商提出的变更，但应接受承包商提出的保证工程安全方面的变更建议。

4.5.10   *In Question*
该，这

E.g.: It is common for Tenders to be identified by such a tender reference or contract number as shall be added to link the Tender to the Project in question.

例：通常为了把投标书和有关工程项目联系在一起，投标书应标明投标参考编号或合同号。

4.5.11   *The Above-Mentioned, Said, Aforesaid*
上述的，前述的

E.g.1: Party A shall make delivery of the goods in accordance with the above-mentioned arrangement.

E.g.2: Party A grants Party B an exclusive license to manufacture products by using the invention of the said letter of Patent.

E.g.3: The Licensee shall keep full and adequate books of account containing all particulars that may be necessary for the purpose of showing the amount of royalty payable to the Licensor. The aforesaid books of account shall be kept at the licensee's place of business.

例1：甲方将按照上述安排交货。

例2：甲方授予乙方独占许可证，利用上述专利证书中的发明专利制造产品。

例3：被许可方应完整地、详尽地记录会计账目，账目应包括所有旨在向许可方说明应付的使用费的细节。以上会计账目应在被许可方营业地保存。

4.5.12 *Undersigned*
以下签名方，在末尾签名的

E.g.1: The sponsors of the undersigned company will draw up the terms and conditions of the organization.

E.g.2: The undersigned party agrees to continue to be responsible for paying the balance of payment.

例1：署名的公司发起人将草拟公司组织的条款。

例2：以下签名方同意继续负责，支付未付清的欠款。

4.5.13 *In Consideration Of*
考虑到、鉴于、由于

E.g.1: In consideration of the licenses and technical assistance provided, the Joint Venture will pay Party A technical assistance fees in the form of the Euro.

E.g.2: In consideration of the right to publish cheap edition, the publisher will pay to the author 25% of the retail price of one copy sold of the edition.

例1：考虑到许可证以及在此提供的技术援助，合资企业将以欧元支付甲方技术援助费。

例2：考虑到出版廉价版本的权利，出版商将付给作者25%的版税。

4.5.14 *Subject to=Depending on...as a Condition*
以……作为条件

E.g.1: Subject to the terms of this Agreement, the Producer agrees to be bound by the terms to the following marketing agreement.

E.g.2: Subject to Clause 5, no variation in or modification of the terms to the Contract shall be made except by written amendment signed by the parties.

E.g.3: Subject to the above stipulations, the profits, losses and risks of the Joint Venture shall be borne by the parties in proportion to their respective contributions to the registered capital of the Joint Venture.

E.g.4: We make you the following offer, subject to change without notice.

例1：在本协议的条款下，制造商同意接受下列营销协议各项条款的约束。

例2：根据第5条规定，合同的任何条款的变更或修改，必须以双方签订的修改本为准。

例3：在上述规定的范围内，各方按各自对合资企业的注册出资比例分享合资企业的利润，并承担合资企业遭受的损失和风险。

例4：我方报盘如下，如有变动不另行通知。

4.5.15　*To Be Entitled to= to Give Sb. the Right to Sth.*
有，有资格

E.g.1: Chairman and Directors are entitled to have such positions in other companies, which will not be the competitors of the company.

E.g.2: If one or more of the following events of default shall occur and be continuing, the Agent and the Banks shall be entitled to the remedies set forth in Article 2 Item 3.

E.g.3: The Seller shall be entitled to terminate this license in the event of failure by the Buyer to comply with any of the conditions states in this Article.

E.g.4: The Tenant shall not be entitled to any such reimbursement in accordance with the Clause 5. 3 to this agreement.

例1：公司的董事长及董事有资格在其他公司担任同样的职务，但其任职的公司不得是本公司的竞争对手。

例2：如果发生下列一种或几种违约事件，且违约事件正在继续，代理人以及各银行应行使第2条第3款规定的补救方法。

例3：如果买方违反本条款所规定的任何条件，卖方有权终止该特许权。

例4：按照本协议第5条第3款的规定，承租人无权获得任何此类补偿。

4.5.16　*Notwithstanding=Although, though or even If*
尽管……，即使

E. g. 1: Notwithstanding the above provision, this Agreement shall terminate if the Joint Venture enters into liquidation.

E.g.2: Anything to the contrary notwithstanding, it is expressly agreed that on any default as provided in this paragraph, the Seller shall have the right to rescind this Agreement, and the Seller, at his option, may retake such goods.

例1：虽有前述条款，如果合资企业停业清算，则本协议应终止生效。

例2：尽管有与之相反的情形，双方明确同意，如果违反本段条文规定，卖方有权废除本协议，卖方可自行决定收回这些货品。

4.5.17　*Save=Except (For)*
除外

E.g.1：The Contractor shall not cut or alter the work of any other Contractor save with the consent of the Engineer.

E.g.2：Save as is provided in this Ordinate, no claim within the jurisdiction of the Board shall be actionable in any court.

例1：除非得到工程师的同意，否则该承包商不应消减或改变任何其他承包商的工程。

例2：除非本条例另有规定，否则凡属仲裁处司法管辖权范围内的申诉，不得在任何法庭进行诉讼。

4.5.18 *In Respect Of*
对于，关于，有关……的

E.g.1: The Voting Trustees shall, in respect of any stock possess all stockholders' right of every kind.

E.g.2: Contractor shall not be relieved from any obligation/responsibility and/or liability under the Contract in respect of any part of the Work performed by a Subcontractor.

E.g.3: Party A will make, declare or pay any distribution or payments of any kind in respect of its capital stock:

例1：股权受托人拥有各类股票的全部股东权利。

例2：按照合同规定，由分包商执行的任何工程部分，承包商不能推卸其义务、责任和/或债务。

例3：甲方将实行、宣布或支付有关其股本的任何分配或款项。

Exercises

Chapter 4 即测即评

Ⅰ.Translate the following sentences into English.

1.董事会表决中如遇投票数均等平分，主席（董事长）可投票决定。

2.如果任何一方有任何违反本协议之处，另一方有权索取因对方违反协议而造成的损失赔偿费。

3.合同价格意指第××款中所提及的总计价格，可根据下文所列条款酌情予以增减。

4.对于最低产量或有关专利费的支付要求必须按比例分配。

5.此种买卖应服从下列条款。

6.考虑到包含于此的相互协议，缔约双方特此同意如下事项。

7.该项不动产包括土地连同地面上的一切建筑物和辅助设施。

8.工程师应该为此按公司规定的标准价格得到报酬。

9.高级职员或董事不得在卖方业务中使用的或从属于该业务的商标或商号中占有任何利益。

10.由于没有满足该项要求，这笔债务应视为到期应付款。

Ⅱ.Translate the following sentences into Chinese.

1.By adding hereto one or more of the commodities, and fixing the current prices thereof, the Manufacturer may amend or change the price schedule.

2.When decisions are made by the Engineer, the Contractor shall comply therewith.

3.The Joint Venture shall have the Agreement executed and become bound thereby on the date.

4. The restriction provided for in this paragraph shall only apply to the Customers named in the aforesaid list.

5. If you are prepared to accept it, please indicate on the copy of this letter enclosed herewith in the space provided.

6. In the event of failure to the Operator to comply with the obligations to correct, the Company shall have the right to forthwith make such correction at the costs and expenses of the Operator.

7. The cost of such remedial actions will be for Contractor's account if and to the extent the aforesaid reasons are attributable to Contractor.

8. In the event of litigation, against Party B on account, of any claim of infringement arising out of the use of licensed products, Party A agrees to do so.

9. Testimony must be heard in the presence of all the parties relating to this License Agreement, unless a hearing is waived in the submission or by the written consent of the parties.

10. All and every other interest of or belonging to or due to each of the constituent corporations shall be deemed to be transferred to Buyer without further act or deed.

Chapter 5

Translation of International Business Contracts
国际商务合同的翻译

Learning Objectives

◆   重点掌握从句的翻译技巧；掌握句子的翻译技巧；了解合同翻译的准则。

Guide Case

Taylor v. Caldwell

3 B. & S. 826, 112 Eng. Rep. 309 (1863)

Action for the breach of a written agreement by which defendants contracted to "let" the Surrey Gardens and Music Hall, at Newington, Surrey, to plaintiffs, for four days, for the purpose of giving four "grand concerts" and "day and night fetes" in the hall; plaintiffs agreed to pay £100 at the close of each day. The defendants agreed to furnish a band and certain other amusements in connection with plaintiffs' entertainments, but the plaintiffs were to have all moneys paid for entrance to the music hall and gardens. The plaintiffs alleged the defendants' breach, whereby the plaintiffs lost much money paid by them for printing advertisements of and in advertising the concerts, and also lost a lot of expenses incurred by them in preparing for the concerts and otherwise in relation thereto, and on the faith of the performance by the defendants of the agreement on their part. The defendants pleaded that the Surrey Gardens and Music Hall were accidentally destroyed by fire on June 11, 1861, without the default of the defendants or either of them. A verdict was returned for the plaintiffs, with leave reserved to enter a verdict for defendants. Further facts were stated in the opinion.

The judgment of the Court was now delivered by Blackburn, J. In this case the plaintiffs and defendants had, on the 27th May, 1861, entered into a contract by which the defendants agreed to let the plaintiffs have the use of the Surrey Gardens and Music Hall on four days then to come, viz., the 17th June, 15th July, 5th August and 19th August, for the purpose of giving a series of four grand concerts, and day and night fetes at the Surrey Gardens and Music Hall on those days respectively. And the plaintiffs agreed to take the Surrey Gardens and Music Hall on those days, and pay £ 100 for each day. (The court interprets the agreement not to be a lease, and concludes that the entertainments provided for in the agreement could not be given without the existence of the Surrey Gardens and Music Hall.)

After the making of the agreement, and before the first day on which a concert was to be given, the Hall was destroyed by fire. This destruction, which we must take on the evidence, was without the fault of either party, and was so complete that in consequence the concerts could not be given as intended. And the question we have to decide is whether, under these circumstances, the loss which the plaintiffs have sustained is to fall upon the defendants. The parties when framing their agreement evidently had not presented to their minds the possibility of such a disaster, and have made no express stipulation with reference to it, so that the answer to the question must depend upon the general rules of law applicable to such a contract.

There seems no doubt that where there is a positive contract to do a thing, not in itself unlawful, the contractor must perform it or pay damages for not doing it, although in consequence of unforeseen accidents, the performance of his contract has become unexpectedly impossible. The law is so laid down in 1 Roll Abr. 450, Condition(G), and in the note (2) to Walton v. Waterhouse, 2 Wms. Saund. 421 a. 6th ed., and is recognized as the general rule by all the Judges in the much discussed case of Hall v. Wright (E. B. & E. 746). But this rule is only applicable when the contract is positive and absolute, and not subject to any condition either express or implied and there are authorities which, as we think, establish the principle that from the nature of the contract, it appears that the parties must from the beginning have known that it could not be fulfilled unless when the time for the fulfillment of the contract arrived some particular specified thing continued to exist, so that, when entering into the contract, they must have contemplated such continuing existence as the foundation of what was to be done; there, in the absence of any express or implied warranty that the thing shall exist, the contract is not to be construed as a positive contract, but as subject to an implied condition that the parties shall be excused in case, before breach, performance becomes impossible from the perishing of the thing without default of the contractor.

There seems little doubt that this implication tends to further the great object of making the legal construction such as to fulfill the intention of those who entered into the contract. For in the course of affairs men in making such contracts in general would if it were brought to their minds, say that there should be such a condition. Accordingly, in the civil law, such an exception is implied in every obligation of the class which they call "obligatio de certo corpore". The rule is laid down in the Digest, lib. XLV., tit. l, de verborum obligationibus, 1.33. "Si Stitchus cero die dari promissus, ante diem moriatur: non tenetur promissor." The principle is more fully developed in 1.23. "Si ex legati causa, aut ex stipulatii hominem certum mihi debeas: non aliter post mortem ejus tenearis mihi, quam si per te steterit, quominus vivo eo eum mihi dares: quod ita fit, is auto interpellators non deistic, auto occident elm." The examples are of contracts respecting a slave, which is the common illustration of a certain subject used by the Roman lawyers, just as we are apt to take a horse; and no doubt the propriety, one might almost say necessity, of the implied condition is more obvious when the contract relates to a living animal, whether man or brute, than when it relates to some inanimate thing (such as in the present case a theatre) the existence of which is not so obviously precarious as that of the live animal, but the principle is adopted in the civil law as applicable to every obligation of which the subject is a certain thing. The general subject is treated by Pothier, who in his Traite des Obligations, Partied 3, Chap. 6, Art.3, Sec.668 states the result to be that the debtor corporis certi is freed from his obligation when the thing has perished, neither by his act, nor his neglect, and before he is in default, unless by some stipulation he has taken on himself the risk of the particular misfortune which has occurred.

Although the civil law is not of itself authority in an English Courts, it affords great assistance in investigating the principles on which the law is grounded. And it seems to us that the common law authorities establish that in such a contract the same condition of the continued existence of the thing is implied by English law.

There is a class of contracts in which a person binds himself to do something which requires to be performed by him in preson; and such promises, e.g. promises to marry, or promises to serve for a certain time, are never in practice qualified by an express exception of the death of the party; and therefore in such cases the contract is in terms broken if the promisor dies before fulfillment. Yet it was very early determined that, if the performance is personal, the executors are not liable; Hyde v. The Dean of Windsor (Cro. Eliz. 552, 553). See 2 Wms. Exors. 1560, 5th ed., where a very apt illustration is given. "Thus," says the learned author, "if an author undertakes to compose a work, and dies before completing it, his executors are discharged from this contract: for the undertaking is merely personal in its nature, and, by the intervention of the contractor's death, has become impossible to be performed." These are instances where the implied condition is of the life of a human being, but there are others in which the same implication is made as to the continued existence of a thing. For example, where a contract of sale is made amounting to a bargain and sale, transferring presently the property in specific chattels, which are to be delivered by the vendor at a future day; there, if the chattels, without the fault of the vendor, perish in the interval, the purchaser must pay the price and the vendor is excused from performing his contract to deliver, which has thus become impossible. In (Williams v. Lloyd (Jones, 179)) the court, which in assumption allied that the plaintiff had delivered a horse to the defendant, who promised to redeliver it on request. Breach, that though requested to redeliver the horse he refused. Plea, that the horse was sick and died, and the plaintiff made the request after its death; And on demurrer it was held a good plea, as the bailer was discharged from his promise by the death of the horse without default or negligence on the part of the defendant. "Let it be admitted," says the Court, "that he promised to deliver it on request, if the horse died before, that has become impossible by the act of God, so the party should be discharged as much as if an obligation were made conditioned to deliver the horse on request, and he died before it."

It may, we think, be safely asserted to be now English law, that in all contracts of loan of chattels or bailments, if the performance of the promise of the borrower or bailee to return the things lent or bailed, becomes impossible because it has perished, this impossibility (if not arising from the fault of the borrower or bailee from some risk which he has taken upon himself) excuses the borrower or bailee from the performance of his promise to redeliver the chattel.

The great case of Coggs v. Bernard (1 Smith's L. C. 171, 5th ed.; 2 L. Raym. 909) is now the leading case on the law of bailments, and Lord Holt, in that case, referred so much to the civil law that it might perhaps be thought that this principle was there derived direct from the civilians, and was not generally applicable in English law except in the case of bailments; but the case of Williams v. Lloyd (Jones, 179), above cited, shows that the same law had been already adopted by the English law as early as The Book of Assizes. The principle seems to us to be that, in contracts in which the performance depends on the continued existence of a given person or thing, a condition is implied that the impossibility of performance arising from the perishing of the person or thing shall excuse the performance.

In none of these cases is the promise in words other than positive, nor is there any express stipulation that the destruction of the person or thing shall excuse the performance; but that excuse is by law implied, because from the nature of the contract it is apparent that the parties contracted on the basis of the continued existence of the particular person or chattel. In the present case, looking at the whole contract, we find that the parties contracted on the basis of the continued existence of the Surrey Gardens and Music Hall at the time when the concerts were to be given; that being essential to their performance.

We think, therefore, that the Surrey Gardens and Music Hall having ceased to exist, without fault of either party, both parties are excused, the plaintiffs from taking the gardens and paying the money, the defendants from performing their promise to give the use of the Surrey Gardens and Music Hall and other things. Consequently the rule must be absolute to enter the verdict for the defendants.

思考题:

（1）依本案的判决意见，当合同的履行因不可预见的事件的发生而变得难以承担或不可能时，决定当事人可否免责的一般规则是什么? 该规则受到什么样的限制?

（2）支持本案判决的法律规则是什么?

（3）试通过本案说明罗马法对英国法产生的影响。

（4）如果一艘货轮因遭遇台风而延误了航程，未能在海运合同规定的期限之内把货物运至约定的地点，而合同未就承运人可否因此而免责作任何规定，那么法律能否依本案规则进行判决?

5.1 Principles of Contract Translation[①]
合同翻译的准则

On the basis of the standard of "faithfulness, expressiveness and elegance", while translating international business contracts, two standards should be adhered to: first is faithfulness and accuracy, second is expressiveness and smoothness.

在"信、达、雅"标准的基础上，在进行国际商务合同的翻译时，应坚持两个标准：一是准确严谨；二是规范通顺。

5.1.1 *Faithfulness and Accuracy*
准确严谨

Due to the growing professionalism and compatibility of international business contract, the content of the contract is accurate and complete. Especially the translation of legal terms and key words must be paid more special attention in the contract. It is difficult to reflect "faithfulness and accuracy" of the contract language if only loyal to the original. Take two words "offer and accept" for example, translating "offer" into "provide, propose" and translating "accept" into "accept, approval, consent" are correct, which also reflects the intention of the word and already reach "faithfulness". However, in an international business contract, "offer" can only be translated into "invitation", the corresponding "invitation person" is the offerer and offeree is "the invitatee"; "accept" only can be translated into "promise", the corresponding "promise person" is the acceptor, acceptee is "the person who accepts commitments", other translations are wrong.

Translation of a contract is different from literary works, which is generally not particular about literary grace, lasting appeal and rhetoric, etc. It requires faithfulness and accuracy, sometimes in order to avoid ambiguity, the translation of some words must remain the same way of translation, especially terms of the contract and the key words. "Exclusive territory" for example should be translated into exclusive territory, which says that the licensor shall not put the same content of technology license granted to any third party within the region, even the licensor itself can not use this technology in the region. However, exclusive contract is translated into "exclusive contract", which says an agreement between manufacturer and retailer that prohibits the retailer from carring the product lines of firms to firms that are the rivals of the manufacturer. For another example, net income can be translated into "net income"; while "net profit" should be translated into "net profit" (not translated into "net margin").

"Faithfulness and accuracy" of contract translation should include the following two elements:

由于国际商务合同的专业性和兼容性越来越强，因此，合同的内容也就日趋精确和完

---

① 吴敏，吴明忠. 国际经贸英语合同写作［M］. 广州：暨南大学出版社，2002.

备。尤其是合同中的法律术语、关键词语的翻译更应予以特别重视，仅仅"忠实"原文，很难体现出合同语言的"准确严谨"。以 offer 和 accept 这两个词为例，将 offer 译为"提供、提议"，将 accept 译为"接受、认可、同意"都是正确的，也反映了词的本义，可谓已达到了"信"。然而在国际商务合同中，offer 只能译为"要约"，相应的"要约人"是 offerer，offeree 就是"受要约人"；accept 只能译为"承诺"，相应的"承诺人"就是 acceptor，acceptee 就是"接受承诺人"，其他译法都属不妥。

合同的翻译不同于文艺作品的翻译，一般不讲求文采、韵味、修辞等。它要求的是准确严谨。有时为了避免产生歧义，有些词语的翻译必须保持同一种译法，特别是合同中的专业术语和关键词语。如 exclusive territory，应译成"独占区域"，表示许可方不得再把同样内容的技术许可协议授予该地域内的任何第三方，就连许可人本身也不得在该地域使用该技术。但是，exclusive contract 则译为"独家经销合同"，表示制造商和零售商之间的协议禁止零售商携带公司的产品到竞争对手制造商那里。再如，net income 可译成"净收入"，而 net profit 则应译为"纯利润"（不译成"净利润"）。

"准确严谨"的合同译文应具备以下两个要素：

5.1.1.1   Accuracy
词语准确

In the practice of contract translation, there is quite a number of translation error which is produced in the error judgment of the translator and means. For example, in the international purchase and sale contract of goods, generally, a "confirmation" is needed to sign. In a confirmation, "The undersigned Sellers and Buyers have agreed to follow the terms" firstly is set, which can be translated as "The undersigned Sellers and Buyers have agreed to close the following transactions according to the terms and conditions stipulated below". The "clause" in the translation should be translated into the "terms and the conditions", the "conditions" in the phrases cannot be missed, because a contract agreed upon often contains a number of conditions. For example of "payment clause" in the contract, before signing the contract, both the buyer and the seller mainly discuss the terms of payment, the two sides should firstly discuss the mode of payment (such as transfer, collection, or by letter of credit). If using a letter of credit, a sight letter of credit, confirmed letter of credit, transferable letter of credit or by revolving letter of credit should also be further determined, then set the terms. Followed by both parties to negotiate the related conditions, such as when the buyer will open the L/C, if the buyer does not open the L/C in time, what legal consequences will he/she take on etc. As a result, only these related payment terms and conditions combined together can form the payment terms in the contract, i.e., the terms and conditions.

在合同翻译的实践中，有相当多的错译都产生于译者的判断错误和望文生义。例如，在国际货物买卖合同中，一般要签订一份"确认书"。在确认书中，首先规定"兹经买卖双方同意按下列条款成交"，翻译为"The undersigned Sellers and Buyers have agreed to close the following transactions according to the terms and conditions stipulated below"。这个译文中的"条款"一词应译成 terms and conditions，短语中的 conditions 不能漏掉，因为一个合同条款的达成经常包含着若干条件。以合同中的"支付条款"为例，在合同签订前，买卖双方主要商讨付款条件，双方首先要商讨用什么方式支付（如采用转让、托收或信用证）。如果采用信用证方式，还应进一步确定是采用即期信用证、保兑信用证、可转让信用证还是循环信用证，这样就把条款定下来了。紧接着双方还要协商与此有关的条件，比如买方何时开立信用证；如果买方不按时开证，应承担何种法律后果等。因此，这些有关支付的 terms 和 conditions 结合在一起才能构成合同中的"支付条款"，即 terms and conditions。

5.1.1.2 Completeness
译文完整

Translation must maintain the integrity of the contract and never keep the equivalence between the original and the amount of words in the translation.

E.g.1: In case part of or all know-how of the above-mentioned technical contents have been published by Licensor or any third party, the licensee shall no longer be responsible for keeping the opened parts secret.

"Confidential" in this clause shall be translated into "keep secret and confidential", while "confidential" is missed in the translation, which is not very rigorous. In addition, after the translation of "In case part of or all know-how of the above-mentioned technical contents have been published by Licensor or any third party", add "Licensee obtains evidence of such publication". This can make this clause complete because one party must have a reason not to undertake confidential obligations, and must show enough evidence when the other party insisted.

E.g. 2: Shipment during the period beginning on Apr. 1 and ending on Oct. 20 subject to Buyer's Letter of Credit reaching Seller before Mar. 20.

Among the terms above, the time of delivery should include these two days—April 1 and October 20, so "both dates inclusive" should be added in translation. In addition, the arrival date of buyer's L/C also includes the day on March 20, therefore, the preposition before Mar. 20 should add "on" except for "before", which is translated into "subject to Buyer's Letter of Credit reaching Seller on and before Mar. 20". "Subject to" in the sentence here refers to "subject to...", "be valid for". For example: This offer is subject to our final confirmation.

E.g.3: COMMODITY RICE FROM NORTHEAST CHINA, 5,000 M/TONS USD××× PER M/T CIF VANCOUVER IRREVOCABLE SIGHT L/C PROMPT SHIPMENT VALID SUBJECT TO REPLY HERE 30 JUNE, 2023. ("Here" is a key word in "reply here", which must never leak. As to translation of "reply June 30, 2023", it refers to "send on June 30, 2023", and an addition of "here" emphasizes "we received a reply message on June 30, 2023". That is to say, the actual date of replying message advances a few days with a word of "here".)

合同的翻译一定要保持译文的完整性，决不能只求保持原文与译文在词量上的对等。

例1：如果上述专有技术和技术资料中的部分或全部被出让方或第三方公布，受让方对公开部分则不再承担保密义务。

这一条款中"保密"应译成 keep secret and confidential，译文中漏掉一个 confidential

显得不很严谨；另外，在"In case part of or all know-how of the above-mentioned technical contents have been published by Licensor or any third party"之后要增译一句"Licensee obtains evidence of such publication"，这样才使得这一条款完整，因为一方不承担保密义务必须有理由，对方坚持要求时，必须出示足够的证据。

例2：从4月1日起到10月20日止这一期间内交货，但以买方信用证在3月20日前到达卖方为限。

以上条款中交货期间应包括4月1日和10月20日这两天，所以应补译 both dates inclusive；另外，买方信用证到达日期也包括3月20日这一天，因此，3月20日之前的介词除用 before 外还应增加 on，译成 subject to Buyer's Letter of Credit reaching Seller on and before Mar. 20。句中的 subject to 在这里指"以……为准""以……为有效"。例如：本报价以我方最后确认为准。

例3：中国东北大米，5 000公吨，CIF温哥华，每公吨×××美元，不可撤销即期信用证付款，立即装船，2023年6月30日复到我方有效。（reply here 中的 here 是个关键词，决不可漏译。如译为"reply June 30，2023"是指"2023年6月30日发出"，而增加一个 here 则强调"2023年6月30日我方收到复电"，也就是说，用了一个 here 把实际复电日期提前了几天。）

5.1.2　*Expressiveness and Smoothness*
规　范　通　顺

The contract English belongs to the solemn style, which can't allow arbitrary text. So to make the contract language expressive and smooth, first of all, the use of contract terms are required of expressiveness in accordance with conventional meaning.

E.g.1: By Irrevocable Letter of Credit available by Seller's documentary bill at sight to be valid for negotiation in China until 15 days after date of shipment, the Letter of Credit must reach the Sellers 30 days before the contracted month of shipment.

The original translation:"以不可取消的信用证，凭卖方即期附有单据的票据协商，有效期应为装运期15天后在中国到期，该信用证必须于合同规定的装运月份前30天到达卖方。"

There were at least four wrong points around the original translation.

Firstly,"Irrevocable Letter of Credit"refers to"A Letter of Credit which cannot be altered or canceled once it has been negotiated between the buyer and his bank". The original translation"不可取消的信用证"can also express the original text, but the professional words should be"不可撤销的信用证".

Secondly, the translation of"documentary bill at sight"as"即期附有单据的票据"is not clear, because the"bill"is pointed out that the drawer makes signature on the bill, agrees upon themselves or entrusts others, to unconditionally pay a certain amount of money for the purpose of securities."Bill"in the international business contract refers to"draft". Therefore, the bill in the treaty should be understood as"draft". As for"documentary bill", it refers to"a bill to which the documents are attached"which should be translated as"跟单汇票".

Thirdly, "negotiation" in the settlement refers to "the giving of value for bills (drafts) of the documents by the bank authorized to negotiate", whose professional words should be translated into "议付".

Fourthly, "until 15 days after the date of shipment" should be "15 days after the shipment date".

After the review, the original translation changes to: "以不可撤销的信用证，凭卖方即期跟单汇票议付，有效期应为装运期后15天在中国到期。该信用证必须于合同规定的装运月份前30天到达卖方。"

E.g.2: 乙方保证是本合同规定提供的一切专有技术和技术资料的合法所有者，并有权向甲方转让。如果发生第三方指控侵权，由乙方负责与第三方交涉，并承担法律上和经济上的全部责任。

The original translation: "Party B guarantees that he is the legitimate owner of the know-how and technical documentation supplied to Party A in accordance with the Contract and that he has the right to transfer them to Party A. If the third party accuses Party B of infringement, Party B shall take up the matter with the third party and bear all legal and economic responsibilities arising therefrom."

Let's analyze the above English translation sentence by sentence:

Firstly, in "Party B guarantees that he...", the subject "he" in the object clause seems somewhat ambiguous, which should repeat "Party B" again.

Secondly, "supplied to Party A" should be added translation of "Party B" after the participle "supplied", which makes the whole sentence completely clear.

Thirdly, the original meaning of "in accordance with the Contract" is "clauses stipulated in the Contract", so it should be changed into "in accordance with the stipulations of the Contract" which can reflect with the consistency of the original. "he has the right to transfer them to Party A", this translation is not like "jargon". In addition, two pronouns in the sentence should also be replaced by the noun, because in English contracts, pronouns are not needed to replace nouns as far as possible in order to avoid misunderstanding. "Party B has the right to transfer" should be translated into "Party B is lawfully in a position to transfer", which can emphasize Party B's absolute legitimacy for technology and material.

Fourthly, in "if the third party accuses Party B of infringement", obviously there are two errors:

① "The third party" gives a person an impression that Party A and Party B seem to know who the "third party" is, but the actual is not the case, so it should be changed to "any/a third party";

② "To accuse sb. of sth." generally refers to accuse someone who violates the criminal law, while "accuse" only refers to the general civil tort, so it should be changed into "to bring a charge of infringement".

Fifthly, the translation of "take up sth. with sb." refers to "take up sth. with sb. orally or in written form", which can not exactly bring out meaning in the original text of "Party B shall be responsible for dealing with the third party" so it should be changed into "Party B shall be responsible for dealing with the third party". In the end, "bear all the legal and economic responsibilities arising therefrom", "full responsibility" refers to "due to the above" reasons occurring, Party B shall bear the responsibility, so it should choose "full" instead of "all". In addition, "the resulting legal and economic responsibility" should be translated as "bear the legal and financial responsibilities which may arise therefrom".

After the review the sentence should be changed to: "Party B guarantees that Party B is the legitimate owner of the know-how and technical documentation supplied by Party B to Party A in accordance with the stipulations of the Contract, and that Party B is lawfully in a position to transfer the above-mentioned know-how and technical documentation to Party A. If any/a third party brings a charge of infringement, Party B shall be responsible for dealing with the third party and bear the full legal and financial responsibilities which may arise therefrom."

合同中的英语属于庄严性文体，不允许文字上的随意性。因此要使合同语言"规范通顺"，首先要求合同的词语运用规范，符合约定俗成的含义。

例1：By Irrevocable Letter of Credit available by Seller's documentary bill at sight to be valid for negotiation in China until 15 days after date of shipment, the Letter of Credit must reach the Sellers 30 days before the contracted month of shipment.

原译文为："以不可取消的信用证，凭卖方即期附有单据的票据协商，有效期应为装运期15天后在中国到期，该信用证必须于合同规定的装运月份前30天到达卖方。"

原译文起码有四处翻译不妥：

第一，Irrevocable Letter of Credit是指一旦被买方和银行议付就无法改变或不可撤销的信用证。原译文用"不可取消的信用证"也能表达原文，但其专业用语应该是"不可撤销的信用证"。

第二，documentary bill at sight译为"即期附有单据的票据"，概念不清，因为"票据"是指出票人签名于票上，约定自己或委托他人，以无条件支付一定金额为目的的有价证券。在国际商务合同中的"票据"主要指"汇票"。因此，该条约中的bill应理解为"汇票"。至于documentary bill是指a bill to which the documents are attached，应译为"跟单汇票"。

第三，negotiation在涉外票据结算中是指账单（汇票）通过被授权的银行议付兑付价值，其专业用语应该是"议付"。

第四，until 15 days after the date of shipment，应该是"装运期后的15天"。

经审校改译为："以不可撤销的信用证，凭卖方即期跟单汇票议付，有效期应为装运期后15天在中国到期。该信用证必须于合同规定的装运月份前30天到达卖方。"

例2：乙方保证是本合同规定提供的一切专有技术和技术资料的合法所有者，并有权向甲方转让。如果发生第三方指控侵权，由乙方负责与第三方交涉，并承担法律上和经济上的全部责任。

原译文为："Party B guarantees that he is the legitimate owner of the know-how and technical documentation supplied to Party A in accordance with the Contract and that he has the right to transfer them to Party A. If the third party accuses Party B of infringement. Party B shall take up the matter with the third party and bear all legal and economic responsibilities arising therefrom."

让我们逐句分析一下以上的原译文：

第一，"Party B guarantees that he..."该句的宾语从句中的主语用he显得有些含混，应重复Party B。

第二，supplied to Party A应在分词supplied后加译Party B，使全句完整明晰。

第三，in accordance with the Contract这句原文的含义是指"按合同中规定的条款"，所以应改成in accordance with the stipulations of the Contract才能体现出与原文的一致性。he has the right to transfer them to Party A的译文不大像"行话"。此外，句中的两个代词也应换成名词，因为在英语合同中，出现过的名词尽量不用代词代替，以免产生误解。Party B has the right to transfer应改译为Party B is lawfully in a position to transfer，这样更能强调乙方对技术和资料占有的绝对合法性。

第四，if the third party accuses Party B of infringement明显有两处错误：

①the third party给人一种甲乙双方似乎都已知道"第三方"是谁的印象，而实际并非如此，所以应改为any/a third party；

②to accuse sb. of sth.一般是指控诉某人触犯刑法，而这句中的"指控"仅指一般的民事侵权，故应改译成to bring a charge of infringement。

第五，"Party B shall take up the matter with the third party"，此译文中的take up sth. with sb.是指"口头或书面向某人提出某事"，没有能确切地译出原文中"由乙方负责与第三方交涉"的本义，故应改译成"Party B shall be responsible for dealing with the third party"。最后，"bear all the legal and economic responsibilities arising therefrom"，"全部责任"指的是"由于上述"原因而发生的乙方应承担的责任，所以"全部"应选用full而不用all。另外，"承担法律上和经济上的全部责任"应译为"bear the full legal and financial responsibilities which may arise therefrom"。

经审校改译为："Party B guarantees that Party B is the legitimate owner of the know-how and technical documentation supplied by Party B to Party A in accordance with the stipulations of the Contract, and that Party B is lawfully in a position to transfer the above-mentioned know-how and technical documentation to Party A. If any/a third party brings a charge of infringement, Party B shall be responsible for dealing with the third party and bear the full legal and financial responsibilities which may arise therefrom."

5.2 Translation of Special Words in English Contracts[①]
英语合同专用词的翻译

There are some special conventional words in English contracts. "Offer" is one of the key words in English contracts. At the time of English-Chinese translation, we should pay attention to "offer" and the translation of the phrase (see Table 5-1).

---

① 宋德文. 国际贸易英文合同文体与翻译研究 [M]. 北京：北京大学出版社，2006.

Table 5-1   **The Translation of "Offer" and Its Phrase**

offer		要约，报盘
offeror		要约人，发盘人
offeree		受要约人，受盘人
offering		出售物
offer	by description	附加发盘
	CIF	报成本加保险费和运费价
	for sale	提供销售
	sample	发盘附样
	under seal	密封发盘
	for sale by tender	投标代销发盘
	subject to prior sale	先售发盘
	goods until withdrawal	有效至撤回
buying	offer	买方发盘
selling		卖方发盘
combining		搭配发盘
counter		还盘
firm		实盘
lump		综合发盘
accept		接受发盘
decline		谢绝发盘
extend		延长发盘
entertain		准备发盘
reinstate		重新报盘
withdraw		撤销发盘
renew		恢复发盘

There are some special words in English contracts, whose meanings are relatively fixed in the contract. These words appear frequently in the contract, the utilization rate is very high, and they are similar in form, similar in meaning, so in translation, especially in English-Chinese translation, attention should be paid to them in the accuracy of the Chinese expression. These words are: hereby, herein, hereon, hereof, hereinafter, hereto, hereupon, herewith, hereafter; therein, thereby, thereunder, thereon, thereof, therebefore, thereinafter, therefrom, thereupon; whereon, whereof, whereby, whereas, etc. Stylistic features of these words are serious and simply clear. Now the comprehensive analysis about the meaning of these words and their translation is as follows:

英语合同中有一些约定俗成的专用词语，如 offer。offer 是英语合同中的关键词之一，在英汉互译的时候要注意 offer 及其构成的短语的翻译（见表 5-1）。

英语合同有一些专用词语，在合同中的意思较为固定。这些词语在合同文本中的使用率很高，而且它们在形式上相似，在意思上相近，因此在翻译的时候，尤其在英译汉的时候，要注意它们在汉语表达上的准确性。这些词语有 hereby, herein, hereon, hereof, hereinafter, hereto, hereupon, herewith, hereafter; therein, thereby, thereunder, thereon, thereof, therebefore, thereinafter, therefrom, thereupon; whereon, whereof, whereby, whereas 等。这些词语的文体特点是：庄重严肃、简洁明确。现将有关这些词语的含义及翻译综合分析如下：

5.2.1 Compound Adverb: Hereby, Herein, Hereon, Hereof, Hereinafter, Hereto, Hereupon, Herewith, Hereafter

复合副词：hereby, herein, hereon, hereof, hereinafter, hereto, hereupon, herewith, hereafter

"Here" means "this", whose meaning in the English contract is "this writing (contract)". "Here" refers to the file (laws, contracts, treaties, etc.), and "there" refers to another file.

E.g.1: Attachments hereof shall be made an integral part of this Contract and effective as any other provisions of this Contract herein. (herein =in which)

E.g.2: Party A hereby concluded to pay to Party B in accordance with the construction and completion of the Project herein the price associated or other cost happened according to the Contract in time provided by the Contract. (herein=in accordance with this Contract; by means of the agreement stipulated)

E.g.3: After arrival of the goods at the port of destination, the Buyer shall apply to General Administration of Customs of the People's Republic of China (hereinafter referred to as GAC）for a further inspection as to the specifications and quantity/weight of the goods.

here 意即 this，在英语合同中的意思为文本（合同）。here 就是指本文件（法律、合同、条约等），there 指另外的文件。

例 1：本合同的附件是合同的一部分，与此合同的其他部分一样，有同等效力。（herein 意为 in which）

例 2：（因此）甲方根据合同约定在合同规定的期限内，按合同规定的价格和其他成本向乙方支付本项目施工和竣工的费用。（herein 意为 in accordance with this Contract，by means of the agreement stipulated）

例 3：货到目的港后，买方将申请中华人民共和国海关总署（以下简称 GAC）对货物的规格和数量/重量进行检验。

5.2.2　Compound Adverb: Thereby, Thereunder, Thereon, Thereof, Therebefore, Thereinafter, Therefrom

复合副词: thereby, thereunder, thereon, thereof, therebefore, thereinafter, therefrom

"There" means "that", which means that writing (contract, article) in the English contract, and generally refers to the text or the file other than this contract. Use these words to express "in that writing, to that writing, according to that writing or of that writing".

E.g.1: Either party may terminate this Agreement immediately without incurring thereby any liable to the other, by merely serving a notice of termination on the other in any of the following events. (thereby= by that)

E.g.2: Upon receipt the Defaulting Party shall, at its own expense promptly take all action necessary to remedy such failure. If the Defaulting Party thereof shall fail to correct such default or if immediate correction is not possible to commence and diligently continue effective action to correct such default within ×× days following notification thereof from the Aggrieved Party, the Aggrieved Party may terminate this Agreement.

E.g.3: However, the Seller shall inform the other party of its occurrence in written form as soon as possible and thereafter send a certificate of the Force Majeure issued by the relevant authority to the other party but no later than 15 days after its occurrence.

there 的意思是 that，在英语合同中的意思为文本（合同，条款），一般是指本合同书以外的文本或文件。用这些词来表示 in that writing，to that writing，according to that writing 或 of that writing。

例1：在下列情况下任何一方可通知对方立即终止协议并无须对另一方承担责任。（thereby 意为 by that）

例2：收到（通知）后，未履行责任方应自费迅速采取必要措施弥补这类失误。如果未履行责任方不能弥补失误或不能立即弥补，不能在接到被侵害一方的通知后××天内采取有效措施改正失误，被侵害一方可终止协议。

例3：但卖方应尽快地将所发生的事件通知对方，并应在事件发生后15天内将有关机构出具的不可抗力事件的证明寄交对方。

5.2.3　Compound Adverb: Whereas, Whereby, Wherein, Whereof, Whereon

复合副词:whereas,whereby,wherein,whereof,whereon

"Whereas" means "according to, considering/concerning that". "Whereby" means "on the basis, in accordance with/by credit". "Wherein" means "in terms and the conditions mentioned". "Whereof" means "of/about the point noted". "Whereon" means "therefore, on/to the point referred".

E.g.1: This contract is made by and between the Sellers and the Buyers, whereby the Sellers agree to sell and the Buyers agree to buy the under-mentioned goods according to the terms and conditions stipulated below and overleaf.

E.g.2: Party C as well as other members of the management team of the Company wherein are both liable for the normal operation of the Company's business and the maintenance of the Company's interest and benefit after the signature of the Agreement. If any action occurs which is conflicting to the terms and conditions of the Agreement, or if any action occurs which is harmful to the Company or to the benefits of Party A, or Party B, then either Party A or Party B has the right to terminate the Agreement. Whereof any results caused from the above action shall be born by Party C. ("Wherein" refers to "the management team of the Company". "Whereof" refers to "any results caused".)

E.g.3: Whereas the Seller agrees to sell and the Buyer agrees to buy the undermentioned commodity according to the terms and conditions stated below.

E.g.4: Whereas the Buyer agrees to buy and the Seller agrees to sell the undermentioned commodity subject to the terms and conditions stipulated below.

whereas 意即根据、鉴于。whereby 意即根据、按照。wherein 意即在（所提及）之中。whereof 意即关于、所指（那一项）。whereon 意即因此、鉴于。

例 1：买卖双方签订本合同，并同意按下列条款进行交易。

例 2：本合同签订后，丙方及公司其他管理层有义务保证企业的正常运转并维护企业利益，如发生任何与本合同项下股权转让相冲突的行为或任何损害公司或甲乙双方利益的行为，甲乙双方任何一方有权利终止本合同，因此造成的一切后果，由丙方承担。（wherein 指"公司管理层"。whereof 指"造成的一切后果"。）

例 3：双方同意按照下述条款由卖方出售、买方购进下列商品。

例 4：买卖双方同意按下述条款交易下列商品。

5.3　Translation of Usual Phrases in English Contracts 英语合同常用短语的翻译

5.3.1　By and Between 双方（签订）

E.g.1: This Contract is hereby made and concluded by and between the Seller and the Buyer and the Seller whereby agrees to sell and the Buyer agrees to buy the undermentioned commodity under the terms and conditions specified as follows.

E.g.2: This contract is made by and between the Sellers and the Buyers according to the terms and conditions stipulated below and overleaf.

例 1：兹经买卖双方同意按照以下条款由买方购进、卖方售出以下商品。

例 2：买卖双方签订本合同并同意按下列条款进行交易。

5.3.2   *Terms and Conditions*
条款

E. g. 1: The Contract is made out, in Chinese and English, both versions being equally authentic, by and between the Seller and the Buyer whereby the Seller agrees to sell and the Buyer agrees to buy the undermentioned goods subject to terms and conditions set forth hereinafter as follows.

E. g. 2: Unless otherwise agreed and accepted by the Buyer, all other matters related to this Contract shall be governed by Section Ⅱ, the Terms of Delivery which shall form an integral part of this Contract. Any supplementary terms and conditions that may be attached to this Contract shall automatically prevail over the terms and conditions of this Contract if such supplementary terms and conditions come in conflict with terms and conditions herein and shall be binding upon both parties.

例 1：本合同由买卖双方缔结，用中英文写成，两种文体具有同等效力，按照下述条款，卖方同意售出、买方同意购进以下商品。

例 2：除非经买方同意和接受，本合同其他一切有关事项均按第二部分交货条款之规定办理，该交货条款为本合同不可分的部分。本合同如有任何附加条款将自动地优先执行附加条款，如附加条款与本合同条款有抵触，则以附加条款为准。

5.3.3   *Secret and Confidential*
秘密

E.g.1: All the information provided by the Company relating to the manufacture and sale of its products is provided secret and confidential, and the Consultant agrees not to disclose such information without the Company's authorization.

E.g. 2: Licensee agrees that licensee shall keep the know-how supplied by Licensor under secret and confidential conditions within the validity period of the contract. In case a part or the whole is published by Licensor to any third party and Licensee obtains evidence of such opened parts, Licensee shall no longer be responsible for having the secret and confidential obligations to the opened parts.

例 1：对公司提供的所有有关制造及产品销售的信息，市场（调研）顾问有保密义务，未经授权，不能泄露。

例 2：（技术转让）受让人在合同有效期内对出让人的技术保密。如果受让人有证据证明出让人将技术公开或泄密于第三者，受让人不再向获密一方承担保密义务。

5.3.4   *Provided That*=on the Condition That; *Stipulated*
但是，但规定，规定

E.g.1: This agreement is governed by the law of England, provided that matters affecting the organization of Company are governed by the law of Japan. (provided that=except that)

E.g. 2: All expenses (including inspection fees) and losses arising from the return of the goods or claims should be borne by the Seller. In such case, the Buyer may, if so requested, send a sample of the goods in question to the Seller, provided that sampling is feasible. (provided that=on the condition that)

E.g.3: Provided that the Buyer may apply to General Administration of Customs of the People's Republic of China for a further inspection as to the specifications and quantity/weight of the goods in question. (provided that= stipulating that)

例1：本合同适用英国法律，但是，有关公司设立事项的部分以日本法为准据法。（provided that意为"但是"）

例2：因退货或索赔引起的一切费用（包括检验费）及损失均由卖方负担。在此情况下，凡货物适于抽样者，如卖方要求，买方可将样品寄交卖方，但是，样品应属可交寄的物品。（provided that意为"但是"）

例3：按照（本合同）规定，买方可以向中华人民共和国海关总署申请对其货物的规格和数量/重量进行检验。（provided that意为"进一步规定"）

5.3.5 By and Before
在此（包括此月、日）之前

E.g.: If the Buyer asks to increase the insurance premium or scope of risks, the Buyer should get the permission of the Seller by and before time of loading, and all the charges thus incurred should be borne by the Buyer.

例：买方如要求增加保额或扩大保险范围，应于装船前经卖方同意，因此而增加的保险费由买方负责。

5.3.6 By and under=in Accordance with; under; Pursuant to Make Amendments and Revision
在此（包括此月、日）后（下）；根据……

E.g. 1: One month prior to the time of shipment, the Buyer shall open with the Bank of _____ irrevocable Letter of Credit in favour of the Seller payable at the issuing bank against presentation of documents as stipulated by and under Clause 18 Art.A of Section Ⅱ the Terms of Delivery of this Contract after departure of the carrying vessel. The said Letter of Credit shall remain in force till the 15th day after shipment. （"by and under" expresses "emphasis"）

E.g.2: The amendments and revision of the contract shall come into force only after a written agreement has been signed by Party A and Party B and approved by the original examination and approval authority.

例1：买方于货物装船时间前一个月通过_____银行开出以卖方为抬头的不可撤销信用证，卖方在货物装船起运后凭本合同第二部分交货条款第18条A款所列单据在开证银行议付货款。上述信用证有效期将在装船后15天截止。（by and under表示强调）

例2：只有经甲乙双方书面同意和重新确认并经审批机关批准，才能对合同进行修改并生效。

5.3.7 *Fulfill or Perform*
履行（义务），付诸实施（条款）

It is rare in general English. In common English, "carry out" is often used.

E.g. 1: Party A and Party B in this contract shall fulfill or perform the obligations above-mentioned by and under this contract.

E.g. 2: When either of the two parties fails to fulfil or perform the contract or the contract obligations according to the terms stipulated, that is, breaks the contract, it must pay a breach penalty of USD500 (or the equivalent in CNY).

这是在普通英语中很少见的。在普通英语中，一般用 carry out 来表示。

例1：本合同中的甲乙双方均应履行合同规定的各项义务。

例2：签约人任何一方未能履行合同和合同规定的各项义务，则视为违约，违约一方应付500美元（或相当于500美元的人民币）的违约金。

5.3.8 *Sole and Exclusive*
独家（经营、专营、特许）

The meaning of sole and exclusive, which generally do not post in general English, is close, but in the English contract, in order to avoid ambiguity, using "sole and exclusive" to limit the content of terms within a certain scope.

E.g. 1: Party A shall complete processing works and deliver products to Party B, and Party B shall own sole and exclusive rights in respect of the production and marketing of such products worked out by Party A.

E. g. 2: Products may be sold on overseas markets through the following channels: The cooperative venture company may directly sell its products on the international market. The cooperative venture company may sign sales contracts with Chinese foreign trade companies, entrusting them to be the sales agencies or sole and exclusive sales agencies. ("Sole" in general English means "only" and "unique". In international business contracts, the "sole" as the "exclusive" right, generally refers that "authorized person" shall not give licenses to any person or entity other than "authorized person" in a certain region, but "authorized person" is not made restrictions. "Exclusive" indicates that the licensor shall not use the same content of the license agreement granted in the region of any third party, and even the licensor himself/herself shall not use the technology in the region.)

sole 与 exclusive 意思相近，在普通英语中一般不连用，但在英语合同中为了避免歧义，使用 sole and exclusive，以在一定范围内限定条款的内容。

例1：甲方应该完成产品的所有制作过程，并将产品交于乙方。乙方对甲方生产的该产品有独家拥有和独家销售的权利。

例2：产品可以通过下列渠道在海外销售：合资公司在国际市场上可以直接销售其产品；合资公司可以与中国外贸公司签订销售合同，委托中国外贸公司为销售代理商或独家销售代理。（sole 在一般英语中的意思是"唯一的""独有的"。在国际商务合同中，sole 为

"独家"（享有）权利，一般指在某一区域范围内"授权人"不得再将许可证发放给"授权人"以外的任何人或实体，但对"授权人"未作限制规定。exclusive 表示，许可方不得再把同样内容的使用许可证协议授予该地域的任何第三者，就连许可人自己也不得在该地域使用该项技术。）

5.3.9　*Null and Void (Latin)=No Avail, Invalid, Invalid after, Fail*
　　　　无效，失效（拉丁语）

E.g.1: The contract and such any attachments shall be valid for 4 years from the effective date of the contract. On the expiring date of the contract, the contract shall become null and void accordingly.

E.g.2: The contract shall become null and void if Buyer fails or becomes unable to fulfil or perform the obligations under the contract and such default or inability is not cured within 30 days on receiving the notice from the Seller.

例1：本合同有效期为4年，从合同生效之日算起。有效期满后，本合同将自动失效。

例2：如果买方未能履行合同所规定的义务，或买方在接到卖方通知30天后仍然未履行其义务，本合同将视为失效。

5.3.10　*In Respect of = Concerning, About*
　　　　关于，对于；至于

In general English, "in respect of" means "with regard to that question; in consideration of". In contract English, "in respect of" is a fixed phrase and means "concerning, about", that is "regards, as far as". It is often used in English contract.

E.g.1: No entity or individual may suppress the application of an inventor or designer for a patent in respect of an invention-creation that is not job-related.

E.g.2: The formation, validity, interpretation, execution and settlement of disputes in respect of, this contract shall be governed by the relevant laws of the People's Republic of China.

The above is the explanation of frequent conventional fixed phrases commonly used in the English contract and the comparison of English - Chinese translation. Due to the limitation of length, some of the other special words fail to summarize. Other formal special phrases are as follows: be liable for, unless otherwise, be deemed to, in question, in case, be liable to, in the event that, in the event of, in the case where, etc.

在一般英语中，in respect of 的意思是 with regard to that question；in consideration of。in respect of 在英语合同中是一个固定短语，意思是 concerning 或 about，意即关于，对于；至于。它在英语合同中的使用是比较频繁的。

例1：对于发明人或者设计人的非职务发明创造专利申请，任何单位或者个人不得压制。

例2：关于解决争议的形式、有效期限、解释原则、执行裁决，本合同适用中华人民共和国相关法律。

以上是对英语合同中常用和频繁出现的约定俗成的固定短语的解释和英汉翻译对比。

由于篇幅所限，未能概括其他的一些专用词语。其他正式专用短语还有：be liable for, unless otherwise, be deemed to, in question, in case, be liable to, in the event that, in the event of, in the case where等。

5.3.11   Such, Such...As

这样的，如此的；例如，比如

In modern English, "such" is generally used to give emphasis. To use "such" before the "adjective + noun" emphasizes the meaning of adjectives.

在现代英语中，such一般用来加强语气。such用在"形容词+名词"前，以强调形容词的意思。

5.3.11.1   Such
这样的，如此的

E.g.1: It is such a nice deal!

E.g.2: Both parties agree to attempt to resolve all disputes between the parties with respect to the application or interpretation of any term hereof of transaction hereunder, through amicable negotiation. If such disputes cannot be resolved in this manner to the satisfaction of the Seller and the Buyer within a reasonable period of time, maximum not exceeding 90 days after the date of the notification of such dispute, the case under dispute shall be submitted to arbitration if the Buyer should decide not to take the case to court at such a place of jurisdiction that the Buyer may deem appropriate. Unless otherwise agreed upon by both parties, such arbitration shall be held in Beijing, China and shall be governed by the rules and procedures of arbitration stipulated by the Foreign Trade Arbitration Commission of the China Council for the Promotion of International Trade. The decision by such arbitration shall be accepted as final and binding upon both parties. The arbitration fees shall be borne by the losing party unless otherwise awarded.

例1：这是桩好生意!

例2：双方同意对那些因执行或解释本合同条款所发生的争议，努力通过友好协商解决。在争议发生之日起一个合理的时间内，最多不超过90天，协商不能取得买卖双方都满意的结果时，如买方决定不向他认为合适的有管辖权的法院提出诉讼，则该争议应提交仲裁。除双方另有协议，仲裁应在中国北京举行，并按中国国际贸易促进委员会对外贸易仲裁委员会所制定的仲裁规则和程序进行仲裁。该仲裁为终局裁决，对双方均有约束力。仲裁费用除非另有决定，否则由败诉一方负担。

5.3.11.2   Such...That...
如此……以至于……

(1)Such+a+Adjective+Singular Countable Nouns+That Clause

E.g.: He is such a nice guy that all the bosses like him.

(2)Such+Adjective+Plural Noun+That Clause

E.g.: These are such attractive pictures of goods in the exhibition that the buyers are reluctant to leave.

(3)Such+Adjective+Uncountable Noun

E.g.: It was such bad weather that the goods would not be delivered on time.

（1）such+a+形容词+可数名词单数+that从句

例：他是如此好的一个人以至于所有的老板都喜欢他。

（2）such+形容词+名词复数+that从句

例：展览会上这些产品的照片这么漂亮，以至于买家都不愿离开。

（3）such+形容词+不可数名词

例：天气太糟糕了，货不能准时装运了。

5.3.11.3　"As", "Such as" and "Such...as" Used in English Contracts
as、such as和such...as在英语合同中的使用

(1)As

E.g.: There are several kinds of shellfish goods, as scallops, oysters, crabs and lobsters.

(2)Such as, "Noun+Such as+Noun=Such+Noun+as+Noun"

E.g.1: This lot of goods includes kinds of crops such as wheat, corn, cotton and soybeans.

E.g.2: There are many clauses in international business contract, such as packing and shipment clause.

E.g.3: Should the Seller fail to load the goods on board or to deliver the goods under the tackle of the vessel booked by the Buyer, within the time as notified by the Buyer, after its arrival at the port of shipment, the Seller shall be fully liable to the Buyer and responsible for all losses and expenses such as dead freight, demurrage, and consequential losses.

(3)Such...as=That, Which

The reason why "such...as" is used in English contracts is that the structure has a very strong limit function to avoid ambiguity.

E.g.1: The above-mentioned price refers to the gross invoice price of Contract Products sold otherwise disposed of by Licensee in normal, bonafide, commercial transactions without any deduction other than such expenses and charges as sales discounts, rebates, returns, commissions, indirect taxes, insurance premiums, freights, packing expenses, transportation charges, duties on the imported raw materials, intermediate goods, parts and components for the manufacture of Contract Products and other expenditures directly relating to the sale of Contract Products.

E.g.2: Should the Seller fail to load the goods, within the time as notified by the Buyer, on board the vessel booked by the Buyer after its arrival at the port of shipment, such expenses as dead freight, demurrage, etc. and consequences thereof shall be borne by the Seller.

Thus, "such...as..." structure in terms of the English contract plays an extremely limited function, and it can be locked by modified words to avoid disputes. At this point, the contract English is different from general English. "Which" or "that" is usually used to guide the limit of the object or subject in clauses in general English.

（1）例如

例：水生贝壳类动物货物有好几种，如蛤、牡蛎、蟹和龙虾。

（2）例如、比如，"名词+such as+名词=such+名词+as+名词"

例1：这批货物包括各种农作物，如麦子、玉米、棉花和大豆。

例2：商务合同中有很多条款，像包装与装运条款。

例3：如买方所订船只到达装运港后，卖方不能在买方所通知的装船时间内将货物装上船只或将货物交到吊杆之下，卖方应负担买方的一切费用和损失，如空舱费、滞期费及由此而引起的一切损失。

（3）如此……以至于

such...as之所以用于英语合同，是因为该结构有很强的限定作用，用来避免发生歧义。

例1：上述价格是指合同产品的总发票价格，否则由许可方在没有扣除其他任何费用情况下，正常、诚意地去处理，除了销售折扣、返利、回报、佣金、间接税、保险费、装卸费、包装费用、运输费用，以及为生产合同产品而需要的进口原材料、中间产品、零部件的关税和其他直接与销售合同产品相关的费用以外。

例2：如买方所订船只到达装港后，卖方不能按买方所通知的时间如期装船，则空舱费及滞期费等一切费用和后果均由卖方负担。

由此可见，such...as...结构在英语合同条款中起着极强的限定作用，它可以把被修饰的词语锁定，避免发生争议。在这一点上，合同英语与普通英语不同。在普通英语中一般常用which或that来引导限定从句中的宾语或主语。

5.3.11.4　Other Usage of "Such"
　　　　　such的其他用法

(1)Such as to +Verbs, to Express Degree or Result

E.g.: The delaying delivery was not such as to cause contract cancellation. =The delaying delivery was not so serious as to cause contract cancellation.

(2)Such as It Is (Was, Were, Etc.)=but So or That's All

E.g.: You can use my contract model, such as it is.

(3)As Such=in That Capacity

E.g.: He is a shipper, and must be treated as such.

(4)As Such=in Itself or in Themselves

E.g.1: He is the boss, and as such must be obeyed.

E.g.2: Article as such is too often neglected.

E.g.3: I didn't sign a contract as such.

E.g.4: I am a general manager, and as such have a high sense of duty to help develop company's future business.

(5)As Such=also or Think So

E.g.: Don't thank me, I would do as such for any buyers.

(6)Such and Such

E.g.1: Such and such a contract partner doesn't keep his promise.

E.g.2: Such and such results follow from such and such wrong clauses.

E.g.3: When you are studying clauses, you learn that such and such a bad result to such and such a wrong clause.

（1）such as to+动词原形，表示程度或结果

例：拖延装运还没有严重到取消合同的地步。

（2）不过如此，如此而已

例：尽管我的合同模板不怎么好，请凑合用吧。

（3）照其资格

例：他是承运人，必须这样对待。

（4）其本身

例1：他是老板，因此必须服从他。

例2：这样的条款常被忽略。

例3：我不会像这样签合同的。

例4：我是总经理，正因为如此，我才有高度的责任感去帮助发展公司未来业务。

（5）同样、这样（想）

例：不要感谢我，对任何买家我都会这样做的。

（6）某某，这样或那样，等等

例1：这样的合同合伙人没有遵守其诺言。

例2：这样的结果来自错误的条款。

例3：当你研究条款时，你会知道这样的坏结果是由于如此错误的条款。

5.4 Sentence Translation Techniques[①]
句子的翻译技巧

Because there are larger differences between English and Chinese in the aspects of syntax and expressions, in order to translate international business contracts more accurately and more professionally, you need not excessively accommodate the original structure and word order of the original arrangement, should jump out of the original frame, the common basic skills of translation-conversion method, and adjust composition and structure of sentences in order to make the contract translation more smooth and more normative.

由于英汉两种语言在句法和表达方式等多方面存在较大的差异，为了更准确、更专业地翻译国际商务合同，你不必过于迁就原文的句子结构和词序排列，跳出原来的框框，应用翻译中常见的基本技巧——转换法，对句子成分和结构形式作一些调整，使合同的译文更加通顺、更加规范。

---

① 刘川，王菲. 英文合同阅读与翻译 [M]. 北京：国防工业出版社，2010.

5.4.1 Conversion of Sentence Patterns and Part of Speech in International Business Contracts' Translation[①]
国际商务合同翻译中的句型和词性的转换

The translation method of parts of speech conversion refers to the translation method in which a certain part of speech of words in original language are translated into the target language which belongs to another part of speech of words. For example, the nouns of the original language are translated into the verbs of the target language and adjectives are translated into adverbs of the target language. Both belong to the parts of speech conversion method. The most common is that nouns in English are translated into verbs in Chinese.

E.g.: We have found the application form for the exportation of the goods.

Because the sentence structure and expression way in English and Chinese languages are different, in order to make the translation smooth, normal, it is necessary to convert one of the English components into another Chinese component or vise versa.

词类转换翻译法是指在翻译中将源语中属于某种词性的词语翻译成目的语中属于另一种词性的词语的翻译方法。比如，将源语中的名词翻译成目的语中的动词，将源语中的形容词翻译成目的语中的副词等，都属于词类转换翻译法。最常见的是把英语中的名词转化成汉语的动词。

例：我们找到了出口这批货物的申请表。

由于英汉两种语言的句子结构和表达方式不同，翻译时，为了使译文通顺、规范，有必要将英语的某一成分转换为汉语的另一成分，或将汉语的某一成分转换成英语的另一成分。

5.4.1.1   Convert Subject into Predicate
主语转化为谓语

A subject of the original is often a verbal noun, and uses the passive voice. When translated into Chinese, the English passive voice need to be adjusted to Chinese active voice for transforming translation.

E.g.1: Delivery must be effected within the time stated on the purchase order, otherwise the Buyer may at its option cancel the order without cost to him, and charge the Seller for any loss incurred as a result of the latter failure to make such delivery. (Note: The original noun "delivery" for the subject, is converted into the translation of "delivery" as a predicate verb, while "the Seller" is translated in the subject position.)

E.g.2: Payment shall be made by net cash against sight draft with the bill of lading attached showing the shipment of the goods. Such payment shall be made through Bank of China, Yantai Branch. The bill of lading shall not be delivered to the Buyer until such draft is paid. (Note: The original words "payment" for the subject, can be translated into a Chinese verb.)

---

① 兰天. 国际商务合同翻译教程［M］. 大连：东北财经大学出版社，2007.

E. g. 3: Partial shipments shall be permitted upon presentation of a clean set of shipping document. (Note: The original subject "shipment" can be converted into Chinese verbs, the original "partial" which modifies the subject can be converted into adverbials.)

原文的主语往往是动作性名词，且采用被动语态。译成汉语时，需将英语的被动语态调整为汉语的主动语态，进行转换翻译。

例1：卖方必须在购货订单规定的时间内交货；否则，买方可取消订货，而不承担任何损失，并要求卖方赔偿因不交货所造成的一切损失。（说明：原文的名词delivery做主语，转换为译文的动词"交货"做谓语，同时在主语的位置翻译了"卖方"二字。）

例2：凭即期汇票和所附表明货物发运的提单通过中国银行烟台分行以现金支付。汇票支付之前，提单不交给买方。（说明：原句中的payment做主语，可译为汉语的一个动词。）

例3：可以允许分批发货，但须提供一套清洁的装运单据。（说明：原文中的主语shipment转换为汉语的动词，原文中修饰主语的partial转换为状语。）

5.4.1.2　Convert Subject into Object
主语转换为宾语

The original subject is often a common noun, and often in the passive voice. When translated into Chinese, English passive voice is converted into active voice, and subject is converted into object.

E. g. 1: If any terms and conditions of this Contract are breached and the breach is not corrected by the breaching party within 30 days after a written notice thereof is given by the other parly, then the non-breaching party shall have the option to terminate this Contract by giving the written notice thereof to the breaching party.

E. g. 2: Progress review meeting will be held at the Seller's plant with the Buyer's representatives as necessary during the manufacturing of the Equipment. At such meeting, the Seller shall report progress and indicate completion status against schedule.

原文的主语往往为普通名词，且常为被动语态。译成汉语时，将英语的被动语态改译为汉语的主动语态，主语转换为宾语。

例1：如果一方违反本合同的任何条款，并且在接到另一方的书面通知后30日内不予以补救，未违约方有权选择向违约方书面通知终止本合同。

例2：在设备制造期间，如有必要，将邀请买方代表参加在卖方工厂举行的进展评定会，会上由卖方报告进展情况与计划完成情况。

5.4.1.3　Convert Object into Subject
宾语转换为主语

Some verb objects in the original English contract sentences should logically illustrate the main body. In order to make it outstanding and eye-catching, generally it will be translated into Chinese subject.

E. g. 1: Licensee shall keep true and accurate records, files and book of account containing all of the data reasonably required for the full computation and verification of the amount to be paid here under and the information to be given in the statements herein provided for.

E.g.2: The Seller shall deliver the Equipment and Materials in accordance with the Contract from the 19th (nineteenth) month to the 27th (twenty-seventh) month from the date of signing the Contract in 5 (five) lots.

E.g.3: Party A shall send twice its technical personnel to Party B's factory for training, and the total number of the participants shall not exceed 320 (excluding the interpreter).

原文英语合同句中的某些动词宾语，在逻辑上是应说明的主体，为使其突出和醒目，翻译时一般将其转换为汉语的主语。

例1：被许可方的记录、档案以及会计账簿必须保持真实、准确。其中会计账簿内容包括：为计算和稽核本协议范围所付款项所必需的全部合理数据，以及为所规定的财务报表提供所需的材料。

例2：依据合同，卖方的设备和材料应当自合同签订之日起第19个至第27个月内分5批交付。

例3：甲方的技术人员将分两批赴乙方工厂接受培训，参加培训人员的总数不超过320人（翻译人员除外）。

5.4.1.4　Convert Object into Predicate
宾语转换成谓语

If the predicate verb of the original is unfavorable to be translated into Chinese predicate and the object of the original is nouns containing the meaning of verbs, the Chinese translation of the object of the original can be converted into Chinese predicate or Chinese predicate with the original verbs.

E. g. 1: The Contractor shall perform the inspection and examination of all equipment, machinery and materials including spare parts required for the construction of the plant.

E.g.2: The Licensor will, at its own cost, take such actions to eliminate infringement of the Licensed Patents as may be reasonably necessary and proper in its own opinion.

E.g.3: The Seller shall make delivery of the goods strictly within the period stipulated herein. In the event of delay in delivery, the Buyer may cancel the Contract and claim damages for breach of the Contract.

In addition to the above transformations, there are often the subject into the attributive, the predicate into the subject, the attribute into the predicate, and so on, which the translator should translate flexibly in accordance with the requirements of prose and context coherent.

如果原文的谓语动词不宜处理成汉语的谓语，而原文中的宾语又是含有动作意义的名词，则译成汉语时可将原文中的宾语转换成汉语的谓语或与原文动词一起合译为汉语的谓语。

例1：承包商应进行检验，并检查建设工厂所需的一切设备、机械和材料，其中包括各种备用零部件。

例2：许可方应在其认为有必要的时候，以适当的方式，自费采取行动，消除对特许产品的侵权。

　　例3：卖方应当严格按规定的期限交货，若迟交，买方有权撤销本合同，并向卖方提出由此所造成的损失赔偿请求。

　　除上述成分转化外，还经常有主语转化为定语、谓语转化为主语以及定语转化为谓语等情况，译者应根据行文需要和上下文的连贯，灵活翻译。

5.4.1.5　Adjusting of the Predicative
　　　　　表语的转换

(1)Convert Predicative into Chinese Subject

In English, when using a noun as a predicative, the content expressed by the subject and predicative is always consistent. When translated into Chinese, in order to make the context coherent, or highlight the content stated by predicative, the predicative in the original sentence can be converted into the Chinese subject.

E.g.1: Agent oriented toward a single geographic market searching for products to import and market in the home Country is an import agent.

E.g.2: The date of registration of the Joint Venture shall be the date of the establishment of the board of directors of the Joint Venture.

E.g.3: This is the final arbitration award and binding on both Contracting Parties.

(2)Convert Predicative into Chinese Predicate

When using prepositional phrases as a predicative, an appropriate Chinese verb generally should be chosen as a object in order to facilitate translation.

E.g.1: In the course of arbitration, the Contract shall be continuously executed by both parties except the part of the Contract which is under arbitration.

E.g.2: Whereas Party B is in the real estate business, and the two Parties are in consideration of the mutual conventions and agree to enter into this Contract under the terms and conditions set forth as follows.

E.g.3: The Buyer is of the opinion that if the result of packing in cartons turns out to the satisfaction of the buyer's clients, the Seller may continue using this packing in the future.

（1）表语转换为汉语的主语

在英语中，当用名词做表语时，主语和表语所表达的内容往往是一致的。在译成汉语时，为使上下文连贯，或突出表语所述的内容，可将原句中的表语转换为汉语的主语。

　　例1：进口代理商是面向某一个地区市场，寻找能进口到本国销售的产品的代理人。

　　例2：合资公司成立日期，以合资公司注册登记之日为准。

　　例3：仲裁裁决是终局性的，对双方均有约束力。

（2）表语转换为汉语的谓语

当用介词短语作表语时，一般都应选择一个适当的汉语动词做谓语，这样有利于处理译文。

例1：在仲裁过程中，除了正在仲裁的部分条款外，合同的其他条款应继续执行。

例2：鉴于乙方经营房地产业务，双方考虑相互的惯例，同意按下列条款签订本合同。

例3：买方认为，如果纸板箱包装的效果使买方用户满意，则卖方在今后的业务中可继续使用这种包装。

5.4.1.6　Adjusting of the Attributive
　　　　　定语的转换

(1)Convert Attributive into Chinese Predicate

In Chinese, adjectives can be used as a predicate. Therefore, when English adjectives are as front attributive, it is hard to turn it into smooth Chinese. At this point, if the attributive is converted into Chinese predicate to form the main predicate group with the nouns modified, it can make the translation fluent and normative.

E.g.1: The sample of the machine submitted by the Seller is featured by novel shape, easy operation, high calorific efficiency and low fuel consumption.

E.g.2: We look forward to an ever increasing volume of business with your glass factories.

E.g.3: We claim for shortage in weight and low quality on the consignment of wheat shipped per s.s "Princess Victoria".

(2)Convert Attributive into Chinese Adverbial

In English, if a certain noun containing action meaning is translated into Chinese verbs, the adjectives or participles before the original nouns as attributive can be converted into Chinese adverbial.

E.g.1: The Joint Venture's products to be sold in China may be handled by the Chinese Materials and Commercial Departments by means of agency or exclusive sales, or direct sale by the Joint Venture.

E.g.2: Payment for the goods specified herein shall not mean a full acceptance thereof by the Buyer with regard to its quality. All goods shall be accepted only after the Buyer's close inspection.

（1）定语转换为汉语的谓语

在汉语里，形容词是可以做谓语的。因此，当英语的形容词做前置定语时，很难将其译成通顺的汉语。此时，如果把定语转换为汉语的谓语，使之和所修饰的名词一起构成汉语的主谓词组，则可以使译文流畅规范。

例1：卖方提交的样机的特点是造型新颖、操作简便、热效率高、油耗低。

例2：我方盼望与你方玻璃厂的交易额日渐增加。

例3："维多利亚公主"号轮装运的小麦短重且质量低劣，我方对此提出索赔。

（2）定语转换为汉语的状语

在英语中，如果将某一含有动作意义的名词转译为汉语的动词，那么，原来名词前做定语的形容词或分词，即可转为汉语的状语。

例1：合资公司内销产品可由中国物资部门和商业部门代销或包销，或由合资公司直接销售。

例2：对合同规定的货物付款不意味着买方已完全接受货物的质量，所有货物要经过买方仔细检验后方可接受。

5.4.1.7 Adjusting of the Adverbial
状语的转换

(1)Convert Adverbial into Chinese Subject

When some prepositional phrases in English contracts are as adverbial in the sentence, usually they are closely linked with subjects in meaning. In order to emphasize its position in the sentence, such adverbials are often converted into Chinese subject when in translation.

E. g. 1: The conditions for establishment of the Joint Venture and the total amount of investment and registered capital are stipulated in this Contract.

E.g.2: For the purpose of this Contract, the Party B desires to introduce the Patent and engage a production cooperation in accordance with the technical know-how specified in the Patent.

E.g.3: The products fair will be held at the Standard Electrical Co., Madrid, Spain with the Buyer's representatives.

(2)Convert Adverbial into Chinese Attributive

In English, some preposition phrases are adverbial in form, but in reality they are closely connected with the nouns in the sentence. When translating the adverbial into Chinese, processing them into attributive seems to be more exact.

E.g.: In this Contract, the Packing Clause stipulates for one gallon to a polythene bag, covered with paper box, 50 paper boxes to an inner carton, 2 cartons to a wooden case.

（1）状语转换为汉语的主语

英语合同中有些介词短语在句中做状语时，往往在意义上和主语有密切的联系。为了强调其在句中的地位，翻译时常将这类状语转换成汉语的主语。

例1：本合同规定了设立合资公司的条件以及投资总额与注册资本。

例2：本合同的目的在于乙方希望引进专利，按专利提供的技术诀窍进行合作生产。

例3：买方代表将参加在西班牙马德里标准电气公司举行的产品博览会。

（2）状语转换为汉语的定语

英语中某些介词短语在形式上是状语，但实际上与句中的某些名词有密切的联系，这类状语在译成汉语时，处理成定语似乎更确切些。

例：合同中的包装条款规定为：每一个聚乙烯袋装一加仑，然后装入纸盒。50盒装一纸箱，两纸箱装一木箱。

5.4.1.8 Adjusting of Clauses
从句的转换

Conjunction "where" guides place adverbial clause, and in the translation of international business contract, sometimes it is considered as a conjunction guided the conditional adverbial clauses. If put into "if" or "whether", it becomes Chinese conditional clauses.

E. g. 1: All disputes in connection with or in the execution of this contract shall be settled through friendly negotiations.Where no settlement can be reached, the disputes shall be submitted to arbitration.

E.g.2: Where one party to the Joint Venture assigns all or part of his investment, the other party has preemptive right.

连词where引导地点状语从句，而在翻译国际商务合同时，有时却被看成引导条件状语从句的连词。如果把它译成"如果"或"若"，就变成了汉语中的条件从句。

例1：所有与合同有关或者在履行合同中发生的争议，均应通过友好协商解决。如果得不到解决，应提交仲裁。

例2：如果合资一方转让其全部或部分出资额，那么合资的另一方有优先购买权。

5.4.1.9　Adjusting of Words
　　　　　 词语的转换

(1)Conversion of Conjunction

Under normal circumstances, we translate the word "after" into "after...", but in international business contracts, it is translated into "before...". "Before" in contracts is also translated into "only after...can..." by adjusting measures to local conditions.

E.g.: After the Buyer receives the relative documents issued by the Shipping Company, the Seller shall pay the Buyer within 20 days.

(2)Convert Nouns into Verbs

E.g.1: A company with an impressive development plan requires large imports of capital goods, technology, raw materials and other inputs to carry out the plan effectively.

E.g.2: We will see what is to be done after the termination of the contract period agreed on.

(3)Convert Adjectives into Adverbs

E.g.1: The President of Board of Directors has meticulous preparation for this contract negotiation.

E.g.2: Warm discussion arose every comer as to his achievements.

E.g.3: He asked me for a full account of the contract.

(4)Convert Adjectives into Verbs

There are a lot of adjectives constituted by the verb plus suffixes in English, which are so-called homologous adjective verbs, such as "reckon - reckonable, dominate - dominant, create - creative" and so on. When these adjectives, especially psychological or mental adjectives such as "grateful" "ignorant" "hopeful", are used with the verbs "be" "feel" "become" etc., they can replace the function of the action verbs and can be converted into verbs when translated into Chinese.

E.g.1: As you are aware, the British Electrical and Allied Manufacturers' Association is the organization that represents many firms in the sector of British industry which manufactures equipment for the generation, transmission, distribution and utilization of electrical power.

In addition, when a lot of adjectives related to thinking, emotion, desire, perception etc. in English are translated into Chinese, they often can be translated into Chinese verbs. These adjectives are:

① Adjectives related to thinking and perception, such as: aware, conscious, sure, mindful, alert and so on.

② Adjectives related to emotional, such as: glad, pleased, cautious, exhilarate, happy, excited, confident, thankful, grateful, concerned, eager, afraid, doubtful, sorry, etc.

③ Adjectives related to the desire, such as: desirous, anxious, keen, enthusiastic, zealous, etc.

E. g. 2: The prospect of earning five thousand dollars a month stimulated the sporting and commercial instinct of the staffs in the company.

(5)Convert Adjectives into Nouns

To translate English adjectives into Chinese nouns, in fact, is to put the original description of abstract specific. This flexible technique is often used in the process of English - Chinese translation.

E.g.: Article 7 of Contract No.765: Since silver and gold are inconvenient to carry and to assay for purity and for weight, it became customary for each state to stamp out in coin form a specified number of ounces of gold carrying the seal of the state to guarantee purity and weight.

(6)Convert Prepositions as Predicative into Verbs

When English prepositional phrases are as predicative in sentences, if they are separated from the specific meaning of the original and extended as an abstract meaning, without exception, the translator should convert them into Chinese verbs.

E.g.1: The best way to guard against large financial loss is through insurance.

E.g.2: Most of the items listed in the catalog are currently on sale.

(7)Prepositional Phrases as Adverbial

As adverbial and predicative, prepositional phrases need to be converted into sentences after being converted into verbs when translated into Chinese.

E.g.1: With the changing of the world market, the prospects of chemicals market become very dim in our company.

E. g. 2: Your company's representatives expressed interest in our products and asked that additional details to be sent for further consideration.

(8)Convert Verbs into Nouns

Because of the different expressions in English, the corresponding verbs of some verbs such as "aim at" "behave" "characterize" "impress" "interest" and so on can't be found in Chinese, therefore, they should be translated into nouns in the process of translation.

E.g.1: However, the negotiations which were begun in London in 1946 and aimed at setting up a world trade organization failed because the United States held that they were in conflict with its domestic law.

E.g.2: This strategy targets a specific segment of buying public by carrying products only in a specific price range.

E.g.3: For the last 2 years, our company has spent more than it has taken in.

(9)Convert Nouns into Adverbs

English nouns are translated into adverbs, which are used to handle the noun phrases modified by infinitive phrases. In translation, nouns can be translated into an adverb according to Chinese writing practices to modify the back of the infinitive verbs.

E.g.1: If you give us the agency, we should spare no effort to further your trading interests in America.

E.g.2: The 1990s say something of a reversal of this export prosperity.

Due to no similar expression, the subject nouns can only be converted into Chinese adverbial and rearrange the sentence.

（1）连词的转换

after一词在通常情况下，我们把它译成"在……之后"，而国际商务合同的行文习惯是把它译成"……之日起"。before在合同中也"因地制宜"地被译成"……后，才能……"。

例：买方应从收到航运公司出具的有关单据之日起，20天内向卖方支付款项。

（2）名词转换成动词

例1：一个具有宏伟发展计划的公司，为了有效地实施其发展计划，可能要大量进口资本货物、技术、原材料以及其他投入品。

例2：在过了合同约定的这一段时间后，我们再看下一步如何进行。

（3）形容词转译成副词

例1：董事长周密地安排了此次合同谈判。

例2：到处都在热烈地讨论他的成就。

例3：他详细地向我询问合同的情况。

（4）形容词转化为动词

英语中有不少形容词是由动词加后缀构成的，即所谓的动词的同源形容词，如reckon-reckonable、dominate-dominant、create-creative等。这些形容词，特别是表示心理或精神状态的形容词如grateful、ignorant、hopeful在与系动词be、fed、become等连用时，均代替行为动词的功能，在译成汉语时可以转换成动词。

例1：你们都了解，英国电气联合制造商协会代表了英国工业中很多公司，生产发电设备、输电设备、配电设备以及电力使用设备。

另外，英语中很多与思维、情感、欲望、知觉等有关的形容词在被翻译成汉语时，往往可以转译成汉语里的动词。这些形容词有：

①与思维和知觉有关的形容词，如aware、conscious、sure、mindful、alert等。

②与情感有关的形容词，如glad、pleased、cautious、exhilarate、happy、excited、confident、thankful、grateful、concerned、eager、afraid、doubtful、sorry等。

③与欲望有关的形容词，如desirous、anxious、keen、enthusiastic、zealous等。

例2：眼看能每个月挣到5 000美元，公司职员都动了碰运气赚钱的念头。

（5）形容词转换成名词

将英语中的形容词转换成汉语中的名词实际上是将原文描写的抽象、模糊的事情具体化了。这种在英汉翻译过程中的变通手法是经常使用的。

例：第765号合同第7条：由于金银携带不方便以及难以测定金银的纯度和重量，因此，以往通常的做法是，每个国家把特定数量盎司的黄金冲压成金币，同时印上该国的印记以保证纯度和重量。

（6）介词做表语时转换成动词

英语介词短语在句中做表语时，如果已脱离原来的具体含义而引申为一种抽象含义，译者应无一例外地将之转换为汉语的动词。

例1：防范重大财务损失的最好办法是投保。

例2：目录中的大多数商品目前有售。

（7）介词短语做状语

介词短语做状语与做表语一样，翻译成汉语时需要转换为动词后变为句子。

例1：随着世界市场的改变，我公司化工产品出口的前景变得十分暗淡。

例2：贵公司代表对我们的产品有兴趣，并要求我们寄送更详细的资料以便作进一步考虑。

（8）动词转化成名词

由于表达方式不同，英语中有些动词或词组如 aim at、behave、characterize、impress、interest 等在汉语中找不到对应的动词，因而，在翻译过程中要转译成名词来表达。

例1：然而，1946年开始在伦敦举行的谈判，目标在于建立一个世界性的贸易组织，但是却未取得成功，因为美国认为这些谈判与其国内法律相抵触。

例2：这一策略是以消费群体中特定阶层为目标，只经营特定价格范围的商品。

例3：过去2年中，我们公司的支出大于收入。

（9）名词转换为副词

英语名词转译为副词多用于处理不定式短语所修饰的名词词组。翻译时可按照汉语行文习惯将名词转译为副词，以修饰后面的不定式动词。

例1：如果贵方授予我方代理权，我们将不遗余力地扩大贵公司在美国的贸易利益。

例2：20世纪90年代这种出口繁荣出现复苏的势头。

由于汉语并无类似的表达法，翻译时只能将主语名词转换为汉语中的状语并重新安排句式。

5.4.2 *Addition and Deletion in International Business Contract Translation*
国际商务合同翻译中的增词与减词

We know that there are very big differences between the structure of words and sentences when expressing the same concept or idea in English and Chinese, therefore when translating, some existing words are often added, which are not in the original or omitted. This is the translation skill of addition and deletion. The key to addition and reduction is to add words without adding meanings and reduce words without reducing meanings. As for English contract translation, generally we can consider addition and reduction words in the following aspects.

我们知道，英语和汉语在表达同一概念或同一思想时所用的词句结构差异很大，因而翻译时常要增加一些原文没有的或省略一些原文已有的词语。这就是翻译技巧上讲的增词和减词。增词和减词的关键是增词不增意，减词不减色。就商务类英语合同翻译而言，一般可以从以下几个方面考虑增减文字。

5.4.2.1　Addition
增词

Addition is the method commonly used in the process of translation. Its purpose is to make the translation of the grammar structure, expression, rhetoric, tone conforms to the Chinese expression habit while maintaining the meaning of the original, rather than "adding". Addition is to add words, phrases or sentences which are not in the original text but have the meaning.

(1)Addition Considering the Differences Between Two Languages

In business English, we may encounter some vague connotation words. In the process of translation, in order to make its embodiment, we need to add some category words to make virtual meaning real.

E. g. 1: Your corporation's representatives asked additional details to be sent to your corporation for future consideration. (Note: In this sentence, the translator will translate "details" into "data in details", adding the word "data", which makes the sentences smooth. Without the word, the sentence will be difficult to understand.)

E. g. 2: ×× interest rates now depend greatly on the attitudes and actions of investors and policy makers in ××. (Note: In this sentence, the translator adds "change" behind the "interest rate", which makes the sentence very smooth. If there is not the word "change", the sentence seems to be very hard and doesn't accord with our language habits.)

(2)Add Explanatory Words Considering the Need of the Content

The implication is clear from the context of the original, but literal translation may not be understood or misunderstood. Under this situation, some explanatory words are needed to add so that the implicit in the original can be explicitly expressed.

E.g.1: Some contractors think modern economies can just close gates, but the movement of capital and ideas knows no borders. (Note: In this sentence, the translator will translate "close gates" into "closed management behind closed doors", which adds a few words of "closed management". This translation is for the further interpretation of the "close gates", which is better than simple "behind closed doors" or "closed".)

E.g.2: As Japan's bubble burst, a downsizing of expectations was taking place for the world's third-largest capitalist economy. (Note: That "Japan's bubble burst" is translated into "Japan's economic bubble burst" can explain "bubble" further. If the word "economy" isn't added, there will be understanding obstacles of the whole sentence.)

(3)Add the Original Words Omitted Considering the Need of the Translation's Structure

According to the English writing practices, the same words which we have already mentioned before are often omitted in the later article, or the same words of the coordinate structure are merged to avoid unnecessary repetition. But Chinese, on the other hand, with the need of structure, in the same situation is likely to be repeated using the same words, otherwise may cause the meaning expression of the translation not clear or not smooth. So when encountering this kind of situation in translation, you need add words omitted in the original.

E.g.1: It's more expensive than it was last time but not as good.

E.g.2: The application of the goods in automobile industry has brought about great increase of the consumption.

E.g.3: Germany is the biggest of the medium-sized economies, bigger than, but basically in the same class as, France. (Note: The translator supplemented the word "France" to make the meaning clearer in dealing with this sentence.)

增词法是合同翻译过程中常用的方法。其目的是使译文的语法结构、表达方式、修辞、语气在保持原文的意思同时，又符合汉语表达习惯，而并非"添油加醋"。增词是增加原文虽无但有其义的词、词组或句子。

（1）考虑两种语言差异增词

在商务英语中常会碰到一些内涵空泛的词语。在翻译过程中为了使其具体化，我们要增加一些范畴词，化虚为实。

例1：贵公司的代表要求我们寄送更为详细的资料，以便作进一步考虑。（说明：在这一句中，译者将details译成"详细资料"，加上了"资料"一词，使得句子很流畅。若没有这个词，句子就会很难懂。）

例2：目前××利率的变化很大程度上取决于××投资者和政策制定者的态度和行为。（说明：这一句中，译者在"利率"后面加入了"变化"一词使得句子变得十分通顺。如果没有"变化"一词，句子显得很生硬，不符合我们的语言习惯。）

（2）考虑内容需要，增加解释性词语

原文的寓意在上下文中很明确，但如果照字面直译过来可能会令人看不明白或产生误解，这种情况下需要加上一些解释性词语，以便将原文中的隐义明确表达出来。

例1：有些合约者认为现代经济尽可关起门来封闭经营，但是资本的流通与观念的传播却不分国界。（说明：本句中译者将close gates翻译成了"关起门来封闭经营"，加入了"封闭经营"几个字。这样的译法是对close gates进行了进一步的解释，比译成单纯的"关起门来"或者"封闭"都要好。）

例2：随着日本泡沫经济的破灭，对这个位居世界第三的资本主义经济大国的期望值也在下降。（说明：将Japan's bubble burst译成"日本经济泡沫的破灭"是对bubble一词作了进一步的解释，如果不加入"经济"一词，对全句的理解会有障碍。）

（3）考虑译文结构的需要，添加原文省略的词语

按照英语行文习惯，在后文中往往省略前文中已提及的相同词语，或对并列结构中的相同词语加以合并，以避免不必要的重复。但汉语则相反，由于结构需要，在同一情况下往往要重复使用相同词语，否则可能造成译文句意表达不清楚或不通顺。因此翻译中遇到这种情况，需要将原文省略的词语补充上。

例1：价钱比上次高，但质量却比上次差。

例2：此货物在汽车工业上的使用大大增加了此货物消费量。

例3：德国经济在中等国家中居首位，实力强于法国，但仍与法国同属于一个层次。（说明：译者在处理这个句子的时候增补了"法国"一词，使意思更加清楚。）

5.4.2.2   Word Reduction
减词

Due to the difference between two language expression habits, copying every word in translation will tend to be redundant, sluggish or will not conform to the writing habits, and even produce ambiguity. Word reduction can make translation brief. In English, some parts of speech such as articles, pronouns, verbs, etc., sometimes play a role of grammar in words only and without meaning for use or ideographic function is not big, and this kind of words can be considered to be omitted in translation without affecting the original.

(1)Reduce Pronouns

The following two types of pronouns can be considered to save translation. One is the possessive pronouns. According to the English grammar, in a sentence, when refering to the above subject's relationships, or to the logic subject or object's relationships, possessive pronouns must be used in accordance with the subject, but there are no hard and fast rules in this aspect in Chinese. Sometimes to omit in translation may accord with Chinese expression habit.

E.g.1: We are in receipt of your fax of May 8th, offering us 200,000 yards of Cotton Piece Goods Art. No.C−342.

E.g.2: We assure you of our prompt attention to this matter.

E.g.3: You are kindly requested to let us have your best quotation for the canned fish.

E.g.4: All those in favour of the contract raise your hands.

(2)Reduce Verbs

In English sentences, some of the predicate verbs are only used with noun phrases of honest meaning, which are ideographic with little or no effect. This kind of verbs can be omitted when they are translated into Chinese, while translating nouns (phrases) into Chinese verbs.

E.g.1: We take this opportunity to inform you that we are now in a position to make prompt shipment of the merchandise.

E.g.2: Delivery must be effected within the time stated on the purchase order.

E.g.3: No failure or delay on the part of the Agent in exercising any right hereunder shall operate as a waiver of any such right.

(3)Reduce Prepositional Phrases

Prepositional phrase plays an important role in the English sentences, but there are few Chinese prepositions and its phrases. There are many places that need prepositions and prepositional phrases in English, where Chinese will replace with a verb, or won't use. Because the context in the process of translation or verbs can fully express the meaning of the original, the part of prepositional phrases can be not translated.

E.g.1: The price of the products should be set according to the price in the international market. It should be fixed by the two parties at a level that will bring profit to both.

E.g.2: All members shall settle their international disputes by peaceful means in such a manner that international peace and security, and justice, are not endangered.

E.g.3: He held up a contract in his hand.

由于两种语言表达习惯不同，翻译时如果一字不漏地照搬，往往会显得累赘、拖沓、冗杂或不合行文习惯，甚至产生歧义。采取减词译法可以使译文言简意赅。在英语中，有些词类如冠词、代词、动词等，有时在句中只起语法作用而无表意作用或表意作用不大，这类词在不影响原意的情况下可考虑省略不译。

（1）减去代词

下面两类代词可以考虑省去不译。一是所有格代词。按照英语语法，在一个句子中，指代前述主语表明所有关系，或指代前述主语表明动作的逻辑主语或宾语关系时，必须用与主语一致的所有格代词。但汉语在这方面无硬性规定，有时候省略不译可能更符合汉语的表达习惯。

例1：现收到贵方5月8日传真，报盘20万码C-342货号棉布。

例2：我们保证立即处理此事。

例3：请报鱼罐头最优惠价。

例4：赞成此合同的请举手。

（2）减去动词

在英语句子中，有些谓语动词只同具有实义的名词词组搭配使用，本身表意作用很小或根本无表意作用，这类动词汉译时可以省略不译，而将名词（词组）转译为汉语动词。

例1：兹奉告，该商品可即期装运。

例2：必须在购货订单确定的时间内交货。

例3：代理行没有或延迟行使本合同项下的权利不应视为放弃上述权利。

（3）减去介词短语

介词短语在英语句中起着重要的作用，汉语介词及其短语很少。英语中很多需要介词和介词短语的地方，汉语要么用动词代替，要么不用。在翻译过程中，由于上下文或动词已经能充分表达了原文的意思，因此介词短语的部分可以不译出来。

例1：产品价格应该根据国际市场由双方共同商定，须照顾到双方利益。

例2：各会员国应以和平方式解决其国际争端，避免危及国际和平、安全及正义。

例3：他举起一份合同。

5.4.3 Translation Skills of Long Sentences

长句翻译技巧

5.4.3.1 Reasons for the Formation of Long Sentences in English Contracts
英语合同长句的形成原因

① Contract is a form of legal documents, which itself is more complex on the grammatical structure: long sentences, big sentences link with small sentences, and small sentences link with clauses, multiple levels of language structure. Sometimes a word will account for half a page or a page.

② To avoid omission or being evaded by others, drafters often like to write very tedious and complex sentences and use more modifiers to qualify a noun to avoid the possibility of a second meaning no matter how to understand this noun.

③ In order to make the contract's content as accurate as possible and not to produce ambiguity, drafters are trying to make all possibilities in the process of implementation or performance included in the contract. So use more synonyms repetition, paratactic structure etc. A long sentence often includes non-predicate verbs, composite structures, prepositional phrases, subject clauses, object clauses, predicative clauses, adverbial clauses, and other ingredients. Thereinto, to use of attributive and adverbial structure widely is one of the reasons that language structure is complex and lengthy sentences overlap in business contracts.

Considering all possibilities when writing a sentence in the contract, it is natural to make the sentence longer. If the organization is not good, long sentence is likely to cause confusion, misunderstanding and ambiguity.

① 合同是法律文件的一种形式,法律文件本身在语法结构上比较复杂:句子长,大句套小句,小句套分句,语言结构层次多。有时一句话就占了半页甚至一页。

② 起草人为避免遗漏或被别人钻空子,往往喜欢将句子写得烦琐而又复杂,使用较多的修饰语来限定一个名词,让这个名词无论怎样理解都不会出现有第二种意思的可能性。

③ 起草人为了使合同包含的内容尽可能准确,不产生歧义就试图将合同在实施或执行过程中的一切可能性都包括在内,因此较多地使用同义词重复、并列结构等成分。一个长句往往包括非谓语动词、复合结构、介词短语、主语从句、宾语从句、表语从句、状语从句等多种成分。其中定语结构和状语结构的大量使用是商务合同语言结构复杂、句子冗长重叠的原因之一。

在写合同中句子时，如果考虑执行的可能性，自然可以让句子更长。如果组织不好，长句子可能会造成混淆、误解和歧义。

5.4.3.2   Analysis of English Long Sentences
英语长句的分析

A large number of long sentences in English business contract are mainly divided into three categories: simple long sentences, complex sentences and compound sentences.

The analysis methods of long sentences in contracts should abide by the following steps concretely: Firstly, the translator is to find out the subject, the predicate and the object of the whole sentence, i.e. the main structure of the sentence. Secondly, find out all the predicate structures, non-predicate structures, prepositional phrases and guide words of clauses in the sentence, and then analyze the function of the clauses and phrases, i.e., whether it is a subject clause, an object clause, a predicative clause, or an adverbial clause, etc. as well as the relationship between the words, phrases and clauses. Finally, analyze the sentence whether there is a fixed collocation, parenthesis, and other ingredients.

E.g.1: If a Party breaches any of the representations and warranties given to it in Articles 18.1 or repeated in 18.2, then in addition to any other remedies available to the other Party under this contract or under Applicable Laws, it shall indemnify and keep indemnified the other Party and the company against any losses, damages, costs, expenses, liabilities and claims that such Party or the Company may suffer as a result of such breach.

(Note: When we encounter such a long sentence, we first split it. The first step is to find out the main clause in the sentence. We know that:

① "It shall indemnify and keep indemnified the other Party and the company against any losses, damages, costs, expenses, liabilities and claims that such Party or the Company may suffer as a result of such breach." This is the main clause in the sentence.

② In the main clause, there is an attributive clause "that such Party or the Company may suffer as a result of such breach" to modify the previous "any losses, damages, costs, expenses, liabilities and claim". The predicate verb in the sentence is the verb phrases "indemnify sb. against sth.".

③ A conditional adverbial clause is led by "if". In the conditional adverbial clause, "given to it in Articles 18.1 or repeated in 18.2" is the rear attributive modifying "the representations or warranties".

④ What "in addition to" guide is a supplement ingredient, and core word "remedies" is also followed by the rear attributive "available to the other Party under this contract or under Applicable Laws".

⑤ Fixed structure "indemnify sb. against..." means "make sb. not suffer from...".

According to our analysis of this sentence and the language habits of Chinese, i.e., the principles of the conditions former, the result later, attributive former, we got the translation.)

E.g.2: In the event that the Company's operations are reduced substantially from the scale of operation originally anticipated by the parties, or the Company experiences substantial and continuing losses resulting in negative retained earnings not anticipated by the Parties in the agreed Business Plan, or in any other circumstance permitted under Applicable Laws or agreed by the Parties, the Parties may agree to reduce the registered capital of the Company on a pro data basis.

(Note: This is also a sentence consisting of 74 words.

① The main clause of the sentence is short. The main clause is "the Parties may agree to reduce the registered capital of the Company on a pro data basis". In the main clause, "the parties" is the subject, "agree to reduce" is a predicate, object is "the registered capital of the Company", "on a pro data basis" is adverbial.

② "In the event that" is a phrase of conjunction, which leads a conditional adverbial clauses. "In the event of" followed by a noun is a phrase which leads a similar adverbial clause.

③ "In the event that" is the condition adverbial clause of the sentence, made up of three parallel conditional adverbial clauses, which are connected by a "or". This is the key to understand this sentence, and remember protasis coordination is connected by "or", rather than our usual understanding "and".)

E.g.3: Party A, in consideration of the agreement hereinafter contained of Party B, contracts and agrees with Party B, that he will deliver, in good and marketable condition, to Party B, during the month of March of next year, five thousand cases of tea, in the following lots, and on the following specified terms: one thousand cases by the eighth of March, one thousand cases additional by the fifteenth of the month, one thousand cases more by the twenty‑second of the month, and the entire five thousand cases to be all delivered by the thirtieth of March. (Note: In the above long sentence, the backbone of the sentence is "Party A...contracts and agrees with Party B", then there is a long object clause guided by "that". After we understood the sentence structure, we found that the attributive modified subject is too long. We must do proper segmentation in translation.)

E.g.4: The Buyer shall pay the Seller USD350,000 within 20 days after Bank of China has received the following documents from the Seller and found them in order, but not earlier than 12 months after the date the Contract Plant for the first time reached 95% of guaranteed capacity of the whole Contract Plant according to the guaranteed quality indices as per Annex VI to the Contract, or 65 months after the date of signing the contract, whichever is earlier. (Note: This sentence contains a very complicated time adverbial, which defines the time of the buyer to bear the payment obligation. From the perspective of pragmatics, actually the part at the back of "but" is a supplement of the former, namely "within 20 days after Bank of China has received the following documents from the Seller and found them in order", there is adversative relation in semantics. From the English structure and expression, so lengthy English adverbial in the end of the sentence does not pose any problem to writing criterions and to be understood by readers. But if such a lengthy adverbial is mechanically translated into Chinese intact and put before the predicate verb in accordance with Chinese writing practice again, it will make the translation appear messy, which is difficult to express. Therefore, when translating the sentence, modular approach can be used to convert the longer part of supplement content into Chinese compound sentence, and the core of predicate modified by the time adverbial in the original part, namely the "payment" transplant for the subject of compound sentences.)

英语商务合同中使用的大量长句主要分为三大类：简单长句、复合长句和并列长句。

合同长句的分析方法具体要遵循以下步骤：首先，译者要找出全句的主语、谓语和宾语，即句子的主干结构。其次，要找出句子中所有的谓语结构、非谓语结构、介词短语和从句的引导词。再次，分析从句和短语的功能，即是否是主语从句、宾语从句、表语从句或状语从句等，以及词、短语和从句之间的关系。最后，分析句子中是否有固定搭配、插入语和其他成分。

例1：如果一方违反任何其根据第18.1条或18.2条所作的陈述及担保，则另一方除根据本合同或相关法律寻求任何可能的救济之外，违约方应当赔偿另一方或合营公司因此种违反而招致的任何损失、损害、成本、费用、责任或索赔。

（说明：遇到这样一个长句，我们首先对句子进行拆分。第一步我们先找出句子中的主句。我们知道：

①"It shall indemnify and keep indemnified the other Party and the company against any losses, damages, costs, expenses, liabilities and claims that such Party or the Company may suffer as a result of such breach"是本句中的主句。

②在这个主句中有一个定语从句"that such Party or the Company may suffer as a result of such breach" 来修饰前面的 "any losses, damages, costs, expenses, liabilities and claims"。在这个句子中谓语动词使用了 indemnify sb. against sth. 这个动词短语。

③"if" 引导的是一个条件状语从句，在这个条件状语从句中 given to it in Articles 18.1 or repeated in 18.2 作为后置定语修饰 the representations or warranties。

④in addition to 引导的是增补成分，其核心词 remedies 也跟了后置定语 available to the other Party under this contract or under Applicable Laws。

⑤固定结构 indemnify sb. against... 意为 "使某人不受……"。

根据我们对此句的分析以及汉语的语言习惯，即条件在前、结果在后、定语在前的原则，我们得出了上述的翻译。）

例2：如果合营公司的经营规模比双方原来预期的规模有大幅度缩减，或合营公司持续遭受严重亏损，导致双方商定的业务计划中所未预期的盈余保留负数，或在任何相关法律允许或双方一致同意的情况下，双方可以协议按原有出资比例减资。

（说明：这同样是一个由74个单词组成的句子。）

①这个句子的主句很短。主句为 the Parties may agree to reduce the registered capital of the Company on a pro data basis。在这个主句中，the parties 是主语，agree to reduce 是谓语，宾语是 the registered capital of the Company，on a pro data basis 是状语。

②in the event that 是一个起连词作用的短语，引起条件状语从句。in the event of 后接名词，是一个引起类似条件状语从句的短语。

③in the event that 是这个句子的条件状语从句，由三个并列的条件状语从句构成，它们由 or 连接，这是理解这个句子的关键，要记住条件从句的并列是由 or 来连接的，而不是我们平时理解的 and 来连接。）

例3：鉴于乙方的允诺，甲方特与乙方订立协议并同意：由甲方负责，于定约之翌年3月份1个月之内向乙方运送质地优良、符合行销标准的5 000箱茶叶，并按下列期限分批交货：到3月8日交货1 000箱，到3月15日另交货1 000箱，到3月22日再交货1 000箱，至3月30日全部5 000箱茶叶如数交迄。（说明：在上述长句中，句子的主干是 Party A... contracts and agrees with Party B...，其后又有一个 that 引导的冗长的宾语从句。理解了句子结构之后，我们发现修饰主语的定语过长，翻译时必须对其进行适当的切分。）

例4：买方须于中国银行收到卖方下列单据，并经审核证实无误后的20天内向卖方支付350 000美元，但此款项的支付不得早于合同工厂首次达到附件Ⅵ所规定之质量保证指标的95%以后的12个月，或本合同签名后的65个月，以早到的日期为准。（说明：此句中含有一个非常复杂的时间状语，界定了买方承担付款义务的时间。从语用学的角度来看，but 后面的部分实际上是对前一部分，即 within 20 days after Bank of China has received the following documents from the Seller and found them in order 的补充，同时语义上有转折关系。从英语的结构及表述方式上看，英语的状语放在句末，如此冗长的状语对行文规范及读者的理解都不构成任何问题，但如果机械地将如此冗长的状语原封不动地译成汉语并按照汉语行文习惯置于谓语动词之前，就会使译文显得拖泥带水，难以达意。因此，翻译此句时可以采用化整为零的手法，将表示补充内容的较长部分转换成汉语的并列句，并将原文中时间状语所修饰的谓语部分的核心，即 "支付款项" 移植为并列句的主语。）

5.4.3.3　Translation Methods of English Long Sentences 英语长句的翻译方法

In the translation of long sentences, complicated relationships in English sentences can be dealt with according to Chinese way. Processing methods can be roughly divided into two kinds: one is to translate basically according to the order of the English original sentence structure, the other is to translate according to the time sequence and logical order of Chinese translation.

(1)Order Method in Translation of Long Sentences

If an English long sentence describes a series of actions according to the arrangement of time order, or logical relationship, and if the expression of Chinese is consistent, it can be translated in the original order.

E.g.1: In international buying and selling of goods, there is a number of risks, which, if they occur, will involve traders in financial losses.

(Note: According to the relationship of meaning, the sentence can be divided into three parts:

①"In international buying and selling of goods" is the place clause in the sentence.

②"There is a number of risks" is the main structure of this sentence, "there be" structure is also the backbone of the sentence.

③"Which, if they occur, will involve traders in financial losses" is a restrictive attributive clause of conditional clause. "Which" in the sentence modifies antecedent "risks" and "they" is a subject of the conditional clause, which represents the front "risks". The logical relationship of the original sentences and expression order are consistent with Chinese, so the sentence can be translated in the original order.)

E.g.2: The Buyer shall be entitled to send his inspectors at his own expense to the Seller's country to join the Seller's representatives in the quality inspection and test of the Equipment and Materials in the manufacturer's workshops.

(Note: According to the relationship of meaning, the sentence can be divided into:

①"The Buyer" is the subject of the sentence.

②"Shall be entitled to send" is the predicate of the sentence.

③"His inspectors" is the object of this sentence.

④"At his own expense" is the manner adverbial of "send" in this sentence.

⑤"To the Seller's country" is the place adverbial of "send" in this sentence.

⑥"To join the Seller's representatives" is the objective adverbial of "send" in this sentence.

⑦"In the quality inspection and test of the Equipment and Materials in the manufacturer's workshops" is the place adverbial of "join".

Because the arrangement of this sentence is similar to Chinese, order translation can be used. Order translation refers to arrange translation according to time order and logical order. Because this kind of translation is basically the same as Chinese expression order and the difference is not big, the translator can translate in sequence order.

(2)Reverse Order Method in the Translation of Long Sentences

"Reverse order translation" is also called "inversion translation", which refers that there are some back to front inversion problems in the translation of some sentences. These sentences are recombined according to the national language habits of the target language in the translation, and the original order will be disrupted in the process of combination. This is because Chinese generally narrate actions according to the order of action, while English will use more various grammatical means to disrupt the action sequence. This requires that we must translate from the behind of the original and against the original order. This translation is usually called reverse translation. (Note: About reverse method in the translation of long sentences, we can reverse all or partly reverse according to different situations of sense-group.)

E. g. 1: The Owner may request the removal and replacement of any person employed, in accordance with the Contractor, if such person on the site is guilty of misconduct, incompetence or negligence, and ensure the accomplishment of the project. (Note: In order to comply with the Chinese language habits of reasons in front and results back, we will put the result section "the owner may request the removal and replacement of any person employed" firstly appeared in the original at the end of the translation sentence, and will put clause section "such person on the site is guilty of misconduct, incompetence or negligence" on the front. This sentence arrangement is in line with Chinese language habits.)

E. g. 2: The Seller shall not be responsible for the delay of shipment or non-delivery of the goods due to Force Majeure, which might occur during the process of manufacturing or in the course of loading or transit. (Note: The writing style of the original here is to focus the information at the beginning of the sentence. Firstly, illustrate the seller's exceptions "the Seller shall not be responsible for the delay of shipment or non-delivery of the goods", then stipulate reason under which "due to Force Majeure" provisions for failure or delay of delivery would escape, and limit Force Majeure "which might occur during the process of manufacturing or in the course of loading or transit" as well. And according to Han nationality habits of thinking, we often talk reasons at first, then tell conclusions. Therefore, when translating, the translator should adopt reverse order method to move the original which represents exception condition of "due to Force Majeure, which might...of loading or transit" to the beginning of the sentences. Moreover, when translating the English restrictive attributive clause "which might occur...of loading or transit" into Chinese, you can still translate into attributive before words and can handle for other components as well.)

(3)Division Techniques of Translation

Division techniques of translation are to divide a sentence of the original text into a few sentences to translate, or translate one longer modifier into a word or a few words separately. When the main clause and the clause in the English long sentences, or a prepositional phrase and participle phrase has multilayer meanings and the relationship between words modified is not very close, and each has a relatively independent significance, if using a Chinese sentence to translate the original, it is easy to cause the sentence's chaos, at this time, we can decompose various meaning layers of the original according to the Chinese habit that a small sentence expresses a layer of meaning, and then arrange in chronological order or logical order, which you can add or reduce appropriate words for cohesion between sentences. It not only conforms to the Chinese habit of more short sentences used but also can make the sentence meaning more clear.

E.g.1: Either Party may terminate the contract in case of failure on the part of the other Party to fulfill or perform any of its obligations hereunder and in the event that such failure remains unremedied sixty (60) days after the service of a written notice as described in Article × below by the non-defaulting Party to the other Party specifying the failure in question and requiring it to be remedied. (Note: The original is the clauses about the term and termination in business contract, according to tell the conclusion first, namely either Party in the contract has the right to "either Party may terminate the contract" and then list the conditions of implementation of the right "in case of failure...and in the event that" ....But the Chinese habits of writing are often conditions first and conclusion after, so the reverse method should be adopted on the whole. Namely: the default behavior is not corrected within 60 days, from the date since a written notice of no responsible party delivered, no responsible party has pointed out that the other party's defaults in the written notice and requests the correction and so on. If the content is not decomposed, it may lead to chaos of sentence meaning. Therefore, to translate this sentence, division techniques of translation should be adopted to state the original meaning clearly.)

E.g.2: The project involved the weekly production of about 50 million screw-worms at a specially constructed "fly factory" and the use of 20 light airplanes to fly arranged flight patterns, five to six hours daily, each plane carrying a thousand paper cartons, each carton containing 200 to 400 irradiated flies. (Note: Pay attention to the comprehension and translation of the long sentences, first layered understanding, and then used reverse method of translation. Two parallel objects followed behind "involved" in this sentence: "the weekly production of" and "the use of". "Each plane carrying a thousand paper cartons" and "each carton containing 200 to 400 irradiated flies" are two independent nominative structure as an adverbial. These two structures can be translated into two clauses.)

(4)Synthesis Method

The above three different kinds of methods of translation are not entirely separate in the process of translation. Simply using one kind method of translation cannot translate idiomatic Chinese. At this time, the whole sentence should be carefully analyzed, deliberated, or dealt with synthetically according to time order or logical order, in sequence or reversed order.

在翻译长句时，要按汉语的表达方式来处理英语句子里错综复杂的关系。处理方法大致可归纳为两种：一种是基本上按英语原句的结构顺序翻译；另一种是按汉语的时间顺序和逻辑顺序翻译。

（1）用顺序译法来翻译长句

有些英语长句叙述的一连串动作按发生的时间先后安排，或按逻辑关系安排。如果汉语的表达方式比较一致，可按原文顺序译出。

例1：在国际货物贸易中存在各种各样的风险，这些风险的发生将会给有关的商人们带来经济损失。

（说明：按意群的关系，该句可以拆分为三部分：

①in international buying and selling of goods是本句中的地点状语。

②there is a number of risks是本句的主要结构，there be结构，也是本句的主干。

③which，if they occur，will involve traders in financial losses是带有条件从句的非限定性定语从句。句子中which修饰先行词risks，they是条件从句中的主语代表前面的risks。原文各句的逻辑关系、表达次序与汉语基本一致，因此可以按原文顺序译出。）

例2：买方有权自行出资派遣检验人员到卖方国家，会同卖方代表一起在制造方的车间对设备和材料的质量进行检验和测试。

（说明：根据意群的关系，本句可以拆分成：

①the Buyer是本句的主语。

②shall be entitled to send是本句的谓语。

③his inspectors是本句的宾语。

④at his own expense是本句中send的方式状语。

⑤to the Seller's country是本句中send的地点状语。

⑥to join the Seller's representatives是本句中send的目的状语。

⑦in the quality inspection and test of the Equipment and Materials in the manufacturers workshops，整个短语都作join的地点状语。

由于这一句的排列同汉语的排列很相似，故可以采用顺序译法来翻译。顺序译法指按时间顺序、逻辑顺序安排翻译。由于这种译法与汉语的表达顺序基本相同，差别不大，译者可以按顺序翻译。）

（2）用逆序译法来翻译长句

"逆序译法"又称"倒置译法"，主要指由于英汉两种语言在表达方面存在差异，有些译文的句子就出现了前后倒置问题。这些句子在翻译时按照目标国家的语言习惯重新组合，在组合过程中，原文的一些语句顺序将被打乱。这是因为汉语在叙述动作时一般按照动作发生的先后顺序排列，而英语在叙述动作时更多的是使用各种语法手段将动作的先后顺序打乱。这就要求我们必须从原文的后面译起，逆着原文的顺序翻译。这种译法通常称之为逆序译法。（说明：在长句的翻译中，我们可根据不同的情况按意群进行全部逆序或部分逆序。）

例1：为了保证工程完成，若业主认为工地上承包商的雇员品行不端，不能胜任工作或者有失职行为，可按照本合同，要求承包商将此人调离或更换。（说明：为了符合汉语原因在前、结果在后的语言习惯，我们将在原句中首先出现的结果the owner may request the removal and replacement of any person employed部分放到了译文句子的末尾，而将从句部分such person on the site is guilty of misconduct，incompetence or negligence放到了前面。这种句子的排列符合汉语的语言习惯。）

例2：凡在制造或装船运输过程中，因不可抗力致使卖方推迟或不能交货的，卖方不负责任。（说明：这里原文的行文方式是把信息的重心放在句首。首先表明卖方的免责事项the Seller shall not be responsible for the delay of shipment or non-delivery of the goods，接着再规定由于什么原因引起的不能交货或延迟交货才会免责——due to Force Majeure，而对不可抗力又作了限定：which might occur during the process of manufacturing or in the course of loading or transit。而按照汉民族的思维习惯，我们往往是先谈原因，再讲结论。因此，翻译时译者应采用逆序的方法将原文表示免责条件的 due to Force Majeure，which might...of loading or transit 移到句首。再者，英语中的非限制性定语从句 which might occur...of loading or transit 翻译成中文时，可以仍翻译成定语放在所修饰的词之前，也可处理为别的成分。）

（3）分译法

分译法就是将原文一个句子分成几个句子来翻译，或者将其中某个较长的修饰成分单独翻译成一句或几句。当英语长句中的主句与从句或介词短语及分词短语等有多层意思且所修饰的词与词之间的关系不是很密切，并且各具有相对的独立意义时，如果采用一个汉语句子对原文进行翻译，容易导致句义混乱，此时我们可根据汉语一个小句表达一层意思的习惯，对原文的各个意思层进行分解，再按时间顺序、逻辑顺序安排，可增减适当的词语以便于短句之间的衔接。这样做也符合汉语多用短句的习惯，同时也可以使句子意思表达得更清楚明了。

例1：如果一方未完成或未履行其在本合同项下的任何义务，而且未按照下述第×条规定在另一方向其送达书面通知，指出其违约行为并要求其予以改正后六十（60）天内，其仍未予以改正，另一方则可以终止本合同。（说明：原文是商务合同中有关期限和终止的条款，按照先讲结论，即合同任一方具有的权利"either Party may terminate the contract"，然后再列举实施此权利的条件"in case of failure...and in the event that..."的顺序行文。而汉语的行文习惯往往是先条件后结论，所以译文在整体上应采用逆序法，即违约行为60天内未改正，60天是从无责任方书面通知送达之日算起，书面通知中无责任方已指出对方违约行为并要求其改正等。如不对内容进行分解，则可能导致句义混乱。因此，翻译此句时应采用分译法，将原文意思表述清楚。）

例2：这项计划包括每周在专门建造的"蝇厂"生产大约5 000万只螺旋锥蝇，用20架轻型飞机按照预定的航线每天飞行5至6个小时，每架飞机运载纸盒1 000个，每个纸盒装有经过辐射处理的螺旋锥蝇200~400只。（说明：注意这个长句的理解与翻译，首先分层理解，然后再用分译法翻译。本句的 involved 后面跟两个平行的宾语：the weekly production of 和 the use of。each plane carrying a thousand paper cartons 和 each carton containing 200 to 400 irradiated flies 是两个独立主格结构作状语。这两个结构可以译成两个分句。）

（4）综合法

上述三种不同的翻译方法在翻译过程中并非截然分开。单纯地使用一种译法不能译出地道的汉语。这时就要对全句进行仔细分析、推敲，或按时间或逻辑顺序，有顺有逆地进行综合处理。

5.5 Translation of Passive Voice[①]
被动语态的翻译

Because the active voice is natural, clear, direct and powerful, it is often used in the English contract. But the use of passive voice in English contract is also required in the language structure. In English contract, the concept expressed by passive voice is mostly used by the active voice when it is translated into Chinese. In practical translation, the flexible use of translation skills should be both faithful to the content of the original and standardly smooth in language form. There are several translation methods of passive voice as follows.

由于主动语态比较自然、明确、直接和有力，因此英语合同中主动语态用得较多。但英语合同中被动语态的使用在语言结构中也是必需的。在英语合同中，被动语态所表达的概念被译成汉语时大多采用主动语态表示。在实际翻译工作中，要灵活运用翻译技巧，既做到在内容上忠实于原文，又在语言形式上规范通顺。被动语态的翻译方法有以下几种。

5.5.1 Conversion Translation of Passive Voice
被动语态的转换翻译

The following should be paid attention to when using conversion translation of the passive voice:

运用转换法翻译被动语态要注意以下几点：

5.5.1.1 Convert the Sender of the Action into the Subject of Chinese
把动作的发出者转换为汉语的主语

In some of passive sentences of an English contract, phrases arisen from "by or between" often appear in the sentence as adverbial. The noun is the parties to a behavior to highlight the senders of action in the sentence, which can be converted into subject.

E.g.1: If any terms and conditions to this Contract are breached and the breach is not corrected by any party within 15 days after a written notice thereof is given by the other party, then the non-breaching party shall have the option to terminate this Contract by giving a written notice thereof to the breaching party.

E.g.2: All the payments shall be made in the U.S. Currency by the Buyer to the Seller by telegraphic transfer to the Seller's designated account with Bank of China, Beijing Branch.

在英语合同中的一些被动句子中，往往会出现 by 或 between 引起的短语，在句中作状语。其中的名词是本句涉及的行为当事人，为突出句中动作的发出者，可将它转换为主语。

---

① 乔焕然. 英语合同阅读指南——英语合同的结构、条款、句型与词汇分析 [M]. 最新增订版. 北京：中国法制出版社，2015.

例1：如果一方违背本合同的任何条款，并且在另一方发出书面通知后15日内不予补救，未违约方有权选择向违约方书面通知终止本合同。

例2：买方应以美元支付卖方货款，并以电汇的方式汇至卖方指定的在中国银行北京分行的账户。

5.5.1.2　Convert the Adverbial of an English Sentence into the Subject of Chinese
把英语句中的某一状语转换为汉语的主语

When there is inclusive relationship between the adverbial of passive voice and subject, in order to make the translation smooth, adverbial part can be translated into Chinese subject.

E. g. 1: The cost of the non‐returnable containers of the goods sold under this Contract/hereunder is included in the prices herein specified.

E. g. 2: The production design, technology of manufacturing, means of testing, materials prescription, standard of quality and training of personnel shall be stipulated in Chapter 4 in this contract.

E. g. 3: The establishment, remuneration and the expenses of the staff of the preparation and construction office, when agreed by both parties, shall be covered in the project budget.

在被动语态的状语与主语之间有包容关系时，为了使译文通顺，可将状语部分译成汉语的主语。

例1：所定价格包括依照本合同所售装货用的一次性容器费。

例2：本合同第4章规定了产品设计、制造工艺、测试方法、材料配方、质量标准以及人员培训。

例3：经甲乙双方同意后，工程预算应包括筹建办公室工作人员的编制、报酬及费用。

5.5.1.3　Convert the English Subject into the Chinese Object
把英语句中的主语转换为汉语的宾语

If the original sentence is not involved in the parties of the contract, the English passive sentences can be treated without the subject sentence into Chinese, and the original subject is converted into object.

E. g. 1: In case the quality, quantity or weight of the goods is found not in conformity to those stipulated in this Contract after reinspection by General Administration of Customs of the People's Republic of China within 15 days after the arrival of the goods at the port of destination, the Buyer shall return the goods to, or lodge claim against the Seller for compensation of losses upon the strength of General Administration of Customs of the People's Republic of China with the exception of those claims for which the insurers or the carriers are liable.

E. g. 2: Upon the expiration of the duration or termination before the date of expiration of the Joint Venture, liquidation shall be carried out according to relevant law. The liquidated assets shall be distributed in accordance with the proportion of investment contributed by Party A and

Party B.

如果原句中没有涉及合同的当事人，可将这样的英语被动句处理成汉语的无主语句，原句的主语被转换为宾语。

例1：货到目的港后15天由中国海关总署复检，如发现货物的质量、数量或重量与本合同规定不符，除保险公司和船运公司负责赔偿的部分外，买方凭中国海关总署出具的检验证明书，向卖方提出退货或索赔。

例2：合同期满或提前终止合营时，应依照有关法律进行结算，并根据甲乙各方投资的比例分配结算后的财产。

5.5.2 Linear Translation of Passive Voice
被动语态的顺序翻译

In the translation of international business contract, in order to make the translation conform to the contract style of Chinese expression, the passive voice in the original text can be translated according to the sequence of the original sentence.

在翻译国际商务合同时，为了使译文符合合同文体的汉语表达方式，可将原文中的某些被动语态按原句的语序顺译。

5.5.2.1 To Translate into Chinese Active Voice
译成汉语的主动语态

The passive voice in English contracts can be changed into active voice under the condition of unchanging the original subject, without adding any words in translation.

E.g.: The Seller shall be entitled to terminate this Contract in the event of failure by the Buyer to comply with any terms or conditions stated in this Article.

英语合同的某些被动语态，可在不改变原文主语的情况下，翻译时将被动语态改成主动语态，无须添加任何词。

例1：如果买方违反本条款所规定的条件，卖方有权终止此合同。

5.5.2.2 To Translate into Chinese Passive Sentences
译成汉语的被动句

English passive sentences are made up of "be+v.+ed". Because there is no verb inflexion in Chinese, it is illustrated only by adding a certain amount of words when being translated into Chinese passive voice.

E.g.1: The term for the technology transfer agreement is signed by Joint Venture and Party B and it shall be approved by the approval authority.

E.g.2: All the equipment and materials supplied by the Seller shall be inspected by the Buyer and the quality certificates and inspection and test records shall be issued by the manufacturer.

英语的被动句是由"be+v.+ed"构成的。因汉语的动词无词形变化，所以译成汉语被动语态时，只能通过添加一定的词汇手段来表示。

例1：技术转让协议的期限由合资公司与乙方签订并经审批机关批准。

例2：卖方所提供的全部设备和原材料将由买方负责检验；品质证书、检验和试验记录应由制造商出具。

5.5.2.3　Translation of Structure"It Is + P.P." "it is +p.p."结构的翻译

Sometimes some special passive patterns are also used in the English Contract, whose structure is "it is+p.p.+that clause". This kind of pattern has basically formed a fixed translation method.

E.g.1: It is mutually agreed that the certificate of quality and quantity or weight issued by the manufacturer shall be part of the documents for payment with the adopted Letter of Credit.

E.g.2: It is essentially stressed that the Buyer is requested to sign and return the duplicate of this Contract within 3 days from the date of receipt. In the event of failure to do this, the Seller reserves the right to cancel the Contract.

E.g.3: It is strictly understood that the number of employees to be trained by the Contractor at any one time shall be no more than_____.

英语合同中有时还常用一些特殊的被动句型，其结构为"it is+p.p.+that clause"。这种句型已基本形成了固定的译法。

例1：经双方同意，制造商出具的品质、数量或重量证书作为有关信用证项下付款所需的单证的一部分。

例2：必须强调：买方应于收到本合同之日起3日内签名并退还合同的副本，如买方不这样做，卖方保留撤销合同的权利。

例3：严格明确承包商任何时候所培训的雇员人数不得超过____人。

5.6　Translation of Clauses[①] 从句的翻译

There are differences in translation of English contract clauses besides common points like other style clauses' translation. Generally speaking, the English clauses can be divided into three categories: noun clauses, adverbial clauses and adjective clauses. Adverbial clause mainly appear in contract English, the second are attributive clauses.

英语合同中的从句翻译，除具有与其他文体从句翻译的共同点外，也有其不同点。通常来讲，英语的从句可分为名词性从句、副词性从句、形容词性从句三大类。在英语合同中出现的主要是状语从句，其次是定语从句。

5.6.1　*Translation of Adverbial Clauses* 状语从句的翻译

English adverbial clauses include various clauses of time, cause, condition, concession,

---

① 吕昊，刘显正，罗萍. 商务合同写作及翻译［M］. 武汉：武汉大学出版社，2005.

purpose etc. The usage of adverbial clause in the English contract is very exquisite in order to prevent the adverse economic and legal consequences, prevent omissions or change without permission and disputes happened in the future. Because English and Chinese language habits are different, there are many differences in word order and sentence structure. English focuses on hypotaxis, extensive use of clausal structure while Chinese pays attention to parataxis, of which word order is fixed, generally time first, location later; first occurs in the former and after behind; reason in the former, the result behind, conditions in the former, facts after. Single adverbs as adverbials in English contract are seldom used at the beginning of the sentences. At this point, it is different from common English. In order to make the translation smooth and easy to understand, translation can not be constrained by the original structure and the relationship between the structures. It is important to seize semantics which they express, and then reappear according to the Chinese expressions habits. In order to comply with Chinese expression habits, Chinese phrases or correlative words which present logic relations can be added. At the same time, also for the same reason, original phrases which are unnecessary in Chinese translation can be omitted.

The commonly used adverbial clauses in the English contract are conditional adverbial clauses, time adverbial clauses, concession adverbial clauses. [①]

英语状语从句包括表示时间、原因、条件、让步、目的等各种从句。英语合同中状语从句使用上十分讲究，为的是防止带来不良经济和法律后果，防止遗漏或擅自更改以及日后发生纠纷。由于英汉语言表达习惯不同，在词序和句子结构方面均有许多差异。英语注重形合，大量使用关联词。而汉语注重意合，语序比较固定，一般是先说时间，后说地点：先发生的在前，后发生的在后；原因在前，结果在后，条件在前，事实在后。在英语合同中作状语的单个副词很少用于句首。在这一点上与普通英语有所不同。为了使译文通顺易懂，翻译可不必拘泥于原文结构形式以及结构之间的关系。重要的是：要抓住它们所表达的语义，然后按照汉语表达习惯再现出来。为了符合汉语表达习惯，可增添表示逻辑关系的汉语词组或关联词。同时，也出于同样的原因，可将原文中虽有但在汉语译文中成为多余的词组省略。

在英语合同中常用的状语从句有条件状语从句、时间状语从句和让步状语从句。

5.6.1.1 The Translation of Condition Adverbial Clauses
条件状语从句的翻译

An international business contract is a written document which contract parties agree on mutual rights and obligations relations. The written document mainly agrees to the rights which can be enjoyed and obligations which should be fulfilled. But the exercise of the rights and the implementation of obligations are provided with a variety of conditions. Therefore, the conditional adverbial clauses extensively appear and are used in the English contract. There are a lot of conjunctions which guide conditional adverbial clauses, we emphasize to introduce the following:

---

① 王相国. 鏖战英文合同——英文合同的翻译与起草 [M]. 最新增订版. 北京：中国法制出版社，2014.

(1)If

Adverbials of conditional adverbial clauses are usually put behind the conjunction "if" or "when" and so on, but in front of clauses, conditional adverbials are usually translated as "if". These words are correlative words which commonly say "condition" or "assume" in Chinese. On the tone, "as long as/only" is the strongest while "if" is the weakest. In English, the preposition·or post position of "condition" and the "assume" clause is more flexible, while such Chinese clauses are generally preposed.

E.g.1: If, during air transportation, the Documentation is found lost or damaged, Party B shall, within 30 days after receiving Party A's written notice, supply Party A free of charge with the Documentation again.

E.g.2: If, at any time during the execution of the Contract, either of the Parties to the Contract is to be prevented from executing the Contract by cases of Force Majeure such as war, serious fires, flood, typhoon and earthquake, etc., the time for execution of the Contract shall be extended for a period equal to the effect of those causes.

E.g.3: If the Force Majeure event lasts over 40 days, the Buyer shall have the right to cancel the Contract or the undelivered part of the Contract.

E.g.4: If any change is required regarding the terms and conditions to this Agreement, both parties shall negotiate in order to find a suitable solution, provided however, that any change to this Agreement shall be subject to the approval by the Chinese Government.

E.g.5: Claims, if any, shall be submitted by fax within fourteen days after the arrival of the goods at destination. (Note: In English contracts, elliptical sentences led by "if" are often encountered. There are also other kinds of elliptical sentences led by "if required", "if possible", "if necessary", and "if agreeable" etc., but subject should be highlighted when being translated.)

E.g.6: Contingent shares, if any, to be issued hereunder shall be determined on the basis of the after-tax consolidated earnings of Seller.

E. g. 7: Said amount shall be reduced by the sum of the difference, if any, between the inventory value of small equipment and the closing inventory value thereof.

(2)In Case

When it indicates conditional adverbial clauses, "in case" usually emphasizes the possibility that the conditions are ripe , which are smaller than in the "if" clause.

E.g.1: In case the Buyer fails to carry out any of the terms and conditions to this Contract with the Seller, the Seller shall have the right to terminate all or any part of this Contract with the Buyer or postpone shipment or stop any goods in transit and the Buyer shall in every such case be liable to the Seller for all losses, damages and expenses thereby incurred. (Note: "In case of" in the contract can be used as an adverbial, which can be translated into "if" etc.)

E.g.2: In case of any divergence of interpretation, the Chinese text shall prevail.

E.g.3: In case of quality discrepancy, claims shall be filed by the Buyer within 30 days after the arrival of the goods at the port of destination.

(3)In the Event That

E.g.1: In the event that deficiencies in the Equipment become evident, such deficiencies shall be corrected by ABC during the two days per week during which the Purchaser will not be testing.

E.g.2: In the event that the Documents supplied by Party B are not in conformity with the stipulations in Sections 8.2, Party B shall, within the shorted possible time but not later than 30 clays after the receipt of the Party A's written notice, dispatch free of charge to Party A the missing or the correct and legible Documents.

E.g.3: In the event of graft or serious dereliction of duty on the part of the general manager and/or deputy general managers, the Board of Directors shall have the power to dismiss them at will.

(4) "Should+Subject+Verb" Structure

The structure belongs to non‐real condition clauses. When using this kind of condition sentences in the English contract, its main clause generally is in indicative mood. The structure shows that the possibility mentioned in condition clauses is very small, and if the conditions mentioned happen, then the issues set in the main clause must be completed.

E.g.1: Should any of the stipulations to the Contract be altered, amended, supplemented or deleted the same shall be negotiated between and agreed upon by both parties and written documents shall be signed by the representatives of both parties.

E.g.2: Should the effect of Force Majeure continue more than one hundred and twenty (120) consecutive days, both parties shall settle the further execution of the Contract through friendly negotiations as soon as possible.

(5)Unless

It is equivalent to "if not, except if, except when" which leads to clauses that use the present tense to express the future tense, and generally don't use virtual conditional sentences. The subject and the verb "be" of "unless" clause are often left out.

E.g.1: Unless expressly agreed to, the port of shipment is at the Seller's option.

E.g.2: Unless otherwise stated thereafter, the accounting principles employed shall be the same as those applied in the preceding years.

E.g.3: Neither party shall have the right to represent the other party unless otherwise arranged.

(6)Provided That...

When "provided that..." leads to clauses stating condition, it often expresses the conditions that the parties hope.

E.g.1: No salary shall be paid and charged against the operating expenses, provided that the commission or brokerage of the Second Party shall be paid and charged as a part of the operating expenses.

E.g.2: Provided that Party B desires to continue leasing the flat, Party B shall notify Party A in writing two months in advance of expiry of the lease and a new contract shall be signed. (Note: Along with "where" and "when" can also lead to conditional adverbial clauses in English contract, said "if" and "if" , etc.)

国际商务合同是合同各方就相互权利、义务关系达成一致意见而订立的书面文件。这种书面文件主要约定双方应享有的权利和应履行的义务，但这种权利的行使和义务的履行，均附有各种条件，因此，在英语合同中大量地出现和使用条件状语从句。引导条件状语从句的连词很多，我们重点来介绍以下几个：

（1）若，如果

条件状语从句中的状语通常应放在连词 if 或 when 等词的后面，但放在从句的前面。条件状语在汉语中一般翻译成"要是""如果""假如"等，这些都是汉语表示"条件"或"假设"的常用关联词。在语气上，"只要/只有"最强，"如果"最弱。英语中表示"条件""假设"的从句前置或后置比较灵活，汉语中这类从句一般前置。

例1：在空运过程中，如果有关资料丢失、损坏，乙方应在收到甲方书面通知后30天内，再次免费补寄或重寄给甲方。

例2：在合同期的任何时候，合同双方的任何一方，由于受到如战争、严重火灾、洪水、台风、地震等不可抗力事件的影响而不能执行合同，履行合同的期限应予以延长，延长的期限应相当于事件所能影响的时间。

例3：若不可抗力事件持续40天以上，买方有权撤销本合同或本合同中未完成的部分。

例4：如需对本协议条款进行修改，双方应协商解决，但对协议的任何修改必须经中国政府批准方为有效。

例5：若有索赔，买方应于货物到达目的地后14天内以传真方式提出。（注意：在英语合同中，常常会遇到 if 引起的省略句。这类 if 的省略句还有 if required、if possible、if necessary、if agreeable 等，但在翻译时要突出主语。）

例6：下述或有股票，如果有的话，是否发行，必须在卖方缴纳税金后的综合收入基础上来决定。

例7：必须从该数量中扣除小型设备的存货价值与期末存货价值间的差额，如果有这种差额的话。

（2）如，若，如果

in case 在表示条件状语从句的时候，通常是强调其条件成熟的可能性要比用 if 从句小。

例1：倘若买方未能履行与卖方所订合同的任何条款，卖方有权终止与买方的全部或部分合同，或延期交货，或截留运输中的货物。在任何一种情况下，买方须负责赔偿卖方由此发生的损失、损坏和相应的费用。（注意：in case of 在英语合同中可用作状语，译成"若""如果"等。）

例2：若对解释产生异议，以中文文本为准。

例3：若发生质量索赔，买方的索赔必须在货物到达目的港的30天内提出。

（3）若，如果，假如

例1：若发现设备有明显缺陷，应由 ABC 用每周买方不进行实验的这两天时间对设备予以校正。

例2：若乙方提供的技术资料不符合本合同第8条第2款的规定，乙方必须在收到甲方书面通知后尽快在不超过30天的时间内，免费将所缺的或正确和清晰易读的技术资料寄给甲方。

例3：若总经理和/或副总经理有营私舞弊或严重失职，董事会有权随时将其撤换。

（4）"should+主语+动词"结构

这个结构属于非真实条件从句。在英语合同中使用这种条件句时，其主句一般为陈述语气。该结构表明，发生条件从句中所述情况的可能性很小，如果该条件从句所述的情况发生了，那么主句所设的事宜必须完成。

例1：本合同条款的任何变更、修改或增删，须经双方协商同意，并由双方代表签署书面文件为有效。

例2：如不可抗力事件延续到120天以上，双方应通过友好协商方式尽快解决继续履行合同的问题。

（5）除非

unless相当于if not、except if、except when，它引出的从句用现在时表示将来，一般不用虚拟条件句。unless从句中的主语和动词be常省去。

例1：运货港由卖方选择，除非双方有明确规定。

例2：除非后文另有说明者外，所运用的会计原则应与以往各年所应用的会计原则相同。

例3：除另有安排者外，任何一方无权代表另一方。

（6）若

provided that引出从句表示条件时，常表示当事人所希望的条件。

例1：若想把支付第二方的佣金或手续费作为营业费用的一个部分，则不应在营业费用中支付和计算薪金。

例2：乙方若续租该套公寓，须于合同期满前2个月内书面通知甲方并另订租赁合同。（注意：连同where和when在英语合同中还可以引出条件状语从句，表示"如果""若"等。）

5.6.1.2　Translation of Time Adverbial Clauses
　　　　时间状语从句的翻译

When translating the adverbial clause which contains time, we should first notice the position adjustment to avoid writing structure loose, and semantic ambiguity and time definition indistinct. In the context of the contract, the contracting parties often have "tacit understanding" of the obligations and rights between each other. The key of the terms lies in its timeliness. That is to say, the whole sentence is not in the center of the action of the sentence, but in the time of the action, namely what to do at what time. So when translating it into Chinese, we should use "subject+time adverbial+predicate+object" to highlight the timeliness of behavior.

(1)After

The time adverbial clause led by "after" is generally translated into "since..." in the English contract, which conforms with the language rigour of legal documents.

E.g.1: Within six months after the Effective Date of the Contract, the Seller shall submit to the Buyer the final delivery schedule in six (6) copies, which shall include the following items.

E.g.2: In case the contract cannot come into force within six months after the date of signing the contract, the contract shall be binding neither to Party A, nor to Party B.

(2)**Before**

An time adverbial clause is usually translated into "after... can..." . Such a translation method emphasizes the duty of one party in the contract.

E.g.1: Both Parties shall apply to their respective government authorities for approval before the Contract is officially signed.

E.g.2: The negotiation which lasted about four hours before the contract was concluded.

(3)**When**

"When" can lead a time adverbial clause, but in the business contract, it is regarded as a conjunction which guides conditional adverbial clauses. The shift is a good combination of basic translation skills and profession. So, "when" in the contract is translated into "if" .

E.g.1: When one party to the Joint Venture assigns all or part of its investment, the other party has preemptive right.

E.g.2: The Contractor shall notify the insurers of changes in the nature, extent or program for the execution of the Works and ensure the adequacy of the insurance at all times in accordance with the terms of the Contract and shall, when required, produce to the Employer the insurance policies in force and the receipts for payment of the current premiums.

(4)**Subject To**

The way of language expression is different in different style of paper. Combined with the different expressions in English and Chinese languages, the differences are more obvious. The meaning of a typical phrase "subject to" is "under the condition that..." . In different business contracts, the translation of this phrase is flexible, but its core is still around conclusion and execution of a contract.

E.g.1: Subject to the prior delivery of the Parent Guarantee from the contractor, the contract will come into effect upon the signature of this contract.

E.g.2: Subject to the terms and conditions set out in this Agreement, the Seller shall sell to the Buyer One Million (1,000,000) shares of _____(name of the company from which the shares are issued) at the price of Five CNY (CNY5) per share, and in an aggregate price of Five Million CNY (CNY5,000,000).

In some contracts, authors use prepositions phrases instead of clauses in order to reduce the length of the article. Still they can be translated into Chinese in accordance with clauses, and don't simply translate them into phrases.

(5)**As Soon As**

E.g.1: As soon as the new price-lists are ready, we shall be sending copies to all customers. (Note: From the above example, we can see that the location of the time adverbial is as well as Chinese word order.)

E.g.2: We will get the goods ready as soon as the contract is concluded. (Note: In the translation of this sentence, the location of a time adverbial clause is premised, so we can see the location of a time adverbial clause is decided according to the needs, which is very flexible, not necessarily according to the order of the original position.)

在翻译含有时间的状语条款时，应首先注意到位置的调整，以避免行文结构松散，语义含混，时间界定不清。在合约的语境下，缔约双方该承担的义务和权利相互之间往往已"心照不宣"。条款的关键是在于其时效性。也就是说，整个句子的中心不在于句子的动作，而在于动作发生的时间，即在什么时限内做什么。因此在翻译成汉语时应采用"主语+时间状语+谓语+宾语"，以此来突出行为的时效性。

（1）……之日起

由after引出的时间状语从句，在英语合同中一般被翻译成"……之日起"，这合乎法律文书的语言严谨性。

例1：在本合同生效之日起6个月内，卖方应向买方提交最终交货计划一式六份，包括下列内容。

例2：本合同自签名之日起6个月内仍不能生效，双方有权取消合同。

（2）……后，才能……

由before引出的时间状语从句，一般被译成"……后，才能……"。这样的翻译方法在合同中强调一方应尽的义务。

例1：合同双方应分别向本国的政府当局申请，经批准后，才能签订正式合同。

例2：谈判持续了约4个小时之后，合同达成。

（3）如果，倘若

when可以引导时间状语从句，但在商务合同中，却被看成是引导条件状语从句的连词，这种转变是基本翻译技能与专业的较好结合。所以，在合同中when就被译成"如果"或"倘若"。

例1：如果合资公司一方拟转让其全部或部分出资额，另一方有优先购买权。

例2：承包商应把工程施工的性质、范围或进度计划方面的变化情况通知承保人，保证按合同条款在整个期间内有完备的保险，并在需要时，向业主出示生效保险单及本期保险费的支付收据。

（4）以……为条件

不同文体的文章，其语言表达的方式有较大的差异，再加上英汉两种语言表达方式的不同，这种差异就更加明显了。一个非常典型的短语subject to，其原意是"以……为条件"。在不同的商务合同中，该短语的翻译却要灵活多变，但其核心仍然是围绕着合同的订立和执行。

例1：只有在承包商向母公司提交保函后，本合同才能自签名之日起生效。

例2：依据本合约所规定之各项条件，买方将自己所持_____（发行股票公司名称）公司之壹佰万股（1 000 000）股份，以每股人民币5元、总价人民币500万元之价格出售给买方。

在有些合同中作者为了减少文章的篇幅采用介词短语来代替从句。在译成汉语时还可以按照从句来翻译，不要单纯译成一个短语。

（5）一旦，一旦……就……

例1：一旦新的价格单备妥，我们就寄给所有的客户。（说明：从上面的例子中我们可以看到，时间状语所在的位置同汉语的语序一样。）

例2：一旦合同达成我们就备货。（说明：这一句的译文中，将时间状语从句的位置前提了，因此我们可以看到时间状语从句的位置是根据需要而定的，位置十分灵活，并不一定按照原文的顺序。）

5.6.2　*Translation of Attributive Clauses*
定语从句的翻译

Attributive clauses can be divided into two kinds, restrictive attributive clauses and the non-restrictive attributive clauses. Because contract language requires accuracy and norm, so in order to meet the terms of the contract of semantic integrity, attributive clauses in English contracts are indispensable. English contracts generally use restrictive attributive clauses and rarely use non-restrictive attributive clauses, which is due to the stylistic characteristics of English contracts. Restrictive attributive clauses' structure is precise and meaning is clear, which can avoid ambiguity while the word's definiteness modified by a non-restrictive attributive is not strong, even will lose definiteness.

E.g.1: In lieu of payments as provided for in Clause 4 above, the Joint Venture shall have the option of satisfying such obligation to pay by either.

E.g.2: The seller shall get the signed B/L from the forwarding agent, a copy of which will be sent to the buyer by airmail. (Note: The attributive clause in the sentence is translated into independent clauses to explain the handling information of the bill of lading previously mentioned.)

E.g.3: The Sales Representative will comply with the Manufacturer's guidelines on prices, charges, terms, and conditions for the sale of the Goods, which are subject to change from time to time.

E.g.4: Repacking, which is often considered as a trouble, is sometimes a help in the delivery. (Note: Although this sentence in English is an attributive clause, but in Chinese it is translated into a concession adverbial clause. This kind of translation method adopts the Chinese pattern of modifier-head type sentence.)

E.g. 5: For any order the volume of which exceeds USD10,000, we'll allow 5% special discount. (Note: This sentence also adopts the Chinese modifier-head type sentence structure to translate the original English prepositional phrases into assuming adverbial clauses.)

定语从句可分为限定性定语从句和非限定性定语从句两大类。由于合同语言要求准确和规范，因此为了实现合同条款语义完整，定语从句在英语合同中是不可缺少的。在英语合同中一般使用限定性定语从句，很少使用非限定性定语从句，这是由英语合同文体特点所决定的。限定性定语从句结构严谨，意思明确，可以避免引起歧义；非限定性定语从句对所修饰的词语限定性不强，甚至失去限定作用。

例1：合营公司有权选择使用下述任何一种支付办法，取代上述第4条规定的支付办法，以履行其该项义务。

　　例2：卖方应向装运代理领取签署的提单，并将其中一份航寄买方。（说明：这一句中的定语从句部分译成了独立的分句来解释前面提到的提单的处理情况。）

　　例3：销售代表在商品的销售价格、销售费用、销售条件方面应当遵循生产商的指导，这些指导可能随时改变。

　　例4：重新包装虽然常被认为是一种麻烦，但有时却有助于装运。（说明：这一句在英语中虽然是定语从句，但在汉语中译成了让步状语从句。这种翻译方法采用了汉语的偏正句的句式。）

　　例5：对金额超过1万美元的订单，我们可以给予5%的特殊折扣。（说明：这个句子同样采用了汉语偏正句的结构，将原来英语中的介词短语部分译成了假设状语从句。）

5.6.2.1　Translation of Restrictive Attributive Clauses
　　　　　限定性定语从句的翻译

The relationship between restrictive attributive clauses and the antecedents is very close. In translation, adopt the method of combination techniques of translation to translate this kind of sentences into Chinese "of..." and put them in the front of the modifiers.

E.g.1: Party B guarantees that the technical documents to be supplied by Party B are the latest technical information which has been put into practical use by Party B.

E.g.2: Shipment shall be commenced within 10 months counting from the date when the contract has come into force and completed within 16 months.

E.g.3: Net Selling Price means the price at which the product is sold by Party B from time to time after deduction of packing, installation and freight charges, trade and quantity discount, commission, insurance and commodity tax, if any, directly applicable of Product.

E.g.4: The Seller ensures that all the equipments listed in Appendix One to the Contract are brand-new products whose performance shall be in conformity with the Contract and which are manufactured according to current Chinese National Standards or Manufacturer's Standard.

E.g.5: All drawings, designs, specifications and all other technical details made available under this Contract by Party B shall be kept strictly confidential by Party A who shall not sell, transfer or divulge them in any manner to anyone except those of its own employees who will be using it in a manufacture of the Product, without prior written consent of the Party B.

　　限定性定语从句与先行词的关系十分紧密。在翻译时，要采用合译的方法，把这类句子译成汉语的"……的"，并置于被修饰词的前面。

　　例1：乙方保证所提供的技术资料是乙方经过实际使用的最新技术资料。

　　例2：自合同生效之日算起，10个月内装运，16个月内交付完毕。

　　例3：净销售价是指在扣除合同产品的包装费、安装费、运输费、商业和数量折扣、佣金、保险费和商品税之后，乙方通常销售合同产品的价格。

　　例4：卖方保证本合同附件一所列全部设备都是新产品，是根据现行的中国国家标准或厂商的标准制造的，其性能符合合同规定。

例5：乙方根据本协议所提供的一切图纸、设计、说明书及其他技术资料，甲方均须严格保密。未得乙方的书面同意，甲方不得以任何方式出售、转让或泄漏给任何人，但不包括甲方生产合同产品而使用技术资料的雇员。

5.6.2.2　Translation of Non-Restrictive Attributive Clauses 非限定性定语从句的翻译

The relationship between non-restrictive attributive clauses and the antecedents is not very close, which only acts as a supplement. Therefore, the translation of non-restrictive attributive clause basically adopts the method of division techniques of translation. In division techniques of translation, antecedent may be repeated or omitted.

E.g.1: If, through the Seller's default, the shipment is delayed beyond 30 days, the Buyer shall then be entitled to make other purchase of the same sort of goods at any lower market price; or he may cancel its order through a fax to the Seller, which is required to get to the latter prior to the beginning of any shipment.

E.g.2: If within thirty days of the giving such notice, no successor Agent shall have been so appointed and accepted such appointment, the retiring Agent may appoint a successor Agent, which shall be a bank having a combined capital and surplus of at least USD50,000,000, or the equivalent thereof in another currency, or an affiliate of such a bank.

非限定性定语从句与它所说明的先行词关系并不很密切，只是起一种补充说明的作用，因此，非限定性定语从句的翻译基本上是采用分译的方法处理。分译时可重复先行词或省译先行词。

例1：如果由于卖方违约，装船延期超过30天，在此期间，买方有权以任何更低的市场价格另行购买同类货物，买方也可以用传真通知卖方取消订货，但此传真须在装运之前到达卖方。

例2：如果在作出上述通知的30天内，接替的代理行没有被指定或没有接受这种指定，则已卸任的代理行可指定一个接替的代理行，这个接替代理行的联合资本和盈余至少有5 000万美元或与其值相当的其他货币，或者是这家银行的附属机构。

5.6.3　*Translation of Short Forms in Clauses* 从句简略形式在句中的翻译

If the subordinate clause in the sentence is short form, the subordinate clause should be inserted in the main sentence, after "shall", before the action verbs. Translate according to Chinese language habits of the contracts.

E.g.: The Contractor shall, if called upon so to do, enter into and execute the Contract Agreement to be prepared and completed at the cost of the Employer, in the form annexed to these conditions with such modification as may be necessary.

若从句是简略形式，从句应插入主句之中，应放在shall之后，行为动词之前。翻译时，按照汉语的合同语言习惯来做。

例：在被邀请签约时，承包商应同意签订并履行合同协议书，该协议书是由业主按照本合同条件所附格式拟订的，如有必要，可对其进行修改。该协议书的拟订和签订费用由业主承担。

Exercises

Chapter 5 即测即评

Ⅰ.**Translate the following into English.**

1.每家银行每年都由政府部门的会计检查账目。

2.你最好派你公司会计去查对一下报表。

3.我方不得不为这批发货受损向你提出索赔。

4.法院判令甲方对乙方所受损失支付1万英镑赔偿费。

5.如果需要聘请其他国家的审计师对年度财务报表进行审查,甲方应予以同意。其所需费用由乙方负担。

6.第一次技术服务应始于本合同生效之日起第6天。乙方应派遣一名技术人员赴甲方工厂,提供12个工作日的技术指导。

7.凡因为履行本合同而在甲方国家以外发生的一切税费,均由乙方负担。

8.倘若合同中的交货时间只是估计的时间,任何一方可在距估计日期尚有1/3的时间时,用书面要求另一方同意一个确定的时间。

9.制造商应对货物的质量、规格、性能、数量、重量进行细致和全面的检验,出具检验证书,证实检验的技术数据和结论后,才能发货。

Ⅱ.**Translate the following into Chinese.**

1.Clean shipped on board Ocean Bill of Lading in full set made out to order of shipper is blank enclosed.

2.If the anticipated progress has not been maintained in accordance with the schedule, the Contractor shall advise the reasons therefore and suggest means to eliminate the causes of delay.

3.The issuing bank shall have a reasonable time to examine the documents.

4.On close inspection, it was found out to be a forgery.

5.The Contractor shall perform the inspection and examination of all equipment, machinery and materials including spare parts required for the construction of the plant.

6.This is the final arbitration award and binding on both Contracting Parties.

7.When either party contributes his capital goods or industrial property as investment, Party A and Party B shall conclude a separate contract to be a part of this main contract.

Chapter 6

Drafting International Business Contracts
国际商务合同的起草

Learning Objectives

◆   重点掌握国际商务合同中容易出现的问题的解决方案（如合同要有明确的权利和义务、必要的条款等）；了解国际商务中合同在哪些方面容易出现问题；了解国际合同中中方常出现的以及可能出现的错误，并熟悉相应的解决办法。

Guide Case

A Collision Between the Applicant and the Issuing Bank

In May 2006, an export company in China concluded a contract of 31 metric tons of antimony slabs, unit price USD 2,750 CFR Karachi. On June 8, the importer opened an irrevocable L/C through a local bank, L/C amount USD 85,250, partial shipment not allowed, latest date of shipment August 10, expiry date of the L/C August 25, the market price for antimony slab slumped to USD 2,000 CFR Karachi per metric ton.

After the establishment, the importer telexed the exporter three times on end asking for cancellation of the contract and even the credit. What was more, the importer threatened to go bankrupt if the exporter did not cancel the contract and repeatedly declared that they would not retire the documents even if the goods had arrived at Karachi.

Feeling embarrassed, the exporter consulted the negotiating bank for advice. The negotiating bank held that UCP600 stipulates that an irrevocable credit can be neither amended nor canceled without the agreement of the beneficiary and that the issuing bank must make payments as long as the documents comply with the terms and conditions of the credit. Whether the applicant retires the documents or not is the matter between the applicant and the issuing bank. The issuing bank cannot discharge itself from the primary liability for the reason that the applicant goes bankrupt or refuses to redeem the documents. In conclusion, the export company should arrange for the shipment, documentation and negotiation as scheduled. Once the documents comply with the credit, the issuing bank has no reason to refuse to pay.

Due to short supply of the goods, the exporter was unable to ship the goods in one lot. The exporter had contacted the importer for amendment of the credit to allow partial shipment. Not until one Sunday did the importer reply by turning down the request and asking for a clearance certificate issued by the beneficiary to state that the goods are in line with the current price of the international market.

After study, the export company believed that the importer demanded the certificate with the aim of producing an excuse for refusal of payment and rejected the request.

On August 23, the export company presented the full set of documents to the negotiating bank who examined the documents with great care to ensure their invulnerability. During the validity period of the credit, the negotiating bank presented the documents to the issuing bank for reimbursement. Since the documents fully agreed with the credit terms and with one another, the issuing bank had no choice but make the payment.

资料来源　王秉乾. 国际商事合同[M]. 北京：对外经济贸易大学出版社，2013.

思考题：

（1）信用证的修改在什么情况下才可接受？

（2）从这个申请人与开证行串通的案例中我们应吸取什么教训？

6.1　Considerations for Parties to the Transaction[①]　交易各方注意事项

In international business transactions, buyers and sellers need to pay attention to the main items, including positioning, profit calculation and attorney consultation, etc.

In sales transactions, rights and obligations in contracts of the parties concerned commonly only bind on both the buyer and the seller, and the third party cannot be filed for enforcing the contract even if there is a joint interest relationship between the third party and the parties to a contract, which is one of the important principles of contract law, namely "the contract relativity principle".

The following is an example of how to conduct profit accounting and the factors to be considered in the consultation of lawyers to briefly describe the major considerations for buyers and sellers in international business.

The buyer: first of all, the buyer as a consumer in the whole consumption chain may be in the middle link or the final consumer. Secondly, the buyer's target is the lowest price for the best or relatively good products and services, and the main factors influencing the price depend on the supply and demand of the market. Finally, before signing the contract, the investigation of the seller's credit standing is a kind of effective means to protect their own interests.

---

① 王立非. 国际商务合同实践教程［M］. 上海：上海外语教育出版社，2012.

The Seller: First of all, the seller may be in the whole consumption chain of the original part or the intermediate links. Secondly, the seller's goal is to keep the low cost, and sell products and services at the best price, and the main factors influencing the price also depend on the supply and demand of the market. Finally, the seller needs to use appropriate means to achieve the price expected.

Make the profits: Both buyers and sellers will deduct freight, customs clearance, insurance and other costs of additional hidden costs. The parties should know why to consult a lawyer, when to consult a lawyer, how to choose a lawyer, and what to consult. For example, before negotiations, during transactions and before contracts are signed, both buyers and sellers should consult lawyers about their own and other countries' trade regulations, to ensure their rights under the contract. In the aspect of customs clearance, transportation, and declare dutiable goods, etc., the lawyer cannot provide more detailed consultation, the parties should consult the corresponding professional visitors.

在国际商务交易中，买卖双方需要注意的主要事项包括在交易中的定位、利润核算及律师咨询等问题。

在销售交易中，合同项下的权利和义务一般只对买卖双方当事人产生拘束力，而第三方当事人不能诉请强制执行该合同，即使第三方当事人与合同当事人之间存在连带利益关系，这就是合同法的重要原则之一，即"合同相对性原则"。

以如何进行利润核算和在律师咨询时需要考虑的因素为例，简述在国际商务贸易中买卖双方主要的注意事项。

买方：首先，买方作为消费者在整个消费链中可能居于中间环节或作为最终消费者；其次，买方的目标是以最低价格购得最好的或相对较好的产品和服务，而影响价格的主要因素取决于市场的供求关系；最后，签订合同前对卖方进行资信调查是保护自身利益的一种有效手段。

卖方：首先，卖方可能居于整个消费链的最初环节或者中间环节；其次，卖方的目标是保持较低成本，并以最优价格出售产品和服务，而影响价格的主要因素为市场的供求关系；最后，卖方需要使用适当的推销手段以获得期望价格。

利润核算：买卖双方要将运费、通关、保险及其他额外花销等交易的隐性成本扣除。当事人应该了解为什么咨询律师、什么时候咨询律师、怎么选择律师，以及咨询什么内容。例如，在谈判前、交易中及合同签署前，买卖双方应就本国和对方国家的贸易法规等问题咨询律师，以保证自己合同项下的权益；在通关、运输，以及报税等方面，律师则无法提供更详细的咨询内容，当事人应该去咨询相应领域的业内人士。

6.2 Key Issues in International Business Contracts[①]
签订国际商务合同应注意的问题

For the body text, both parties of the contract should pay attention to the following aspects in

---

① 李爽，于湛波. 商务谈判 [M]. 北京：清华大学出版社，2015.

the contract. As the parties in a contract, they should conclude a contract in writing. After establishing the relationships of a contract, they should fulfil their obligations to verify the other party of the contracting ability through some terms of the contract, (such as disclaimer clauses) to reduce their risks. The contents of the contract should be complete and accurate. In the process of executing a contract, if the content is changed, both sides should modify the agreement in writing. Conclude the applicable law clauses in the contract so that the no - fault party obtains corresponding relief in the event of a dispute. In addition, as lawyers of parties in a contract, in review of the contract, they should pay attention to investigating the background of the other party. Attention should also be paid to the payment terms in the contract: transfer risks, relevant state policies and regulations of import and export, and market circulation requirements.

International business involves many parties, complicated legal relations and the application of laws in different countries. Therefore, parties should take special care in the process of signing and performing contracts to avoid unnecessary losses. As for how to sign a contract correctly, naturally there are different requirements under different situations. Generally speaking, the following seven aspects should be paid attention to:

① Before signing the contract, we should carefully review the other party's true identity, sincere willingness and ability of performance.

② Ensure that the contract is signed in the appropriate form and the basic terms are complete, make every effort to express clearly, definitely and completely, must not be vague, incomplete or ambiguous, which will bring some hidden troubles to a dangerous precedent for the fulfillment of the contract.

③ Review the legality of means and content of the contract. If they are illegal, the contract will be invalid.

④ Agree on dispute jurisdiction and applicable law clauses.

⑤ Default clauses are expressly agreed upon breach liability, for potential future litigation and rights to lay a good foundation. The default clause is clear in the interest of arrears or liquidated damages. However, the penalty in the default clause due to breach of contract should not be exorbitant. If a dispute arises over excessive penalty, the other party will ask the court to cancel this clause on the grounds of violating the principle of fairness, making it impossible to realize this clause.

⑥ Agree on the ownership retention clause. As a condition of sales, the supplier can keep the legal ownership of the goods until the buyer pays full payment for the transfer to the buyer.

⑦ If necessary and possible, the parties in a contract may agree on the terms of the guarantee so as to guard against credit risk.

If there is a dispute after concluding the sales contract, it is bound to affect the performance of the contract or the realization of the expected benefits. Therefore, appropriate preventive clauses must be concluded in the contract to prevent the possibility of disputes or problems. Exporters, for example, in order to ensure that the other party can deliver the goods on time, stipulate in the contract in accordance with requirements that the L/C must reach the buyer before deadline. In addition to the preventive clauses according to the requirement of the specific situation, general transactions often stipulate a time limit for objection to the non-conformity of the goods and the provisions on the basis of claims, as well as the exemption clauses for non-performance of the contract due to natural disasters or accidents or other force majeure. As for how to deal with disputes, this is also a very important problem.

After signing the contract, the parties in a contract should review the key points and matters need attention: firstly, the parties should make it clear whether signing a contract is just to complete a transaction or to establish a long-term cooperation relationship with each other, because different trading purposes can lead to differences in the contract content and the tone of the contract. Secondly, confirm whether the other party has the right to sign a contract. Finally, the parties have to review whether the contract includes such important clauses as specification, price, delivery, payment, customs clearance, transportation, quality assurance and after-sales service, transfer and termination of a contract, and remedy for breach of contract. Reviewing contracts is a process which can not be ignored. Especially for bilingual international business contracts, we should pay attention to the review of language, business and legal aspects.

Common legal and commercial problems in international contracts mainly include: ①relationship commitment; ②the contract power; ③basic terms; ④the inspection of goods; ⑤the terms of delivery; ⑥the specifications; ⑦customs clearance; ⑧shipment and insurance; ⑨guarantee and return; ⑩transfer; ⑪termination rights; ⑫default relief; ⑬independent consulting; ⑭intellectual property rights.

After such a dispute occurs, it is better to negotiate and solve friendly by both parties or the third party agreed by both parties. In addition, the dispute can also be brought to court or settled by an arbitration institution. Compared with court lawsuit, the arbitration has the advantages of simple procedure, low cost, quick handling of cases, moderate atmosphere and better legal effect. According to the practices and the law of some countries, when the arbitration method is used to deal with disputes, the parties must have an arbitration agreement before the arbitration institution can accept it. When the parties make an arbitration agreement, it can eliminate the court's right to accept. As for the arbitration agreement conclusion, it is more convenient and easier to obtain an agreement before the dispute occurs than after. The arbitration agreement concluded after the event is sometimes rejected by the damaged party, while the damaged party goes to court. So, in the general sales contract, clauses shall be concluded that both sides can settle the dispute through arbitration if negotiation fails, including the place of arbitration, the arbitration organization, arbitration proceedings and the effectiveness of the verdict. In the trade agreement between the governments of our country and other countries, if there is an arbitration clause, it can be omitted in the sales contract. If there is a dispute, it shall be dealt with according to the terms of the agreement between the governments.

Parties in the process of signing a contract should pay attention to the following aspects of contents:

Before signing the contract, you should carefully review each other's true identity, sincere willingness and ability of performance. In international business, drafting a contract precisely and completely is very important, it is not possible to cover all the clauses and possible problems in the contract. In a contract, the perfect terms are impossible, but you can draw up a clear contract as far as possible, covering the complete content as much as possible to avoid the possible differences and disputes. The role of body parts in a contract is to help to find out the ambiguity of the terms and how to strive to precise expressions. Specific draft depends on the specific environment of the parties.

To draft a business contract, first of all, you should be familiar with the format and the structure of the contract, understand the basic materials, use clear and standard contract language to draw up the terms of the contract, clarify contract details and language. For common terms in a contract, it is necessary to pay attention not only to their complete expression and accurate wording, but also to understand the meaning of relevant legal terms and understand why standard terms should be drafted according to the contract template and the legal consequences of using incomplete terms. At the same time, we should also note that the grammar structure of the terms of the contract is more complex. There are often long sentences, large sets of small sentences, a small set of clauses, and sometimes even one word is a clause. For the characteristics of contract language, we should be aware of differences of thinking between English and Chinese, and express the complete terms of the contract clearly and accurately. Contract text can be divided into two parts. The first part mainly introduces the terms of the contract format. The attention should be paid to the shortcomings of these terms and conditions in order to protect their rights in the event of a dispute. The second part is the body of the text, that is, the structure of terms and the precise terminology. The terms of the contract mainly include the following content: (accept) to sign contracts, order of contracts; cargo description (number, category, color, composition, specification, etc.); goods quality (merchant ability, industry standards, technical standards and other prices); delivery and shipment (time, location, trade terms); insurance; ownership transfer; risk (time); return of the goods; customs clearance; inspection rights.

Issues which parties shall clarify when drafting the contract: Get to know whether the other party has the right to sign the contract; Ensure the product specification description is accurate; Force majeure risks defined in the contract; Express complete contract content with accurate language; Do correctly understand the content before signing the contract; Act in accordance with the contract, etc. The parties in a contract may also seek a lawyer to help.

对于正文，合同的买卖双方当事人在合同订立时应该注意以下几方面：合同当事人应该以书面形式订立合同；在确立合同关系后再履行义务，以核实对方当事人的缔约能力，并通过一些合同条款（如免责条款）减轻自身所承担的风险；合同的内容应该完整、准确；在合同履行过程中，如发生内容变更，双方应以书面形式达成变更协议；在合同中要订立法律适用条款，这样在发生争议时无过错一方才能获得相应的救济。另外，作为合同当事人的律师，在对合同进行审核时应注意以下几个方面：对另一方当事人做背景调查；要注意合同中的支付条款，即风险转移、与进出口相关的国家政策与法规，以及市场流通要求。

　　国际贸易涉及的当事人较多，法律关系复杂，还涉及不同国家的法律适用等问题，所以当事人在签订合同及履行合同过程中应该特别谨慎，以免发生不必要的损失。关于如何正确地签订合同，在不同的情况下自然有不同的要求。总的来讲，合同双方当事人在签订合同过程中，应该注意以下七个方面的内容：

　　① 在签订合同以前，应认真审查对方的真实身份、诚信意愿和履约能力。

　　② 保证合同签订形式的适当和基本条款的完备，要力求表达得清晰、明确、完整，决不能含糊不清、残缺不全或者模棱两可，给合同的履行埋下隐患。

　　③ 审查合同的订立手段和内容是否合法，合同订立手段如果不合法或约定内容不合法，将会带来合同无效的结果。

　　④ 约定争议管辖权和准据法条款。

　　⑤ 约定违约条款，即明确约定违约的责任，为将来可能的诉讼与维权打下良好的基础。违约条款中可以明确约定违约金或欠款的利息。但是，违约条款中的违约金不宜过高。过高的违约金如果引发争议，对方当事人会以违反公平原则为由要求法院撤销该条款，使得该条款无法实现。

　　⑥ 约定所有权保留条款。作为销售的条件，供应商可以规定保留货物的法定所有权，直到购买者付清全部货款后所有权才转移给购买者。

　　⑦ 如有必要且有可能，合同的当事人可以约定担保条款，以防范信用风险。

　　销售合同订立以后，倘若发生争议，势必影响合同的履行或预期效益的实现。因此，对合同订立后可能发生的争议或问题，须在合同中订立适当的预防性条款。例如，出口方为了保证对方能按时交付货物，在合同中规定符合要求的信用证必须在最后期限前送达买方。除了根据具体情况需要规定的预防性条款外，一般交易通常都规定对货物不符提出异议的期限和索赔依据的条款，以及因自然灾害或意外事故等不可抗力原因造成的不能履行或不能如期履行合同的免责条款等。至于发生争议时如何处理，这也是一个十分重要的问题。

　　合同签订后，合同当事人应审核合同的重点及注意事项。首先，各方要明确签订合同只是为了完成一次交易，还是要与对方建立长期合作关系，因为交易目的不同会导致合同内容和基调产生差别；其次，确认对方是否有权签订合同；最后，当事人要审核合同是否已包括商品规格、价格、交货、付款、通关、运输、质量保证及售后服务、合同转让及终止、违约补救等重要条款。审核合同是订立合同过程中不可忽视的环节，用双语起草的国际商务合同，尤其应该重视语言、商务、法律等多方面的审核。

　　国际合同常见的法律和商务问题主要包括：①关系承诺；②合同权利；③基本条款；④货物检验；⑤交货条款；⑥货物规格；⑦清关；⑧运输和保险；⑨保证和退货；⑩转让；⑪终止权利；⑫违约救济；⑬独立咨询；⑭知识产权。

　　争议发生后，双方友好协商解决或由双方同意的第三者调解是较好的办法。此外还可以向法院提起诉讼或由仲裁机构解决争议。仲裁较之法院诉讼，有程序简便、费用低、处理案件迅速、气氛缓和、法律效果较好等优点。根据惯例和一些国家的法律，凡采用仲裁方法处理争议，当事人之间必须订有仲裁协议，仲裁机构方能受理。当双方当事人订有仲裁协议时，一般可以排除法院对该争议案的受理权。在争议发生前订立仲裁协议比在争议发生之后订立更为方便且易达成一致。事后订立仲裁协议有时会遭到受损方的拒绝，而由受损方诉诸法庭。所以，在一般的销售合同中都应订立"如有争议，双方协商不成时通过仲裁解决"的条款，包括仲裁地点、仲裁机构、仲裁程序及裁决的效力等内容。在我国与对方国签订的政府间贸易协定中，如订有仲裁条款，则在销售合同中可以省略，发生争议时按政府间协定的条款办理。

双方在签订合同的过程中应该注意以下几个方面的内容：

在签订合同之前，应该仔细审查对方的真实身份、真诚的意愿和履行合同的能力。在国际贸易中，准确和完整地起草一份合同是非常重要的，合同中不可能覆盖所有条款和可能出现的问题。在一份合同中，不可能有完美的条款，但是你可以制定一个明确的、内容尽可能完整的合同，尽量避免可能出现的分歧和争端。合同正文的作用在于帮助找出条款的模糊性，以及如何力求措辞严谨。具体的内容还要看当事人所处的具体环境。

起草一份商业合同，首先应该熟悉合同的格式和结构，了解基本材料，使用清晰、标准的合同语言拟定合同条款，明确合同细节和语言。对于合同中常见的条款，不仅要注意其完整的表达和准确的用词，也要理解相关法律术语的含义，理解按照模板起草的合同标准条款和使用不完整的条款的法律后果。与此同时，我们也应该注意到合同条款的语法结构更加复杂，经常出现一些长句子、大句子套小句子、一小组条款，有时一个单词也会是一个条款。关于合同语言的特点，我们应该意识到英语和汉语之间的思维差异，要清晰、准确地表达完整的合同条款。合同文本可以分为两部分。第一部分主要介绍合同条款的格式，要注意这些条款的缺点，在发生争端时可以保护自身的权利。第二部分是正文，即条款的结构和准确的术语。合同的条款主要包括以下内容：（接受）签订合同，合同订单；货物描述（数量、类别、颜色、成分、规格等）；货物质量（适销性、行业标准、技术标准和其他价格）；交货和运输（时间、地点、贸易术语）；保险；所有权转移；风险（时间）；退货；清关；检验权利。

起草合同时双方应阐明的问题：了解对方是否有签订合同的资格；确保产品规格描述准确；合同中定义的不可抗力风险；以准确的语言完整地表达合同内容；在合同签署之前正确理解合同内容；按合同行事等。合同当事人也可寻求律师帮助。

6.3　Drafting Precise Contract Provisions[①]
用准确的语言起草合同条款

6.3.1　*Normal Steps of Writing a Business Contract*
撰写商务合同的一般步骤

Step 1: Summarize the basic terms of your agreement in writing. Before making a business contract, you need a final agreement on all the terms. If possible, confirm these terms with the other party by email or fax. For complicated business contracts such as license agreements, equipment sales contracts, engineering project contracts, related parties should meet and negotiate the commercial contract and all technical appendices.

---

① 王立非. 国际商务合同实践教程 [M]. 上海：上海外语教育出版社，2012.

Step 2: Find samples of the relevant business contract online. Depending on the type of business contract, there may be existing templates on the web you can use. You can find over 1,000 different types of professional business agreements or business contracts in Chinese, English and some other languages at this website: http://www.biztree.coni/store. You should modify these business contract templates to suit your needs and specific terms.

Step 3: Draft a business contract using a sample agreement from Step 2 or create your own new contract using clear language. If you have a simple business contract, you may not need a sample agreement—it may be easier to make your own letter as an agreement that is signed by all parties.

Step 4: Include all terms and specific agreements within your business contract. Read the contract. Confirm that you have written about the Who, What, When, Where, Why and How in the terms of the contract.

Step 5: Consider what the scenario is. Check that if you have accounted for nonperformance, lateness, and default. Discuss any changes or new terms with the other party, if applicable.

Step 6: Send the contract for a large business deal to your attorney for review. For big investments such as a house or investment purchase, equipment purchase, license agreement, it's best to work with an attorney to ensure that your contract is compliant with the law.

Step 7: If you are not able to sit together to sign the agreement, send two originals to the other party with a short cover letter. All parties should initial each page of the agreement, and sign and date the last page. Follow up to get the signed contract back quickly. After the other party has initialed and signed the contracts, sign them and send one original back to them for their records. Complete your side of the deal and enforce the agreement.

步骤1：总结书面协议的基本条款。在起草一份商业合同之前，你需要所有条款的最终协议。如果可能的话，通过电子邮件或传真跟对方确认这些条款。对于像许可协议、设备销售合同、工程合同这样的复杂商务合同，相关各方应见面协商商务合同和所有的技术附件。

步骤2：在网上找到相关的商务合同样本。根据商务合同的类型，可以使用网络现有的模板。你可以在网站 http://www.biztree.coni/store 找到超过1 000个不同类型的中文、英文和一些其他语言的专业商务协议或合同。你应该修改这些商务合同模板来适应你的需求和具体条款。

步骤3：使用步骤2中的协议样本起草商务合同或用清晰的语言创建自己的新合同。如果你有简单的商务合同，你可能不需要协议样本，你可以更容易地撰写由各方签署的书面协议。

步骤4：确保商务合同包含所有的条款和具体协议。阅读合同，确认你将与交易有关的人、对象、时间、地点，以及原因和过程写进了合同。

步骤5：考虑场景是什么。核查你是否阐述了不作为、延迟和违约。与另一方讨论任何适用的更改或新条款。

步骤6：大型交易的合同要寄给你的律师审查。对于像房产买卖、投资采购、设备购买、许可协议这样的大型投资，最好与律师合作，确保合同符合法律。

步骤 7：如果你们不能够坐在一起签署协议，向另一方寄送两份原件和一封简短附信。各方应在协议的每个页面签字，在最后一页签字并标出日期。跟进并迅速拿回签字后的合同。在另一方签署合同后，在合同上签字并将合同正本寄回给他们备案。完成你的交易并执行该协议。

6.3.2 *Useful Tips for Drafting Business Contracts*
起草商务合同的有用提示

Reading contracts can be tedious and confusing; drafting them can be even more challenging. But well-drafted contracts are vital to your business. A well-drafted contract spells out the rights and obligations of each party and protects you and your business to the most practical extent. A good contract can increase your business, earn you respect, and make money for you. A bad contract, on the other hand, can be disastrous. Following tips will give you a head start.

阅读合同可能会感到乏味和困惑，起草合同则更具挑战性，但好的合同对交易至关重要。撰写得好的合同会说明双方的权利和义务，能最大限度地在实际中保护你和你的交易。好的合同可以增加你的业务，为你赢得尊敬，为你赚钱；相反，糟糕的合同可能是灾难性的。以下提示会对你有益。

6.3.2.1 General Tips for Making a Business Contract
撰写商务合同的一般提示

① Make sure the names of all parties are accurate. State the correct legal names of the parties in the first paragraph. As obvious as this is, it is one of the most common problems in contracts. For individuals, legal names include full first and last name, and middle initials if available, and other identifying information, if appropriate, such as "Jr. MLD", etc. For corporations, check with the registered local authority.

② Identify the parties by nicknames. Giving or defining each party a nickname in the first paragraph will make the contract easier to read. For example, Shanghai Bao Shan Iron & Steel Corporation Limited would be nicknamed "Baosteel"; Bank of China would be nicknamed "BOC".

③ Be careful when using nicknames for legal terms. Do not use "Contractor" as a nickname unless that party is legally a contractor. Do not use "Agent" unless you intend for that party to be an agent, and if you do, then you had better specify the scope of authority and other agency issues to avoid future disagreements.

④ Include a blank for the date in the first paragraph. Putting the date in the first paragraph makes it easy to find after the contract is signed. This also makes it easier for contracts to be described in other documents in a precise way, such as the "October 8, 202×, Contract for Sale of Steel Rolling Mill".

⑤ Include the background. Recitals are the "whereas" clauses that precede the body of a contract. They provide a simple way to bring the contract's reader (party, judge or jury) up to speed on what the contract is about, who the parties are, why they are signing the contract, etc. The first paragraph in the body of the contract can incorporate the recitals by reference and state that they are true and correct. This will avoid a later argument as to whether or not the recitals are a legally binding part of the contract.

⑥ Outline the contract by writing out and underlining paragraph headings in their logical order. The paragraphs should flow in logical, organized fashion. It is not necessary to write them all at once; you can write them as you think of them. Try to group related concepts in the same paragraphs or in adjacent paragraphs.

⑦ Complete each paragraph by writing the contract terms that apply to that paragraph. This is simple. You learned this in elementary school. Write the contract paragraph by paragraph to show what the parties agree to do or disagree to do.

⑧ Keep a pad at hand to remember clauses to add. It is normal to think of additional clauses, wording and issues while writing a contract. Jot these down on a pad as you write; they are easily forgotten. Also keep your outline and other forms in front of you as you write, and check off items as you write them.

⑨ Repeat yourself only when repetition is necessary to improve clarity. Ambiguity is created by saying the same thing more than once; it is almost impossible to say it twice without creating ambiguity. Only if the concept is a difficult one should you write it in more than one way. In addition, if you use an example to clarify a difficult concept or formula, be sure that all possible meanings are considered and the example is accurate and consistent with the concept as worded.

⑩ Title it "Contract". If your client wants a contract, call it a contract. A judge now sitting on the federal bench once ruled that a document entitled "Proposal" was not a contract even though it was signed by both parties. The lesson learned is: "Say what you mean." If you intend the document to be a legally binding contract, use the word "Contract" in the title.

⑪ Sentences should be short to avoid unnecessary complexity and ambiguity. Short sentences are easier to understand than long ones.

⑫ Write in active tense, rather than passive. Sentences in active voice are shorter, more efficient, and have more clear meanings. The example of active: "Sellers shall sell the Property to Buyers." The example of passive: "The Property shall be sold to Buyer by Sellers."

⑬ Don't use the word "biweekly". It has two meanings: twice a week and every other week. The same applies to "bimonthly". Instead, write "every other week" or "twice a week".

⑭ Don't say things like "advanced technology and equipment". Avoid ambiguity by writing "advanced technology and advanced equipment" or "equipment and advanced technology". When adding a modifier like "advanced" before a compound of nouns like "technology and equipment", be sure to clarify whether you intend the modifier to apply to both nouns or just the first one. If you intend it to apply to both, use parallel construction and write the modifier in front of each noun. If you intend it to apply to just one noun, place that one noun at the end of the list and the modifier directly in front of it.

⑮ Don't say "Leaser" and "Leasee". These are bad nicknames for a lease, because they are easily reversed or mistyped. Use "Landlord" and "Tenant" instead. The same applies to lienor and lienee, mortgagor and mortgagee, grantor and grantee, licensor and licensee, Party A and Party B. This is where you can use your creativity to come up with a different nickname for a party, as long as you use it consistently throughout the contract.

⑯Watch out when using "herein". Do "wherever" used "herein" means "anywhere" in the contract or "anywhere" in the paragraph? Clarify this ambiguity if it matters.

⑰Write numbers as both words and numerals: ten (10). This will reduce the chance for errors.

⑱When you write "including", consider adding "but not limited to". Unless you intend the list to be all-inclusive, you had better clarify your intent that it is merely an example. For instance: "Erection means the installation of the equipment, including but not limited to placing and connecting the parts to their positions." "Should contract equipment be found defective before the expiration of mechanical warranty period, including but not limited to latent defect or the use of unsuitable materials, the buyer has the right..."

⑲Don't rely on the rules of grammar. The rules of grammar that you learned in school are not universal. The judge or jury interpreting the meaning of your contract may have learned different rules. Write the contract so that no matter what rules they learned, the contract is clear and unambiguous.

⑳Don't be creative with words. Contract writing is not creative writing. It is not meant to provoke reflective thoughts or controversies about nuances of meaning. Contract writing is clear, direct and precise. Therefore, use common words and common meanings.

㉑Be consistent in using words. If you refer to the subject matter of a sales contract as "goods", use that term throughout the contract; do not alternately call them "goods" and "items". Maintaining consistency is more important than avoiding repetition. Don't worry about putting the reader to sleep; worry about the opposing lawyer hunting for ambiguities to get your contract into court a year from now.

㉒Consider including choice of law, venue or arbitration selection, and attorneys fee clauses.

㉓Define a word by capitalizing it and putting it in quotes. Capitalizing a word indicates that you intend it to have a special meaning. The following are two sample clauses for defining terms:

Wherever used in this contract, the term "Contract Goods" shall mean the goods that Buyer has agreed to purchase from Seller under this contract.

Buyer hereby agrees to purchase from Seller ten (10) sets of machine tools, hereinafter called the "Contract Goods".

㉔Define terms or words either in the beginning of the contract or when first used. This will avoid misunderstanding or different interpretations of the meaning of the terms.

㉕Explain technical terms and concepts. Remember that the parties might understand the technical jargon, but the judge and jury who interpret and apply the contract do not. Therefore, explain the contract's terms and concepts within the contract itself.

㉖Check spelling, paragraph numbering, and cross references both manually and with your computer's spelling and grammar checker. This almost goes without saying today, especially since the computer word processor now checks your spelling and grammar as you type. But do not simply trust your computer. Unfortunately sometimes it also may change "without doubt" into "with our doubt", if you fail to watch it closely.

㉗ Let your secretary or paralegal read it. Not only will your staff frequently find spelling and grammar errors missed by your word processor 's spell checker, but also they will find inconsistencies and confusing areas that you missed when drafting.

㉘ Print the contract on 80 gram paper instead of 70 gram copier paper. Using a heavier paper will make it easy to tell the original contract from copies. It will also last longer.

㉙ Print on pages using the same paper, and if pages are changed, reprint the document using the same paper. This will avoid an argument that pages were substituted after the contract was signed.

㉚ Identify the parties and witnesses who sign by providing blank lines below their signature lines for their printed names and addresses. This will make it easier to find the witnesses if the contract is contested.

㉛ Make sure that corporate officers include their titles, the corporate name and the word "as". Failure to do this can result in personal liability of the officer. The proper way to sign in a representative capacity is as follows:

ABC Corporation, a Florida corporation

By:

John Jones, as its President

① 确保所有当事方的名字是准确的。在第一段陈述当事方正确的法定名字。显然地，它是合同中最常见的问题之一。个人名称包括可用的完整的名和姓、中间名字的缩写，以及其他证明身份的信息，如"Jr. MLD"等。公司名称可通过注册地当局核查。

② 确定合同双方的简称。在合同第一段给出各方简称将使合同更容易阅读。例如，将上海宝山钢铁有限公司简称为"宝钢"，将中国银行简称为"中行"。

③ 小心使用法律术语的简称。不要将"合约方"作为简称，除非当事方是法定的合约方。不要使用"代理"，除非你想让当事方成为法定的代理方；如果你这么做了，那么你最好明确授权的范围和其他问题以避免将来的争议。

④ 在合同的第一段要为书写签约日期留下空格。把日期放在合同的第一段，这样在合同签署之后你就很容易发现它了。这也使得合同在其他文件中更容易被精确地描述，如"202×年10月8日，轧钢厂销售合同"。

⑤ 包括背景陈述。陈述语是指那些放在合同主体前面的"鉴于"条款。它们以简单的方式使合同的读者（当事方、法官或陪审团）快速了解合同的当事方是谁，他们为什么签订合同，等等。合同正文的第一段可以通过引用来体现陈述语，并表明它们是真实和正确的。这将避免以后出现关于陈述语是否是合同的一部分的争议。

⑥ 按逻辑顺序列出合同段落的标题词。段落应该按照逻辑顺序有条理地排列。没有必要把内容一次性地全部写出来，你可以先写出你想到的，再尝试将相关的概念放在同一段落或相邻的段落。

⑦ 撰写适用于每一段落的合同条款。这是简单的，你在小学就学过这一点。通过一段一段地撰写合同来说明合同双方同意做什么，或不同意做什么。

⑧在手边保留便笺簿，以便记下需要添加的条款。在撰写合同时，想起一些附加条款、措辞和问题是正常的，你可以在便笺簿上记下这些，否则很容易忘记。在撰写合同时，把大纲和其他一些表格放在眼前，以便检查各项内容。

⑨只有在需要提高清晰度时才重述内容。同样的事情说不止一次就会产生歧义，只有在要表达的概念很难的时候，你才会以不止一个方式把它写出来。此外，如果你使用一个例子来阐明一个很难的概念或公式，你要确保已经考虑到所有可能的含义，并且这个例子是准确的，措辞与概念相一致。

⑩以"合同"为标题。如果你的客户需要的是合同，就以"合同"为之命名。联邦法院法官曾裁定，标题名为"提议"的文件即使被双方签署也不是合同。我们得到的教训是："要把意思表达出来。"如果你想要文件成为一个具有法律约束力的合同，那么就使用"合同"作为标题。

⑪句子尽量简短以避免不必要的复杂性和模糊性。短句子比长句子更容易理解。

⑫用主动语态而不用被动语态。主动语态的句子更简短，更有效，并且意义更明晰。主动语态的例子："卖方将把财产卖给买方。"被动语态的例子："财产将由卖方卖给买方。"

⑬不使用"双周的"这个词。这个词有两个含义：每周两次和每两周一次。这同样适用于"双月的"。正确的写法是："每隔一周"或"每周两次"。

⑭不要使用诸如"先进技术和设备"的说法。为避免含糊不清，应采用"先进技术和先进设备"或"设备和先进技术"的表达方式。当在复合名词前添加修饰词时，如果在"技术和设备"之前添加"先进的"，你一定要明确修饰词是适用于这两个名词还是只适用于第一个名词。如果你打算令修饰词适用于这两个名词，那么使用平行结构并在每个名词前写出修饰词。如果你打算令修饰词只适用于其中一个名词，那么把该名词放在词组串的末尾，并且把修饰词直接放在该名词的前面。

⑮不要使用"出租方"和"承租方"。对于租赁合同来说，这是不合适的简称，因为它们容易被颠倒或者出现打印错误。可以用"房东"和"房客"来称呼他们。这同样适用于留置权人和被留置权人、抵押人和抵押权人、让与人和受让人、许可方和被许可方、甲方和乙方。只要你在整个合同中一直使用简称，你可以使用你的创造力想出不同当事方的简称。

⑯谨慎地使用"此处"一词。在任何地方都使用"此处"，是指在合同中的"任何地方"还是段落中的"任何地方"？如果这么使用就要澄清这个模棱两可的问题。

⑰写数目时需要文字和阿拉伯数字并用，如"拾（10）"。这将减少一些不必要的错误。

⑱当你写"包括"这个词时，应考虑加上"但不限于"。除非你的列表是详尽的，否则你最好明确你的意图，即它仅仅是一个例子。例如，"建造意味着设备的安装，包括但不限于放置和连接零件。""如果在设备保修期期满前，发现合同设备有缺陷，包括但不限于潜在的缺陷或使用不合适的材料，买方有权利……"

⑲不要依赖语法规则。你在学校学到的语法规则并不是普遍的。解释合同意义的法官或陪审团可能已经精通了不同的语法规则。无论他们精通什么语法规则，你都要把合同撰写得清晰、明确。

⑳不要创造词语。合同文书不是创造性作品，不应该因意义间的细微差别而引起反思或争论。合同文书应该是清晰、直接和准确的。因此，要使用普通的词语，表达普通的意思。

㉑用词一致。如果你在整个合同中使用"货物"这个词来指代销售合同的标的物，不要再交替地称之为"货物"和"物品"。保持用词一致性比避免重复更加重要。别担心把读者催眠了，要担心的是一年后对方律师因为你的合同含糊不清而把你告上法庭。

㉒考虑法律的选择、地点或仲裁的选择，以及律师费用条款。

㉓通过大写来定义一个词，并用引号把它标出。将词语的开头字母大写以表明它有特别的意义。以下是两个术语定义的例子：

凡在本合同中使用的"合同货物"，指买方已同意向卖方购买的货物。

据此买方同意向卖方购买的拾（10）套机床，为以下文中所称的"合同货物"。

㉔在合同开头或第一次使用的时候定义术语或词汇。这将避免对术语的含义产生误解或不同的解释。

㉕解释技术术语和概念。记住，合同双方可能会理解合同中的术语，但是法官和陪审团却不懂合同中的术语。因此，要解释合同中的术语和概念本身。

㉖手动检查，并用计算机的拼写和语法检查器检查合同中的拼写、段落编号和交叉引用。如今，毫无疑问地，当你打字的时候，计算机的文字处理器就在检查你的拼写和语法。但不要简单地信任你的计算机，如果你没有密切关注它，有时它也可能作出错误的修改。

㉗让你的秘书或法律助理阅读合同。你的员工不仅会经常发现拼写和语法错误——这些错误是你的计算机的拼写和语法检查器遗漏的，他们还会找到你起草合同时没有察觉到的矛盾和混淆之处。

㉘用80克而不是70克的复印纸打印合同。使用更重的纸使合同正本和副本更易于辨别。而且这样合同保存的时间会更长。

㉙使用同样的纸打印页面，如果页面内容改变，使用相同的纸重印文档。这将避免合同签署后页面被偷换的争议。

㉚确定当事人和证人，他们在合同签名栏下方留下的一些空白行上签下他们印刷的名字和地址。一旦合同发生纠纷，这将更易于找到证人。

㉛公司的管理人员一定要签上他们的头衔、公司名字。未能这样做会导致该管理人员个人责任的缺失。签名的正确方法如下：

ABC公司，佛罗里达公司

董事长：约翰·琼斯

6.3.2.2　Tips for Reviewing a Business Contract
审核商务合同的提示

In situations where you do not generate the form of the contract but are entering into an agreement with another business or individual, you should typically:

① Read the contract over carefully and highlight anything that is ambiguous or vaguely worded for further clarification and/or possible deletion.

② List any additions you feel are necessary to include in the contract.

③ Discuss all changes to the contract with the other party or parties.

④ Make sure any requested and orally agreed changes have been added to the contract prior to signing as oral agreements can be very tricky and are not always binding.

⑤ Consult an attorney, especially if the agreement is complicated.

当你还没有生成合同形式，但正要与另一个企业或个人签订协议的时候，你通常应该：

① 仔细阅读合同，对任何含糊不清以至于需要进一步说明和/或可能需要删除的地方作突出标记。

② 列出你认为合同中有必要增加的内容。

③ 与另一方或各方讨论合同的所有更改内容。

④ 因为签订口头协议是非常复杂的，并且不总是具有约束力，所以签名前确保任何请求和口头同意的更改已经被添加到合同中。

⑤ 咨询律师,尤其在协议很复杂的时候。

6.3.2.3　Tips for Negotiating a Business Contract
商务合同谈判的提示

Certain fundamental strategies will assist you in the day-to-day negotiation that all business persons perform, in contracts and other business transactions. The following are a few suggestions to get you started on the road to effective negotiation tactics.

① Always have clear objectives. It helps to make a list of goals before meeting the other.

② It is important to go to a negotiation having done your research. Know relevant law, facts, and figures.

③ Consider what you really need to get from the other party, and decide in what areas you are willing to compromise.

④ Build trust with the other party. Trust will aid communication.

⑤ You may want to have a first draft of a written agreement before meeting with the other party.

⑥ Try to keep the discussion ordered when meeting with the other party. Make a checklist of topics that should be reached during the negotiation.

⑦ Listen to the other party and their concerns.

在合同和其他商务交易中，某些基本策略将有助于你进行日常谈判，这是所有商人都会做的。以下的一些建议可以为你开启有效谈判的大门。

① 总是有明确的目标。会见另一方之前列出目标清单会对你有所帮助。

② 在谈判之前作一些研究很重要。要了解相关法律、事实和数据。

③ 考虑你真正需要从另一方那里得到什么,并决定在哪些方面你愿意妥协。

④ 与对方建立信任。信任将有助于沟通。

⑤ 与对方会面之前,你可能需要一份协议的书面初稿。

⑥ 当会见另一方时,尽量保持讨论次序。列出一个在谈判过程中需要达成的话题清单。

⑦ 倾听对方及他们的关注点。

6.3.2.4 Tips for Signing a Business Contract
签署商务合同的建议

① Proofread or double-check the contract manually prior to signing.

② All parties should sign the contract, including business titles if applicable.

③ In addition to the formal signatures of all parties on the signature page or signature block of the contract, also initial every page of the contract. Having each party initial each page of the contract will make it less likely that anyone could claim a page was changed after the contract was signed.

④ If the contract is not signed by all parties at the same time in a same place, you should try to let other parties to sign the contract first.

⑤ Pages of the contract should be numbered. Avoid the appearance that pages could have been added after the agreement was signed.

⑥ Sign the contract in blue ink, not black ink. This, too, will make it easier to differentiate the signed original contract from photocopies.

⑦ Under any circumstances, keep a signed original copy of every contract that you signed.

① 签署合同前，手工校对或再次核对合同。

② 各方应在合同上签名，如适用，签名应包括商务头衔。

③ 各方当事人除了在合同签名页或签名区正式签名外，也应在合同的每一页用姓名的首字母签名。这样做可以防止有人怀疑合同在签署后被更改过。

④ 如果合同各方不能在同一时间在同一个地方签名，你应该试着让其他方先签名。

⑤ 合同页码应编号，避免在协议签订之后还能添加页面。

⑥ 用蓝墨水而不是黑墨水签署合同。这也能让你更容易地区分出哪个是合同正本，哪个是影印副本。

⑦ 在任何情况下，都要保留一份你签署的合同的正本。

6.3.2.5 Procedures of Drafting a Business Contract
起草商务合同的步骤

The following twelve steps in drafting a business contract are the key to success in your business transaction.

① Label the document. Use the terms "Contract" or "Agreement" to distinguish your contract from other legal documents in your files.

② Separate the document parts into segments that identify each paragraph's purpose or intent. Label these segments with numbers or letters to clarify them from one another.

③ List the parties involved in the contract. Include contact information as you list the parties. As you refer to the parties later in the contract, you can shorten their identification or names.

④ Write out the purposes of the contract prior to providing the details. The purposes include the services provided, the product created, the labor exerted or any other focuses that pertain to the purposes of the agreement.

⑤ Indicate any monetary issues. These may include cost payment arrangements or interest charges for late or deferred payments. Due dates and amounts should be addressed with specific information. For instance, if a payment is due in the middle of the month, the contract should say "by the 15th of the month".

⑥ Identify all deadlines associated with the contract along with the contract enactment date. Project completion, product delivery or other timelines should be clearly written out for the protection of all parties within the contract.

⑦ Explain the expiration date, along with any renewal terms, if applicable. Many contracts expire, such as lease agreements. The details of the expiration should be explained in detail.

⑧ Write any consequences for the breach of contract for both parties into the contract. Consequences often include payment for services not rendered, reimbursement for damages and automatic termination of the contract. It includes details about all consequences and possible consequences of breach of contract.

⑨Include a confidentiality clause if any part of the partnership should be kept private. Many transactions should not be open to the public. A confidentiality clause prevents either party from sharing details about the contract and the business partnership.

⑩ Consider a mediation and arbitration clause. In the event of a dispute, it may be advantageous to include a provision that requires the parties to enter either mediation or arbitration, or both. Mediation is a voluntary process where both parties try to work out their issues directly, with the help of a neutral third party mediator. Arbitration is a more adversarial process where the arbitrator (sometimes a panel of arbitrators) hears both sides' arguments and makes a decision that both parties must abide by.

⑪Provide termination conditions. Most contracts can be terminated through modifications or other requests. Write specifics about how the contract may be terminated and any consequence that might result from the termination.

⑫Create signature lines for all parties of the contract. Provide space for printed names and dates along with an area for a witness signature. Require that all parties sign the contract before it can be enacted.

以下起草商务合同的12个步骤是你交易成功的关键。

① 给文档贴上标签。在你的文件里，使用术语"合同"或"协议"来区分合同和其他法律文件。

② 找出每一段的目的或意图，将文件分成几个部分。用数字或字母给这些部分贴上标签以区分它们。

③ 列出合同当事人，并像列出当事人信息一样列出合同信息。如果你在之后的合同中还要提到当事人，可以简化他们的身份证明或名字。

④ 在提供细节之前，先把合同的目的写清楚。目的包括所提供的服务、所制造的产品、所使用的劳动力或与本协议目的相关的任何其他重点内容。

⑤ 标明任何货币问题。这些可能包括成本支付安排或逾期、延期付款的利息费用。

到期日和金额应注明具体信息。例如,如果付款是在本月中旬到期,合同中就应该写明"到本月 15 日"。

⑥ 确定所有与合同相关的到期日及合同生效日期。为了保护各方利益,在合同中应明确写入项目完成时间、产品交付时间或其他的时间期限。

⑦ 解释到期日期,以及任何续期条款(如果适用)。许多合同涉及到期问题,如租赁协议。对过期问题的细节应该详细解释。

⑧将双方违约的后果写进合同中。后果通常包括未提供服务的费用、损害赔偿,以及合同的自动终止。内容应包括一切后果的详细信息和违约可能带来的后果。

⑨如果合作方应保密的话,合同应包括保密条款。许多交易都不应该对公众开放。保密条款能够防止任何一方分享关于合同和其业务伙伴的细节信息。

⑩考虑添加调解和仲裁条款。在发生纠纷时,如果合同中有这个条款可以要求当事人调解或仲裁,或两者兼而有之,这样会更好一些。调解是一个自愿的过程,在一个中立的第三方中介的帮助下双方都试图直接地解决他们的问题。仲裁是一个更具对抗性的过程,仲裁员(有时是一个仲裁员小组)听取双方的观点,然后作出双方必须遵守的决定。

⑪提供终止条件。大多数合同可以因修改或其他请求终止。将终止合同的方式及终止合同可能带来的后果写进合同。

⑫为合同各方创建签名行。提供打印姓名和日期的空间,以及供证人签名的区域。要求各方在合同生效前签字。

6.3.3   *Common Clauses in International Business Contracts*
国际商务合同中的基本条款

6.3.3.1   Name of Commodity and Quality Clauses
品名与品质条款

Both parties in international trade of goods should not only specify the name of the commodity, but also specify its specific quality. Otherwise there is no way to confirm the material basis of the sales contract, and the transaction will not normally perform.

(1)**Name of Commodity**

The name of the commodity, namely contract mark, is indispensable to constituting a valid contract. In accordance with relevant laws and practices, the name of the commodity is a description of the commodity, which constitutes a major part of the commodity description. It is the basis of the transfer of goods between the seller and the buyer and it is related to the rights and obligations of buyers and sellers. If the seller's delivery of the goods does not conform to the provisions of the contract or the name of the specification, the buyer shall have the right to refuse, cancel the contract and claim damages. Therefore, to clear the name of the goods in the contract has an important role of law.

E.g.: Name of Commodity: High-Quality Rice.

(2)**Quality of the Goods**

The quality of the goods refers to the synthesis of inner quality and appearance of the commodity. The quality of the goods will not only affect the selling price and market, but also affect an enterprise and even a country's reputation. Quality conditions of the contract are an important part of the commodity description and the basis of the transfer of goods between the seller and the buyer. In international trade, there is a wide variety of goods with different characteristics. Therefore, there are many ways to express quality. To sum up, there are two categories and seven subcategories represented by physical and statement.

①Sale by sample.

E.g.: Quality should strictly comply with the sample supplied by the seller on June 5, 2016, the sample label: HM06 stuffed toy doll.

②Sale by specification.

E.g.: Bleached cotton cloth 30×36 count, 72×69.38 inches×121.5 yards.

③Sale by grade.

E.g.: The northeast rice, A grade quality.

④Sale by standard.

E.g.: The northeast soybeans, fair average quality.

⑤Sale by descriptions and illustrations.

E.g.: The quality and technical data must be strictly in conformity with product specifications provided by the seller.

⑥Sale by brand name or trademark.

E.g.: Lining sneakers.

⑦Sale by the name of origin.

E.g.: Shaoxing carved wine.

国际货物买卖双方在进行交易时，不仅应明确货物的名称，还要规定其具体品质，否则就无从肯定买卖合同的物质基础，交易也就无法正常进行。

（1）品名

品名即合同标的，是构成有效合同不可缺少的条件。有关法律与惯例都有规定，品名是对成交商品的描述，是构成商品说明的一个主要组成部分，是买卖双方交接货物的依据，它关系到买卖双方的权利和义务。如果卖方交付的货物不符合合同规定的名称或说明，买方有权拒收、撤销合同并要求损害赔偿。因此，在合同中明确货物的名称具有重要的法律作用。

例：品名：优质大米。

（2）商品的品质

商品的品质是指商品的内在素质和外观形态的综合。商品的品质的好坏不仅会影响其销售价格和销路，还会影响一个企业乃至一个国家的声誉。合同中的品质条件是构成商品说明的重要组成部分，是买卖双方交接货物的依据。在国际贸易中，商品种类繁多、特点各异，所以表示品质的方法也多种多样。归纳起来，商品种类包括凭实物表示和凭说明表示的两大类、七小类。

①凭样品买卖。

例：质量应严格符合卖方于2016年6月5日提供的样品质量标准，样品标号：HM06

填充玩具娃娃。

②凭规格买卖。

例：漂白棉布30支×36支，72英寸×69.38英寸×121.5码。

③凭等级买卖。

例：东北大米，一级品。

④凭标准买卖。

例：东北大豆，良好平均品质。

⑤凭说明书买卖。

例：品质和技术数据必须与卖方所提供的产品说明书严格相符。

⑥凭商标或品牌买卖。

例：李宁运动鞋。

⑦凭产地名称买卖。

例：绍兴花雕酒。

6.3.3.2　Quantity Clauses
数量条款

In international business, because the cargo types, features, and country's weights and measures are different, calculation units and calculation methods are also diverse.

(1)Kinds of Quantity Clauses

According to the nature of the commodity and different measuring units, there are six kinds of common quantity clauses in the contract.

①Weight.

To conclude a deal according to weight, the commonly used units are: Gram, KG or Kilogram, Ounce, Pound, Metric Ton, Long Ton, Short Ton, etc. Weight units are commonly used in general natural products, such as wool, cotton, grain, minerals, oil, salt and medicine, etc. and some industrial products.

E.g.: iron ore, 5,000 metric tons.

②Capacity.

Volumetric units mainly include: Litre, Gallons, Bushel, etc. Transactions of grain and some of the fluid, gas items, etc. commonly use this kind of measurement unit, such as wheat, corn, kerosene, gasoline, beer, hydrogen peroxide, and natural gas, etc.

E.g.: gasoline, 1,000 litres.

③Number.

Number units are: Piece, Pair, Set, Dozen, Gross, Ream, Roll, Coil, etc. Number units are often used in general daily industrial products, as well as grocery products, such as stationery, paper, toys, automobiles, tractors, and live animals.

E.g.: shirt, 1,000 Pieces.

④Length.

Units in transactions according to the length are: Meter, Foot, Yard, etc. This kind of unit is mostly used in the trade of gold folded rope, textiles, wire and cable, etc.

E.g.: white bleached cloth, 5,000 feet.

⑤Area.

Units in transactions according to measurement are: Square Meter, Square Foot, Square Yard, etc. Area units are used for wood, glass, carpets, wire and other goods, and some still need to illustrate thickness, such as wood.

E.g.: compound floor, 1,000 square feet.

⑥Volume.

Volume measurement units are: Cubic Meter, Cubic Foot, Cubic Yard, Cubic Inch, etc. Trading goods in volume as the calculating unit are not much, mainly are chemical gas and wood, etc.

E.g.: gas, 2,000 cubic meters.

(2)Quantity Allowance

In actual import and export business, sometimes due to the nature of the product, the quantity concluded, natural conditions, packing, loading and unloading capacity and means of transport and other factors, the quantity of actual delivery goods of the seller often can not completely conform to a certain number of the provisions of the contract. To make the contract be performed smoothly, and avoid disputes in delivery quantity in the future, for some goods with large volume and difficult to calculate accurately, such as wheat, soybeans, corn, coal, ore, crude oil, etc., both the seller and the buyer also often illustrate the quantity allowance of the delivery goods in the contract. There are two kinds of methods: one is the weight tolerance, the second is the approximate quantity.

①More or less clauses.

More or less clauses refer to the more or less percentage which can be specified in the quantity clauses in the sales contract, but the more or less range is not more than a certain percentage. For example, 100,000 yards, 5% more or less at the seller's option. More or less clauses can also be replaced by symbols of plus or minus.

The main content of more or less clauses is: the more or less percentage, the more or less options, the price for the more or less parts. It is the seller that decides more or less, i.e. at Seller's Option. But in the case of a ship dispatched by the buyer, to adapt to the ship loading ability, it can also be specified by the buyer (at Buyer's Option). In the FOB contract, such as, the buyer abroad often requires to determine the more or less loading in the mobile range. In special cases, some more or less loading of bulk cargoes can be chosen by the ship. The pricing of the more or less part can be counted according to the market price if it is not specified. On the contrary, it can be calculated according to the contract price.

②About/circa/approximate clauses.

Approximate clauses refer to the quantity allowance of adding the word "about" before the delivery quantity. But in the world, there are different interpretations of the meaning of the word "about", some interpreted as 2.5%, some interpreted as 5%. In order to prevent disputes in the future, it should be explicitly stipulated in the contract when both parties negotiate.

在国际贸易中，由于货物的种类、特性和各国度量衡的不同，计算单位和计算方法也多种多样。

（1）数量条款的种类

根据商品性质和计量单位的不同，合同中常用的数量条款有以下六种。

①重量。

按重量交易，其常用单位有克、千克、盎司、磅、公吨、长吨、短吨等。重量单位多应用于一般天然产品（如羊毛、棉花、谷物、矿产品、油类、盐及药品等）及部分工业制品。

例：铁矿石，5 000公吨。

②容积。

容积的计量单位主要有升、加仑、蒲式耳等。谷物类及部分流体、气体物品等交易一般采用此种单位计量，如小麦、玉米、煤油、汽油、啤酒、过氧化氢及天然气等。

例：汽油，1 000升。

③数量。

数量的计量单位有件、双、组、打、篓、令、卷、捆等。数量单位常用于一般日用工业制品，以及杂货类产品，如文具、纸张、玩具、车辆、拖拉机及活牲畜等。

例：衬衫，1 000件。

④长度。

交易中使用的长度计量单位有米、英尺、码等。这种单位多用于金属绳索、纺织品、电线、电缆等交易。

例：白色漂布，5 000英尺。

⑤面积。

交易中使用的面积计量单位有平方米、平方英尺、平方码等。面积单位多用于木板、玻璃、地毯、铁丝等货物，有的还需要另列厚度，如木板。

例：复合地板，1 000平方英尺。

⑥体积。

体积的计量单位有：立方米、立方英尺、立方码、立方英寸等。以体积为计算单位的交易商品不多，主要是化学气体、木材等。

例：天然气，2 000立方米。

（2）数量机动幅度

在实际进出口业务中，有时由于产品的特性、成交的数量、自然条件、包装方式、装卸能力及运输工具等多种因素的限制，卖方实际交货的数量常常不能完全符合合同规定的某一数量。为使合同能顺利履行，避免日后因交货数量而发生争议，对于某些成交数量大、计算不易准确的货物，如小麦、大豆、玉米、煤炭、矿石及原油等，买卖双方还常在合同数量条款中阐明交货数量的机动幅度，具体有两种方法：一是溢短装；二是约量。

①溢短装条款。

溢短装条款是指在买卖合同的数量条款中明确可以增减的百分比，但增减幅度以不超过某一百分比为限。例如，100 000码，卖方可溢装或短装5%。溢短装条款也可用增加或减少符号代替。

溢短装条款的主要内容有溢短装的百分比、溢短装的选择权、溢短装部分的作价。溢短装条款一般规定由卖方决定是溢装还是短装，即卖方选择。但是在由买方派船装运的情况下，为了便于适应船的装载能力，也可规定由买方决定。例如，在FOB合同中，国外买方往往要求在机动幅度内由他们决定多装或少装的数量。在特殊情况下，某些散装货可由船方选择。对于溢短装部分的作价办法，如果没有指定价格，可按装船时或货到时的市价计算；反之，可按合同价格计算。

②约量条款。

约量条款即在交货数量前加"约"字以表示机动幅度。但国际上对"约"字的含义解释不一，有的解释为浮动2.5%，有的解释为浮动5%。为防止日后发生纠纷，交易双方协商时应在合同中对其作出明确规定。

6.3.3.3　Price and Payment Clauses
价格与支付条款

Price clauses are mainly composed of four parts: the currency of amount, unit, unit price and trade terms, which specify goods. In addition to the four basic contents, if buyers and sellers in the trade also involve the provisions of the commission and discount, corresponding provisions should also be made. International trade terms are often used to indicate the unit price of goods, for example, in the regulation of unit price of USD 500 per metric ton CIF New York, the weight of the unit is metric tons, the currency is dollars, the unit price is USD 500, the port of destination is New York, the price structure is the cost plus freight and insurance of the goods. The total amount of sales of goods contract is the unit price multiplied by the number of traded goods. Price clauses are the main basis for determining the buyer's payment obligation.

(1)Price

Because the stability of the currency is affected by various factors, if you use a foreign currency settlement, the currency exchange rate must be agreed in advance in the contract, in order to avoid exchange rate risk in the future.

E.g.1: Unit price: USD 145.00 FOB trimmed Qinhuangdao per metric ton and based on 6%–10% if the percentage of ash contents is lower than 6%, 10 (ten) pence will be added to the unit price for every one percentage and if the percentage of ash contents is higher than 10%, 10 (ten) pence will be deducted from the unit price for every one percent. Any portion, which is less than one percent, will be taken into account according to the above-mentioned proportion.

E.g.2: Unit price: USD 1, 890.00 per metric ton CFR Huangpu.

(2)Payment

Due to various reasons, each company's finance department has a time limit for payment. Many companies, especially large ones, have strict control over the payment process, and the payment of a sum may have to go through several links for examination. In addition, the contract of foreign currency payment needs to obtain tax payment or tax exemption certificates issued by the tax bureau, and the tax bureau needs a certain amount of time for review. Therefore, it is necessary to remind the parties concerned to pay attention to the payment time, which should not be too short. Otherwise, it may cause a delayed payment in the future, which may not only lead to a penalty due to breach of contract, but also impact the company's credibility.

E.g.1: The Buyers shall open through a bank acceptable to the Sellers an Irrevocable Sight Letter of Credit to reach the Sellers 30 days before the shipment, valid for negotiation in China until the 15th day after the month of shipment.

E.g.2: Payment should be made by Irrevocable Letter of Credit for 90% of the total invoice value of the goods to be shipped, in favor of the Sellers, payable at the issuing bank against the Seller's draft at sight accompanied by the shipping documents stipulated in the Credit. The balance of 10% of the proceeds is to be paid only after the goods have been inspected and proved at the port of destination.

价格条款主要由规定货物的计价货币、计价单位、单价和贸易术语四部分组成。除了四项基本内容外，如买卖双方在交易中还涉及佣金与折扣，也应作出相应的规定。国际贸易术语常常被用来表示货物的单价。例如，"每公吨500美元CIF纽约"的单价中，重量的单位是公吨，计价货币是美元，单位价格金额是500美元，目的港是纽约，价格构成是货物的成本加运费和保险费。货物买卖合同的总价是以单价乘以交易商品的数量。价格条款是确定买方支付义务的主要依据。

（1）价格

由于计价货币的稳定性受各种因素的影响，所以如果使用外币结算，那么一定要在合同中事先约定该货币的汇率，以避免日后的汇率风险。

例1：单价：每公吨145.00美元秦皇岛港FOB价（理舱费），条件是粉尘含量在6%~10%之间。如果粉尘含量低于6%，每低一个百分点，价格提高10便士；如果粉尘含量高于10%，每高一个百分点，价格降低10便士。少于1%的部分根据上面提到的比例给予考虑。

例2：单价：每公吨成本加运费到黄埔港价格1 890.00美元。

（2）支付

由于种种原因，每个公司的财务部都会对支付时间有要求。很多公司，特别是大公司，对支付的流程控制得很严格，一笔款项的支付可能需要通过好几个环节审批。此外，由外币付款的合同需要先取得税务局签发的完税凭证或免税凭证，而税务局需要一定的时间进行审核。因此，需要提醒当事人注意支付的时限不能过短；否则，可能造成日后的支付延迟，不仅可能产生违约金，而且会给公司的信誉造成影响。

例1：买方应在装运前30天通过卖方可接受的银行开立不可撤销的即期信用证并送达卖方，至装运月份后15天在中国议付有效。

例2：按运输货物金额的90%开立以卖方为受益人的不可撤销的信用证，凭卖方即期汇票向银行议付，其余10%的货款在货物到达目的港检验合格后付清。

6.3.3.4 Packing Clauses
包装条款

Packing clauses generally include packaging materials and ways of packaging. For example: in international standard tea boxes, 20 boxes on a pallet, 10 pallets in a container.

The following needs to be paid attention to:

① The packing clauses shall be specific.

② Choose the packing element according to the goods' characteristics and different modes of transportation.

③ Clarify the related matters of packaging materials supplied and cost burden.

④ Clarify the packing count and its proportion.

⑤ Clarify the specific marks. According to the convention on international trade, shipping mark generally is specified by the seller, and it is not necessary to make specific provisions in the contract.

⑥ Issues of brand, no brand and neutral packing.

⑦ Specify the suitable current laws and regulations of relevant countries and regions.

包装条款一般包括包装材料和包装方式。

例：国际标准茶叶，纸箱装，20纸箱一托盘，10托盘一集装箱。

订立包装条款需要注意以下问题：

①包装条款应明确具体。

②要结合货物特点和不同运输方式选择包装要素。

③明确包装材料的提供与费用负担的相关事项。

④明确装箱系数及配比。

⑤明确唛头的指定。按照国际贸易惯例，唛头一般由卖方指定，不必在合同中作出具体规定。

⑥定牌、无牌和中性包装问题。

⑦明确有关国家和地区的现行法律、法规。

6.3.3.5 Shipment Terms
装运条款

The shipment terms in the contract usually include the time of shipment, the port of loading and the port of destination, partial shipment and transshipment, shipping advice, demurrage and dispatch clauses, etc. Examples of common terms of shipment are as follows:

E.g.1: Shipment during Aug./Sep. 202× in two about equal lots, transshipment allowed.

E.g.2: Shipment during Mar./Apr./May with partial shipment and transshipment allowed.

E. g. 3: Shipment within 45 days after receipt of the L/C. The buyers must open the L/C to reach the sellers before ×× (date).

E. g. 4: Shipment before Aug. 202× from Shanghai via Hong Kong to London by container vessel. 5,000 M/T shipment to be effected in three equal consignments at an interval of about 20 days.

合同中的装运条款通常包括装运时间、装运港（地）和目的港（地）、分批装运和转运、装运通知、滞期和速遣条款等内容。常见的装运条款示例如下：

例1：202×年8/9月份分两批平均装运，允许转运。

例2：3/4/5月份装运，允许分批装运和转运。

例3：收到信用证后45天内装运，买方必须最迟于××（日期）将信用证开抵卖方。

例4：202×年8月前装运，由上海经香港至伦敦集装箱运输，5 000公吨分三批等量装运，每批相隔20天。

6.3.3.6　Insurance Clauses
保险条款

In the import and export business, when CIF or CIP terms are used in export contracts and FOB, CFR are used in import contracts, or FCA, CPT terms are used, insurance formalities and contract matters will be dealt with by us.

① In contracts concluded under FOB, CFR or FCA, CPT term, the buyer is responsible for the insurance and insurance premium payment. Because it does not involve the interests of the seller, the insurance clause in the sales contract may be specified as:"Insurance to be effected by the buyer." If the seller entrusts the buyer to cover the insurance, the insurance amount, the insurance coverage, the applicable insurance clauses and insurance premium which shall be borne by the buyer, shall be expressly provided.

② In the contract concluded under CIF or CIP trade terms, the buyer is responsible for the risk of the transportation from the port of shipment to the port of destination, and the seller is responsible for the insurance and insurance premium payment. Insurance involves the interests of buyers and sellers, therefore, insurance clauses in the sales contract should explicitly stipulate the following four contents: who deal with insurance, the insurance coverage, the insured amount, the applicable clauses. For example, in the prescribed clauses in the contract: "Insurance to be covered by the sellers for ××% of total invoice value against ×× as per and subject to the relevant Ocean Marine Cargo (Clauses of the People's Insurance Company of China dated 1/1/1981)."

If the buyer requires to cover insurance in accordance with the London Institute Insurance Clauses, then the insurance clause in the contract should be as follows: "Insurance to be covered by the sellers for ××% of total invoice value against ×× as per Institute Cargo (Clauses ×× dated 1/1/1982)."

在进出口业务中，当出口合同使用CIF或CIP术语，进口合同使用FOB、CFR术语或FCA、CPT术语时，保险手续及合同事宜由我方办理。

① 以FOB、CFR或FCA、CPT等贸易术语成交的合同，买方负责办理保险并支付保险费。由于不涉及卖方的利益，因此买卖合同中的保险条款可规定为："保险由买方负责。"如果卖方委托买方代为投保，则应明确规定保险金额、保险险别、适用的保险条款，以及保险费由买方承担等问题。

② 以CIF或CIP贸易术语成交的合同，买方承担货物自装运港（地）至目的港（地）运输途中的风险，而卖方负责办理保险、支付保险费。保险涉及买卖双方的利益，因此，在销售合同的保险条款中应明确规定下列四项内容：谁办理保险、保险险别、保险金额、适用的保险条款。例如，在合同的保险条款中订明："保险由卖方按发票金额的××%投保××险（险别），××险以中国人民保险公司1981年1月1日的海洋运输货物保险条款为准。"

如果买方要求按照伦敦保险协会保险条款投保，则合同中的保险条款为："保险由卖方按发票金额的××%投保××险（险别），××险按照伦敦保险协会1982年1月1日货物××险条款负责。"

6.3.3.7　Means of Payment Terms
　　　　　付款方式

At present, there are three payment modes mainly used in Chinese import and export business: remittance, collection and L/C. In addition, the buyer can also use bank guarantee, standby letter of credit, international factoring services, and the combination of several methods used for payment. Payment terms' samples are as follows:

(1)Remittance Payment Terms

E.g.1: The buyers shall pay 100% of the sales proceeds in advance by demand draft to reach the sellers not later than June 25.

E.g.2: The buyers shall pay 30% of the sales proceeds by telegraphic transfer. The remaining part will be paid to the sellers within 5 days after receipt of the fax concerning original B/L by the buyers.

(2)Collection Payment Terms

E.g.1: Upon the first presentation, the buyers shall pay against the documentary draft drawn by the sellers at sight. The shipping documents are to be delivered against payment only.

E.g.2: The buyers shall duly accept the documentary draft drawn by the sellers at 90 days sight upon the first presentation and make payment on its maturity. The shipping documents are to be delivered against acceptance after it has been made.

(3)L/C Payment Terms

E.g.1: By confirmed irrevocable L/C for 100% invoice value available by sight draft. The L/C is to reach sellers not later than May 20.

E.g.2: By irrevocable L/C available by the seller's documentary draft at ×× days after sight, to be valid for negotiation in China until the 15th day after the date of shipment. The L/C must reach the sellers 30 days before the contracted month of shipment.

目前，我国进出口业务中所使用的支付方式主要是汇款、托收和信用证三种方式。此外，买方还可以采用银行保函、备用信用证、国际保理服务，以及这几种方法的结合来进行支付。支付条款示例如下：

（1）汇款支付条款

例1：买方应不迟于6月25日用即期汇票的方式将100%的货款预付至卖方。

例2：买方应于4月20日前将30%的货款电汇至卖方，其余货款于收到正本提单传真后5日内支付。

（2）托收支付条款

例1：买方根据卖方开具的即期跟单汇票，于见票时立即付款，付款后交单。

例2：买方根据卖方开具的见票后90天内付款的跟单汇票，于提示时承兑，并于汇票到期日付款，承兑后交单。

（3）信用证支付条款

例1：100%保兑的、不可撤销的即期信用证，必须于5月20日前开出并抵达卖方。

例2：以不可撤销信用证，凭卖方开具的见票后××天付款的跟单汇票，有效期限为装运期后15天，在中国议付。该信用证必须于合同规定的装运月份前30天到达卖方。

6.3.3.8　Inspection Clauses
检验条款

Goods inspection is the indispensable important link in international sales of goods when both parties hand over goods. It provides the basis for claims and settlement between the buyer and the seller to resolve disputes and claims, it is also one of the basis for exchanging goods and making payment. The inspection clause is an important clause in an international contract.

E. g.: Certificate of quality/weight/quantity to be issued by the General Administration of Customs of the People's Republic of China shall be taken as final.

货物检验是国际货物买卖中交易双方交接货物时必不可少的重要环节，它为解决买卖双方的争议提供索赔和理赔的依据，同时它也是交换货物和支付货款的依据之一。货物检验条款是国际贸易合同中的一项重要条款。

例：以中华人民共和国海关总署出具的质量/重量/数量证书为最后依据。

6.3.3.9　Dispute and Claim Clauses
争议与索赔条款

In the import and export business, if the goods received by the buyer do not conform to the provisions of the contract or are damaged due to human, natural disasters or other reasons, the buyer shall ask for compensation from the relevant aspects according to the responsibility to compensate for the losses which also include expected losses. There are also some claims made by the seller against the buyer for non-performance of the contract, such as failure to open the L/C on schedule, etc.

E.g.: The certificate of quality and quantity (weight) issued by the General Administration of Customs of the People's Republic of China shall be part of the documents to be presented for negotiation under the relevant letter of credit. Any claim by the buyers regarding the goods shipped shall be filed within ×× days after the arrival of the goods at the port of destination, and supported by a survey report issued by a surveyor approved by the sellers.

在进出口业务中，由于人为、天灾或其他种种原因，而使买方收到的货物不符合合同规定或货物遭受损害，买方依据其责任的归属，向有关方面提出赔偿的要求，以弥补其所受的损失，这种损失也包括期望损失。也有因买方不履行合同，如不按期开立信用证等，而引起卖方向买方提出索赔的情况。

例：中华人民共和国海关总署签发的品质、数量（重量）检验证书应作为有关信用证项下议付所提交单据的一部分。买方对于装运货物的任何索赔，必须于货物到达目的港××天内提出，并需要提供经卖方同意的公证机构出具的检验报告。

6.3.3.10 Arbitration Clauses
仲裁条款

In foreign trade, when the parties to the dispute can not solve the problem through friendly consultations, they usually adopt the method of arbitration. Arbitration clauses generally include five aspects of content: the place of arbitration, the arbitration organization, the arbitration proceedings, the validity of arbitral awards, and arbitration fee burden and so on.

E.g.1: Arbitration clauses which the arbitration takes place in our country: "About disputes in the implementation of this contract or in connection with this contract, both parties shall settle them through friendly negotiation, in case no settlement can be reached, it shall be submitted to the China International Economic and Trade Arbitration Commission to arbitrate according to its rules of arbitration procedure, and the award of the arbitration shall be final and binding upon both parties."

E.g.2: Arbitration clauses which the arbitration takes place in the countries of the defendant: "About disputes in the implementation of this contract or in connection with this contract, both parties shall settle them through friendly negotiation, in case no settlement can be reached, the dispute shall be submitted to arbitration. The arbitration will take place in the defendant's country. In China, it will be arbitrated by the China International Economic and Trade Arbitration Commission for arbitration according to the rules of arbitration procedure. It will be arbitrated in the country ×× (the other party's country name), by ×× (the other party's arbitration organization) under the arbitration rules of procedure of the organization. The award of the arbitration shall be final and binding upon both parties."

E. g. 3: Arbitration clauses which the arbitration takes place in a third country: "About disputes in the implementation of this contract or in connection with this contract, both parties shall settle them through friendly negotiation. In case no settlement can be reached, the dispute shall be submitted to ×× (a third country) by ×× country's arbitration institutions, according to the rules of procedure of the arbitration organization for arbitration. The arbitral award is final and binding upon both parties."

在对外贸易中，当争议双方通过友好协商不能解决问题时，一般采取仲裁的方式来解决。仲裁条款一般包括仲裁地点、仲裁机构、仲裁程序、仲裁裁决的效力和仲裁费用的负担等五个方面的内容。

例1：仲裁地点在我国的仲裁条款："凡因执行本合同所发生的或与本合同有关的一切争议，双方应通过友好协商解决。如果协商不能解决，应提交中国国际经济贸易仲裁委员会，根据其仲裁程序规则进行仲裁。仲裁裁决是终局性的，对双方均有约束力。"

例2：仲裁地点在被告国的仲裁条款："凡因执行本合同所发生的或与本合同有关的一切争议，双方应通过友好协商解决。如果协商不能解决，应提交仲裁。仲裁在被告人所在国进行。在中国，由中国国际经济贸易仲裁委员会根据其仲裁程序规则进行仲裁。在××国（对方所在国名称），由××（对方所在国仲裁机构）根据该组织的仲裁程序规则进行仲裁。仲裁裁决是终局性的，对双方均有约束力。"

例 3：仲裁地点在第三国的仲裁条款："凡因执行本合同所发生的或与本合同有关的一切争议，双方应通过友好协商解决。如协商不能解决，应提交××国（某第三国）由××国仲裁机构根据该仲裁机构的仲裁程序规则进行仲裁，仲裁裁决是终局性的，对双方都有约束力。"

6.3.3.11   Effectiveness Contract Clauses 合同的效力条款

Effectiveness contract clauses are mainly composed of two parts: The first is words used in the contract, copies of the contract, the effectiveness of the various texts；The second is the effective time of the contract, the validity of the modification and supplement of the contract and the effectiveness of the attachment of the contract (if any). It should also be stipulated in the contract that the attachment is an inalienable part of the contract. Otherwise, there are no conditions to constitute the attachment of the contract.

E. g. 1: The agreement is an integral part of Contract No. ×× for machinery and Contract No. ×× for feathers. Both parties shall carry out the terms and conditions agreed upon, and neither party shall terminate this agreement and the attached contracts until all stipulations contained therein have been carried out.

E. g. 2: The appendices attached hereto are hereby made an integral part of this contract and are equally binding on both parties.

E. g. 3: This contract is made out in both the Chinese and English languages, each in two originals and one original of each is held by Party A and Party B. In case of any discrepancies between the Chinese and the English copy, the English copy shall govern.

The effective date of the contract plays an important role in the contract. The contract text sometimes has plenty of modifications on the basis of the original. The contract's rights and obligations of both parties are calculated based on the effective date of the contract.

E. g. 4: This contract comes into effect on the first day of the engaged party's arrival at the ×× University and ceases to be effective at its expiration. If either party wishes to renew the contract, the other party shall be notified in writing one month before it expires. Upon agreement by both parties through consultation, a new contract may be signed between the two parties.

E. g. 5: The contract shall become effective as soon as it is signed by the two parties. The contract is valid for three years (from January 1, 2024 to December 31, 2026). This contract is renewable for a further period of two years upon mutual consent after consultation between the two parties.

E. g. 6: This contract, when duly signed by parties concerned, shall remain in force for two years to be effective from February 1, 2024 to January 31, 2025. If no written objection is raised by either party one month before its expiry, this contract will be automatically extended for another year. Should one of the parties fail to comply with the terms and conditions of this contract, the other party is entitled to terminate this contract.

If there is not an effective date stipulated in the contract, both parties' signing date (signing date of the later party) generally is the effective date of the contract. But sometimes the parties do not hope that the contract takes effect immediately, it is especially necessary to promise the effective date in the contract.

In addition to the specific expression for the date of the contract comes into effect, it can also be agreed that the effective starting point is the occurrence or non-occurrence of an event, which is equivalent to additional conditions which come into force only when conditions attached to set up the contract.

E.g.7: Effective date means the date on which the contract, after it is signed, be approved by the Ministry of Commerce of the People's Republic of China.

E.g.8: This Contract shall come into force after it has been approved by the examination and approval authority of China.

合同的效力条款主要由两部分组成：一是合同使用的文字、合同的份数、各种文本的效力；二是合同的生效时间、对合同修改补充的效力、合同附件（如果有）的效力。合同中还应规定"附件是合同不可分割的一部分"，否则不具备构成合同附件的条件。

例1：本协议是第××号机器合同和第××号羽绒合同不可分割的组成部分。双方应该执行所达成的全部条款。在全部条款执行完毕前，任何一方不得终止本协议和所附的合同。

例2：本合同所有附件为本合同不可分割的组成部分，对双方具有同等约束力。

例3：本合同用中文和英文两种文字写成，每种文字有正本两份，由甲乙双方各持一份。如中文版本与英文版本有异议，以英文版本为准。

合同的生效日期在合同中起着重要的作用。合同协议的文本有时会在原件的基础上有大量的修改。合同中约定合同双方享有的权利和承担的义务都是以合同的生效期作为计算基准日。

例4：本合同自受聘方到××大学之日起生效，到聘期届满时失效。如果一方要求延长聘期，必须在合同期满前一个月以书面形式向对方提出，经双方协商同意后另签延聘合同。

例5：本合同经双方签署后立即生效，其有效期为2年，自2024年1月1日起，至2026年12月31日止。本合同经双方协商同意时可以顺延两年。

例6：本合同经双方签署后立即生效，有效期为两年，自2024年2月1日起，至2025年1月31日止。期满前一个月如果双方均没有提出书面异议，本协议将自动延长一年。如一方未按本条款执行，另一方有权终止本协议。

如果合同中并未约定生效日期，双方签约日期（后一方的签约日期）一般作为合同的生效日期。但有时签约方并不希望合同立即生效，这就尤其有必要在合同中约定生效的日期。

除了以具体的日期表述合同生效日期外，还可以约定以某个事件的发生或者不发生为合同生效起点，相当于附加条件，只有在附加条件成立时合同才生效。

例7：生效日是中华人民共和国商务部批准之日。

例8：本合同经中国有关机构审批后生效。

6.3.3.12   Assignment Clauses
转让条款

Transfer of the contract refers to the transfer of contract rights and obligations. In accordance with the different contents of the assignment, the assignment of contract includes three types: transfer of contract rights, undertaking contract debt, and generalization of contract rights and obligations. Of course, the transfer may be in whole or in part. Because the transfer of the content is different, the condition and the effect are also different. Among the above three conditions, the first is a transfer of creditor's rights; the second is a transfer of debt; the third is the general assumption. The assignment of the contract reflects the features that the creditor - debtor relationship is the property of the dynamic relationship.

E.g.: If either Party A or Party B intends to assign all or part of its investment to a third party, it shall first offer such assignment to the other party which has the right to decide whether or not to acquire the investment of the other party within a period of three (3) months after receipt of the written notice of the party indicating its intention to assign. Upon expiry of the three (3)- month period referred to in the preceding paragraph, the party intending to assign all or part of its investment may assign such investment to the third party provided that:

① The other party has not exercised its preemptive right;

② The terms and conditions of such an assignment to a third party are not more favorable than those offered to the other party;

③ Approval from the examination and approval authority has been obtained for such an assignment.

No assignment shall be effective when there is any violation of the above stipulations.

When writing assignment clauses, the contract should clearly indicate the following:

① In addition to the prior written consent of the party, either party shall not transfer the rights and obligations of the contract to a third party.

② In case the other party transfers the contract to a third party without the other party's consent, it shall be stipulated that "the transfer shall be null and void if the aforesaid provisions are violated".

③ For a legitimate third party who accepts the rights and obligations under the contract, he can take his rights and obligations in accordance with the law. Therefore, it can be stipulated in the contract: "The contract binds upon the legal heirs of the parties or the transferees. After the transfer, the assignee enjoys all rights of the transferor, and undertakes all the obligations of the transferor."

合同转让，是指合同权利、义务的转让。按照所转让的内容不同，合同转让包括合同权利的让与、合同债务的承担以及合同权利与义务的概括转移三种类型。当然，转让可以是全部转让，也可以是部分转让。因为转让的内容有所差异，其条件和效力也有所不同。在上述三种情况中，第一种是债权转让；第二种是债务转移（债务承担）；第三种是概括承受。合同的转让体现了债权、债务关系是动态的财产关系这一特性。

例：如甲方或乙方要向第三方转让其全部或部分出资额，应事先向合营他方转让，合营他方在收到转让方发出书面转让通知之日起3个月内有权决定是否优先购买。在前款提及的3个月期限届满后，有意转让其全部或部分出资额的一方可将其出资额转让给第三方，但出让方须遵守下列各项规定：

①合营他方没有行使其优先购买权。

②向第三方转让出资额的条件不能比向合营他方转让的条件更优惠。

③转让已获审批机关批准。

如果违反上述规定的条款，合同转让无效。

在撰写合同转让条款时，应明确注明以下几点：

① 除事先取得一方的书面同意外，任何一方不得将本合同的权利与义务转让给第三方。

② 对于未经对方同意，另一方将合同转让给第三方的情况，应视为"违反上述规定，其转让无效"。

③ 对于按照合同规定接受合同权利和义务的合法的第三方来说，他可以依法享有和承担他的权利和义务。因此,合同中可以规定:"本合同对双方当事人的合法继承人或受让人均有约束力。转让后受让人享有让与人的一切权利，并承担让与人的一切义务。"

6.3.3.13 Guarantee Clauses
保证条款

Because the content involved is different, the content of the guarantee clauses of English business contracts is also different. The purpose of setting up the guarantee clauses in the international business contract is to supervise the parties to the contract to fulfill the obligations as stipulated in the contract in accordance with the contractual requirements, or to make creditors get certain economic compensation when the debtor fails to perform his obligations. Guarantee clauses are commonly found in international purchase contracts and international technology transfer contracts. In the international contract of buying and selling goods, the seller shall guarantee the quality, specification and nature of the goods.

E.g.1: The sellers shall guarantee that the commodity must be in conformity with the quality and specifications specified in this contract and Letter of Quality Guarantee. The guarantee period shall be 3 months after the arrival of the goods at the port of destination, and during the period the sellers shall be responsible for the damage due to the defects in designing and manufacturing of the manufacturer.

In technology trade contracts, guarantee clauses mainly safeguard the interests of the licensee and strengthen the responsibility of the licensor. Guarantee clauses include two contents: rights guarantee and technical guarantee. Rights guarantee refers that the technology transfer licensor warrants to the licensee that he is the lawful owner of the technology transfer which does not infringe the rights of any third party within the contract area. His technical data provided, which is complete, correct and effective, can achieve the purpose of the agreement. Technical know-how supplied by the licensor is safe and practical, can produce qualified contract products. Otherwise, the licensor should hand in, correct, or modify technology he provided within a time limit free of charge. Failure to hand in, correct, or modify on schedule, each day overdue will be fined. If the quality of the products is not up to the standard of the contract, the licensee shall have the right to refuse to pay fees: if someone is infringing, the licensor shall be responsible for the prosecution. If being charged, the licensor shall be responsible for the respondent.

E. g. 2: Party B guarantees that the document supplied by Party B shall be of the latest technical documentation being used by Party B. Party B shall also supply to Party A the technical information relevant to any development and improvement of the contract product during the validity term of the contract. Party B guarantees that the documentation supplied by Party B shall be complete, legible, and dispatched within the stipulated period in this contract.

If the documentation supplied by Party B is not in conformity with the stipulations in the Annex to this Contract, Party B shall within the shortest possible time but not later than thirty (30) days after the receipt of Party A's written notice, dispatch free of charge to Party A the missing or the correct and legible documents.

Investment recovery guarantee clauses stipulate provisions of investment recovery, recovery method and the recovery period. To ensure the investment recovery of foreign partners, the following methods can be used:

① During the first few years, both sides do not distribute profits and invest profit will be repaid to foreign collaborators;

② Both sides distribute certain profits with the depreciation funds to repay the foreign party's investment;

③ Mainly use depreciation funds to pay, insufficient profit will be recovered by the amount of reoccupying complement;

④ A fixed percentage of the sales of investments is used to repay foreign partners in a monthly or quarterly turnover or each batch of product.

E. g. 3: The Company shall deduct 8% from the total value of production every year for the Foreign Co. to recover its investment and for the renewal and overhaul of equipment. The balance after the expenses are defrayed shall be distributed to the two parties as profit according to the ratio stipulated in Article 2.3 hereof.

由于所涉及的内容不同，英语商务合同的保证条款的内容也不一样。国际商务合同中设立保证条款的目的在于督促签署合同的各方按照合同要求履行合同中规定的义务，或在债务人不履行义务时，使债权人得到一定的经济赔偿。保证条款常见于国际货物买卖合同和国际技术转让合同。在国际货物买卖合同中，卖方应向买方就货物的质量、规格和性能作出担保。

例1：卖方应该保证货物品质规格必须符合本合同及质量保证书之规定。品质保证期为货物到目的港3个月内，在保证期限内，因制造商在设计和制造上的缺陷造成的货物损害应由卖方负责赔偿。

在技术贸易合同中，保证条款主要是为了维护被许可方的利益，加强许可方的责任。它包括权利保证和技术保证两项内容。权利保证是指技术出让方向技术受让方保证他是所转让技术的合法拥有者，这种转让在合同规定的地域内没有侵犯任何第三方的权利。他所提供的技术资料完整、无误、有效，能够达到协议规定的目标。出让方提供的技术是安全实用的，可以生产出合格的合同产品。否则，出让方就应限期免费补交、更正或修改他所提供的技术。如果未能按期补交、更正或修改，每逾期1日就要罚款若干；如果产品质量达不到合同的标准，受让方有权拒付使用费；如果有人侵权，由出让方负责追诉；如果被人控告，由出让方负责应诉。

例2：乙方保证所提供的技术资料是乙方实际使用的最新技术资料，并保证在合同有效期内向甲方及时提供任何关于合同中所列产品的改进和发展的技术资料。乙方保证所提供的技术资料完整、正确、清晰，并保证按合同规定的时间及时交付。

如果乙方提供的技术资料不符合本合同附件的规定，乙方必须在收到甲方书面通知后的最短时间内（不迟于30天）免费将所缺的技术资料或正确、清晰的技术资料寄给甲方。

投资回收保证条款规定了投资回收额、回收方法和回收期限。为保证外国合作者的投资回收，可采用以下几种方法：

①开头几年双方不分利润，用利润来偿还外国合作者的投资；

②双方分配一定的利润，用折旧基金偿还外国合作者的投资；

③主要用折旧基金偿还外国合作者的投资，不足的利润将由再占款补足；

④按销售投资所得的固定百分比以每月或每季的营业额来偿还外国合作者的投资。

例3：公司应从每年的生产总值中抽出8%来偿还外方投资，以及更新和大修设备。支付各种开支后的余额作为利润，按照第二条第三款规定的比率分给双方。

6.3.3.14 Confidentiality Clauses
保密条款

In general, complete confidentiality provisions include: secrecy subject, secrecy object, privacy and confidentiality. When drafting a contract, we must make a detailed agreement according to the customer's actual situation of secrecy subject, secrecy object, secrecy way and secrecy period. Secrecy subject is the contracting party; Secrecy object is data related to the project; Secrecy way is not to disclose to third parties; Secrecy period is several years after the validity of the contract and the termination. This is a simple and complete confidentiality clause.

E.g.1: All information made available under this agreement shall be kept in strict confidence from any third party without prior consent in writing of the other party. The only exception, however, shall be the disclosures forced by the laws, orders or regulations of Governments or Organizations having the necessary authorities, and such disclosures shall not be deemed to constitute a violation of this Article under this Agreement.

E.g.2: For the full term and even after the termination or cancellation of the agreement, Party B shall take all and every necessary care to ensure that such technical information shall not be disclosed to any third party.

通常，一个完整的保密条款包括保密主体、保密客体、隐私和保密性。在草拟合同时，一定要根据客户的实际情况对保密主体、保密客体、保密方式和保密时间进行详细约定。保密主体是签约方；保密客体是与项目有关的数据资料；保密方式是不向第三方披露；保密时间是整个合同有效期及合同终止后数年内。这就是一个简单而完整的保密条款。

例1：在没有预先取得另一方书面同意的情况下，本协议中提供的一切资料必须严格保密，不得向任何第三方泄露。唯一的例外是在政府或者有关权力机构制定的法律、命令、规章之下强制披露的情况，这种披露不得视为构成对本协议条款的违反。

例2：在本合同有效期内，甚至在其终止或者撤销后，乙方仍需注意保密，不得将该项技术资料泄露给任何第三方。

6.3.3.15   Dissolution Clauses
解除条款

The dissolution of an international business contract refers to a legal act in which one party notifies the other party to rescind the legal relationship of the original contract due to the occurrence of a subjective situation that makes the contract performance unnecessary or impossible before the contract is not performed or fully performed. The dissolution of international business contracts mainly includes the following types: first, dissolution of agreement; second, failure to achieve the purpose of the contract due to force majeure; third, delay in performance; fourth, incomplete performance; fifth, refusing to fulfill.

E.g.1: In case there is any breach of the provisions under this agreement by either party during the effective period of this agreement, these parties hereto shall, first of all, try to settle the matter in question as soon and amicable as possible to mutual satisfaction. Unless a settlement is reached within thirty days after the notification of writing of the other party, such other party shall have the right to cancel this agreement and the loss and damage sustained thereby shall be indemnified by the party responsible for such breach.

E.g.2: If the other party fails to perform its obligation in the contract within the time limit agreed upon in this contract, and fails to eliminate or remedy such breach within 15 days following the receipt of the notice thereof from the non-breaching party and still again fails to perform the contract within the period of time allowed for delayed performance, in such case, the non-breaching party shall be entitled to rescind the contract by the written notice to the defaulting party and still have the right to claim damages from the defaulting party.

国际商务合同的解除是指合同未履行或未完全履行前，由于发生导致合同履行成为不必要或不可能的主观情况，当事人一方通知另一方解除原合同法律关系的法律行为。合同的解除是一种单方的法律行为。只要法定或约定的合同解除原因发生，当事人一方就有权通知另一方解除合同。国际商务合同解除大致有以下几种类型：一是协议解除；二是不可抗力致使不能实现合同目的；三是迟延履行；四是不完全履行；五是拒绝履行。

例1：在本协议有效期间，当任何一方对本协议的条款有所违背时，缔约双方首先应尽可能迅速友好地解决问题，使双方都能满意。另一方以书面通知后，如果问题在30天内不能获得解决，则另一方有权取消本协议，由此而遭受的损害和损失应由违约的一方负责赔偿。

例2：如果合同一方未能在合同规定的时限内履行合同义务，并在收到未违约方的通知后15天内未能消除违约或采取补救措施，而且在被允许推迟履行的期限内仍未履行合同，未违约的一方应书面通知违约方解除合同，同时有权要求违约方赔偿损失。

6.3.3.16 Termination Clauses
终止条款

The rights and obligations under the contract shall terminate in any of the following circumstances:

① The debt has been performed in accordance with the contract.

② Termination of the contract.

③ Debt offsets each other.

④ The obligor delivers the subject matter in escrow: In certain cases, the debtor cannot deliver the contract subject matter to the creditor, the debtor can submit the subject matter in escrow to the agency and eliminate the debt. After the subject matter is placed in escrow, the contractual rights and obligations terminate.

⑤ The creditor cancels the debt.

⑥ Credit and debt ascribe to one person.

⑦ Other circumstances as prescribed by law or agreed by the parties concerned to terminate.

E.g. 1: Article 5: No cedant may countervail the liabilities formed by relevant original insurance contracts with the assets formed by reinsurance contracts against.

E.g.2: The validity period of the contract shall be five (5) years from the effectiveness of the contract and shall become null and void automatically upon the expiry of the validity period of the contract.

E.g.3: From the termination of the agreement, the publisher can sell out all existing stock of the adapted works, as described in Schedule 14 (hereafter, the liquidation period). During the liquidation period, the publisher is not allowed to carry out reprints or publications of the adapted works. After the termination of the liquidation period, the publisher is obliged to send within 30 days a sales report that includes the same information as in article 9(b), and any payment due shall be done within 30 days. Possible excess stock of the adapted works after the final liquidation must be destroyed as well as positive films, electronic devices, master tapes, etc. connected to the adapted works.

凡属下列情形之一的，合同的权利和义务终止：

① 债务已经按照合同履行。

② 合同解除。

③ 债务相互抵销。

④ 债务人依法将标的物提存：在某种特定情况下债务人无法向债权人交付合同标的物的，债务人可以将该标的物提交给提存机关而消灭债务。标的物提存后，合同权利和义务终止。

⑤ 债权人免除债务。

⑥ 债权、债务同归于一人。

⑦ 法律规定或者当事人约定终止的其他情形。

例1：第五条：再保险分出人不应当将再保险合同形成的资产与有关原保险合同形成的负债相互抵销。

例2：本合同有效期为合同生效后5年，有效期满后，本合同即自动失效。

例3：从该协议终止之日起，出版商在附表14规定期限内（以下称清算期）出售改编作品的所有现有库存。清算期内，出版商不允许对改编作品进行重印或出版。清算期结束后，出版商必须在30天内将销售报告发送给著作权人，销售报告内容与第九条b款的信息相同，且应付账款应在30天内付清。最终清算后的改编作品的库存余书必须马上销毁，而且与改编作品相关的正片、电子设备、母带等也须予以销毁。

6.3.3.17 Default Penalty Clauses
违约处罚条款

The contract stipulation about liability for breach of the terms and conditions is very important. The default clause is mainly divided into three parts, namely, restrictions, penalty due to breach of contract damages and compensation and remedy.

E.g.1: Should the Seller fail to make delivery on time as stipulated in the contract, with the exception of Force Majeure causes specified in Clause 21 of this contract, the Buyer shall agree to postpone the delivery on the condition that the Seller agrees to pay a penalty which shall be deducted by the paying bank from the payment under negotiation. The rate of penalty is charged at____% for every____days, odd days less than____days should be counted as____days. But the penalty, however, shall not exceed____% of the total value of the goods involved in the delayed delivery. In case the Seller fails to make delivery later than the time of shipment stipulated in the contract, the Buyer shall have the right to cancel the contract and the Seller, in spite of the cancellation, shall nevertheless pay the aforesaid penalty to the Buyer without delay.

The Buyer shall have the right to lodge a claim against the Seller for the losses sustained, if any.

E.g.2: If any invoice remains unpaid more than 15 days after the specified credit term, the unpaid amount will be considered overdue, and the seller reserves the right to levy a late payment charge based on the prevailing interest rate on the overdue amount for the period for which it has been outstanding.

合同中关于违约责任的规定是非常重要的条款。违约条款主要分为三个部分，即赔偿损失、赔偿限制，以及违约金和补救措施。

例1：除合同第二十一条不可抗力原因外，如卖方不能按合同规定的时间交货，买方应同意在卖方支付罚款的条件下延期交货。罚款可由议付银行在议付货款时扣除，罚款率按每____天收____%，不足____天时以____天计算，但罚款不得超过迟交货物总价的____%。如卖方逾期交货，买方有权撤销合同，此时尽管合同撤销，卖方仍应不延迟地按上述规定向买方支付罚款。

买方有权对因此遭受的其他损失向卖方提出索赔。

例2：如果在发票载明的付款期后15日内仍未付款，则未付款部分将被视为付款延迟，卖方保留按照延迟部分的现行利率征收滞纳金的权利。

6.3.3.18 Force Majeure Clauses
不可抗力条款

In concluding the sales contract, generally there is the force majeure clause whose content includes the accident report, the time limitation, the means of evidence documents put forward to the other party by the party suffered from the force majeure accident, and the scope of responsibility of the party suffered from the force majeure accident. If the contract cannot be performed due to force majeure, the contract should be terminated. If majeure is just a temporary block to the contract, we generally adopt the method of postponing the performance of the contract. If any force majeure accident occurs, the parties should try to take remedial measures, but the parties are not liable for compensation if they fail to avoid a loss.

E.g.1: The sellers shall not be held responsible for late delivery or non-delivery of the goods owing to the generally recognized "Force Majeure" causes. However, in such case, the sellers shall notify the buyers immediately and within 14 days deliver to the buyers a certificate of the accident issued by the Government Authorities or the Chamber of Commerce at the place where the accident occurs as evidence thereof.

E.g.2: Any event or circumstance beyond the control of the parties shall be deemed an event of Force Majeure and shall include but not be restricted to fire, storm, flood, earthquake, explosion, war, rebellion, insurrection, epidemic and quarantine restriction. If either party is prevented from performing any of his obligations under this contract due to an event of Force Majeure, the time for performance under this contract shall be extended to a period equal to the period of delay caused by such Force Majeure.

The affected party shall immediately notify the other party of the occurrence of any Force Majeure by fax and shall send to the other party by registered airmail, with fifteen（15）days thereafter, a certificate from the relevant government authorities or departments confirming the occurrence and the cause of such Force Majeure. Should the delay caused by any event of Force Majeure continue for more than 60 consecutive days, both parties shall settle the problem of further performance of this contract through friendly negotiations.

在订立买卖合同时，一般都订有不可抗力条款，其内容包括：遭到不可抗力事故的一方向另一方提出事故报告和证明文件的期限和方式，以及遭遇不可抗力事故一方的责任范围。如遇不可抗力使合同无法履行，则应解除合同。如不可抗力只是暂时阻碍合同履行，则一般采取延期履行合同的方式。凡发生不可抗力事故，在当事方已尽力采取补救措施但仍未能避免损失的情况下，当事方可不负赔偿责任。

例1：由一般公认的不可抗力的原因，致使延迟交货或者不能交货，卖方不承担责任。但在此情况下，卖方要立即通知买方，并在14天内向买方交付一份事故证明书作为证据，该证明书须由出事地点的政府机关或者商会出具。

例2：遇有双方无法控制的事件或情况应视为不可抗力事件，其包括但不限于火灾、风灾、水灾、地震、爆炸、战争、叛乱、暴动、瘟疫和检疫限制。如遇不可抗力事件致使任何一方不能履行本合同项下的义务，应将履行合同的时限按发生不可抗力事件所延误的时间予以延期。

受影响的一方应立即通过传真通知另一方不可抗力事件的发生，并且在事件发生15天内通过挂号航空邮件的方式向另一方发送由相关政府机构或部门出具的证明，证实这种不可抗力的发生和原因。如果任何不可抗力事件引起的延迟超过连续的60天，双方应通过友好协商解决进一步执行本合同的问题。

6.3.3.19　Jurisdiction Clauses
适用法律条款

Jurisdiction clauses are essential clauses in every contract, if both parties can not execute in accordance with the contract, they need to turn to resort to the judicial institutions or quasi-judicial institutions to ensure the enforcement of the contract. Only with the compulsory execution, can the contract be legally binding. Mainly there are two kinds of ways to settle the dispute, one is to submit the dispute to the court that has jurisdiction, and the second is to submit the dispute to an arbitration institution for resolution.

E.g.1: All disputes in connection with this contract or the execution thereof shall be settled amicably through negotiation. In case no settlement can be reached, the case under dispute then be submitted for arbitration. The arbitration shall be conducted in the country of the defendant. If in China, the China International Economic and Trade Arbitration Commission, Beijing, shall execute the arbitration in accordance with the Rules of Procedure of Arbitration of the said Commission. The decision of the arbitration shall be accepted as final and binding upon both parties. The fees for arbitration shall be borne by the losing party unless otherwise awarded.

E.g.2: The formation, interpretation and performance of the contract shall be governed by the laws of the People's Republic of China.

Because each contract serves a different purpose, according to the general international closest relation principle, the applicable law for all kinds of contracts is roughly as follows:

① Agency contracts are governed by the laws of the place where the agency is located. If the agent has no place of business, the contracts are governed by the laws of the place where the agent's domicile or habitual residence is located at the time of establishment of the agency relationship.

② Technology transfer contracts are governed by the laws of the place where the assignee's business is located.

③ Foreign insurance contracts are governed by the laws of the place where the insurance business is located

④ Foreign bank loan contracts or guaranty contracts are governed by the laws of the place where the lending bank or guarantee bank is located.

⑤ Foreign project contracts are governed by the laws of the place where the project is located.

⑥ Complete sets of equipment supply contracts are governed by the laws of the place where the equipment is installed and operated.

⑦ Foreign labor service contracts are governed by the laws of the place where the labor service is to be performed.

⑧ International sales contracts are governed by the laws of the place where the seller's business is located.

⑨ Contracts of carriage are governed by the laws of the place where the carrier's business is located.

⑩ Currency payment and settlement contracts are governed by the laws of the location of payment or settlement.

⑪ Trademark transfer contracts are governed by the laws of the place where the assignor's business is located.

⑫ Copyright transfer contracts are governed by the laws of the place where the copyright owner has his domicile or habitual residence.

⑬ Contracts for the issuance, sale and transfer of bonds are governed by the laws of the place where consumers have their domicile or habitual residence.

⑭ Donative contracts are governed by the laws of the place where the donor has his domicile or habitual residence.

⑮ Trust contracts are governed by the laws of the place of trust administration designated by the grantor, or the laws of the place where the trust property is located, or the laws of the place where the trustee has the business or habitual residence, or the laws of the place where the purpose of trust is realized.

⑯ Agency contracts are governed by the laws of the place where the trustee has his business or residence or habitual residence.

⑰ Exchange business contracts are governed by the laws of the place where the exchange is located.

⑱ Auction contracts are governed by the laws of the auction place.

In addition, the foreign contractual relationship of the real estate should be applied to the laws of the place where the property is situated. If there are no relevant provisions in the law in our country, international practices may be applied.

适用法律条款是每个合同的必备条款，如果双方当事人不能按合同执行，最后就需要求助司法机构或准司法机构来保障合同的强制执行。只有具备了强制执行力，合同才能谈得上有法律约束力。解决争议的方式主要有两种：一是将争议提交给有管辖权的法院，二是将争议提交仲裁机构解决。

例1：凡与本合同或执行本合同有关的一切争议，均应通过友好协商解决。如不能解决，争议的案件可以提交仲裁机构。仲裁需在被告国进行。如在中国进行，由中国国际经济贸易仲裁委员会北京总部按照其仲裁程序规则执行仲裁。仲裁的裁决是终局性的，对双方均有约束力。除非另有规定，仲裁费用由败诉的一方承担。

例2：合同的签订、解释和履行适用中华人民共和国法律。

由于每种合同所要达到的目的不同，根据国际上通用的最密切关系原则，各类合同的适用法律大致如下：

①代理合同，适用代理营业所所在地法律。代理人无营业所的，适用代理关系成立时代理人住所地或惯常居所所在地法律。

②技术转让合同，适用受让人营业所所在地法律。

③涉外保险合同，适用保险人营业所所在地法律。

④涉外银行贷款合同或担保合同，适用贷款银行或担保银行所在地法律。

⑤涉外工程承包合同，适用工程所在地法律。

⑥成套设备供应合同，适用设备安装运转地法律。

⑦涉外劳务合同，适用劳务实施地法律。

⑧国际货物买卖合同，适用合同订立时卖方营业所所在地法律。

⑨运输合同，适用承运人营业所所在地法律。

⑩货币支付与结算合同，适用支付地或结算地法律。

⑪商标使用权转让合同，适用转让人营业所所在地法律。

⑫著作权转让合同，适用著作权所有人住所地或惯常居所所在地法律。

⑬债券的发行与出售或转让合同，适用消费者住所地或惯常居所所在地法律。

⑭赠与合同，适用赠与人住所地或惯常居所所在地法律。

⑮信托合同，适用授予人指定的信托管理地法律，或信托财产所在地法律，或受托人营业所或者惯常居所所在地法律，或信托目的实现地法律。

⑯委托合同，适用受托人营业所或住所或惯常居所所在地法律。

⑰交易所业务合同，适用交易所所在地法律。

⑱拍卖合同，适用拍卖地法律。

此外，有关不动产的涉外合同关系，应适用不动产所在地法律。对于我国法律未作规定的，可以适用国际惯例。

6.4   Concluding International E-Commerce Contracts①
国际电子商务合同的撰写

6.4.1   *Formation and Validity of E-Commerce Contracts*
电子商务合同的构成与有效性

UNCITRAL Model Law on Electronic Commerce stipulates that in the context of contract formation, unless otherwise agreed by the parties, an offer and the acceptance of the offer may be expressed by means of data messages. If a data message is used in the formation of a contract, that contract shall not be denied validity or enforceability on the sole ground that a data message is used for that purpose. As between the originator and the addressee of a data message, a declaration of will or other statements shall not be denied legal effect, validity or enforceability solely on the ground that it is in the form of a data message.

Though the CISG and the Contract Law lack detailed regulations for the formation, signature,

①   涂定武. 国际商贸合同精要 [M]. 杭州：浙江大学出版社，2004.

certification of electronic contracts, and maneuverable articles on the formation of electronic contracts, contracts concluded by means of data messages are approbatory. Article 13 of the CISG validates that "writing" includes telegram and telex. Under Contract Law, "written form" refers to documents of a form in which the content of the contract may be visibly recorded, such as contact instruments, correspondence, and electronic documents (including telegrams, telexes, facsimiles, electronic data interchange and electronic mails).

《联合国国际贸易法委员会电子商务示范法》规定，除非合同当事方另有约定，一项要约和对要约的承诺均可通过数据电文的手段表示。如果使用了一项数据电文来订立合同，则不得仅仅以使用了数据电文为理由而否定该合同的有效性或可执行性。就一项数据电文的发端人和收件人之间而言，不得仅仅以意志声明或其他陈述采用数据电文形式为理由而否定其法律效力、有效性或可执行性。

虽然《联合国国际货物销售合同公约》和合同法缺乏对电子合同的构成、签名、认证和电子合同机动性条款的详细规定，但采用数据电文方式订立合同是被认可的。CISG 第13条确认合同的"书面形式"包括电报和电传。根据合同法，合同的"书面形式"是指可以有形地表示可载内容的形式，如合同书、信件和数据电文（包括电报、电传、传真、电子数据交换和电子邮件）等。

6.4.2 *Acknowledgement of Receipt*
确认收讫

Under Article 14 of UNCITRAL Model Law on Electronic Commerce, if the originator has not agreed with the addressee that the acknowledgement must be given in a particular form or by a particular method, the addressee may give an acknowledgement by any communication or any conduct provided that such communication is sufficient to indicate that the data message has been received. If the originator has stated that the data message is conditional on receipt of the acknowledgement, until the acknowledgement is received, the data message is treated as if it has never been sent. In the event that the originator has not stated that the data message is conditional on receipt of the acknowledgement, and the acknowledgement has not been received by the originator within the time specified or agreed or, if no time has been specified or agreed, within a reasonable time, the originator may give notice to the addressee stating that no acknowledgement has been received and specifying a reasonable time by which the acknowledgement must be received. If the acknowledgement is not received within the time as specified above, the originator may, upon notice to the addressee, treat the data message as if it had never been sent, or exercise any other rights it may have. When the originator receives the addressee's acknowledgement of receipt and the received acknowledgement states that the relevant data message met technical requirements, it is presumed that those requirements have been met, and that the addressee has received the relevant data message, but the presumption does not imply that the data message corresponds to the message received.

In accordance with the above regulations, it is understandable that the receipt of acknowledgement in electronic commercial activities is of great importance, but on the other hand, the receipt of acknowledgement itself does not imply that the acknowledgement has the effectiveness as an acceptance. So, in electronic commercial activities, a coded electronic signature is commonly used to certify the identity of the originator of a data message and to ensure the integrality and incontestability of a data message. For some material transactions in the form of business - to - business (B2B), certification online may be applied to validate the effectiveness of an electronic acknowledgement.

As regards to the time of dispatch and receipt of data messages, Article 15 of UNCITRAL Model Law on Electronic Commerce stipulates that dispatch occurs when it enters an information system outside the control of the originator or of the person who sent the data message on behalf of the originator unless the originator and the addressee agreed otherwise. But the determination of the time of receipt of a data message is quite complex. If the addressee has designated an information system for the purpose of receiving data messages, receipt occurs at the time when the data message enters the designated information system. If the data message is sent to an information system of the addressee that is not the designated information system, the receipt occurs at the time when the addressee retrieves the data message. In the event that the addressee has not designated an information system, receipt occurs when the data message enters an information system of the addressee.

With regard to the place of dispatch and receipt of data messages, it is stipulated in the Article 15 of UNCITRAL Model Law on Electronic Commerce that a data message is dispatched at the place where the originator has its place of business, and received at the place where the addressee has its place of business if the originator and the addressee have not agreed otherwise. If the originator or the addressee has more than one place of business, the place of business is the one that has the closest relationship to the transaction or the principal place of business. In case the originator or the addressee does not have a place of business, its habitual residence shall be regarded to be the place of business. If there is not any principle transaction, a place of its main business shall be regarded as the place of sending or receiving.

《联合国国际贸易法委员会电子商务示范法》第14条规定：如发端人未与收件人商定以某种特定形式或某种特定方法确认收讫，则收件人可通过足以向发端人表明该数据电文已经收到的任何通信方式或任何行为来确认收讫。如发端人已声明数据电文须以收到收讫确认为条件，则在收到确认之前，数据电文可视为从未发送。如发端人并未声明数据电文须以收到收讫确认为条件，而且在规定或商定时间内，或在未规定或商定时间的情况下，在一段合理时间内，发端人并未收到收讫确认，可向收件人发出通知，说明并未收到其收讫确认，并指定必须收到收讫确认的合理时限；如在所规定的时限内仍未收到收讫确认，发端人可在通知收件人之后，将数据电文确认为从未发送，或行使其所拥有的其他权利。当发端人收到收件人的收讫确认，且所收到的收讫确认指出有关数据电文符合商定的适用标准或规定的技术要求时，可推定这些要求业已满足，但这种推断并不含有该数据电文与所收电文相符的意思。

按照上述规定，我们知道确认收讫在电子商务活动中是非常重要的，但是确认收讫本身并不具有承诺的效力。因此，在电子商务活动中，电子签名通常用于认证发起者的身份数据信息，以确保数据的完整性和无可置疑性。对于一些企业对企业（B2B）的电子商务交易模式，可以应用在线认证来验证电子确认的有效性。

关于数据电文的收发时间，《联合国国际贸易法委员会电子商务示范法》第15条规定：除非发端人与收件人另有协定，否则，一项数据电文的发送时间为该数据电文进入发端人或代表发端人的控制范围之外的某一信息系统的时间。但是，确认一项数据电文的收到时间就相当复杂了。如果收件人为接收数据电文指定了某一信息系统，则以数据电文进入该指定信息系统的时间为收到时间。如果数据电文发送给了收件人指定接收该数据电文的信息系统外的另一个系统，则以收件人检索到该数据电文的时间为收到时间。如果收件人并未指定某一信息系统，则以数据电文进入收件人的任一信息系统的时间为收到时间。

关于数据电文的收发地点，《联合国国际贸易法委员会电子商务示范法》第15条也作了明确的规定，即除非收发双方另有协议，否则，数据电文的发出地点为发端人的营业地点，而数据电文的收到地点为收件人的营业地点。如果发端人或收件人有一个以上的营业地点，则以与其基础交易具有最密切联系的营业地为发出地或接收地。如果没有任何基础交易，则以其主要的营业地为发出地或接收地。如果发端人或收件人没有营业地，则以其惯常居住地为准。

6.5　Some Taboos in English Contract Translation/Draft[①]　英语合同翻译/起草中的若干禁忌

The style is the man. The contract translator and drafter not only decide the appearance of the English contract, but also reflect their comprehensive quality at the same time. In order to give customers a professional, precise prose style, the translators and drafters should pay attention to the following matters:

文如其人，合同的翻译者和起草者在决定英语合同面貌的同时，也反映着自身的综合素质。为了给客户带来专业、严谨的行文风格，翻译者和起草者在其翻译和起草工作中应当注意如下事项：

6.5.1　No Abbreviation　忌缩写

Abbreviation for other styles naturally endows writing with a natural and readable characteristic and a friendly tone. But, traditionally, people think that it is inappropriate to use abbreviation in formal legal writing, including the draft of the contract translation. In addition to quoting the words of others in abbreviation, or abbreviations appear in works, please do not use abbreviations in the contract for the purpose of being loyal to the original, or defining terms.

对于其他文体而言，缩写赋予写作一种自然亲切的语调和易读的特征。但是，习惯上，人们认为正式的法律写作，包括合同的翻译在内，使用缩写是不恰当的。除引述他人的言辞或著作时出现缩写外，请勿为忠于原文或定义条款而在合同中使用缩写。

6.5.2　No First Person　忌第一人称

The normative objects of the contract are the parties, who have nothing to do with the interests of the translator or the drafter, it is usually not necessary to use the first person. Moreover, if contracts' translators and drafters could focus on translation and drafting, literary content would be more authoritative. When translators and drafters state the fact with an objective attitude and stipulate the responsibility, the rights and benefits of the parties, the prose of the contract also can reflect the objective and fair appearance. As if when a lawyer makes the trial judge forget his identity, the debate can further judge the heart deeply, to avoid using "we", "us" and "our" can win the trust of the parties. If the contract appears the occasion of the first person, the translators and drafters shall change it into the third person as far as possible.

合同规范的对象是当事人，与翻译者或起草者的利益无关，通常没有必要使用第一人称。此外，合同的翻译者和起草者如果能将重点放在翻译或起草上，内容会更具权威性。当翻译起草者以一种客观的态度来陈述事实，规约当事人的责、权、利时，合同的行文也会体现客观公平的面貌。正如律师若能在庭审中令法官忘记其律师的身份，其辩论必能深入法官内心一般，在语言中避免出现"我"、"我们"及"我们的"也将赢得当事人的信任。如果合同中出现要使用第一人称的场合，翻译者和起草者应当尽量将之转换成第三人称。

6.5.3　*No Rhetorical Question*
忌反问

A rhetorical question refers to a question with an implied answer. This question has a strong and apparent provocation and irony meaning, which is far from the objective and fair spirit of the contract. Also, one of the purposes of the contract is to prevent parties from controversy or designing dispute solutions in advance, not to stir up controversy.

反问句是指隐含答案的问句。此种问句带有强烈、明显的挑衅及讽刺含义，与合同的客观公平精神相去甚远。同时，合同的目的之一是防止签约双方出现争议或者提前设计争议解决方案，而不是挑起争议。

6.5.4　*No Slang*
忌俚语

Slang will be considered as taboo in almost all formal styles of writing, and the contract is also written in a more formal style, so the slang will not take tone into the contract. For example, to express the car of one side "broken" with "wrecked" rather than "totaled"; to express "stole stereo" with "stole" rather than "ripped off"; to express "drunk" with "drunk" or "intoxicated" rather than "smashed". Contract writing or translation is not crosstalk or the pursuit of entertainment effect.

几乎所有正式文体的写作均将俚语列为大忌，合同也属于正式程度较高的文体，所以在合同中使用俚语会显得不协调。比如，表达一方的车"被破坏"，就要用"wrecked"而不要用"totaled"；表达"偷了"立体声音响，就要用"stole"而不要用"ripped off"；表达"喝醉了"就要用"drunk"或成文法中的标准用语"intoxicated"，而不要用"smashed"。合同的写作或翻译不是说相声，不追求娱乐效果。

6.5.5　*No Kidding*
　　忌戏谑

To translate or draft a contract is not kidding, so it should be taken seriously. Even if you are quoting a very funny joke, it could make the parties think you don't take the contract seriously, so the risk of making you smile is very big.

　　翻译或起草合同不是开玩笑，所以应当严肃对待。即使你引用一个非常有趣的笑话，也会使得当事人认为你不认真对待合同，博君一笑的风险是很大的。

6.5.6　*No Footnote*
　　忌脚注

When readers read the contract, eyes transfer from the footer back to the place they just stayed in to continue reading, which not only increases the burden of their reading, but also distracts their attention. The contract is not the paper, and the parties are not interested in the research. If the footnote is necessary to note, try to solve it by other means (such as interlinear notes) in the body as far as possible.

　　读者阅读合同时，目光移转到页脚再回到正文中寻找刚才止住的地方继续阅读，不但会增加阅读负担，还会分散注意力。合同不是论文，当事人的志趣也不在研究。如果非标脚注不可，尽量在正文中通过其他方式（如夹注）解决。

6.5.7　*Avoid Abuse Emphasis*
　　忌滥用强调

Just as using bold, italics or capital letters to emphasize many terms in the contract will backfire, frequently using the underline makes readers can't find the key, and even makes readers angry. The effect of emphasizing everything is to emphasize nothing.

　　正如在合同中对很多术语使用字体加粗、斜体或大写字母来强调会适得其反一样，频繁使用下划线会使读者找不到重点，甚至会令读者恼火。凡事都强调的效果就是什么也没强调。

6.5.8　*Avoid a Fancy Font*
　　忌花哨的字体

Now most people have word processing software with complete functions and various fonts or advanced printing equipment. Using the software and equipment, people can easily produce trendy and beautiful text. But in Anglo-American countries, most lawyers still continue to use the most complex laser printer to print out the contract. This is because the laser printer type font is similar to traditional printer type fonts, which are Roman fonts. This also means that Roman fonts are most commonly accepted by lawyers. For the same reason, italics and bulleted graphics usually are not acceptable.

　　如今多数人都拥有功能完备、字体多样的文字处理软件或先进的打印设备。利用这些软件和设备能够轻松地制作出新潮、美观的文本。但在英美国家，大部分律师仍然沿用最复杂的激光打印机来打印合同。这是因为激光打印机打出的字体与传统打印机打出的字体类似，都是普通的罗马字体，这也表示罗马字体是律师们接受程度最高的字体。基于同样的原因，斜体字及项目符号等图示通常不被接受。

6.5.9   *Careful Right-Aligned Typography*
慎用右对齐排版

Most word processing software programs offer the right-aligned typesetting function, however, unless you have a very good typewriter and typesetting software to ensure accurate word spacing, otherwise don't use the right alignment layout. The disorderly word spacing or too much space will make the contract hard to read. Therefore, if your printer or text editing software technology is primary, please do not use right-aligned typography.

多数文字处理软件都提供右对齐的排版功能，但是，除非你的确有台很好的打字机及排版软件，能够确保精确的字间距，否则不要轻易使用右对齐排版方式。字间距乱无章法或者空格过多会让合同难以阅读。因此，如果你的打印机或文字编辑软件技术还不够高级，请不要使用右对齐排版。

6.5.10   *Avoid Title at the Bottom of the Page*
忌页底标题

Lawyers usually don't start a new page for a certain paragraph in the contract; even will not do so for this paper and the conclusion part separate. In fact, the signature page must be a new page in the contract, and it is rarely necessary to restart a page unless accessories are to be separated from the body.

Anyway, avoid placing the title at the bottom of the page. This requirement is difficult for modern people to do, because the computer allows you to continue typing without realizing the pagination, the inserted data will also change the original paging, and a printer can sometimes change the page you see on the computer screen. Therefore, you have to check your file line by line, before, during, and after printing to make sure the title does appear in the place where you want it to appear. If there is no way to set aside at least two lines of space under a title, please move the title to the head of the next page, and, if a title is not on the head of a page, also please make sure you leave one to two lines above the title.

律师们通常不会为了合同中的某个段落而另起一页，甚至不会为了将本文与结束语部分分开而这样做。实际上，合同中的签名页必须另起一页。除非将附件与正文分离，其他情形下很少有另起一页的必要。

无论如何，避免将标题置于页底。这个要求现代人比较难做到，因为电脑会让你在没有意识到该分页的时候继续打字，而中途插入的数据也将改变原来的分页，而且打印机有时也可以改变你在电脑屏幕上看到的页面。所以你必须在打印前后逐行检查你的文件，以确定标题确实出现在你希望它出现的地方。如果在一个标题底下没有办法预留至少两行空间，那么请将此标题移到下一页的页首。同时，如果一个标题不在一页的页首，也请确定这个标题的上方留有一至两行的空间。

Exercises

Chapter 6 即测即评

Ⅰ.Single-choice.

1.The term - "_____" is a shorthand expression for a fairly complex set of legal rules derived from English Common Law to determine who may enforce contractual rights.

A.privity of contract   B.freedom of contract

C.equality of contract   D.freedom from contract

2.The buyer may be_____of the consuming chain.

A.at the beginning   B.in the middle

C.at the end   D.either B or C

3.The seller maybe_____of the consuming chain.

A.at the beginning   B.in the middle

C.at the end   D.either A or B

4.If there are_____, a buyer will be in a strong position in a negotiation because the suppliers will be in competition for their business.

A.many suppliers and many buyers   B.many suppliers and a few buyers

C.a few suppliers and many buyers   D.a few suppliers and a few buyers

5._____may NOT be the buyer's hidden cost.

A.Customs clearance   B.The stated price of the goods

C.Insurance   D.Hospitality costs

6.The bottom-line answers to the question "why should the contract parties consult a lawyer" is "you could end up in a lot of financial and_____because of your ignorance or innocence".

A.legal trouble   B.political trouble

C.economic trouble   D.business trouble

7.If you take delivery of the goods before they are_____, you will have to satisfy a customs officer of the seller's country.

A.produced B.exported   C.imported   D.sold

8.If you buy goods that are_____to export, you could become criminally liable.

A.legitimate B.lawful   C.illegal   D.intellectual

9.If you_____the contract, you may appear in court in the seller's country where you will have to answer a foreign judge.

A.make   B.conclude   C.perform   D.breach

10.The advice of_____can the buyer's or seller's attorney typically provide?

A.customs   B.transport

C.account and tax filings　　　　　　　　D.remedies

Ⅱ.Gap-filling.

Sales transactions occur between two (1)＿＿＿＿＿(当事人): Buyer and Seller. Sometimes transactions involve more than several parties who are jointly buying or selling goods, but the individual interests of parties acting jointly become melded as a single interest in the sales contract. Thus, for purposes of the sales contract, there is a buyer and a seller. In addition, the buyer and the seller may each be represented by legal counsel.

Other (2)＿＿＿＿＿(利益) of (3)＿＿＿＿＿(第三方), and the individual interests of parties acting jointly, are not directly controlled by the sales contract between the buyer and the seller. These outside interests may be indirectly affected by whether the buyer and the seller perform the (4)＿＿＿＿＿(买卖交易) to the letter of the (5)＿＿＿＿＿(销售合同), but generally the rights and risks of these third persons and individual parties depend on contracts separate from the sales agreement. Thus, if parties are string jointly in a sale of goods, the goods are shipped and accepted by the buyer, the buyer makes payment pursuant to the (6)＿＿＿＿＿(合同条款), but one of the sellers absconds with the (7)＿＿＿＿＿(支付条款), the other seller's recourse is against the absconding party for breach of their joint arrangement, not against the buyer for a second payment. Similarly, if a buyer in a sales transaction in the premises sells the goods to a third-party (8)＿＿＿＿＿(零售商) a certain date, the retailer then arranges to resell those goods accordingly, but the goods are (9)＿＿＿＿＿(交付) two months late and the resales are lost, the third party's recourse is against the buyer. Of course, the buyer (but not the third-party retailer) may also have (10)＿＿＿＿＿(追索权) against the seller for damages caused by the late delivery.

Ⅲ.Discussion.

1.Who are the parties to an international sales transaction?

2.What is the meaning of "privity of contract"?

3.What is the role of a buyer or a seller in consumption?

4.What are the goals of a buyer or a seller in a transaction?

5.What will a buyer do to seek quality assurance and protection against defective or damaged goods or unsatisfactory services?

6.What will a seller do to promote the quality and distinctiveness of the seller's goods or services to command the price he or she desires?

7.When considering the cost of the transaction, what hidden expenses might be covered for a buyer or a seller to add before agreeing to a price?

8.Why should the buyer or the seller consult an attorney?

9.When and how to consult an attorney?

10.What advice will not an attorney usually provide?

Ⅳ.Translate the following long sentences into Chinese.

1.Should any purported obligation or liability of the customer (which, if valid or enforceable, would be the subject of this deed)be or become wholly or in part invalid or unenforceable against the customer on any ground whatsoever including any defect or insufficiency or want of powers of the customer, or irregular or improper purported exercise thereof or breach or want of authority by any person purporting to act on behalf of the customer, or any legal limitation, disability, mental or other incapacity, or any other fact or circumstance, whether or not known to you, or if, for any other reason whatsoever, the customer is not or ceases to be legally liable to discharge any obligation or liability undertaken or purported to be undertaken on the customers' behalf, the covenanter shall nevertheless be liable to you in respect of that obligation or liability or purported obligation or liability as if the same were wholly valid and enforceable and the covenanter was the principal debtor in respect thereof.

2.You are not to be concerned to see or enquire into the powers of the customer or its officers (if the customer is a limited company), employees or agents purporting to act on the customer's behalf and the covenanter agrees that you will thus rely on the acts purportedly carried out on behalf of the customer as being validly binding on the customer so that the covenanter is stopped from taking or raising any point or defense on such matter(s).

V.Case study.

MacPherson v. Buick Motor Co.
Court of Appeals of New York, 1916

The defendant, Buick Motor Company, was sued by Donald C. MacPherson, the plaintiff, who suffered injuries while riding in a Buick automobile that suddenly collapsed because one of the wheels was made of defective wood. The spokes crumbled into fragments, throwing MacPherson out of the vehicle and injuring him. The wheel itself had not been made by Buick Motor Company; It had been bought from another manufacturer. There was evidence, however, that the defects could have been discovered by reasonable inspection and that no such inspection had taken place. Although there was no charge that Buick knew of the defect and willfully concealed it, MacPherson charged Buick with negligence for putting a human life in imminent danger. Keep in mind that MacPherson sued the automobile manufacturer, despite the fact that the automobile was purchased from a retail Buick dealer. The trial court held for MacPherson, and Buick Motor Company appealed.

The question to be determined is whether the defendant owed a duty of care and vigilance to my one but the immediate purchaser. The foundations of this branch of the law, at least in this state, were laid in Thomas v. Winchester. A poison was falsely labeled. The sale was made to a druggist, who in turn sold it to a customer. The customer recovered damages from the seller who affixed the label. "The defendant's negligence," it was said, "put human life in imminent danger." A poison, falsely labeled, is likely to injure anyone who gets it. Because the danger is to be foreseen, there is a duty to avoid the injury. (Emphasis added). Thomas v. Winchester quickly became a landmark of the law. In the application of its principle, there may, at times, have been uncertainty or even error. There has never been doubt or disavowal of the principle itself in this state.

...

We hold, then, that the principle of Thomas v. Winchester is not limited to poisons, explosives, and things of similar nature, to things which in their normal operation are implements of destruction. If the nature of a thing is such that it is reasonably certain to place life and limb in peril when negligently made, it is then a thing of danger. Its nature gives warning of the consequences to be expected. If to the element of danger there is added knowledge that the thing will be used by persons other than the purchaser, and used without new tests, then, irrespective of contract, the manufacturer of this dangerous thing is under a duty to make it carefully...It is possible to use almost anything in a way that will make it dangerous if defective. That is not enough to charge the manufacturer with a duty independent of his contract. There must also be knowledge that in the usual course of events the danger will be shared by others than the buyer. Such knowledge may often be inferred from the nature of the transaction. But it is possible that even knowledge of the danger and of the use will not always be enough. The proximity or remoteness of the relation is a factor to be considered. We are dealing now with the liability of the manufacturer of the finished product, who puts it on the market to be used without inspection by his customers. If he is negligent, where danger is to be foreseen, a liability will follow.

We are not required, at this time, to me that it is legitimate to go back to the manufacturer of the finished product and hold the manufacturers of the component parts. To make their negligence a cause of imminent danger, the independent cause must often intervene; the manufacturer of the finished product must also fail in his duty of inspection. It may be that in those circumstances the negligence of the earlier members of the series is too remote to constitute, as an actionable wrong to the ultimate user...There is no break in the chain of cause and effect. In such circumstances, the presence of known anger, attendant upon a known use, makes vigilance a duty.

We think the defendant was not absolved from a duty of inspection because it bought the wheels from a reputable manufacturer. It was not merely a dealer in automobiles. It was a manufacturer of automobiles. It was responsible for the finished product. It was not at liberty to put the finished product on the market without subjecting the component parts of ordinary and simple tests. The obligation to inspect must vary with the nature of the thing to be inspected. The more probable the danger, the greater the need of caution.

The Court of Appeals of New York, the highest court in the New York state system, affirmed the judgment of the original court and the intermediate review court that the defendant, Buick Motor Company, was liable to Donald C. MacPherson for the injuries he sustained when he was thrown from the vehicle.

资料来源　佚名. MacPherson v. Buick Motor Co.[EB/OL].[2023-11-22]. https://en.wikipedia.org/wiki/MacPherson_v._Buick_ Motor_Co.

Case Discussion:

(1)Who are the seller and the buyer in the contract for the sale of Buick automobiles?

(2)Is there a contractual relationship (privity of contract) between Buick Motor Co. and MacPherson?

(3)Should Buick Motor Company be liable for the injuries suffered by MacPherson? Why?

Main Bibliography
主要参考文献

［1］WEBSTER. Webster's third new international dictionary, unabridged ［M］. New York: Merriam Webster, 2002.

［2］KIAN C T S, CHIM T S. Contract law: A layman's guide ［M］. Singapore: Time Editions, 2000.

［3］CURRY J E. A short course in international negotiating: Planning and conducting international commercial negotiations ［M］. Petaluma: World Trade Press, 1999.

［4］MITCHELL C. A short course in international business culture ［M］. Petaluma: World Trade Press, 1999.

［5］SITARZ D. The complete book of small business legal forms ［M］. Portland: Nova Publishing Co., 1996.

［6］FARNSWORTH E A, YOUNG W F. Selections for contracts: Statutes, restatement second, forms ［M］. New York: Foundation Press, 1980.

［7］BLACK H C. Black's law dictionary ［M］. 5th ed. St. Paul: West Publishing Co., 1979.

［8］哈格德. 法律写作 ［M］. 影印版. 北京：法律出版社，2004.

［9］索普，贝利. 国际商务合同 ［M］. 段佳陆，等译. 中英文双语版. 北京：华夏出版社，2004.

［10］希皮. 国际商务合同 ［M］. 英文版. 上海：上海外语教育出版社，2000.

［11］乔焕然. 英语合同阅读指南：英语合同的结构、条款、句型与词汇分析 ［M］. 最新增订版. 北京：中国法制出版社，2015.

［12］王秉乾. 国际商事合同 ［M］. 英文版. 北京：对外经济贸易大学出版社，2013.

［13］王相国. 鏖战英文合同：英文合同的翻译与起草 ［M］. 最新增订版. 北京：中国法制出版社，2014.

［14］王立非. 国际商务合同实践教程 ［M］. 上海：上海外语教育出版社，2012.

［15］刘川，王菲. 英文合同阅读与翻译 ［M］. 北京：国防工业出版社，2010.

［16］陶博. 法律英语：中英双语法律文书制作 ［M］. 上海：复旦大学出版社，2004.

［17］葛亚军，齐恩平. 合同英语 ［M］. 天津：天津科技翻译出版公司，2002.

［18］吴敏，吴明忠. 国际经贸英语合同写作 ［M］. 广州：暨南大学出版社，2002.

Appendix

附录

Appendix 1

Purchase Contract[①]

Contract No.:

Date:

Signing Place:

Seller:

Address:

Postal Code:

Tel:

Fax:

Buyer:

Address:

Postal Code:

Tel:

Fax:

---

① 凌芳. 国际商务合同模板手册 [M]. 广州：广东经济出版社，2015：55-63.

The Seller agrees to sell and the Buyer agrees to buy the under mentioned commodity on the terms and conditions stated below:

1.Article No.

2.Name of Commodity and Specification

3.Quantity

4.Unit Price

5.Total Price

Total amount with____% more or less both in amount and quantity allowed at the Seller's option.

6.Terms of Delivery

7.Origin and Manufacturer

8.Packing and Standard

The packing of the goods shall be preventive from dampness, rust, moisture, erosion and shock, and shall be suitable for ocean transportation/multiple transportation. The Seller shall be liable for any damage and loss of the goods attributable to the inadequate or improper packing. The measurement, gross weight, net weight and the cautions such as "Do not stack up side down", "Keep away from moisture", "Handle with care" shall be stenciled on the surface of each package with fadeless pigment.

9.Shipping Marks

10.Time of Shipment

11.Port of Loading

12.Port of Destination

13.Insurance

Insurance shall be covered by the_____for____% of the invoice value against_____ Risks and Additional Risks.

14.Terms of Payment

(1)Letter of credit: The Buyer shall_____days prior to the time of shipment/after this Contract comes into effect, open an irrevocable Letter of Credit in favor of the Seller. The Letter of Credit shall expire_____ days after the completion of loading of the shipment as stipulated.

(2)Documents against payment: After shipment, the Seller shall draw a sight bill of exchange on the Buyer and deliver the documents through the Seller's bank and_____ Bank to the Buyer against payment, i.e. D/P. The Buyer shall effect the payment immediately upon the first presentation of the bill(s) of exchange.

(3)Documents against acceptance: After shipment, the Seller shall draw a sight bill of exchange, payable_____days after the Buyer delivers the documents through the Seller's bank and _____ Bank to the Buyer against acceptance. The Buyer shall make the payment on the date of the bill(s) of exchange.

(4)Cash on delivery (COD): The Buyer shall pay to the Seller total amount within_____ days after the receipt of the goods (not applicable for FOB or CIF).

15.Documents Required

The Seller shall present the following documents required to the bank for negotiation/collection:

(1)Full set of clean on board Ocean/Combined Transportation Bills of Lading and blank endorsed marked freight prepaid/to collect.

(2)Signed commercial invoice in_____copies indicating Contract No., L/C No. (Terms of L/C) and shipping marks.

(3)Packing list/weight memo in_____copies issued by_____.

(4)Certificate of quality in_____copies issued by_____.

(5)Certificate of quantity in_____copies issued by_____.

(6)Insurance policy/certificate in_____copies (Terms of CIF).

(7)Shipping advice: The Seller shall, within_____hours after shipment effected, send by each copy of the above-mentioned documents' number.

16.Terms of Shipment

(1)FOB

The Seller shall, 30 days before the shipment date specified in the Contract, advise the Buyer of the Contract No., names of commodity, quantity, amount, packages, gross weight, measurement, and the date of shipment in order that the Buyer can charter a vessel/book shipping space. In the eventss of the Seller's failure to effect loading when the vessel arrives duly at the loading port, all expenses including dead freight and/or demurrage charges thus incurred shall be for the Seller's account.

(2)CIF/CFR

The Seller shall ship the goods duly within the shipping duration from the port of loading to the port of destination. Under CFR terms, the Seller shall advise the Buyer of the Contract No., names of commodity, invoice value, and the date of dispatch two days before the shipment for the Buyer to arrange insurance in time.

17.Shipping Advice

The Seller shall, immediately upon the completion of the loading of the goods, advise the Buyer of the Contract No., names of commodity, loading quantity, invoice value, gross weight, name of vessel, and shipment date within_____hours.

18.Quality Guarantee

The Seller shall guarantee that upon delivery all goods to be delivered by the Seller shall be completely new and shall comply in all material respects with this Contract.

The guarantee period is within_____days after the date of the completion of unloading of the goods at the port of destination. Within the guarantee period, the Seller shall remove all defects of the goods due to design, workmanship and improper material used either by repairing or by placing the defective parts of the goods on his own account.

19.Inspection

The Seller shall have the goods inspected by_____days before the shipment and have the Inspection Certificate issued. The Buyer may have the goods reinserted after the goods' arrival at the destination.

20.Claim

The Buyer shall make a claim against the Seller (including replacement of the goods) by the further inspection certificate and all the expenses incurred therefrom shall be borne by the Seller. The claims mentioned above shall be regarded as being accepted if the Seller fail to reply within _____days after the Seller received the Buyer's claim.

21.Late Delivery and Penalty

The Buyer shall take all reasonable acts in order to enable the Seller to make delivery and shall take over the goods.

Should the Seller fail to make delivery on time as stipulated in the Contract, with the exception of Force Majeure causes specified in Clause 22 of this Contract, the Buyer shall agree to postpone the delivery on the condition that the Seller agrees to pay a penalty which shall be deducted by the paying bank from the payment under negotiation. The rate of penalty is charged at_____% for every_____days, odd days less than_____days should be counted as_____ days. But the penalty shall not exceed_____% of the total value of the goods involved in the delayed delivery. In case the Seller fails to make delivery_____days later than the time of shipment stipulated in the Contract, the Buyer shall have the right to cancel the Contract and the Seller, in spite of the cancellation, shall nevertheless pay the aforesaid penalty to the Buyer without delay.

The Buyer shall have the right to lodge a claim against the Seller for the losses sustained if any.

22.Force Majeure

Either party shall not be held responsible for failure or delay to perform all or any part of this Contract due to flood, fire, earthquake, draught, war or any other events which could not be predicted, controlled, avoided or overcome by the relative party. However, the party affected by the event of Force Majeure shall inform the other party of its occurrence in writing as soon as possible and thereafter send a certificate of the event issued by the relevant authorities to the other party within_____days after its occurrence.

If the event of Force Majeure last over_____days, both parties shall negotiate on the performance or the termination of the Contract. However, if the conditions or consequences of Force Majeure which have a material adverse effect on the affected party's ability to continue to perform for a period in excess of_____days and the parties have been unable to find an equitable solution, the Contract shall terminate automatically.

23.Arbitration

All disputes arising from the execution of this Contract shall be settled through friendly consultations. In case no settlement can be reached, the case in dispute shall then be submitted to the arbitration commission in accordance with its Provisional Rules of Procedure. The decision made by this commission shall be regarded as final and binding upon both parties. Arbitration fees shall be borne by the losing party, unless otherwise awarded.

24.Effectiveness

The Contract shall come into effect immediately when it is signed by duly authorized representatives of both parties.

25.Amendment

This Contract shall not be changed verbally, but only by a written instrument signed by the parties.

Representative of the Buyer: Representative of the Seller:

(Authorized Signature)   (Authorized Signature)

采购合同

合同编号：

日　　期：

签约地点：

卖方：

地址：

邮编：

电话：

传真：

买方：

地址：

邮编：

电话：

传真：

兹经买卖双方同意，按照以下条款由买方购进、卖方售出以下商品：

1.货物号

2.货物名称和规格

3.数量

4.单价

5.总价

由卖方决定货物总金额和数量____%的增减。

6.交货条件

7.原产地及生产商

8.包装和标准

货物包装应防潮、防锈、防水、防腐和防碰，应当适合海洋运输/多式联运。卖方应承担由包装不足或不当而导致的货物损坏和损失。体积、毛重、净重和警告（如"此端向上""切勿受潮""小心轻放"）应当用不褪色的颜色标明在每个包装箱上。

9.装运唛头

10.装运时间

11.装运港

12.目的港

13.保险

保险由_____按发票金额的____%投保_____险和附加险。

14.支付条款

（1）信用证：买方应在装运期亦合同生效后____日，开出以卖方为受益人的不可撤销的信用证。信用证在装船完毕后____日内到期。

（2）付款交单：货物发运后，卖方出具以买方为付款人的付款跟单汇票，按即期付款交单方式，通过卖方银行及_____银行向买方转交单证，换取货物。买方见票后即付。

（3）承兑交单：货物发运后，卖方出具以买方为付款人的付款跟单汇票，付款期限为____日，按即期承兑交单方式，通过卖方银行以及_____银行，经买方承兑后，向买方转交单证。买方在汇票到期时支付货款。

（4）货到付款：买方在收到货物后____天内将全部货款付给卖方（不适用于FOB、CIF贸易术语）。

15.所需要的单据

卖方应将下列单据提交银行议付/托收：

（1）全套已装船清洁海运/联运提单，空白背书注明运费预付/到付。

（2）已签署的商业发票一式____份，并标明合同编号、信用证号（信用证条款）和装运唛头。

（3）由_____开立装箱单/重量单，一式____份。

（4）由_____开立的质量证书，一式____份。

（5）由_____开立的数量证书，一式____份。

（6）保险单或保险凭证，一式____份（CIF贸易术语）。

（7）装船通知：卖方应在装船后____小时内发送以上单证号码。

16.装运条款

（1）FOB

卖方应在合同规定的装船日期前30天通知买方合同号、品名、数量、金额、包装、毛重、体积和装运期，以便买方可以租船订舱。如果卖方未能在装运港装船，那么所有费用（包括空舱费和/或由此产生的滞期费）应由卖方负担。

（2）CIF/CFR

卖方应按时在装运期限内将货物由装运港运至目的港。在CFR贸易术语下，卖方应在装船前两天通知买方合同号、品名、发票金额及开船日期，以便买方及时安排保险。

17.装船通知

卖方应在完成装运货物后____小时内立即通知买方合同号、品名、装载数量、发票金额、毛重、船名和起运日期。

18.质量保证

卖方应保证交付的货物是全新的，所用的材料应与本合同相符。

保证期是货物在目的港完成卸货____天内。在保证期内，卖方应更换由设计、工艺和使用材料的不恰当造成的不合格商品，可通过修理或更换有缺陷的零件或货物，费用自己承担。

19.检验

卖方应在货物装运前____天检验货物并出具检验证书。买方可以在货物到达目的地后加货。

20.索赔

买方凭进一步的检验证书向卖方提出索赔（包括更换货物），由此产生的全部费用应由卖方承担。如果卖方在收到买方提出索赔的____天里未能回复，那么以上提到的索赔应视为已接受。

21.延期交货和罚款

买方应当采取一切合理的行为使卖方交货并接管货物。

除合同第22条不可抗力原因外，如卖方不能按合同规定的时间交货，买方应同意在卖方支付罚款的条件下延期交款。罚款可由议付银行在议付货款时扣除。罚款率按每____天收____%，不足____天时以____天计算。但罚款不得超过迟交货物总价的____%。如果卖方延期交货超过合同规定____天，买方有权撤销合同。此时，卖方仍应毫不延迟地按上述规定向买方支付罚款。

买方有权对因此遭受的其他损失向卖方提出索赔。

22.不可抗力

任何一方不应承担由于洪水、火灾、地震、干旱、战争或任何其他无法预测、控制、避免或克服事件的未履行或延迟履行全部或部分协议的责任。但是，受不可抗力事件影响的一方应当在事件发生后____天内书面通知另一方，之后尽快发送经事件相关部门认定的证明给另一方。

如果不可抗力事件持续超过____天，双方应协商履行或终止合同。然而，如果超过____天，不可抗力的条件或后果对受影响方继续履行合同产生重大不利影响，同时双方未能找到一个合理的解决方案，该合同将自动终止。

23.仲裁

凡有关执行合同所发生的一切争议应友好协商解决。如果协商不能解决，则将分歧提交仲裁委员会按暂行程序规则进行仲裁。仲裁将是终局性的，双方均受其约束。除非另有约定，仲裁费用由败诉方承担。

24.有效性

合同由双方正式授权的代表签署时将立即生效。

25.修改

本合同不得口头修改，仅可进行双方签署的书面修改。

买方代表：　　　　　　　　　　　　　卖方代表：

（授权签名）　　　　　　　　　　　　（授权签名）

Appendix 2

Sales Confirmation[①]
销售确认书

SELLER(卖方):	SHANDONG TEXTILES IMPORT & EXPORT CORPORATION 4 YING CHUN STREET, QINGDAO, CHINA	NO.(编号):	03DRA207
		DATE(日期):	JAN. 20, 202×
BUYER(买方):	NICHIEN CORPORATION 2 - 2 NAKANOSHIMA 3 - CHOME, KITA-KU OSAKA, 632-8620, JAPAN	SIGNED IN(签约地点):	QINGDAO, CHINA

This contract is made by and agreed between the BUYER and the SELLER, in accordance with the terms and conditions stipulated below.

经买卖双方同意成交下列商品，订立条款如下。

Marks & Numbers (唛头)	Description of Goods (货物描述)	Quantity (数量)	Unit Price (单价)	Amount (金额)
			FOB	QINGDAO
N/M	PORTABLE MIXER PM-23 VACUUM CLEANER VC-18 ***************************	100 SETS 100 SETS *************	USD23.00 USD47.00 ********	USD2,300.00 USD4,700.00 ****************
	TOTAL:	200 SETS		USD7,000.00

TOTAL(总值):	U. S. DOLLARS SEVEN THOUSAND ONLY.

TRANSSHIPMENT(转运):

□ Allowed(允许)	☒Not allowed(不允许)

PARTIAL SHIPMENTS(分批装运):

□ Allowed(允许)	☒Not allowed(不允许)

SHIPMENT DATE(装运期):

NOT LATER THAN 30TH JUNE, 202×.

---

① 凌芳. 国际商务合同大全：国际商务合同模板手册［M］. 广州：广东经济出版社，2015：66-70.

Insurance(保险)：

To be covered by the_____ for 110% of the invoice value covering_____ risk, additional_____risk from_____to_____.

由_____按发票金额110%投保_____险，另加保_____险从_____至_____为止。

TERMS OF PAYMENT(付款条件)：

☐ The buyer shall pay 100% of the sales proceeds through sight draft/by T/T remittance to the seller not later than_____.

买方不迟于_____年____月____日前将100%的货款用即期汇票/电汇方式送抵卖方。

☒ The buyer shall issue an irrevocable L/C at__***__sight through_____in favor of the seller prior to_30TH APRIL，202×_ indicating the L/C shall be valid in China through negotiation within_21_ days after the shipment effected，the L/C must mention the Contract Number.

买方须于_202×_年_4_月_30_日前通过_____银行开出以卖方为受益人的不可撤销_即_期信用证，并注明在上述装运日期后 21 天内在中国议付有效，信用证须注明合同号。

☐ Documents against payment (D/P)(付款交单)：

The buyer shall duly make the payment against the documentary draft made out to the buyer at_____days sight by the seller.

买方应对卖方开具的以买方为付款人的见票后____天付款跟单汇票付款。

☐ Documents against acceptance (D/A)(承兑交单)：

The buyer shall duly accept the documentary draft made out to the buyer at____days sight by the seller.

买方应对卖方开具的以买方为付款人的见票后____天承兑跟单汇票承兑。

DOCUMENTS REQUIRED(所需单据)：

The seller shall present the following documents required for negotiation/collection to the banks.

卖方应将下列单据提交银行议付/托收。

☒ Full set of clean on board ocean bills of lading.
全套已装船清洁海运提单。

☒ Signed commercial invoice in_3_copies.
已签署的商业发票一式_3_份。

☒ Packing list/weight memo in_3_copies.
装箱单或重量单一式_3_份。

☐ Certificate of quantity and quality in_____copies issued by_____.
由_____签发的数量与质量证书一式____份。

☐ Insurance policy in____copies.
保险单一式____份。

☐ Certificate of Origin in____copies issued by_____.
由_____签发的原产地证书一式____份。

SHIPPING ADVICE(装运通知)：

The seller shall immediately, upon the completion of the loading of the goods, advise the buyer of the contract No., names of commodity, loaded quantity, invoice value, gross weight, name of vessel and shipment date by telex or fax.

一旦装运完毕，卖方应立即电告买方合同号、品名、已装载数量、发票金额、毛重、船名及起运日期等。

INSPECTION AND CLAIM(检验与索赔):

1.The buyer shall have the quality, specification, quantity of the goods carefully inspected by the Inspection Authority_____, which shall issue Inspection Certificate before shipment.

卖方在装船前由检验机构_____对货物的品质、规格和数量进行严格检验，并出具检验证书。

2.The buyer has the right to have the goods inspected by the local commodity inspection authority after the arrival of the goods at the port of destination. If the goods are found damaged/short/their specifications and quantities not in compliance with that specified in the contract, the buyer shall lodge claims against the seller based on the Inspection Certificate issued by the Inspection Authority_____ within_____ days after the arrival of the goods at the destination.

货物到达目的港后，买方可委托当地的商品检验机构对货物进行复检。如果货物被发现损坏、残缺或规格、数量与合同规定不符，买方须于货物到达目的港的____天内凭检验机构_____出具的检验证书向卖方索赔。

3.The claims, if any regarding to the quality of the goods, shall be lodged within_____days after the arrival of the goods at the destination, if any regarding to the quantities of the goods, shall be lodged within____days after the arrival of the goods at the destination. The seller shall not take any responsibility if any claim concerning the shipping goods is up to the responsibility of the Insurance Company/Transportation Company/Post Office.

如买方提出索赔，凡属品质异议，须于货物到达目的港之日起____天内提出；凡属数量异议，须于货物到达目的港之日起____天内提出。对货物所提任何异议，应由保险公司、运输公司或邮政部门负责的，卖方不负任何责任。

FORCE MAJEURE(不可抗力):

The seller shall not hold any responsibility for partial or total non-performance of this contract due to Force Majeure. But the seller shall advise the buyer on time of such occurrence.

如因不可抗力造成本合同全部或部分不能履约，卖方概不负责；但卖方应将上述发生的情况及时通知买方。

DISPUTES SETTLEMENT(争议之解决方式):

All disputes in connection with this contract of the execution thereof shall be amicably settled through negotiation. In case no amicable settlement can be reached between the two parties, the case under the dispute shall be submitted for arbitration, which shall be held in the country where the defendant resides, or in a third country agreed by both parties. The decision of the arbitration shall be accepted as final and binding upon both parties. The arbitration fees shall be borne by the losing party.

凡因执行本合同或有关本合同所发生的一切争执，双方应协商解决。如果协商不能解决，应提交仲裁。仲裁地点在被告方所在国，或者在双方同意的第三国。仲裁裁决是终局性的，对双方都有约束力。仲裁费用由败诉方承担。

LAW APPLICATION(法律适用):

It will be governed by the law of the People's Republic of China under the circumstances that the contract is signed or the goods while the disputes arising are in the People's Republic of China or the defendant is Chinese legal person, otherwise it is governed by the United Nations Convention on Contracts for the International Sale of Goods.

The terms in the contract are based on INCOTERMS 2020 of the International Chamber of Commerce.

本合同之签订地，或发生争议时货物所在地在中华人民共和国境内或被诉人为中国法人的，适用中华人民共和国法律；除此规定外，适用《联合国国际货物销售合同公约》。

本合同使用的贸易术语系根据国际商会 INCOTERMS 2020。

This contract is in 3 copies, effective since being singed/sealed by both parties.

本合同共 3 份，自双方代表签名（盖章）之日起生效。

The Buyer	**The Seller**
NICHIEN CORPORATION	SHANDONG TEXTILES IMPORT & EXPORT CORPORATION
Y. Bayer	张立

Appendix 3

Sales Contract[①]
销售合同

SELLER(卖方):	GUANGDONG FOREIGN TRADE IMP. & EXP. CORP. 15 - 18/F, 351 TIANHE ROAD, GUANGZHOU, CHINA	NO.(编号):	SHDS03027
		DATE(日期):	. APR. 3RD, 202×
BUYER(买方):	NEO GENERAL TRADING CO. #362 JALAN STREET, TORONTO, CANADA	SIGNED IN(签约地点):	SHANGHAI, CHINA

This contract is made by and agreed between the BUYER and the SELLER, in accordance with the terms and conditions stipulated below.
买卖双方同意按以下条款达成交易。

1. Commodity & Specification (品名及规格)	2. Quantity (数量)	3.Unit Price & Trade Terms (单价及贸易术语)	4. Amount (金额)
		CIFC5	TORONTO
CHINESE CERAMIC DINNERWARE			
DS1511 30-PIECE DINNERWARE AND TEA SET	542 SETS	USD23.50	USD12,737.00
DS2201 20-PIECE DINNERWARE SET	800 SETS	USD20.40	USD16,320.00
DS4504 45-PIECE DINNERWARE SET	443 SETS	USD23.20	USD10,277.60
DS5120 95-PIECE DINNERWARE SET	254 SETS	USD30.10	USD7,645.40
Total:	2,039 SETS		USD46,980. 00

With (允许)	10% MORE OR LESS OF SHIPMENT ALLOWED AT THE SELLER'S OPTION.
5. Total Value (总值)	SAY US DOLLARS FORTY-SIX THOUSAND NINE HUNDRED AND EIGHTY ONLY.
6. Packing (包装)	DS2201 IN CARTONS OF 2 SETS EACH AND DS1511, DS4504 AND DS5120 TO BE PACKED IN CARTONS OF 1 SET EACH ONLY. TOTAL: 1,639 CARTONS.
7. Shipping Marks (唛头)	AT THE BUYER'S OPTION.
8. Time of Shipment & Means of Transportation (装运期及运输方式)	TO BE EFFECTED BEFORE THE END OF APRIL 202× WITH PARTIAL SHIPMENT ALLOWED AND TRANSSHIPMENT ALLOWED.
9. Port of Loading & Destination (装运港及目的地)	FROM: GUANGZHOU, CHINA TO: TORONTO, CANADA
10. Insurance (保险)	THE SELLER SHALL COVER INSURANCE AGAINST WPA AND CLASH & BREAKAGE & WAR RISKS FOR 110% OF THE TOTAL INVOICE VALUE.
11. Terms of Payment (付款方式)	BY IRREVOCABLE SIGHT LETTER OF CREDIT.
12. Remarks (备注)	
The Buyer NEO GENERAL TRADING CO. Y. BAYER	The Seller GUANGDONG FOREIGN TRADE IMP. & EXP. CORP. 张立

---

① 凌芳. 国际商务合同大全：国际商务合同模板手册［M］. 广州：广东经济出版社，2015：51-55.

Appendix 4

Processing Contract[①]

Contract No.:
Signing Date:
Signing Place:

Party A (Party of Processing): _____Company
Legal Address: _____
Tel and Fax: _____
E-mail: _____

Party B (Party of Supplying Materials and Parts): _____ Company
Legal Address: _____
Tel and Fax: _____
E-mail: _____

Party A and Party B, according to the Civil Code of the People's Republic of China and the relevant regulations and the principles of equality and mutual benefit, have held discussion relating to the processing of _____and have reached an agreement on the following contractual clauses:

Article 1　Responsibilities

1.Responsibilities of Party A

(1)Party A shall provide factory space consisting of_____ square meters, field of _____ square meters without covering, _____factory management persons and workers for the first phase. The number of workers shall be increased to_____ twelve months after operation. Within the Contract term, Party A shall process the products for Party B which shall be reexported to Party B.

(2)The water supply and utility equipment required for processing shall be provided by Party A. If additional installations of water and electric facilities are required, the expenses thereof shall be borne by Party B.

(3)Party A shall arrange all the necessary import and export approvals required for processing and assembling, and provide administration and accounting management for the processing plant.

① 李岹. 商务英文合同模板大全［M］. 济南：山东科学技术出版社，2009：242-244.

Party A cannot assign Party A's responsibilities to any other party or individual in any way.

2.Responsibilities of Party B

(1)To provide the equipment with the total value of_____yuan.

(2)To provide the raw materials, the indirect materials and the packaging materials for processing the products. Quantities and specifications are to be specified in the separate processing contracts.

(3)In the event any personnel, including management shows substandard performance and makes no improvement after retraining, Party B shall have the right to request Party A to replace such persons. However, any physical search of the workers shall be regarded as illegal and prohibited.

Article 2　Quantity of Products

During the first year, the total processing fee shall amount to_____yuan. From the second year, the quantity shall be increased. The details shall be specified in the separate processing contracts.

Article 3　Price and Salary

(1)The trial production (including training) period shall be two months. During such period, the workers shall be paid_____of processing fee per month on the basis of_____ working days per month and_____working hours per day.

(2)After the trial production period, the workers' payment shall be calculated according to actual production quantities. On the basis of mutual benefit, both parties shall consider the processing fee, which shall be specified in the separate processing contracts, according to the different kinds of the products, specifications, styles and engineering procedures. In order to ensure the reasonable income of the workers, the workers' monthly salary shall be maintained no lower than_____ yuan. If overtime work is required, the payment shall be calculated separately. However, overtime shall not exceed_____hours a day.

(3)Expenses for water and electricity in Party A's plant shall be borne by Party B.

(4)Every month Party B shall pay_____yuan to Party A for management expenses.

Article 4　Proportion of Damaged Products

(1)During the trial production period, Party B shall absorb the cost of the damaged products.

(2)After the trial production period, the proportion of the damaged products shall be mutually considered and decided by both parties and specified in the separate processing contracts.

Article 5　Shipment of Raw Materials & Finished Products

(1)Every month, Party B shall provide sufficient raw materials and packaging materials according to the contracted processing volume. To ensure the normal production of Party A's plant, Party B shall ship such materials to the plant_____days before the production of each lot of the products. Except for causes of force majeure, the plant shall operate for more than_____days in a month. In case the production is held up for four days due to insufficient supply of raw materials, Party B shall calculate the actual days when the production is shut down and pay to Party A the workers' living expenses at the rate of_____yuan per person per day.

(2)To ensure the normal operation of Party B's business activities, Party A shall deliver the finished products to Party B in accordance with the time of delivery, the quality and the quantity. Except for causes of force majeure, in case the losses to Party B are caused due to Party A's failure to make delivery as mentioned above, Party A shall be responsible for the compensation. The details of such compensation shall be mutually agreed upon in the separate processing contracts.

(3)Both parties shall mutually inspect and document the equipment and materials provided by Party B, such as machinery, ventilation and lighting equipment, and raw materials. After the finished products are inspected and shipped from the plant by Party B, Party A shall be free of any responsibility in regard to specifications, quality and quantity, etc.

Article 6　Method of Payment

The payment of the workers' salary and management fee shall be settled once a month by D/P, which shall be conducted through Bank of China_____Branch by Party B's bank in_____(_____Bank, Account No._____) in accordance with the invoices issued by Party A. In case Party B's payment is delayed for_____ days, Party B shall be responsible for the interest incurred according to the bank's interest rate. In case the payment is not settled for _____consecutive months, Party A shall have the right to suspend the delivery of the finished products or take other measures.

Article 7　Labour Protection & Insurance

(1)The plant shall take safety measures and protect the workers from dirt, smoke and poisonous materials. The factory shall be maintained ventilated and bright, and the surroundings clean and tidy.

(2)The transportation expenses for the machinery, the ventilation and lighting equipment, the raw materials, the packaging materials and the finished products shall be paid by Party B.

(3)All insurance for the transportation and storage of the above materials, machinery and equipment and coverage of the workers operating the machinery shall be arranged through the _____Insurance Company by Party B.

Article 8　Technical Exchange

After the arrival of the equipment at the plant, Party B shall dispatch personnel to install such equipment, while Party A shall arrange personnel to assist the installation. When the trial production begins, Party B shall provide technical personnel to carry out the training until the workers have mastered the technology and the production operates normally. Party B shall be responsible for the technical personnel's salary and all related expenses, and Party A shall provide daily necessities.

Article 9　Contract Period

After this contract is signed and approved, Party B shall present to Party A its Business Registration Certificate and Bank Credit Certificate for Party A to arrange business licence and Customs Registration. The period of this contract shall be_____years, namely from_____to _____. If either party wishes to terminate in advance or extend the contract, the responsible party shall inform the other party three months in advance so that both parties can discuss and settle such termination or extension. If either party terminates the contract before the term expires, the responsible party shall compensate the other party for the losses in such case.

After the contract period expires, the real estate such as the factory building and the dormitory building shall be returned to Party A and the machinery and the equipment delivered by Party B shall be returned to Party B. Customs clearance procedures shall be gone through according to relevant regulations.

Both parties agree that, within_____days after the contract is signed and approved, Party B shall pay Party A the amount of_____yuan as its guarantee to carry out the contract. If, within_____months after Party A's receipt of such amount, Party B still cannot arrange to start production, the amount shall be forfeited to Party A unconditionally and Party A shall have the right to cancel the contract. If Party B can start production on time, the amount will be deducted from the processing fee.

Article 10　Arbitration

Any dispute arising from or in connection with this contract (and including all the separate processing contracts) shall be settled through amicable negotiations. Should no settlement be reached through negotiations, the case shall then be submitted to the China International Economic and Trade Arbitration Commission (CIETAC) Shenzhen Commission for arbitration that shall be conducted in Shenzhen in accordance with the CIETAC's arbitration rules in effect at the time of applying for arbitration. The arbitral award is final and binding upon both parties.

Article 11　Language

The present contract is drawn in Chinese and English as well, both texts being equally authentic. In case of any divergence of interpretation, the Chinese text shall prevail.

Article 12　Amendment and Copies

The contract is made out in three copies respectively held by the Parties and the Custom. They shall have the same force.

If there are other issues not covered in the contract, both parties can discuss to supplement or amend the contract and submit the results to relevant government departments for approval.

Party A:　　　　　　　　　　　　　　Party B:

Authorized Representative:　　　　　　Authorized Representative:

(Signature)　　　　　　　　　　　　　(Signature)

加工合同

合同号：_____

签约日期：_____

签约地点：_____

甲方（加工方）：_____公司

法定地址：_____

电话与传真：_____

电子邮箱：_____

乙方（来料和来件方）：_____公司

法定地址：_____

电话与传真：_____

电子邮箱：_____

根据《中华人民共和国民法典》及相关规定，本着平等互利的原则，双方就加工_____进行了充分协商，一致达成如下合同条款：

第一条　双方责任

1.甲方责任

（1）甲方提供厂房_____平方米；场地_____平方米；工厂管理人员和工人首期____名，工人数量在开业后12个月内增至____名。在合同期内，甲方代乙方加工生产上述产品，并复出口给乙方。

（2）甲方提供加工生产之供水和电力设备，如需额外安装水、电设施，其费用由乙方自行解决。

（3）甲方应负责办理来料加工、装配有关业务的必需的进出口手续，以及对加工工厂实行管理等。甲方不得把工作以任何形式承包给任何第三方单位和个人。

2.乙方责任

（1）提供总值_____元的设备。

（2）提供加工上述产品所需的原料、辅料和包装物料，具体数量、规格在各份具体加工合同中写明。

（3）任何工人（含工厂管理人员）如因工作不力，经再培训无改进者，乙方有权向甲方提出调换，但禁止非法搜查甲方工厂工人的身体。

第二条　产品数量

第一年加工上述产品，加工费约为_____元。从第二年开始的产量应在前一年的基础上有所增加，具体数量应在加工合同中写明。

第三条　价格和工资

（1）试产（包括培训）期为两个月。在试产期内，工人每人每月工缴费暂定为＿＿＿＿元，每月工作＿＿＿日，每天工作＿＿＿小时。

（2）试产期满后，采取按件计算方式。在坚持互利原则的基础上，双方应根据加工的品种、规格、款式和工艺繁简程度不同进行定价，并在加工合同中写明。为确保工人的合理收入，工缴费平均每人每月不低于＿＿＿＿元。需要加班时，加班费另计；但每个工人每天加班时间最长不得超过＿＿＿小时。

（3）甲方工厂消耗的水、电费由乙方负责。

（4）每月乙方支付甲方＿＿＿＿元，作为管理费。

第四条　产品损耗率

（1）试产期内，乙方承担损耗产品的成本。

（2）试产期后的产品损耗率，由双方商定，并在具体加工合同中写明。

第五条　原材料和成品的交货期

（1）乙方按加工合同的加工量，按月提供足够数量的原材料和包装物料。为使甲方工厂能正常生产，乙方必须在每批产品开始加工前＿＿＿天，将所需的原材料和包装物料运抵甲方工厂。除不可抗力原因外，工厂每月开工应多于＿＿＿天。乙方来料不足，停工天数累计不得超过4天；否则，乙方应按在厂工人的停工天数计，每人每天补助生活费＿＿＿元，支付给甲方。

（2）为使乙方能开展正常的业务活动，甲方应向乙方按商定的交货期，按时、按质、按量交货。除不可抗力原因外，甲方不按时、按质、按量交货，造成乙方的经济损失，甲方应负赔偿之责任，赔偿数额可在具体的加工合同中写明。

（3）由乙方提供的机械、通风和照明设备、原材料等，在甲方工厂由双方进行交收登记，建立账册。甲方工厂加工后的成品，在甲方工厂经乙方验收起运后，甲方不负产品规格、质量和数量等方面的任何责任。

第六条　支付方式

工缴费及工人管理费每月结算一次，以付款交单方式结汇，由甲方工厂开具发票后，通过中国银行＿＿＿＿分行向乙方在＿＿＿＿开户的银行（＿＿＿＿银行，账号＿＿＿＿）办理。如果乙方超过＿＿＿天仍未付款给甲方，则按逾期天数，以当时的银行利息一并付给甲方。如果乙方连续＿＿＿个月不结汇，甲方有权停止出货或采取其他措施。

第七条　劳动保护和保险

（1）工厂应做好劳动保护及安全工作，完善防尘、防烟、防毒设施。厂房保持通风明亮，内外环境卫生整洁。

（2）乙方提供的机械、通风和照明设备、原材料、包装物料及甲方工厂加工后的成品运输费用，均由乙方负责。

（3）原材料、包装物料、成品的运输与存储，机械设备，以及操作机械的工人，均由乙方向＿＿＿＿保险公司投保。

第八条 技术交流

在设备运抵甲方工厂后，乙方应尽快派出人员进行安装，甲方派出人员进行协助。当试生产开始时，乙方应派出技术人员到甲方工厂进行技术培训，直到工人能基本掌握生产技术、进行正常生产。乙方负责技术人员的工资及一切费用，甲方提供生活上的方便。

第九条 合同期限

本合同经批准签订后，乙方须将商业登记证及银行资信证明交甲方办理营业执照，经海关备案生效。合同有效期为____年，即从_____至_____。如要提前终止或延长本合同，须提前3个月通知对方，并经双方协商处理终止或延长合同事宜。某方单独提前终止合同，要负责补偿对方的经济损失。

合同期满后，不动资产（如厂房、宿舍）归甲方所有，由乙方不作价提供的机械设备归乙方所有，并按海关和有关规定及时办理核销手续。

双方同意，在本合同经批准签订后____天内，乙方向甲方预付_____元，作为履约保证金。从甲方收到履约保证金之日起____个月内，如果乙方仍不投产开业，履约保证金即无条件归甲方所有；同时，甲方有权废约。如果乙方能按时投产开业，则该履约保证金可作为工缴费抵付给甲方。

第十条 仲裁

凡因本合同引起的或与本合同有关（包括任一加工合同）的任何争议，应通过友好协商解决；协商不能解决，均应提交中国国际经济贸易仲裁委员会深圳分会，按照申请仲裁时该会施行有效的仲裁规则进行仲裁。仲裁裁决是终局性的，对双方均有约束力。

第十一条 语言

本合同用英文和中文书写，两种文本具有同等效力。但在对其解释产生异议时，以中文文本为准。

第十二条 合同的修订和份数

本合同正本一式三份，由甲乙双方和海关各持一份，均具有同等效力。

本合同如有未尽事宜，双方可随时补充或修改，并报政府有关部门批准。

甲方：   乙方：

授权代表：   授权代表：

（签名）   （签名）

Appendix 5

Agency Contract[①]

This contract is made on the day of_____ , between Mr._____ , representative of_____ Corporation (hereinafter called Party A) and Mr._____ , representative of_____Corporation (hereinafter called Party B).

Whereas Party A is willing to appoint Party B as its exclusive sole agent in the territory of_____for selling_____ , it is hereby mutually agreed as follows:

1. Party A appoints Party B as its exclusive sole agent in the territory of_____for selling _____ .

2. Party A shall supply Party B with the finished products of_____ . Party B shall be responsible for the packing and labeling, with the same trademark and labels as the original ones.

3. The monthly sales of Party B shall not be less than_____set/box.

4. This contract shall be canceled at any time should Party B fail to meet the agreed sales quantity for_____months.

5. During the term of this contract, Party A shall not appoint another company or factory to sell in the territory of_____without Party B's consent.

6. Party B shall continue to enjoy the privilege of the agent should they meet the agreed sales quantity every month.

7. Advertising expenses shall be borne by Party B.

8. This contract shall be effective commencing from the date of signing.

9. This contract shall be made in two copies, both in English and Chinese and each party shall keep one copy. In case of any discrepancy between the Chinese and English copy, the English copy shall govern.

10. This contract can be changed when both parties agree to the change.

Party A: Party B:

_____Corporation   _____Corporation

---

① 李峣. 商务英文合同模板大全［M］. 济南：山东科学技术出版社，2009：294-296.

代理合同

    _____公司（以下简称甲方）代表_____先生和_____公司（以下简称乙方）代表_____先生于_____年____月____日签订本合同。

    鉴于甲方愿指定乙方为其在_____地区独家代理销售_____，双方就以下条款达成协议：

1. 甲方指定乙方为甲方在_____地区销售_____的独家代理。

2. 甲方供给乙方_____的成品，由乙方包装并粘贴与原样相同的商标和标签。

3. 乙方每月销售量不少于_____套/箱。

4. 如果乙方不能销售双方协议的数量达____个月，则本合同随时可予撤销。

5. 本合同有效期内，甲方未经乙方同意，不得指派另一家公司或工厂在_____地区销售_____。

6. 若乙方每月销售量达到规定的数量，乙方有权继续担任代理。

7. 广告费由乙方负担。

8. 本合同自签名之日起生效。

9. 本合同用中、英文写成，一式两份，双方各执一份。如中文文本与英文文本发生异议，以英文文本为准。

10. 经双方同意，本合同可以修改。

    甲方：   乙方：

    _____公司   _____公司

Appendix 6

Distribution Agreement①

No.:

This agreement is made as of the _____ day of _____ , 20____ , by and between_____(Supplier), a _____organized and existing under the law of_____, with its principal place of business at _____, and_____ (Distributor), a_____ organized and existing under the law of _____ , with its principal place of business at_____.

Supplier:

Distributor:

1.Definition

There are the following terms in this agreement:

(1)Accessories

Accessories may be deleted from or added to Attachment_____and the Supplier may change the contents of the agreement, by mailing the written notice of such changes to the Distributor. Each change shall become effective within_____ days following the date notice thereof is mailed to the Distributor.

(2)Goods

Which means those items described in Attachment_____. The goods may be deleted from or added to Attachment_____, which may be changed by the Supplier at its sole discretion at any time by mailing the written notice of such changes to the Distributor. Each change shall become effective within_____days following the date notice thereof is mailed to the Distributor.

(3)Spare Parts

Which means all parts and components of the Goods and/or any special device used in connection with the maintenance or servicing of the Goods. The Supplier declares that a complete list of the Spare Parts is set forth in Attachment_____. The Spare parts may be deleted from or added to Attachment_____and their specifications and design may be changed by the Supplier at its sole discretion at any time by mailing the written notice of such changes to the Distributor. Each change shall become effective within_____ days following the date notice thereof is mailed to the Distributor.

---

① 李峣. 商务英文合同模板大全 [M]. 济南：山东科学技术出版社，2009：41-43.

(4)Trademark

Which means any trademark, logo, or service mark, whether or not registered, used to represent or describe the Products of the Supplier, as set forth in Attachment_____.

2.Appointment of Distributor

The Supplier hereby appoints the Distributor as the Supplier's Exclusive Distributor of the Products in the territory. It is understood that the Supplier can lawfully prevent its distributors located elsewhere from supplying the Products for sale or use within the territory and that it has no obligation to do so.

3.Relationship between Both Parties

The Distributor is an independent contractor and is not the legal representative or agent of the Supplier for any purpose and shall have no right or authority (except as expressly provided in this Agreement) to incur, assume or create in writing or otherwise, any warranty on the part of the Supplier. The Supplier shall not exercise any control over any of the Distributor's employees, all of who are entirely under the control of the Distributor. The Distributor shall be responsible for the acts and omissions of the Distributor's employees.

The Distributor shall, at its own expense, during the term of this Agreement and any extension thereof, maintain full insurance under any Labor Law effective in the state or other applicable jurisdiction covering all persons employed by and working for it in connection with the performance of this Agreement, and upon request shall furnish the Supplier with satisfactory evidence of the maintenance of such insurance.

4.Sale of Products

The Distributor shall use its best efforts to distribute the Products and to fully develop the market for the Products within the territory. The parties have consulted together and now agree that if the Distributor's best efforts are used as provided in this Section, a minimum of _____ Products (Annual Market Potential) will be purchased and distributed in the territory during the first year of this Agreement. At the beginning of each subsequent year the parties will consult together in good faith and agree on the Annual Market Potential applicable to that year; provided, however, that if they cannot agree, the Annual Market Potential for the immediately preceding year will apply to the current year.

5.Advertisement

The Distributor shall be entitled, during the term of the distributorship created by this Agreement and any extension thereof, to advertise and hold itself out as an authorized Distributor of the Products. At all times during the term of the distributorship created by this Agreement and any extension thereof, the Distributor shall use the Trademarks in all advertisements and other activities conducted by the Distributor to promote the sale of the Products. The Distributor shall submit samples of all proposed advertisements and other promotional materials for the Products to the Supplier for approval and the Distributor shall not use any such advertisements or promotional materials without having received the prior written consent of the Supplier to do so. The Distributor shall not, pursuant to this Agreement or otherwise, have or acquire any right, title or interest in or to the Supplier's Trademarks.

6.Distributor Sales, Service and Storage Facilities

The Distributor shall, at its expense, engage and maintain a sales, service and parts handling organization in the territory, staffed with such experienced personnel as are necessary to enable the Distributor to perform its obligations under this Agreement.

The Distributor shall, at its expense, maintain facilities and personnel in the territory that will enable it promptly and satisfactorily to perform, at a reasonable price, all inspection, maintenance and other necessary servicing of the Products sold by the Distributor. To assist the Distributor in the discharge of this service and maintenance function, the Supplier shall provide service and maintenance training, without charge, to any reasonable number of the Distributor's personnel as the Distributor shall designate.

The Distributor shall, at its expense, at all times store and maintain its inventory of the Products in accordance with current, applicable instructions issued by the Supplier from time to time. The Distributor shall, at its expense, deliver one copy of the Supplier's current, applicable operation and maintenance manual to each Customer at the time of sale and, at that time, the Distributor shall, at its expense, fully explain and demonstrate to the customer the proper method of operating and maintaining the Products.

The Distributor shall mail to the Supplier, during the term of the distributorship created by this Agreement and any extension thereof, prompt the written notice of the address of each location at which the Products are stored, and the address of each facility established by the Distributor to sell and service the Products. The Supplier may, through its designated agent, inspect all such locations, facilities and operations conducted therein at any time during normal business hours.

7.Spare Parts and Accessories

The Distributor shall keep in stock an adequate supply of the Spare Parts and the Accessories for the servicing of the Goods. No Spare Parts or Accessories not manufactured by the Supplier shall be used in connection with the Goods unless they have been approved in writing by the Supplier.

8.Confidential Information

Written technical datas, drawings, plans and engineering in technical instructions pertaining to the Products are recognized by the Distributor to be secret and confidential and to be the property of the Supplier. Those items shall at all times and for all purposes be held by the Distributor in a confidential capacity and shall not, without the prior written consent of the Supplier, (i) be disclosed by the Distributor to any person, firm or corporation, except those salaried employees of the Distributor who are required to utilize such items in connection with the sale, inspection, repair or servicing of the Products during the term of the distributorship created by this Agreement or any extension thereof, or (ii) be copied or used by the Distributor, its employees or agents at any time following the expiration or termination of this Agreement or any extension thereof. The Supplier may require as a condition to any disclosure by the Distributor pursuant to this Section that any salaried employee to whom disclosure is to be made sign a confidentiality agreement, enforceable by the Supplier, containing terms satisfactory to the Supplier.

9.Purchasing Products

The Distributor shall purchase its requirements for the Products from the Supplier. Such requirements shall include purchasing and maintaining an inventory of the Products that is sufficient to enable the Distributor to perform its obligations hereunder, and at least_____ demonstration model of the Goods and Accessories.

The Supplier shall supply to the Distributor the sufficient Products to enable the Distributor to meet the full demand for the Products in the territory. All orders for the Products transmitted by the Distributor to the Supplier shall be deemed to be accepted by the Supplier at the time such orders are received by the Supplier to the extent that they are in compliance with the terms of this Agreement and the Supplier shall perform in accordance with all accepted orders. The Supplier shall confirm its receipt and acceptance of each order within_____days of receipt of the order.

10.Business Procedures

Each order for the Products issued by the Distributor to the Supplier under this Agreement shall identify that it is an order and shall further set forth the delivery date or dates and the description and quantity of the Products which are to be delivered on each of such dates. An order for the Products shall not provide a delivery date less than_____days after the date that the order is delivered to the Supplier.

11.Termination

Any party wants to terminate the relationship, or any cancellation of orders by the Distributor shall be in writing. If the Distributor cancels an order, which has been accepted by the Supplier, the Distributor shall reimburse the Supplier for any cost incident to such order incurred by the Supplier prior to the time it was informed of the cancellation.

12.Purchasing Prices

The prices for the Goods, and any discount applicable thereto, are set forth in Attachment_____ . The prices for the accessories, together with any discount applicable thereto, are set forth in Attachment _____ . The prices for the Spare Parts, together with any discount applicable thereto, are set forth in Attachment _____ . All prices are FOB (the delivery point). If the price for any product is not set forth in the Attachments and the Distributor nevertheless orders such a product from the Supplier, the parties hereby evidence their intention thereby to conclude an agreement for the sale of that product at a reasonable price to be determined by the parties mutually negotiating in good faith.

13.Price Changes

The Supplier reserves the right, in its sole discretion, to change prices or discounts applicable to the Products. The Supplier shall give the written notice to the Distributor of any price change at least_____days prior to the effective date thereof. The price in effect as of the date of the Distributor's receipt of notice of such price change shall remain applicable to all orders received by the Supplier prior to that effective date.

14.Packing

The Supplier shall, at its expense, pack all Products in accordance with the Supplier's standard packing procedures, which shall be suitable to permit the shipment of the Products to the territory; provided, however, that if the Distributor requests a modification of those procedures, the Supplier shall make the requested modification and the Distributor shall bear any reasonable expense incurred by the Supplier in complying with such modified procedures which are in excess of the expenses which the Supplier would have incurred in following its standard procedures.

15.Delivery

The title and risk of losses of the Products shall pass from the Supplier to the Distributor at the delivery point.

The Supplier shall be responsible for arranging all transportation of the Products, but if requested by the Supplier, the Distributor shall, at the Supplier's expense, assist the Supplier in making such arrangements.

16.Inspection and Acceptance

Promptly upon the receipt of a shipment of the Products, the Distributor shall examine the shipment to determine whether any item or items included in the shipment are in short supply, defective or damaged. Within_____days of the receipt of the shipment, the Distributor shall notify the Supplier in writing of any shortage, defect or damage, which the Distributor claims existed at the time of delivery. Within_____days after the receipt of such notice, the Supplier will investigate the claim of shortages, defects or damage, inform the Distributor of its findings, and deliver the Products to the Distributor to replace any which the Supplier determines, were in short supply, defective or damaged at the time of delivery.

17.Payment

Upon delivery and acceptance of the Products, the Supplier may submit to the Distributor the invoice for those Products. The Distributor shall pay each such proper invoice within_____ days after the Distributor's receipt of that invoice. The payment shall be made in_____to a bank account to be notified in writing by the Supplier to the Distributor.

18.Arbitration

All disputes arising from the execution of this Agreement shall be settled through friendly consultations. In case no settlement can be reached, the case in dispute shall then be submitted to _____for arbitration in accordance with its provisional rules of procedure. The decision made by this Commission shall be regarded as final and binding upon both parties. Arbitration fees shall be borne by the losing party, unless otherwise awarded.

Representative of Supplier: Representative of Distributor:

(Authorized Signature)   (Authorized Signature)

经销协议

编号：

本协议由_____（供应商），根据_____（法律名称）成立和存在的_____（主要经营场所在_____）和_____（经销商），根据_____法律成立和存在的_____（主要经营场所在_____）于_____年____月____日在_____签订。

供应商：

经销商：

1.定义

本协议中有以下术语：

（1）附件

供应商有权在附件____中随时增减部分协议内容，但应通过信函方式书面告知经销商。这种变更在信函寄出____日内生效。

（2）货物

这是指在本协议附件____中所描述的物品。供应商有权在附件____删除或增加部分货物，但应通过信函方式书面告知经销商。这种变更在信函寄出____日内生效。

（3）零配件

这是指货物和（或）维护货物或为货物提供服务所用的特殊装置中所包含的所有配件和零件。供应商声明完整的零配件清单在本协议附件____中列明。供应商有权在附件____中删除或增加部分零配件，也有权改变零配件的规格和设计，但应通过信函方式书面告知经销商。这种变更在信函寄出____日内生效。

（4）商标

这是指在本协议附件____中列明的、在供应商产品上使用或描述的任何商标、标识和服务标记，不论其是否注册。

2.指定经销商

供应商有权阻止位于其他区域的经销商在本区域内销售和使用供应商提供的产品。

3.双方关系

经销商是独立的合同当事人，不是供应商法律上的代表人和代理人，没有权利以书面或其他形式代表供应商承担任何保证（除非有明确的约定）。经销商的员工应由经销商控制，供应商无权使用、控制。经销商应对其员工的行为或过失负责。

在本协议生效或续展期间，经销商应根据当地生效的劳动法规为从事本协议项下工作或与本协议有关的员工购买充分的保险，并在供应商的要求下提供足够的证据证明已购买保险。

4.产品销售

经销商应在本区域内尽力销售产品和充分扩大市场。双方协商并同意经销商尽力在本协议的第一年在本区域内购买和销售最少_____产品（年市场潜力）。在此后每年的年初，双方将友好协商，并确定当年适用的年市场潜力；但如双方意见无法统一，则继续适用上一年的年市场潜力。

5.广告

经销商有权在本协议有效期或续展期内进行广告宣传或表明自己授权经销商的身份，有权在广告或推广活动中使用供应商的商标。经销商应事先将广告或宣传资料的样稿提交供应商批准，经销商不得未经供应商书面同意进行广告宣传。除非本协议另有约定，经销商不得主张或享有供应商商标的任何权益。

6.经销商销售、服务及库存设备

经销商应在本区域内雇用或运营一个销售、服务、处理其他事务的组织，并配备能从事本协议项下工作的有经验的销售人员。

经销商应在本区域内以合理的价格保持设备运行和人员匹配，完成所售产品的检验、维护和其他必要的服务。为帮助经销商承担服务和维护职责，供应商应在合理的限度内，免费对经销商指定的人员提供服务和维护培训。

经销商应根据供应商随时签发的现行适用的清单来保持一定的库存储备量，并自行承担费用。经销商应在销售时向客户提供现行适用的操作维护手册，并向客户充分解释和演示操作及维护的适当方法，费用由经销商承担。

在本协议有效期和续展期内，经销商应向供应商及时报告库存货物数量和为保证销售、服务所配备的设备的地点。供应商可以指定代理人在营业时间测查上述地点、设备和操作方式。

7.配件及附件

经销商应保证货物足够的零配件及附件的库存。非供应商生产的零配件及附件不得在货物上使用，除非获得供应商的书面同意。

8.保密信息

经销商获得的有关产品的技术数据、图纸、计划和工程技术指导是保密的，所有权归供应商。无论任何时候、出于任何目的，经销商仅能秘密地持有这些资料，未经供应商书面同意不得：①向任何人、商行、公司披露，除非经销商员工在本协议有效期或续展期内为了销售、检验、修理、服务的需要而使用。②在本协议或续展期终止后，经销商的员工或代理人复制或使用。供应商根据本款可以要求经销商与接触保密信息的员工签订可执行的保密协议，其内容须满足供应商的要求。

9.产品采购

经销商应向供应商购买必备产品，包括采购、维持经销商能履行本协议义务的一定量的产品的库存，和至少____（套）产品和附件的展示模型。

供应商应提供充足的产品以满足本区域产品需求。经销商向供应商下的符合协议条款要求的订单到达供应商，则视为供应商接受该订单，供应商应按接受的订单履行义务。供应商应在收到订单后____天内确认收到和接受订单。

10.业务程序

经销商下的每张订单都应明示订单性质，并进一步明确交付日期、货物规格和不同日期应发送的数量。交付日期不得早于供应商收到订单后＿＿＿天。

11.业务终止

双方中任何一方要终止业务关系或经销商想取消订单应采用书面形式。如果供应商接受经销商取消订单，则经销商应赔偿供应商因此所产生的截止到通知取消前的所有费用。

12.购买价格

货物的价格和折扣在本协议附件＿＿＿上列明。货物附件的价格和折扣在本协议附件＿＿＿上列明。货物零部件的价格和折扣在本协议附件＿＿＿上列明。所有价格为交付点FOB价。如果经销商向供应商订购附件上没有价格的产品，则双方应通过友好协商确定一个合理的价格，并订立协议。

13.价格变化

供应商有权改变货物的价格或折扣。供应商应最迟在价格生效前＿＿＿天书面通知经销商价格变化。在收到价格变化通知之日起，经销商在价格变化生效前收到的订单执行变化后的价格。

14.包装

供应商按适合运输的包装标准对产品进行包装，费用自行承担。但如果经销商要求改变包装模式，供应商应按要求改变包装，但由此产生的额外费用由经销商承担。

15.交货

货物的所有权和货损风险从交付时起转移给经销商。

供应商应负责安排运输，但如果供应商要求，则经销商应予以安排，费用由供应商承担。

16.检验和收货

在收到货物后，经销商应及时检查货物，确定是否有货物短缺、瑕疵和损坏的情况。如果有上述情况，则经销商应在收到货物后＿＿＿天内书面通知供应商。在收到通知后＿＿＿天内，供应商应调查货物短缺、瑕疵和损坏的情况，并通知经销商结果。如果确认货物在交付时存在短缺、瑕疵和损坏的情况，则供应商应予以更换。

17.付款

在交付和接收产品后，供应商向经销商提交该批货的发票。经销商将在收到发票后＿＿＿天内按发票金额支付货款，用＿＿＿＿＿＿＿支付到供应商书面提供的银行账户。

18.仲裁

在履行协议过程中，如产生争议，双方应友好协商解决。若通过友好协商达不成和解，则提交＿＿＿＿＿＿＿＿＿＿＿＿＿＿＿仲裁，根据暂行程序规则进行仲裁。该仲裁委员会的决定是终局性的，对双方均具有约束力。除另有规定外，仲裁费用由败诉方负担。

供应商代表：　　　　　　　　　　经销商代表：
（授权签名）　　　　　　　　　　（授权签名）